The Politics of Interpretation

Edited by W. J. T. Mitchell

The Politics of Interpretation

The University of Chicago Press
Chicago and London

Most of the articles in this volume originally appeared in the September 1982, December 1982, and March 1983 issues of *Critical Inquiry*.

The University of Chicago Press, Chicago 60637
The University of Chicago Press, Ltd., London

Library of Congress Cataloging in Publication Data
Main entry under title:

The Politics of interpretation.

   Includes index.
   1. Criticism—Political aspects—Addresses, essays,
lectures.   I. Mitchell, W. J. Thomas, 1942–
PN98.P64P64 1983   801′.95   83-3581
ISBN 0-226-53219-4
ISBN 0-226-53220-8 (pbk.)

Contents

Introduction

> It is, of course, well known that the only source of war is politics—the intercourse of governments and peoples; but it is apt to be assumed that war suspends that intercourse and replaces it by a wholly different condition, ruled by no law but its own.
>
> We maintain, on the contrary, that war is simply a continuation of political intercourse, with the addition of other means. We deliberately use the phrase "with the addition of other means" because we also want to make it clear that war in itself does not suspend political intercourse or change it into something entirely different. . . . Do political relations between peoples and between their governments stop when diplomatic notes are no longer exchanged? Is war not just another expression of their thoughts, another form of speech or writing? Its grammar, indeed, may be its own, but not its logic.
>
> —CARL VON CLAUSEWITZ, *On War*

What happens if we substitute the notion of "interpretation" for "war" in this famous passage from Clausewitz? One result would be a discussion something like the one contained in this volume: a collection of essays which explores the proposition that criticism and interpretation, the arts of explanation and understanding, have a deep and complex relation with politics, the structures of power and social value that organize human life. Another result would be that we would have a clear formulation of the fundamental question raised by the claim that interpretation is politics by other means—the question of what belongs to interpretation as an autonomous art or science (what Clausewitz calls a "grammar") and what belongs to the social conditions that mobilize interpretive tactics, the "logic" that governs our assessment of any interpretive maneuver.

It may appear at some moments in the following pages that it would be more accurate to drop politics out of the equation and simply to think of interpretation as *war* by other means, for this book was conceived in conflict, not consensus. It is the product of arguments among the editors, writers, and readers of *Critical Inquiry* about the ideological and ethical implications of various critical strategies and reflects fundamental disputes about the way in which a "politics of interpretation" ought to be conceived. Is "politics" to be understood in a restricted sense as the actions and choices of persons in their roles as citizens and leaders, members of a polis or civil society? Or is it to be understood more broadly as the structures of belief and interest, the ideologies which permeate every level of human existence? Is "interpretation" to be understood strictly as an act of unfolding the meaning of intentional objects and events, or is it to be extended to include scientific explanation, the uncovering of impersonal relations of cause and effect? Finally, is the whole concept of a "politics of interpretation" to be understood as "ideological analysis," the disclosure of political meanings in the "texts" of social and cultural life? Or is it to be construed as a reflection on the processes of interpretation themselves, the ideologies which are built into the very mechanisms and metaphors that organize the production of meanings? And to what extent do the answers to these questions entail discernible political alignments?

If our only goal in this book had been theoretical sophistication in the discussion of these questions, we probably would have limited the contributors to Marxists, feminists, and neoconservatives, for these are the intellectual groups who have made the question of a politics of interpretation most urgent and far-reaching. It is they who have taken a professional, not a passing, interest in interpretation of and as politics, they who have developed the terms and arguments which dominate our thinking about the topic. But our goal was not just theoretical depth. We wanted these essays to dramatize as well as to analyze the politics of interpretation, and thus we tried to select contributors representative of a wide variety of political persuasions. Between the lines of the following pages you should be able to hear the voices of Whigs and Tories, Goldwater Republicans and New Deal Democrats, orthodox and maverick Marxists, utopian socialists and Third World Maoists, masculists and feminists, wishy-washy liberals and committed revolutionaries. Sometimes, to be sure, several of these voices seem to be coming in a polyphonic heteroglossia from the mouth of a single writer. Is Stanley Fish a radical or a conservative? Has Wayne Booth succeeded in shedding masculism for feminism? Is Donald Davie a nineteenth-century liberal or a modern Tory? Is Edward Said a Palestinian socialist or a Western humanist? Said's candid remark that his own identity as a "humanist" is one for which he has "contradictory feelings of affection and revulsion" reveals what is a widespread phenomenon in these pages: a sense that the politics of interpretation is an uncomfortable topic for intellectuals, one which seems forced upon us, leaving us embarrassed, unready, forced to resort (as Stanley Cavell and many others admit) to autobiography and confession, forced to leave the security of the disciplines we have spent a lifetime mastering and to confront the "real world" of social and institutional power which has sustained those disciplines. At times, no doubt, it will seem that this confrontation never quite takes place and that the realms of academic, professional, and institutional politics remain as distant as ever from the arenas of state power and real social change. One purpose of this book is to measure this distance and to assess its meaning.

However we confront the politics of interpretation (and one way is to deny that it exists: see Walter Benn Michaels' "Is There a Politics of Interpretation?"), there is, I think, a firm consensus among the contributors that the relation between politics and interpretation has impressed itself upon the attention of intellectuals and academics in the last ten years. There are several ways of accounting for the recent emergence of this topic: it may be just another phase in the widely felt "loss of innocence" in American cultural life since the Vietnam era; it may stem more remotely from the disintegration of the notion of an "end of ideology" that dominated the social sciences in the fifties; it may be a result of the internal momentum of the various interpretive disciplines which, after several generations of technical innovation in the subtle "decoding" of texts and other cultural productions (formalism, structuralism, and post-structuralism), now feel the need for a renewed historicism in order to scrutinize the values, interests, and powers served by the proliferation of hermeneutic techniques. It may, most fundamentally, be a product of the contemporary political situation itself, in which the emergence of Reaganism has brought the pressure of economic and political reality directly to bear on the practice of criticism and scholarship. The intellectual and academic community, that part of society which lives by and on interpretation, finds itself threatened with loss of power, jobs, and prestige. We can say of the eighties what Orwell could say of the forties: "In our age there is no such thing as 'keeping out of politics.' "

Orwell went on to say that the pervasiveness of politics was very bad for language, that it tended to replace discussion with "a mass of lies, evasions, folly, hatred, and schizophrenia." And we can certainly see the signs of degeneration in the language of intellectual debates in recent years as the political animus has intensified. The modern "battle of the books" between the avant-garde and the rear guard in interpretation has all too often fallen into polemical sloganeering or, even worse, into the ominous silence which signals the continuation of the struggle by other means—the control of jobs, publication, funding, and of opportunities to practice the arts of interpretation. Advocates of interpretive determinacy and objectivity are characterized as authoritarian, puritanical, and fascistic; explorers of interpretive indeterminacy and "freeplay" (most notoriously the deconstructionists) are stigmatized as escapists, obfuscationists, nihilists, and—the all-purpose epithet—fascists. In this sort of atmosphere, the observation that some particular interpretive practice has "political implications," that it is not "innocent" or neutral, has all too often been the occasion for finishing a discussion, not starting one.

The general goal of this volume, then, is quite simple: to make the observation that there is a political bias in some interpretive practice the occasion for starting rather than ending a discussion. We also hope to improve the quality of that discussion by pursuing a number of questions which are frequently begged when the issue of a politics of interpretation is raised. The first of these is: So what? What follows from the discovery that an interpretive practice is politically loaded? What effect does the demonstration that an interpretive procedure is not innocent have on its claims to truth? Is a Marxist or liberal or conservative reading of a text true or false, better or worse, by virtue of its politics? Are there other, relatively nonpolitical criteria to which we may appeal? Or is this way of putting the choice already misleading in its tendency to identify ideology with things like "positions" and "biases"?

A related question which needs to be raised when we claim to have uncovered a politically biased interpretive procedure is: For what? That is, *for what* political value, interest, or purpose has this procedure been developed? This question helps to remind us that politics is not just a matter of power and self or class interest; it is also a matter of values and ideals, conceptions of the good life, the good state, and so forth. The claim that some interpretive strategy is politically loaded, then, is a very weak one indeed if it only amounts to a statement of what is true of every interpretation whatsoever. The hard work of unpacking the concrete affiliations of that strategy remains to be done. And it should be noted that this unpacking can only be done under the auspices of some inter- pretive strategy which will itself not be innocent and which will need to be subjected to reflection in its own right. The prospect of all this hard work is one of the leading temptations to keep the politics of interpreta- tion at a theoretical level where the infinite regress of understanding can be contemplated the way abysses usually are—as thrilling landscapes of the sublime. But the practical imperative of a concern with the politics of interpretation is one that is, I think, acknowledged (if only to resist its force) by almost everyone in this volume: "Always historicize!"

The pursuit of the question, For what? leads us, however, not just into the past but into the future and toward what is the most fundamen- tal aim of these essays: the articulation of a positive sense of the politics of interpretation. "Positive" is, I realize, a word that sounds like a ghostly echo of a bygone era in our age of negativity. But I mean only to suggest that there is considerably more to the politics of interpretation than the negative moment of unveiling concealed ideology. The skeptical un- masking of false claims to neutrality, purity, or nonalignment may be a prelude to the clarification of just what political ideals are worth serving in the production of meaning. Ideology need not be just a shameful secret; it can also be the body of values affirmed by a community. The politics of interpretation need not be just a name for bias, prejudice, and unprincipled manipulation; it can also be an agenda for progressive action, a conception of interpretation as the liberation of suppressed or forgotten meanings, or as the envisioning of new meanings which may give direction to social change. Interpreters, to misquote Shelley only slightly, "according to the circumstances of the age and nation in which they appeared, were called, in earlier epochs of the world, legislators or prophets." Who is to say, in an age which lives by the production and transmission of information, that interpreters and poets may not assume that role again?

Interpretation is not likely to resume the status of either law or prophecy, however, unless it wins for cultural work some common ground for negotiation and struggle between ideologies and disciplines. The staking out of this common ground may well be the most controversial and difficult objective that these essays could attain. For it is precisely the appeal to a background of relatively neutral commonplaces, criteria, and concurrent practices that tends to be denied by a concern with the politics of interpretation. Any such appeal is likely to be denounced as a disguised grab for power, an attempt to seize the political high ground by laying claim to some reserve of scientific, aesthetic, or ethical "purity." But we also need to ask ourselves what the cost will be of failing to acknowledge some principle contrary to the political, some dialectical antithesis to the social, cultural, and historical world that man makes around himself. Some obvious candidates for this position are God, Nature, Logic, and the Individual, notions which are usually dismissed by interpretive politicians. If these notions cannot be recuperated, then we will still have to answer Stanley Cavell's question: Politics as opposed to what? If we could answer that question, Marx's complaint that "philosophers have only interpreted the world [but] the point now is to change it" might be answered with a more than wishful claim that interpretation is itself a way of changing the world.

*   *   *

This volume grew out of *Critical Inquiry*'s special issue *The Politics of Interpretation* (vol. 9, no. 1 [September 1982]), which was based on a symposium by the same name, sponsored by *Critical Inquiry*, and held at the University of Chicago's Center for Continuing Education, October 30, 31, and November 1 of 1981. The speakers at that conference were Wayne C. Booth, Stanley Cavell, T. J. Clark, Donald A. Davie, Ronald Dworkin, Julia Kristeva, Edward W. Said, Stephen Toulmin, and Hayden White. The respondents were Stanley Fish, Michael Fried, E. D. Hirsch, Jr., Walter Benn Michaels, Gayatri Chakravorty Spivak, and Garry Wills. In addition to the essays and critical responses generated by the symposium and printed in the September 1982 issue of *Critical Inquiry*, the present volume contains new essays by Gerald Graff and Garry Wills, and further rejoinders by Gerald Bruns, Stanley Cavell, T. J. Clark, Ronald Dworkin, and Terry Eagleton. The symposium was moderated by Janel Mueller and organized by W. J. T. Mitchell with the generous help of the other editors and many friends of *Critical Inquiry.* Elizabeth Abel, Wayne C. Booth, Robert Streeter, and Robert von Hallberg worked especially hard in the planning of the symposium and the recruiting of participants. Others who provided timely advice and moral support included James Chandler, Joyce Feucht-Haviar, Raymond Geuss, Ranlet Lincoln, Françoise Meltzer, Elsie Newton, Jay Schleusener, Mark Schwehn, Joel Snyder, Richard Strier, and John Wallace.

The symposium would not have been possible without the unwavering support of the University of Chicago Press, particularly Morris Philipson, Director, and Jean Sacks, Assistant Director and Manager of Journals, and the benevolent encouragement of the Division of Humanities, Karl J. Weintraub, Dean. The complex logistics of the symposium were expertly managed by Carolyn Williams, and the subsequent editing of the manuscripts was ably handled by her, Janet Silver, and Toby Gordon. Finally, special thanks is due to the Rockefeller Foundation, the Exxon Education Foundation, and the National Endowment for the Humanities for their generous support of this project.

W. J. T. Mitchell

Opponents, Audiences, Constituencies, and Community

Edward W. Said

Who writes? For whom is the writing being done? In what circumstances? These, it seems to me, are the questions whose answers provide us with the ingredients making for a politics of interpretation. But if one does not wish to ask and answer the questions in a dishonest and abstract way, some attempt must be made to show why they are questions of some relevance to the present time. What needs to be said at the beginning is that the single most impressive aspect of the present time—at least for the "humanist," a description for which I have contradictory feelings of affection and revulsion—is that it is manifestly the Age of Ronald Reagan. And it is in this age as a context and setting that the politics of interpretation and the politics of culture are enacted.

I do not want to be misunderstood as saying that the cultural situation I describe here caused Reagan, or that it typifies Reaganism, or that everything about it can be ascribed or referred back to the personality of Ronald Reagan. What I argue is that a particular situation within the field we call "criticism" is not merely related to but is an integral part of the currents of thought and practice that play a role within the Reagan era. Moreover, I think, "criticism" and the traditional academic humanities have gone through a series of developments over time whose beneficiary and culmination is Reaganism. Those are the gross claims that I make for my argument.

A number of miscellaneous points need to be made here. I am fully aware that any effort to characterize the present cultural moment is very likely to seem quixotic at best, unprofessional at worst. But that, I submit, is an aspect of the present cultural moment, in which the social and historical setting of critical activity is a totality felt to be benign (free, apolitical, serious), uncharacterizable as a whole (it is too complex to be described in general and tendentious terms), and somehow outside history. Thus it seems to me that one thing to be tried—out of sheer critical obstinacy—is precisely *that* kind of generalization, *that* kind of political portrayal, *that* kind of overview condemned by the present dominant culture to appear inappropriate and doomed from the start.

It is my conviction that culture works very effectively to make invisible and even "impossible" the actual *affiliations* that exist between the world of ideas and scholarship, on the one hand, and the world of brute politics, corporate and state power, and military force, on the other. The cult of expertise and professionalism, for example, has so restricted our scope of vision that a positive (as opposed to an implicit or passive) doctrine of noninterference among fields has set in. This doctrine has it that the general public is best left ignorant, and the most crucial policy questions affecting human existence are best left to "experts," specialists who talk about their specialty only, and—to use the word first given wide social approbation by Walter Lippmann in *Public Opinion* and *The Phantom Public*—"insiders," people (usually men) who are endowed with the special privilege of knowing how things really work and, more important, of being close to power.[1]

Humanistic culture in general has acted in tacit compliance with this antidemocratic view, the more regrettably since, both in their formulation and in the politics they have given rise to, so-called policy issues can hardly be said to enhance human community. In a world of increasing interdependence and political consciousness, it seems both violent and wasteful to accept the notion, for example, that countries ought to be classified simply as pro-Soviet or pro-American. Yet this classification— and with it the reappearance of a whole range of cold war motifs and symptoms (discussed by Noam Chomsky in *Towards a New Cold War*)— dominates thinking about foreign policy. There is little in humanistic culture that is an effective antidote to it, just as it is true that few humanists have very much to say about the problems starkly dramatized by the 1980 Report of the Independent Commission on International Development Issues, *North-South: A Programme for Survival.* Our political discourse is now choked with enormous, thought-stopping abstractions,

1. See Ronald Steel, *Walter Lippmann and the American Century* (Boston, 1980), pp. 180–85 and 212–16.

Edward W. Said, Parr Professor of English and Comparative Literature at Columbia University, is the author of *Beginnings, Orientalism, Covering Islam,* and the forthcoming *Criticism between Culture and System.*

from terrorism, Communism, Islamic fundamentalism, and instability, to moderation, freedom, stability, and strategic alliances, all of them as unclear as they are both potent and unrefined in their appeal. It is next to impossible to think about human society either in a global way (as Richard Falk eloquently does in *A Global Approach to National Policy* [1975]) or at the level of everyday life. As Philip Green shows in *The Pursuit of Inequality,* notions like equality and welfare have simply been chased off the intellectual landscape. Instead a brutal Darwinian picture of self-help and self-promotion is proposed by Reaganism, both domestically and internationally, as an image of the world ruled by what is being called "productivity" or "free enterprise."

Add to this the fact that liberalism and the Left are in a state of intellectual disarray and fairly dismal perspectives emerge. The challenge posed by these perspectives is not how to cultivate one's garden despite them but how to understand cultural work occurring within them. What I propose here, then, is a rudimentary attempt to do just that, notwithstanding a good deal of inevitable incompleteness, overstatement, generalization, and crude characterization. Finally, I will very quickly propose an alternative way of undertaking cultural work, although anything like a fully worked-out program can only be done collectively and in a separate study.

My use of "constituency," "audience," "opponents," and "community" serves as a reminder that no one writes simply for oneself. There is always an Other; and this Other willy-nilly turns interpretation into a social activity, albeit with unforeseen consequences, audiences, constituencies, and so on. And, I would add, interpretation is the work of intellectuals, a class badly in need today of moral rehabilitation and social redefinition. The one issue that urgently requires study is, for the humanist no less than for the social scientist, the status of *information* as a component of knowledge: its sociopolitical status, its contemporary fate, its economy (a subject treated recently by Herbert Schiller in *Who Knows: Information in the Age of the Fortune 500*). We all think we know what it means, for example, to *have* information and to write and interpret texts containing information. Yet we live in an age which places unprecedented emphasis on the production of knowledge and information, as Fritz Machlup's *Production and Distribution of Knowledge in the United States* dramatizes clearly. What happens to information and knowledge, then, when IBM and AT&T—two of the world's largest corporations—claim that what they do is to put "knowledge" to work "for the people"? What is the role of humanistic knowledge and information if they are not to be unknowing (many ironies there) partners in commodity production and marketing, so much so that what humanists do may in the end turn out to be a quasi-religious concealment of this peculiarly unhumanistic process? A true secular politics of interpretation sidesteps this question at its peril.

1

At a recent MLA convention, I stopped by the exhibit of a major university press and remarked to the amiable sales representative on duty that there seemed to be no limit to the number of highly specialized books of advanced literary criticism his press put out. "Who reads these books?" I asked, implying of course that however brilliant and important most of them were they were difficult to read and therefore could not have a wide audience—or at least an audience wide enough to justify regular publication during a time of economic crisis. The answer I received made sense, assuming I was told the truth. People who write specialized, advanced (i.e., New New) criticism faithfully read each other's books. Thus each such book could be assured of, but wasn't necesssarily always getting, sales of around three thousand copies, "all other things being equal." The last qualification struck me as ambiguous at best, but it needn't detain us here. The point was that a nice little audience had been built and could be routinely mined by this press; certainly, on a much larger scale, publishers of cookbooks and exercise manuals apply a related principle as they churn out what may seem like a very long series of unnecessary books, even if an expanding crowd of avid food and exercise aficionados is not quite the same thing as a steadily attentive and earnest crowd of three thousand critics reading each other.

What I find peculiarly interesting about the real or mythical three thousand is that whether they derive ultimately from the Anglo-American New Criticism (as formulated by I. A. Richards, William Empson, John Crowe Ransom, Cleanth Brooks, Allen Tate, and company, beginning in the 1920s and continuing for several decades thereafter) or from the so-called New New Criticism (Roland Barthes, Jacques Derrida, et al., during the 1960s), they vindicate, rather than undermine, the notion that intellectual labor ought to be divided into progressively narrower niches. Consider very quickly the irony of this. New Criticism claimed to view the verbal object as in itself it really was, free from the distractions of biography, social message, even paraphrase. Matthew Arnold's critical program was thereby to be advanced not by jumping directly from the text to the whole of culture but by using a highly concentrated verbal analysis to comprehend cultural values available only through a finely wrought literary structure finely understood.

Charges made against the American New Criticism that its ethos was clubby, gentlemanly, or Episcopalian are, I think, correct only if it is added that in practice New Criticism, for all its elitism, was strangely populist in intention. The idea behind the pedagogy, and of course the preaching, of Brooks and Robert Penn Warren was that everyone properly instructed could feel, perhaps even act, like an educated gentleman. In its sheer projection this was by no means a trivial ambition. No amount of snide mocking at their quaint gentility can conceal the fact that, in order to accomplish the conversion, the New Critics aimed at nothing less than the removal of *all* of what they considered the specialized rubbish—put there, they presumed, by professors of literature—standing between the reader of a poem and the poem. Leaving aside the questionable value of the New Criticism's ultimate social and moral message, we must concede that the school deliberately and perhaps incongruously tried to create a wide community of responsive readers out of a very large, potentially unlimited, constituency of students and teachers of literature.

In its early days, the French *nouvelle critique,* with Barthes as its chief apologist, attempted the same kind of thing. Once again the guild of professional literary scholars was characterized as impeding responsiveness to literature. Once again the antidote was what seemed to be a specialized reading technique based on a near jargon of linguistic, psychoanalytic, and Marxist terms, all of which proposed a new freedom for writers and literate readers alike. The philosophy of *écriture* promised wider horizons and a less restricted community, once an initial (and as it turned out painless) surrender to structuralist activity had been made. For despite structuralist prose, there was no impulse among the principal structuralists to exclude readers; quite the contrary, as Barthes' often abusive attacks on Raymond Picard show, the main purpose of critical reading was to create new readers of the classics who might otherwise have been frightened off by their lack of professional literary accreditation.

For about four decades, then, in both France and the United States, the schools of "new" critics were committed to prying literature and writing loose from confining institutions. However much it was to depend upon carefully learned technical skills, reading was in very large measure to become an act of public dispossession. Texts were to be unlocked or decoded, then handed on to anyone who was interested. The resources of symbolic language were placed at the disposal of readers who it was assumed suffered the debilitations of either irrelevant "professional" information or the accumulated habits of lazy inattention.

Thus French and American New Criticism were, I believe, competitors for authority within mass culture, not other-worldly alternatives to it. Because of what became of them, we have tended to forget the original missionary aims the two schools set for themselves. They belong to precisely the same moment that produced Jean-Paul Sartre's ideas about an engaged literature and a committed writer. Literature was about the world, readers were in the world; the question was not *whether* to be but *how* to be, and this was best answered by carefully analyzing language's symbolic enactments of the various existential possibilities available to human beings. What the Franco-American critics shared was the notion that verbal discipline could be self-sufficient once you learned to think pertinently about language stripped of unnecessary scaffolding; in other words, you did not need to be a professor to benefit from Donne's metaphors or Saussure's liberating distinction between *langue* and *parole*. And so the New Criticism's precious and cliquish aspect was mitigated by its radically anti-institutional bias, which manifested itself in the enthusiastic therapeutic optimism to be observed in both France and the United States. Join humankind against the schools: this was a message a great many people could appreciate.

How strangely perverse, then, that the legacy of both types of New Criticism is the private-clique consciousness embodied in a kind of critical writing that has virtually abandoned any attempt at reaching a large, if not a mass, audience. My belief is that both in the United States and in France the tendency toward formalism in New Criticism was accentuated by the academy. For the fact is that a disciplined attention to language can only thrive in the rarefied atmosphere of the classroom. Linguistics and literary analysis are features of the modern school, not of the marketplace. Purifying the language of the tribe—whether as a project subsumed within modernism or as a hope kept alive by embattled New Criticisms surrounded by mass culture—always moved further from the really big existing tribes and closer toward emerging new ones, comprised of the acolytes of a reforming or even revolutionary creed who in the end seemed to care more about turning the new creed into an intensely separatist orthodoxy than about forming a large community of readers.

To its unending credit, the university protects such wishes and shelters them under the umbrella of academic freedom. Yet advocacy of *close reading* or of *écriture* can quite naturally entail hostility to outsiders who fail to grasp the salutary powers of verbal analysis; moreover, persuasion too often has turned out to be less important than purity of intention and execution. In time the guild adversarial sense grew as the elaborate techniques multiplied, and an interest in expanding the constituency lost out to a wish for abstract correctness and methodological rigor within a quasi-monastic order. Critics read each other and cared about little else.

The parallels between the fate of a New Criticism reduced to abandoning universal literacy entirely and that of the school of F. R. Leavis are sobering. As Francis Mulhern reminds us in *The Moment of Scrutiny,* Leavis was not a formalist himself and began his career in the context of generally Left politics. Leavis argued that great literature was fundamentally opposed to a class society and to the dictates of a coterie. In his view, English studies ought to become the cornerstone of a new, fundamentally democratic outlook. But largely because the Leavisites concentrated their work both in and for the university, what began as a healthy oppositional participation in modern industrial society changed into a shrill withdrawal from it. English studies became narrower and narrower, in my opinion, and critical reading degenerated into decisions about what should or should not be allowed into the great tradition.

I do not want to be misunderstood as saying that there is something inherently pernicious about the modern university that produces the changes I have been describing. Certainly there is a great deal to be said in favor of a university manifestly not influenced or controlled by coarse partisan politics. But one thing in particular about the university—and here I speak about the modern university without distinguishing between European, American, or Third World and socialist universities—does appear to exercise an almost totally unrestrained influence: the principle that knowledge ought to exist, be sought after, and disseminated in a very divided form. Whatever the social, political, economic, and ideological reasons underlying this principle, it has not long gone without its challengers. Indeed, it may not be too much of an exaggeration to say that one of the most interesting motifs in modern world culture has been the debate between proponents of the belief that knowledge can exist in a synthetic universal form and, on the other hand, those who believe that knowledge is inevitably produced and nurtured in specialized compartments. Georg Lukács' attack on reification and his advocacy of "totality," in my opinion, very tantalizingly resemble the wide-ranging discussions that have been taking place in the Islamic world since the late nineteenth century on the need for mediating between the claims of a totalizing Islamic vision and modern specialized science. These epistemological controversies are therefore centrally important to the workplace of knowledge production, the university, in which *what* knowledge is and how it ought to be discovered are the very lifeblood of its being.

The most impressive recent work concerning the history, circumstances, and constitution of modern knowledge has stressed the role of social convention. Thomas Kuhn's "paradigm of research," for example, shifts attention away from the individual creator to the communal restraints upon personal initiative. Galileos and Einsteins are infrequent figures not just because genius is a rare thing but because scientists are borne along by agreed-upon ways to do research, and this consensus encourages uniformity rather than bold enterprise. Over time this uniformity acquires the status of a discipline, while its subject matter becomes a field or territory. Along with these goes a whole apparatus of techniques, one of whose functions is, as Michel Foucault has tried to show in *The Archaeology of Knowledge,* to protect the coherence, the territorial integrity, the social identity of the field, its adherents and its institutional presence. You cannot simply choose to be a sociologist or a psychoanalyst; you cannot simply make statements that have the status of knowledge in anthropology; you cannot merely suppose that what you say as a historian (however well it may have been researched) enters historical discourse. You have to pass through certain rules of accreditation, you must learn the rules, you must speak the language, you must master the idioms, and you must accept the authorities of the field—determined in many of the same ways—to which you want to contribute.

In this view of things, expertise is partially determined by how well an individual learns the rules of the game, so to speak. Yet it is difficult to determine in absolute terms whether expertise is *mainly* constituted by the social conventions governing the intellectual manners of scientists or, on the other hand, mainly by the putative exigencies of the subject matter itself. Certainly convention, tradition, and habit create ways of looking at a subject that transform it completely; and just as certainly there are generic differences between the subjects of history, literature, and philology that require different (albeit related) techniques of analysis, disciplinary attitudes, and commonly held views. Elsewhere I have taken the admittedly aggressive position that Orientalists, area-studies experts, journalists, and foreign-policy specialists are not always sensitive to the dangers of self-quotation, endless repetition, and received ideas that their fields encourage, for reasons that have more to do with politics and ideology than with any "outside" reality. Hayden White has shown in his work that historians are subject not just to narrative conventions but also to the virtually closed space imposed on the interpreter of events by verbal retrospection, which is very far from being an objective mirror of reality. Yet even these views, although they are understandably repugnant to many people, do not go as far as saying that everything about a "field" can be reduced either to an interpretive convention or to political interest.

Let us grant, therefore, that it would be a long and potentially impossible task to prove empirically that, on the one hand, there could be objectivity so far as knowledge about human society is concerned or, on the other, that all knowledge is esoteric and subjective. Much ink has been spilled on both sides of the debate, not all of it useful, as Wayne Booth has shown in his discussion of scientism and modernism, *Modern Dogma and the Rhetoric of Assent.* An instructive opening out of the impasse—to which I want to return a bit later—has been the body of techniques developed by the school of reader-response critics: Wolfgang Iser, Norman Holland, Stanley Fish, and Michael Riffaterre, among others. These critics argue that since texts without readers are no less incomplete than readers without texts, we should focus attention on what happens when both components of the interpretive situation interact. Yet with the exception of Fish, reader-response critics tend to regard interpretation as an essentially private, interiorized happening, thereby inflating the role of solitary decoding at the expense of its just as important social context. In his latest book, *Is There a Text in This Class?,* Fish accentuates the role of what he calls interpretive communities, groups as well as institutions (principal among them the classroom and pedagogues) whose presence, much more than any unchanging objective standard or correlative of absolute truth, controls what we consider to be knowledge. If, as he says, "interpretation is the only game in town," then it must follow that interpreters who work mainly by persuasion and not scientific demonstration are the only players.

I am on Fish's side there. Unfortunately, though, he does not go very far in showing why, or even how, some interpretations are more persuasive than others. Once again we are back to the quandary suggested by the three thousand advanced critics reading each other to everyone else's unconcern. Is it the inevitable conclusion to the formation of an interpretive community that its constituency, its specialized language, and its concerns tend to get tighter, more airtight, more self-enclosed as its own self-confirming authority acquires more power, the solid status of orthodoxy, and a stable constituency? What is the acceptable humanistic antidote to what one discovers, say, among sociologists, philosophers, and so-called policy scientists who speak only to and for each other in a language oblivious to everything but a well-guarded, constantly shrinking fiefdom forbidden to the uninitiated?

For all sorts of reasons, large answers to these questions do not strike me as attractive or convincing. For one, the universalizing habit by which a system of thought is believed to account for everything too quickly slides into a quasi-religious synthesis. This, it seems to me, is the sobering lesson offered by John Fekete in *The Critical Twilight,* an account of how New Criticism led directly to Marshall McLuhan's "technocratic-religious eschatology." In fact, interpretation and its demands add up to a rough game, once we allow ourselves to step out of the shelter offered by specialized fields and by fancy all-embracing mythologies. The trouble with visions, reductive answers, and systems is that they homogenize evidence very easily. Criticism as such is crowded out and disallowed from the start, hence impossible; and in the end one learns to manipulate bits of the system like so many parts of a machine. Far from taking in a great deal, the universal system as a universal type of explanation either screens out everything it cannot directly absorb or it repetitively churns out the same sort of thing all the time. In this way it becomes a kind of conspiracy theory. Indeed, it has always seemed to me that the supreme irony of what Derrida has called logocentrism is that its critique, deconstruction, is as insistent, as monotonous, and as inadvertently systematizing as logocentrism itself. We may applaud the wish to break out of departmental divisions, therefore, without at the same time accepting the notion that one single method for doing so exists. The unheeding insistence of René Girard's "interdisciplinary" studies of mimetic desire and scapegoat effects is that they want to convert all human activity, all disciplines, to one thing. How can we assume this one thing covers everything that is essential, as Girard keeps suggesting?

This is only a relative skepticism, for one can prefer foxes to hedge-

hogs without also saying that all foxes are equal. Let us venture a couple
of crucial distinctions. To the ideas of Kuhn, Foucault, and Fish we can
usefully add those of Giovanni Battista Vico and Antonio Gramsci. Here
is what we come up with. Discourses, interpretive communities, and
paradigms of research are produced by intellectuals, Gramsci says, who
can either be religious or secular. Now Gramsci's implicit contrast of
secular with religious intellectuals is less familiar than his celebrated
division between organic and traditional intellectuals. Yet it is no less
important for that matter. In a letter of 17 August 1931, Gramsci writes
about an old teacher from his Cagliari days, Umberto Cosmo:

> It seemed to me that I and Cosmo, and many other intellectuals at
> this time (say the first fifteen years of the century) occupied a cer-
> tain common ground: we were all to some degree part of the
> movement of moral and intellectual reform which in Italy stemmed
> from Benedetto Croce, and whose first premise was that modern
> man can and should live without the help of religion . . . positivist
> religion, mythological religion, or whatever brand one cares to
> name. . . .[2] This point appears to me even today to be the major
> contribution made to international culture by modern Italian in-
> tellectuals, and it seems to me a civil conquest that must not be lost.[3]

Benedetto Croce of course was Vico's greatest modern student, and it
was one of Croce's intentions in writing about Vico to reveal explicitly
the strong secular bases of his thought and also to argue in favor of a
secure and dominant civil culture (hence Gramsci's use of the phrase
"civil conquest"). "Conquest" has perhaps a strange inappropriateness to
it, but it serves to dramatize Gramsci's contention—also implicit in
Vico—that the modern European state is possible not only because there
is a political apparatus (army, police force, bureaucracy) but because
there is a civil, secular, and nonecclesiastical society making the state possible, providing the state with something to rule, filling the state with its
humanly generated economic, cultural, social, and intellectual production.

  Gramsci was unwilling to let the Vichian-Crocean achievement of
civil society's secular working go in the direction of what he called "im-
manentist thought." Like Arnold before him, Gramsci understood that if
nothing in the social world is natural, not even nature, then it must also
be true that things exist not only because they come into being and are
created by human agency (*nascimento*) but also because by coming into
being they displace something else that is already there: this is the com-
bative and emergent aspect of social change as it applies to the world of
culture linked to social history. To adapt from a statement Gramsci

  2. Antonio Gramsci to Tatiana Schucht, in Giuseppe Fiori, *Antonio Gramsci: Life of a
Revolutionary,* trans. Tom Nairn (London, 1970), p. 74.
  3. Gramsci to Schucht, *Lettere dal Carcere* (Turin, 1975), p. 466; my translation.

makes in *The Modern Prince,* "reality (and hence cultural reality) is a product of the application of human will to the society of things," and since also "everything is political, even philosophy and philosophies," we are to understand that in the realm of culture and of thought each production exists not only to earn a place for itself but to displace, win out over, others.[4] All ideas, philosophies, views, and texts aspire to the consent of their consumers, and here Gramsci is more percipient than most in recognizing that there is a set of characteristics unique to civil society in which texts—embodying ideas, philosophies, and so forth—acquire power through what Gramsci describes as diffusion, dissemination into and hegemony over the world of "common sense." Thus ideas aspire to the condition of acceptance, which is to say that one can interpret the meaning of a text by virtue of what in its mode of social presence enables its consent by either a small or a wide group of people.

The secular intellectuals are implicitly present at the center of these considerations. Social and intellectual authority for them does not derive directly from the divine but from an analyzable history made by human beings. Here Vico's counterposing of the sacred with what he calls the gentile realm is essential. Created by God, the sacred is a realm accessible only through revelation: it is ahistorical because complete and divinely untouchable. But whereas Vico has little interest in the divine, the gentile world obsesses him. "Gentile" derives from *gens,* the family group whose exfoliation in time generates history. But "gentile" is also a secular expanse because the web of filiations and affiliations that composes human history—law, politics, literature, power, science, emotion—is informed by *ingegno,* human ingenuity and spirit. This, and not a divine *fons et origo,* is accessible to Vico's new science.

But here a very particular kind of secular interpretation and, even more interestingly, a very particular conception of the interpretive situation is entailed. A direct index of this is the confusing organization of Vico's book, which seems to move sideways and backward as often as it moves forward. Because in a very precise sense God has been excluded from Vico's secular history, that history, as well as everything within it, presents its interpreter with a vast horizontal expanse, across which are to be seen many interrelated structures. The verb "to look" is therefore frequently employed by Vico to suggest what historical interpreters need to do. What one cannot see or look at—the past, for example—is to be divined; Vico's irony is too clear to miss, since what he argues is that only by putting oneself in the position of the maker (or divinity) can one grasp how the past has shaped the present. This involves speculation, supposition, imagination, sympathy; but in no instance can it be allowed that something other than human agency caused history. To be sure,

4. Gramsci, *Selections from the Prison Notebooks,* trans. Quintin Hoare and Geoffrey Nowell Smith (New York, 1971), p. 171.

there are historical laws of development, just as there is something that Vico calls divine Providence mysteriously at work inside history. The fundamental thing is that history and human society are made up of numerous efforts crisscrossing each other, frequently at odds with each other, always untidy in the way they involve each other. Vico's writing directly reflects this crowded spectacle.

One last observation needs to be made. For Gramsci and Vico, interpretation must take account of this secular horizontal space only by means appropriate to what is present there. I understand this to imply that no single explanation sending one back immediately to a single origin is adequate. And just as there are no simple dynastic answers, there are no simple discrete historical formations or social processes. A heterogeneity of human involvement is therefore equivalent to a heterogeneity of results, as well as of interpretive skills and techniques. There is no center, no inertly given and accepted authority, no fixed barriers ordering human history, even though authority, order, and distinction exist. The secular intellectual works to show the absence of divine originality and, on the other side, the complex presence of historical actuality. The conversion of the absence of religion into the presence of actuality is secular interpretation.

2

Having rejected global and falsely systematic answers, one had better speak in a limited and concrete way about the contemporary actuality, which so far as our discussion here is concerned is Reagan's America, or, rather, the America inherited and now ruled over by Reaganism. Take literature and politics, for example. It is not too much of an exaggeration to say that an implicit consensus has been building for the past decade in which the study of literature is considered to be profoundly, even constitutively nonpolitical. When you discuss Keats or Shakespeare or Dickens, you may touch on political subjects, of course, but it is assumed that the skills traditionally associated with modern literary criticism (what is now called rhetoric, reading, textuality, tropology, or deconstruction) are there to be applied to *literary* texts, not, for instance, to a government document, a sociological or ethnological report, or a newspaper. This separation of fields, objects, disciplines, and foci constitutes an amazingly *rigid* structure which, to my knowledge, is almost never discussed by literary scholars. There seems to be an unconsciously held norm guaranteeing the simple essence of "fields," a word which in turn has acquired the intellectual authority of a natural, objective fact. Separation, simplicity, silent norms of pertinence: this is one depoliticizing strain of considerable force, since it is capitalized on by professions, institutions, discourses, and a massively reinforced consistency of specialized fields. One corollary of this is the proliferating orthodoxy of separate fields. "I'm sorry I can't understand this—I'm a literary critic, not a sociologist."

The intellectual toll this has taken in the work of the most explicitly political of recent critics—Marxists, in the instance I shall discuss here—is very high. Fredric Jameson has recently produced what is by any standard a major work of intellectual criticism, *The Political Unconscious*. What it discusses, it discusses with a rare brilliance and learning: I have no reservations at all about that. He argues that priority ought to be given to the political interpretation of literary texts and that Marxism, as an interpretive act as opposed to other methods, is "that 'untranscendable horizon' that subsumes such apparently antagonistic or incommensurable critical operations [as the other varieties of interpretive act] assigning them an undoubted sectoral validity within itself, and thus at once cancelling and preserving them."[5] Thus Jameson avails himself of all the most powerful and contradictory of contemporary methodologies, enfolding them in a series of original readings of modern novels, producing in the end a working through of three "semantic horizons" of which the third "phase" is the Marxist: hence, from *explication de texte*, through the ideological discourses of social classes, to the ideology of form itself, perceived against the ultimate horizon of human history.

It cannot be emphasized too strongly that Jameson's book presents a remarkably complex and deeply attractive argument to which I cannot do justice here. This argument reaches its climax in Jameson's conclusion, in which the utopian element in all cultural production is shown to play an underanalyzed and liberating role in human society; additionally, in a much too brief and suggestive passage, Jameson touches on three political discussions (involving the state, law, and nationalism) for which the Marxist hermeneutic he has outlined, fully a negative as well as a positive hermeneutic, can be particularly useful.

We are still left, however, with a number of nagging difficulties. Beneath the surface of the book lies an unadmitted dichotomy between two kinds of "Politics": (1), the politics defined by political theory from Hegel to Louis Althusser and Ernst Bloch; (2), the politics of struggle and power in the everyday world, which in the United States at least has been won, so to speak, by Reagan. As to why this distinction should exist at all, Jameson says very little. This is even more troubling when we realize that Politics 2 is only discussed once, in the course of a long footnote. There he speaks in a general way about "ethnic groups, neighborhood movements, . . . rank-and-file labor groups," and so on and quite

5. Fredric Jameson, *The Political Unconscious* (Ithaca, N.Y., 1981), p. 10; all further references to this work will be included in the text. Perhaps not incidentally, what Jameson claims for Marxism here is made the central feature of nineteenth-century British fiction by Deirdre David, *Fictions of Resolutions in Three Victorian Novels* (New York, 1980).

perspicaciously enters a plea for alliance politics in the United States as distinguished from France, where the totalizing global politics imposed on nearly every constituency has either inhibited or repressed their local development (p. 54). He is absolutely right of course (and would have been more so had he extended his arguments to a United States dominated by only two parties). Yet the irony is that in criticizing the global perspective and admitting its radical discontinuity with local alliance politics, Jameson is also advocating a strong hermeneutic globalism which will have the effect of subsuming the local in the synchronic. This is almost like saying: Don't worry; Reagan is merely a passing phenomenon: the cunning of history will get him too. Yet except for what suspiciously resembles a religious confidence in the teleological efficacy of the Marxist vision, there is no way, to my mind, by which the local is necessarily going to be subsumed, cancelled, preserved, and resolved by the synchronic. Moreover, Jameson leaves it entirely up to the reader to guess what the connection is between the synchrony and theory of Politics 1 and the molecular struggles of Politics 2. Is there continuity or discontinuity between one realm and the other? How do quotidian politics and the struggle for power enter into the hermeneutic, if not by simple instruction from above or by passive osmosis?

These are unanswered questions precisely because, I think, Jameson's assumed constituency is an audience of cultural-literary critics. And this constituency in contemporary America is premised on and made possible by the separation of disciplines I spoke about earlier. This further aggravates the discursive separation of Politics 1 from Politics 2, creating the obvious impression that Jameson is dealing with autonomous realms of human effort. And this has a still more paradoxical result. In his concluding chapter, Jameson suggests allusively that the components of class consciousness—such things as group solidarity against outside threats—are at bottom utopian "insofar as all such (class-based) collectivities are *figures* for the ultimate concrete collective life of an achieved Utopian or classless society." Right at the heart of this thesis we find the notion that "ideological commitment is not first and foremost a matter of moral choice but of the taking of sides in a struggle between embattled groups" (pp. 291, 290). The difficulty here is that whereas moral choice is a category to be rigorously de-Platonized and historicized, there is no inevitability—logical or otherwise—for reducing it completely to "the taking of sides in a struggle between embattled groups." On the molecular level of an individual peasant family thrown off its land, who is to say whether the desire for restitution is exclusively a matter of taking sides or of making the moral choice to resist dispossession. I cannot be sure. But what is so indicative of Jameson's position is that from the global, synchronic hermeneutic overview, moral choice plays no role, and, what is more, the matter is not investigated empirically or historically (as Barrington Moore has tried to do in *Injustice: The Social Basis of Obedience and Revolt*).

Jameson has certainly earned the right to be one of the preeminent spokesmen for what is best in American cultural Marxism. He is discussed this way by a well-known English Marxist, Terry Eagleton, in a recent article, "The Idealism of American Criticism." Eagleton's discussion contrasts Jameson and Frank Lentricchia with the main currents of contemporary American theory which, according to Eagleton, "develops by way of inventing new idealist devices for the repression of history."[6] Nevertheless, Eagleton's admiration for Jameson and Lentricchia does not prevent him from seeing the limitations of their work, their political "unclarity," their lingering pragmatism, eclecticism, the relationship of their hermeneutic criticism to Reagan's ascendancy, and—in Jameson's case especially—their nostalgic Hegelianism. This is not to say, however, that Eagleton expects either of them to toe the current ultra-Left line, which alleges that "the production of Marxist readings of classical texts is class-collaborationism." But he is right to say that "the question irresistibly raised for the Marxist reader of Jameson is simply this: How is a Marxist-structuralist analysis of a minor novel of Balzac to help shake the foundations of capitalism?" Clearly the answer to this question is that such readings won't; but what does Eagleton propose as an alternative? Here we come to the disabling cost of rigidly enforced intellectual and disciplinary divisions, which also affects Marxism.

For we may as well acknowledge that Eagleton writes about Jameson as a fellow Marxist. This is intellectual solidarity, yes, but within a "field" defined principally as an intellectual discourse existing solely within an academy that has left the extra-academic outside world to the new Right and to Reagan. It follows with a kind of natural inevitability that if one such confinement is acceptable, others can be acceptable: Eagleton faults Jameson for the practical ineffectiveness of his Marxist-structuralism but, on the other hand, meekly takes for granted that he and Jameson inhabit the small world of literary studies, speak its language, deal only with its problematics. Why this should be so is hinted at obscurely by Eagleton when he avers that "the ruling class" determines what uses are made of literature for the purpose of "ideological reproduction" and that as revolutionaries "we" cannot select "the literary terrain on which the battle is to be engaged." It does not seem to have occurred to Eagleton that what he finds weakest in Jameson and Lentricchia, their marginality and vestigial idealism, is what also makes him bewail their rarefied discourse at the same time that he somehow accepts it as his own. The very same specialized ethos has been attenuated a little more now:

6. Terry Eagleton, "The Idealism of American Criticism," *New Left Review* 127 (May–June 1981): 59.

Eagleton, Jameson, and Lentricchia are literary Marxists who write for literary Marxists, who are in cloistral seclusion from the inhospitable world of real politics. Both "literature" and "Marxism" are thereby confirmed in their apolitical content and methodology: literary criticism is still "only" literary criticism, Marxism only Marxism, and politics is mainly what the literary critic talks about longingly and hopelessly.

This rather long digression on the consequences of the separation of "fields" brings me directly to a second aspect of the politics of interpretation viewed from a secular perspective rigorously responsive to the Age of Reagan. It is patently true that, even within the atomized order of disciplines and fields, methodological investigations can and indeed do occur. But the prevailing mode of intellectual discourse is militantly antimethodological, if by methodological we mean a questioning of the structure of fields and discourses themselves. A principle of silent exclusion operates within and at the boundaries of discourse; this has now become so internalized that fields, disciplines, and their discourses have taken on the status of immutable durability. Licensed members of the field, which has all the trappings of a social institution, are identifiable as belonging to a guild, and for them words like "expert" and "objective" have an important resonance. To acquire a position of authority within the field is, however, to be involved internally in the formation of a canon, which usually turns out to be a blocking device for methodological and disciplinary self-questioning. When J. Hillis Miller says, "I believe in the established canon of English and American Literature and the validity of the concept of privileged texts," he is saying something that has moment by virtue neither of its logical truth nor of its demonstrable clarity.[7] Its power derives from his social authority as a well-known professor of English, a man of deservedly great reputation, a teacher of well-placed students. And what he says more or less eliminates the possibility of asking whether canons (and the imprimatur placed upon canons by a literary critic) are more methodologically necessary to the order of dominance within a guild than they are to the secular study of human history.

If I single out literary and humanistic scholars in what I am saying, it is because, for better or worse, I am dealing with texts, and texts are the very point of departure and culmination for literary scholars. Literary scholars read and they write, both of which are activities having more to do with wit, flexibility, and questioning than they do with solidifying ideas into institutions or with bludgeoning readers into unquestioning submission. Above all it seems to me that it goes directly against the grain of reading and writing to erect barriers between texts or to create monuments out of texts—unless, of course, literary scholars believe

7. J. Hillis Miller, "The Function of Rhetorical Study at the Present Time," *ADE Bulletin* 62 (September 1979): 12.

themselves to be servants of some outside power requiring this duty from them. The curricula of most literature departments in the university today are constructed almost entirely out of monuments, canonized into rigid dynastic formation, serviced and reserviced monotonously by a shrinking guild of humble servitors. The irony is that this is usually done in the name of historical research and traditional humanism, and yet such canons often have very little historical accuracy to them. To take one small example, Robert Darnton has shown that

> much of what passes today as 18th century French literature wasn't much read by Frenchmen in the 18th century. . . . We suffer from an arbitrary notion of literary history as a canon of classics, one which was developed by professors of literature in the 19th and 20th centuries—while in fact what people of the 18th century were reading was very different. By studying the publisher's accounts and papers at [the Société Typographique de] Neufchatel I've been able to construct a kind of bestseller list of pre-revolutionary France, and it doesn't look anything like the reading lists passed out in classrooms today.[8]

Hidden beneath the pieties surrounding the canonical monuments is a guild solidarity that dangerously resembles a religious consciousness. It is worth recalling Michael Bakunin in *Dieu et l'état:* "In their existing organization, monopolizing science and remaining thus outside social life, the *savants* form a separate caste, in many respects analogous to the priesthood. Scientific abstraction is their God, living and real individuals are their victims, and they are the consecrated and licensed sacrificers."[9] The current interest in producing enormous biographies of consecrated great authors is one aspect of this priestifying. By isolating and elevating the subject beyond his or her time and society, an exaggerated respect for single individuals is produced along with, naturally enough, awe for the biographer's craft. There are similar distortions in the emphasis placed on autobiographical literature whose modish name is "self-fashioning."

All this, then, atomizes, privatizes, and reifies the untidy realm of secular history and creates a peculiar configuration of constituencies and interpretive communities: this is the third major aspect of a contemporary politics of interpretation. An almost invariable rule of order is that very little of the *circumstances* making interpretive activity possible is allowed to seep into the interpretive circle itself. This is peculiarly (not to say distressingly) in evidence when humanists are called in to dignify dis-

8. Robert Darnton, "A Journeyman's Life under the Old Regime: Work and Culture in an Eighteenth-Century Printing Shop," *Princeton Alumni Weekly,* 7 September 1981, p. 12.

9. Michael Bakunin, *Selected Writings,* ed. and trans. Arthur Lehning (London, 1973), p. 160.

cussions of major public issues. I shall say nothing here about the egregious lapses (mostly concerning the relationship between the government-corporate policymakers and humanists on questions of national and foreign policy) to be found in the Rockefeller Foundation–funded report *The Humanities in American Life.* More crudely dramatic for my purposes is another Rockefeller enterprise, a conference on "The Reporting of Religion in the Media," held in August 1980. In addressing his opening remarks to the assembled collection of clerics, philosophers, and other humanists, Martin Marty evidently felt it would be elevating the discussion somewhat if he brought Admiral Stansfield Turner, head of the CIA, to his assistance: he therefore "quoted Admiral Turner's assertion that United States intelligence agencies had overlooked the importance of religion in Iran, 'because everyone knew it had so little place and power in the modern world.'" No one seemed to notice the natural affinity assumed by Marty between the CIA and scholars. It was all part of the mentality decreeing that humanists were humanists and experts experts no matter who sponsored their work, usurped their freedom of judgment and independence of research, or assimilated them unquestioningly to state service, even as they protested again and again that they were objective and nonpolitical.

Let me cite one small personal anecdote at the risk of overstating the point. Shortly before my book *Covering Islam* appeared, a private foundation convened a seminar on the book to be attended by journalists, scholars, and diplomats, all of whom had professional interests in how the Islamic world was being reported and represented in the West generally. I was to answer questions. One Pulitzer Prize–winning journalist, who is now the foreign news editor of a leading Eastern newspaper, was asked to lead the discussion, which he did by summarizing my argument briefly and on the whole not very accurately. He concluded his remarks by a question meant to initiate discussion: "Since you say that Islam is badly reported [actually my argument in the book is that "Islam" isn't something to be reported or nonreported: it is an ideological abstraction], could you tell us how we should report the Islamic world in order to help clarify the U.S.'s strategic interests there?" When I objected to the question, on the grounds that journalism was supposed to be either reporting or analyzing the news and not serving as an adjunct to the National Security Council, no attention was paid to what in everyone's eyes was an irrelevant naiveté on my part. Thus have the security interests of the state been absorbed silently into journalistic interpretation: expertise is therefore supposed to be unaffected by its institutional affiliations with power, although of course it is exactly those affiliations—hidden but assumed unquestioningly—that make the expertise possible and imperative.

Given this context, then, a constituency is principally a clientele: people who use (and perhaps buy) your services because you and others belonging to your guild are certified experts. For the relatively un-marketable humanists whose wares are "soft" and whose expertise is almost by definition marginal, their constituency is a fixed one composed of other humanists, students, government and corporate executives, and media employees, who use the humanist to assure a harmless place for "the humanities" or culture or literature in the society. I hasten to recall, however, that this is the role voluntarily accepted by humanists whose notion of what they do is neutralized, specialized, and nonpolitical in the extreme. To an alarming degree, the present continuation of the humanities depends, I think, on the sustained self-purification of humanists for whom the ethic of specialization has become equivalent to minimizing the content of their work and increasing the composite wall of guild consciousness, social authority, and exclusionary discipline around themselves. Opponents are therefore not people in disagree-ment with the constituency but people to be kept out, nonexperts and nonspecialists, for the most part.

Whether all this makes an interpretive *community*, in the secular and noncommercial, noncoercive sense of the word, is very seriously to be doubted. If a community is based principally on keeping people out and on defending a tiny fiefdom (in perfect complicity with the defenders of other fiefdoms) on the basis of a mysteriously pure subject's inviolable integrity, then it is a religious community. The secular realm I have presupposed requires a more open sense of community as something to be won and of audiences as human beings to be addressed. How, then, can we understand the present setting in such a way as to see in it the possibility of change? How can interpretation be interpreted as having a secular, political force in an age determined to deny interpretation any-thing but a role as mystification?

3

I shall organize my remarks around the notion of *representation,* which, for literary scholars at least, has a primordial importance. From Aristotle to Auerbach and after, mimesis is inevitably to be found in discussions of literary texts. Yet as even Auerbach himself showed in his monographic stylistic studies, techniques of representation in literary work have always been related to, and in some measure have depended on, social formations. The phrase "la cour et la ville," for example, makes primarily *literary* sense in a text by Nicolas Boileau, and although the text itself gives the phrase a peculiarly refined local meaning, it nevertheless presupposed both an audience that knew he referred to what Auerbach calls "his social environment" and the social environment itself, which made references to it possible. This is not *simply* a matter of reference, since, from a verbal point of view, referents can be said to be equal and equally verbal. Even in very minute analyses, Auerbach's view does, however, have to do with the *coexistence* of realms—the literary, the social, the personal—and the way in which they make use of, affiliate with, and represent each other.

With very few exceptions, contemporary literary theories assume the relative independence and even autonomy of literary representation over (and not just from) all others. Novelistic verisimilitude, poetic tropes, and dramatic metaphors (Lukács, Harold Bloom, Francis Ferguson) are representations to and for themselves of the novel, the poem, the drama: this, I think, accurately sums up the assumptions underlying the three influential (and, in their own way, typical) theories I have referred to. Moreover, the organized study of literature—*en soi* and *pour soi*—is premised on the constitutively primary act of literary (that is, artistic) representation, which in turn absorbs and incorporates other realms, other representations, secondary to it. But all this institutional weight has precluded a sustained, systematic examination of the coexistence of and the interrelationship between the literary and the social, which is where representation—from journalism, to political struggle, to economic production and power—plays an extraordinarily important role. Confined to the study of one representational complex, literary critics accept and paradoxically ignore the lines drawn around what they do.

This is depoliticization with a vengeance, and it must, I think, be understood as an integral part of the historical moment presided over by Reaganism. The division of intellectual labor I spoke of earlier can now be seen as assuming a *thematic* importance in the contemporary culture as a whole. For if the study of literature is "only" about literary representation, then it must be the case that literary representations and literary activities (writing, reading, producing the "humanities," and arts and letters) are essentially ornamental, possessing at most secondary ideological characteristics. The consequence is that to deal with literature as well as the broadly defined "humanities" is to deal with the non-political, although quite evidently the political realm is presumed to lie just beyond (and beyond the reach of) literary, and hence *literate,* concern.

A perfect recent embodiment of this state of affairs is the 30 September 1981 issue of *The New Republic.* The lead editorial analyzes the United States' policy toward South Africa and ends up supporting this policy, which even the most "moderate" of Black African states interpret (correctly, as even the United States explicitly confesses) as a policy supporting the South African settler-colonial regime. The last article of the issue includes a mean personal attack on me as "an intellectual in the thrall of Soviet totalitarianism," a claim that is as disgustingly McCarthyite as it is intellectually fraudulent. Now at the very center of this issue of the magazine—a fairly typical issue by the way—is a long and decently earnest book review by Christopher Hill, a leading Marxist historian. What boggles the mind is not the mere coincidence of apologies for apartheid rubbing shoulders with good Marxist sense but how the one antipode includes (without any reference at all) what the other, the Marxist pole, performs unknowingly.

There are two very impressive points of reference for this discussion of what can be called the national culture as a nexus of relationships between "fields," many of them employing representation as their technique of distribution and production. (It will be obvious here that I exclude the creative arts and the natural sciences.) One is Perry Anderson's "Components of the National Culture" (1969);[10] the other is Regis Debray's study of the French intelligentsia, *Teachers, Writers, Celebrities* (1980). Anderson's argument is that an absent intellectual center in traditional British thought about society was vulnerable to a "white" (antirevolutionary, conservative) immigration into Britain from Europe. This in turn produced a blockage of sociology, a technicalization of philosophy, an idea-free empiricism in history, and an idealist aesthetics. Together these and other disciplines form "something like a closed system," in which subversive discourses like Marxism and psychoanalysis were for a time quarantined; now, however, they too have been incorporated. The French case, according to Debray, exhibits a series of three hegemonic conquests in time. First there was the era of the secular universities, which ended with World War I. That was succeeded by the era of the publishing houses, a time between the wars when Galimard-NRF—agglomerates of gifted writers and essayists that included Jacques Rivière, André Gide, Marcel Proust, and Paul Valéry—replaced the social and intellectual authority of the somewhat overproductive, mass-populated universities. Finally, during the 1960s, intellectual life was absorbed into the structure of the mass media: worth, merit, attention, and visibility slipped from the pages of books to be estimated by frequency of appearance on the television screen. At this point, then, a new hierarchy, what Debray calls a mediocracy, emerges, and it rules the schools and the book industry.

There are certain similarities between Debray's France and Anderson's England, on the one hand, and Reagan's America, on the other. They are interesting, but I cannot spend time talking about them. The differences are, however, more instructive. Unlike France, high culture in America is assumed to be above politics as a matter of unanimous convention. And unlike England, the intellectual center here is filled not by European imports (although they play a considerable role) but by an unquestioned ethic of objectivity and realism, based essentially on an epistemology of separation and difference. Thus each field is separate

10. See Perry Anderson, "Components of the National Culture," in *Student Power,* ed. Alexander Cockburn and Robin Blackburn (London, 1969).

from the others because the subject matter is separate. Each separation corresponds immediately to a separation in function, institution, history, and purpose. Each discourse "represents" the field, which in turn is supported by its own constituency and the specialized audience to which it appeals. The mark of true professionalism is accuracy of representation of society, vindicated in the case of sociology, for instance, by a direct correlation between representation of society and corporate and/or governmental interests, a role in social policymaking, access to political authority. Literary studies, conversely, are realistically *not* about society but about masterpieces in need of periodic adulation and appreciation. Such correlations make possible the use of words like "objectivity," "realism," and "moderation" when used in sociology or in literary criticism. And these notions in turn assure their own confirmation by careful selectivity of evidence, the incorporation and subsequent neutralization of dissent (also known as pluralism), and networks of insiders, experts whose presence is due to their conformity, not to any rigorous judgment of their past performance (the good team player always turns up).

But I must press on, even though there are numerous qualifications and refinements to be added at this point (e.g., the organized relationship between clearly affiliated fields such as political science and sociology versus the use by one field of another unrelated one for the purposes of national policy issues; the network of patronage and the insider/outsider dichotomy; the strange cultural encouragement of theories stressing such "components" of the structure of power as chance, morality, American innocence, decentralized egos, etc.). The particular mission of the humanities is, in the aggregate, to represent *noninterference* in the affairs of the everyday world. As we have seen, there has been a historical erosion in the role of letters since the New Criticism, and I have suggested that the conjuncture of a narrowly based university environment for technical language and literature studies with the self-policing, self-purifying communities erected even by Marxist, as well as other disciplinary, discourses, produced a very small but definite function for the humanities: to represent humane marginality, which is also to preserve and if possible to conceal the hierarchy of powers that occupy the center, define the social terrain, and fix the limits of use functions, fields, marginality, and so on. Some of the corollaries of this role for the humanities generally and literary criticism in particular are that the institutional presence of humanities guarantees a space for the deployment of free-floating abstractions (scholarship, taste, tact, humanism) that are defined in advance as indefinable; that when it is not easily domesticated, "theory" is employable as a discourse of occultation and legitimation; that self-regulation is the ethos behind which the institutional humanities allow and in a sense encourage the unrestrained operation of market forces that were traditionally thought of as subject to ethical and philosophical review.

Very broadly stated, then, noninterference for the humanist means laissez-faire: "they" can run the country, we will explicate Wordsworth and Schlegel. It does not stretch things greatly to note that noninterference and rigid specialization in the academy are directly related to what has been called a counterattack by "highly mobilized business elites" in reaction to the immediately preceding period during which national needs were thought of as fulfilled by resources allocated collectively and democratically. However, working through foundations, think tanks, sectors of the academy, and the government, corporate elites according to David Dickson and David Noble "proclaimed a new age of reason while remystifying reality." This involved a set of "interrelated" epistemological and ideological imperatives, which are an extrapolation from the noninterference I spoke about earlier. Each of these imperatives is in congruence with the way intellectual and academic "fields" view themselves internally and across the dividing lines:

1. The rediscovery of the self-regulating market, the wonders of free enterprise, and the classical liberal attack on government regulation of the economy, all in the name of liberty.
2. The reinvention of the idea of progress, now cast in terms of "innovation" and "reindustrialization," and the limitation of expectations and social welfare in the quest for productivity.
3. The attack on democracy, in the name of "efficiency," "manageability," "governability," "rationality," and "competence."
4. The remystification of science through the promotion of formalized decision methodologies, the restoration of the authority of expertise, and the renewed use of science as legitimation for social policy through deepening industry ties to universities and other "free" institutions of policy analysis and recommendation.[11]

In other words, (1) says that literary criticism minds its own business and is "free" to do what it wishes with no community responsibility whatever. Hence at one end of the scale, for instance, is the recent successful attack on the NEH for funding too many socially determined programs and, at the other end, the proliferation of private critical languages with an absurdist bent presided over paradoxically by "big name professors," who also extol the virtues of humanism, pluralism, and humane scholarship. Retranslated, (2) has meant that the number of

11. David Dickson and David Noble, "By Force of Reason: The Politics of Science and Policy," in *The Hidden Election,* ed. Thomas Ferguson and Joel Rogers (New York, 1981), p. 267.

jobs for young graduates has shrunk dramatically as the "inevitable" result of market forces, which in turn prove the marginality of scholarship that is premised on its own harmless social obsolescence. This has created a demand for sheer innovation and indiscriminate publication (e.g., the sudden increase in advanced critical journals; the departmental need for experts and courses in theory and structuralism), and it has virtually destroyed the career trajectory and social horizons of young people within the system. Imperatives (3) and (4) have meant the recrudescence of strict professionalism for sale to any client, deliberately oblivious of the complicity between the academy, the government, and the corporations, decorously silent on the large questions of social, economic, and foreign policy.

Very well: if what I have been saying has any validity, then the politics of interpretation demands a dialectical response from a critical consciousness worthy of its name. Instead of noninterference and specialization, there must be *interference,* a crossing of borders and obstacles, a determined attempt to generalize exactly at those points where generalizations seem impossible to make. One of the first interferences to be ventured, then, is a crossing from literature, which is supposed to be subjective and powerless, into those exactly parallel realms, now covered by journalism and the production of information, that employ representation but are supposed to be objective and powerful. Here we have a superb guide in John Berger, in whose most recent work there is the basis of a major critique of modern representation. Berger suggests that if we regard photography as coeval in its origins with sociology and positivism (and I would add the classic realistic novel), we see that

> what they shared was the hope that observable quantifiable facts, recorded by experts, would constitute the proven truth that humanity required. Precision would replace metaphysics; planning would resolve conflicts. What happened, instead, was that the way was opened to a view of the world in which everything and everybody could be reduced to a factor in a calculation, and the calculation was profit.[12]

Much of the world today is represented in this way: as the McBride Commission Report has it, a tiny handful of large and powerful oligarchies control about ninety percent of the world's information and communication flows. This domain, staffed by experts and media executives, is, as Herbert Schiller and others have shown, affiliated to an even smaller number of governments, at the very same time that the rhetoric of objectivity, balance, realism, and freedom covers what is being done. And for the most part, such consumer items as "the news"—a

12. John Berger, "Another Way of Telling," *Journal of Social Reconstruction* 1 (January–March 1980): 64.

euphemism for ideological images of the world that determine political reality for a vast majority of the world's population—hold forth, untouched by interfering secular and critical minds, who for all sorts of obvious reasons are not hooked into the systems of power.

This is not the place, nor is there time, to advance a fully articulated program of interference. I can only suggest in conclusion that we need to think about breaking out of the disciplinary ghettos in which as intellectuals we have been confined, to reopen the blocked social processes ceding objective representation (hence power) of the world to a small coterie of experts and their clients, to consider that the audience for literacy is not a closed circle of three thousand professional critics but the community of human beings living in society, and to regard social reality in a secular rather than a mystical mode, despite all the protestations about realism and objectivity.

Two concrete tasks—again adumbrated by Berger—strike me as particularly useful. One is to use the visual faculty (which also happens to be dominated by visual media such as television, news photography, and commercial film, all of them fundamentally immediate, "objective," and ahistorical) to restore the nonsequential energy of lived historical memory and subjectivity as fundamental components of meaning in representation. Berger calls this an alternative use of photography: using photomontage to tell other stories than the official sequential or ideological ones produced by institutions of power. (Superb examples are Sarah Graham-Brown's photo-essay *The Palestinians and Their Society* and Susan Mcisalas' *Nicaragua*.) Second is opening the culture to experiences of the Other which have remained "outside" (and have been repressed or framed in a context of confrontational hostility) the norms manufactured by "insiders." An excellent example is Malek Alloula's *Le Harem colonial*, a study of early twentieth-century postcards and photographs of Algerian harem women. The pictorial capture of colonized people by colonizer, which signifies power, is reenacted by a young Algerian sociologist, Alloula, who sees his own fragmented history in the pictures, then reinscribes this history in his text as the result of understanding and making that intimate experience intelligible for an audience of modern European readers.

In both instances, finally, we have the recovery of a history hitherto either misrepresented or rendered invisible. Stereotypes of the Other have always been connected to political actualities of one sort or another, just as the truth of lived communal (or personal) experience has often been totally sublimated in official narratives, institutions, and ideologies. But in having attempted—and perhaps even successfully accomplishing—this recovery, there is the crucial next phase: connecting these more politically vigilant forms of interpretation to an ongoing political and social praxis. Short of making that connection, even the best-intentioned and the cleverest interpretive activity is bound to sink back into the murmur of mere prose. For to move from interpretation to its politics is in large measure to go from undoing to doing, and this, given the currently accepted divisions between criticism and art, is risking all the discomfort of a great unsettlement in ways of seeing and doing. One must refuse to believe, however, that the comforts of specialized habits can be so seductive as to keep us all in our assigned places.

Poet: Patriot: Interpreter

Donald A. Davie

The man without a country is a corpse without a grave.
—PUBLILIUS

Fifteen or twenty years ago, when I was a fellow of a Cambridge College, my physicist colleagues would from time to time bring to lunch or to dine physicist colleagues of theirs visiting from the Soviet Union; and I would be introduced to Anatoli from Leningrad or Dmitri from Kharkov. Seeing alike on the British and the Russian faces the shine of pleasure at making human contact with persons otherwise and earlier known only as names appended to papers in professional journals, I found such occasions touching, even exalting. There I saw in living fact what university presidents and such paid glib lip-service to as "the international community of scholars." It was plain that in certain important fields of their experience my British colleagues and their Russian opposite numbers felt more community with each other than either felt with his next-door neighbour in a British or a Russian street. And I felt wistfully that, if I were ever in the position of bringing to dine a Russian poet or literary historian, the situation could not be the same—the language of literary studies was not, and could not be, an international language such as that in which British and Russian physicists could communicate. Later, however, when I pondered such occasions, I wondered about a conflict of interests such as surely must arise for my colleagues—if not in actual fact, at least in not outlandish imaginings. There was, surely, a community of interests with the next-door neighbour which at all events could, even if it never did, conflict with the community of interests felt between

atomic physicists world-wide. How did my colleagues resolve such a conflict or contemplate resolving it if they were ever compelled to do so?
And of course the newspapers of a few years before told of resolutions
which had been found unacceptable: the so-called atom spies, Klaus
Fuchs, Alan Nunn May, and Pontecorvo, who had (so one version went)
allowed their allegiance to international physics to override their at least
equal obligations, as citizens, to "the guy next door." What I found
myself puzzling about, in fact, was what status, if any, remained for the
concept of patriotism in the context of an "international community of
scholars." I have not ceased to puzzle about this; my puzzlement is what I
now share with those who care to listen.

One brutally obvious solution was available to me from the first, and
of course over the years it has been pressed on me many times. It consists
in denying that patriotism, in the straightforward sense of loyalty to the
patria, has any claims on us now; that it belongs in phases of political
organization and consciousness which have been conclusively superseded; and that it is indeed only a pretty and affecting name for what is
more accurately known under the ugly names "chauvinism" or
"nationalism." On this showing Fuchs and Nunn May and Pontecorvo,
along with other alleged or convicted or self-confessed "traitors," not all
of them scientists, were simply victims, if not indeed heroic martyrs,
immolated on a false principle which they had enlightenedly outgrown
whereas their societies benightedly had not. For without loyalty there
can be no question of disloyalty; without patriotism there cannot be
treachery. This, however, may be contested. If we ask whether within the
professional world of international scholarship there can be conduct
which can rightly be called "treacherous," most of us will agree that there
can be such conduct; one can be treacherous to a colleague, one may
betray him, by stealing his unpublished findings and publishing them
over one's own name or by wilfully misrepresenting his findings so that
he stands convicted of opinions that he does not hold. Or again (much
more dubiously to be sure) one can still hear of "class traitors," of
treachery to the cause of the international working-class. Thus it appears
that loyalty and treachery are words still meaningful to us; what is disputed is whether they still have meaning in relation to the patria, the
homeland, the nation.

The first thing to be said of such an attitude is that it is a luxury,

---

Donald A. Davie, the distinguished poet, is Andrew W. Mellon Pro-
fessor of the Humanities at Vanderbilt University and honorary fellow
of Saint Catharine's College, Cambridge and of Trinity College, Dublin.
He has edited *The New Oxford Book of Christian Verse,* and his *Collected
Poems 1950–1970* appeared in 1972. His latest publications are *Dissentient
Voice* and *These the Companions; Recollections.*

available only to people like ourselves and to be voiced only in such a specially privileged ambience as the one where we find ourselves. We all know—whether we are American, British, Russian, or whatever—that the vast majority of our fellow-citizens do believe in loyalty to the patria and that the legal codes which presuppose such a belief accurately reflect the consensus of thought in our societies. Accordingly, if we scorn such beliefs as long ago superseded by historical developments, we are taking an extremely élitist attitude—which may be okay, only we ought to know what we are doing. Another consideration, which I must admit weighs with me a great deal more, is that by thus loftily declaring ourselves "citizens of the world," we cut ourselves off not just from the majority of our fellow-citizens at the present day but from the far more numerous multitude of the dead. For there can be no doubt that to Virgil and Dante and Machiavelli, to Milton and Wordsworth, to Washington and Jefferson and Walt Whitman, the patria was meaningful, and its claims upon us were real and must be honoured, in just the ways that this sort of modern enlightenment refuses to countenance. The consequences of thus cutting ourselves off from our forebears are dire, and they are all around us, for those who care to look; they manifest themselves in *style*, in our styles of thought and more evidently in our styles of speaking and writing.

For at this point I will come clean and declare myself: I must and do believe in the patria, and in patriotism as a not yet superseded principle in politics, and also in "interpretation." I must do this because I am a student and a practitioner of the linguistic arts, and each extant language of mankind is a vehicle of the national consciousness of those for whom it is the mother tongue. And the female gender in "mother," along with the gender often allotted to the patria (*la belle France*), at least alleviates, if not removes, the bias in the etymology of "pater." All the languages are precious, every one is unique, and so no one is replaceable by any other. And thus I come full circle on the recognition that between me and a Russian poet or literary historian there was not, and there could not be, any such *lingua franca* as a page of equations could constitute for British and Russian physicists. I restate this observation not wistfully but defiantly. For when a poet or a literary scholar, British or American or Australian, addresses not his fellow-Britons or his fellow-Americans or fellow-Australians but the international community of literary scholars, that intention shows up at once in the sort of English that he uses: on the one hand, arcane jargon, caviar to the general; on the other hand, infinitely and immediately translatable, and therefore without any reference to, or resonance from, the generations of usage, British or American or Antipodean, as the case may be, which alone give to English its range of nuance and its wealth of implication. I think I need not give examples: book after book from our university presses and issue after issue of our respectable scholarly magazines are written in this debased and yet pretentious Esperanto or dog-Latin. I am told that a similar debasement is evident in French and that indeed French and Anglo-American infect each other, taking in each other's extremely dirty linen—some evidence of which I do in fact think that I see from time to time. We say of such writers that they use English as if it were a foreign language; and this is exactly so—English as the vehicle of expression for the English-speaking folk through the generations *is* foreign to such writers because they have chosen to make it so, because as they write they are addressing not the person next door or on the next campus but rather (through translation, if need be) Georges in Bucharest or Lucille in Vincennes. If I seem intemperate, you must please bear in mind that in my particular line of business I see such disparities at their most glaring—as when a poem by, say, Andrew Marvell, a miracle of delicate adjustment between the registers of spoken and written seventeenth-century English, is interpreted in English prose that deploys and wheels into action massively mechanized battalions of internationally accredited abstractions.

A brief digression here, to guard against misunderstanding: I am not girding against abstractions as such—after all, "patriotism" is itself an abstraction and one that I am urging be reinstated in our discourse from which it has been for too long conspicuously absent. I am objecting to a sort of abstraction that I call "internationally accredited." Perhaps after all I should give an example—chosen, I assure you, virtually at random:

> We see in this rehearsal of "Foucault" that contemporary criticism cherishes the displacement both of dialectics by diacritics and of totalized organic representations of history by comprehensive graphs of affiliated disciplines in the epistème.[1]

Reading such jaw-breaking propositions—and we all know how commonly they present themselves to us and our students (we have been hearing some of them at this conference)—we find ourselves echoing Ben Jonson when he objected to one of his contemporaries that he "writ no language." For such formulations cannot be said to be written in British English or in American English or in French but only in an ungainly jargon compounded out of all three. I may as well take the risk of giving offence and confess that I think such linguistic enormities became inevitable as soon as "the scholarly paper" and the scholarly "article" became established among us as literary *genres* distinct from the essay on the one hand and the lecture on the other.

At any rate, you already see one way in which I would claim that patriotism, that admittedly assailable sentiment, can be an incentive for those of us who promulgate our findings in discursive English. It incites

1. William V. Spanos, Paul A. Bove, and Daniel O'Hara, intro. to *Boundary 2* 8 (Fall 1979): 3.

us to recognize, through our way of handling our language, that the intellectual endeavour we are engaged in is continuous with that of Edmund Burke maybe or Jonathan Swift, or of Jonathan Edwards and John Adams. In that way it cuts us down to size, it cures us of cocky presumption. Interpretation pursued in this spirit is, no doubt, politically conservative; and I would not dispute the inference that literary studies, of the sort that I respect and try to practise, are of their own nature rather profoundly conservative—they have an inbuilt bias toward preserving, *con*serving, keeping in memory. This does not mean, of course, that they therefore recommend themselves to the political powers behind the status quo at any given time; on the contrary, since such powers often are, or like to think that they are, "progressive" or "innovative," the literary scholar's inbuilt proclivity toward dragging his feet is likely to irritate grant-awarding government agencies more than a little. More generally, "conservative" in the sense of "keeping in mind" has little or nothing to do with what the word means in the mouths of political journalists. The keeping in mind, or bringing back to mind, of principles and liberties long overlooked is just as likely to figure in their vocabulary as "liberal" or "radical."

Patriotic feeling in a scholar, however, can fuel in him incentives of an altogether more momentous sort. I think of the philosopher George Berkeley when, still a student at Trinity College, Dublin, he confided to his Commonplace Book certain statements of Lockean epistemology and then declared: "We Irishmen cannot attain to these truths":

> There are men who say there are insensible extensions.
> There are others who say the fire is not hot.
> ....
>
> We Irishmen are apt to think something and nothing
> are near neighbours.
> The mathematicians think there are insensible lines.
> About them they harangue.
> We Irishmen can conceive no such lines.
> I publish this to see if others have the same ideas as
> we Irishmen.[2]

This declaration is remarkable, in fact astonishing, in several different ways: to begin with, that Irishness which Berkeley so confidently claimed would be disputed, if not explicitly denied him, by most of the marchers in Saint Patrick's Day parades in Boston or New York or (I suppose) Chicago; and, though Berkeley indeed was born on Irish soil and his family had resided in Ireland for two generations, his English cousins,

---

2. George Berkeley, quoted in Joseph Maunsell Hone and Mario M. Rossi, *Bishop Berkeley: His Life, Writings, and Philosophy* (London, 1931), p. 28.

the senior branch of the family, as the philosopher well knew, still occupied their seat in Berkeley, Gloucestershire—from which English
place the family indeed appears to have derived its name. This shows
that for certain people at certain times in certain places the patria is not
anything they are simply stuck with by an accident of birth. It may be
negotiable and a matter of conscious or unconscious choice on the part
of the individual. By the same token, we may declare our allegiance to
two patrias at the same time. No one apparently asks the marchers in
Saint Patrick's Day parades to decide between a patria that is an as yet
unconsummated Republic of All Ireland and another patria that is the
United States of America. Thus we allow people to declare in one sentence "We Welsh" or "We Irish" or "We Scots" or "We English" and in
the next sentence without fear of contradiction (or without *much* fear of
it) "We British"; and in the same way "We Virginians" is not held to be at
odds with "We Americans."

     All the same, as to an American audience the case of the Virginians
may bring home very poignantly, there can arise historical situations in
which the dual allegiance cannot be maintained, in which one is forced to
choose one patria over the other. That choice cannot be other than a
political choice; and if one is an artist or a scholar, it is mere casuistry to
say that the decision is made in one's capacity as a citizen and not in one's
professional capacity. The case of Berkeley is very instructive in this
respect: it was only when modern scholars of Berkeley like A. A. Luce
and T. E. Jessop pondered this entry in his Commonplace Book (along
with other evidence to be sure) that they envisaged the possibility that
Berkeley, so far from extending and driving deeper the furrow that
John Locke had ploughed (which was the view held of Berkeley's epistemology through two centuries), was in fact promoting a radical
alternative to Locke—as it were, Irish common sense as against English
common sense. And the modern revolution in the understanding of
Berkeley derives from that perception: in other words, it was as a philosopher rather than as a citizen that Berkeley proudly declared himself an
Irishman. And while no one would want to maintain that Berkeley's
perception of himself as Irish (distinctively non-English) *originated* his
critique of Locke, still all the evidence is that this perception
strengthened his critique and heartened him in formulating it and
pushing it through—there was, he felt, a consensus that he could appeal
to, in support of it.

     If patriotism can thus be seen as an incentive or as an instigation
even in such a recondite science as epistemology, how much more
readily can it be seen to perform such functions in other studies more
immediately or inextricably bound up with communal human life? I pass
over instances that occur to me—for instance, the Victorian Jesuit,
Father Hopkins, declaring (too shrilly for modern susceptibilities) that
every good poem written by an Englishman was a blow struck for

England—and profit instead, if I may, by the presence among us of Edward Said. I do not know, and it is none of my business to know, what passport Said presents at the international frontier. But it is surely common knowledge among us that he has deep and feelingful and intimate allegiances to the state of Lebanon. Who of us has failed to connect this with his books *Orientalism* and *The Question of Palestine*? The point is that, having made this connection, none of us thinks the worse of Said. On the contrary, we recognize that he has a special stake in such topics and therefore speaks on them with a special authority. Unless I am mistaken, that stake and that authority are, in a perhaps extended sense, *patriotic*. And whatever our speculative objections to the idea and the principle of patriotism, in practice we recognize it and we honour it.

What I am questioning, it will now be plain, is the principle of "disinterest." "The *disinterested* pursuit of knowledge"—it is what in our distinct disciplines all of us have paid lip-service to, and perhaps more than lip-service. But when we come right down to it, is it what we believe? The honest patriot declares an interest; and if we are wise, we take note of the declaration, making allowances and reserving doubts accordingly. But what are we to make of the scholar who declares no interest, who claims implicitly to be truly disinterested? Can we believe him? And if we cannot, what guidance do we have as to what reservations to make, what doubts to entertain? I am of one mind with my Marxist colleagues who, from a political position very far from mine, warn us to be especially suspicious of the scholar who claims to have no axe to grind. We, all of us, have axes to grind; the crucial distinction is between those who know this about themselves and those who don't.

Let me make myself clear. When I urge that the terms "patriotism" and "patriotic" be reinstated in our discourse, and particularly in those forms of our discourse that may be called "interpretation," I do not imply that patriotism is a nobler, a more elevated instigation than sundry others, mostly ideological, of which we are more aware. The point is precisely that of these others we are aware because we share a vocabulary which acknowledges them, whereas "patriotic" has been banished from our vocabulary, and so the reality which the word represents is left out of our calculations. Let me admit for the sake of argument what I do not in fact believe—that patriotism is a concept and a sentiment so besmirched by the unholy uses made of it that, if mankind is to survive, patriotism will have to be eradicated. Even if that were the case, it remains true that patriotic interest and incitement are very far from having been eradicated from the world that we in fact inhabit, and try to interpret, here and now; and if we try to work within a vocabulary that pretends otherwise, we condemn ourselves to producing interpretations that are drastically partial and perhaps disastrously misleading. The point is not whether patriotism is a good thing or a bad thing but simply that it *is;* it exists, as a powerful factor which we all in our hearts acknowledge even as our vocabulary refuses to. And when we speak in this context of "the world," we certainly include in that world ourselves, who offer to interpret it. Every one of our interpretations is coloured by the fact that we, the several interpreters, are British or American, French or Italian or Russian or whatever. If we think otherwise, we deceive ourselves; and yet where, in any of our currently acceptable vocabularies, determined as all of them are by the glib rationalism of the Enlightenment, do we find that momentous fact about ourselves acknowledged? Where is it acknowledged, for instance, in the vocabulary of feminism that "woman," as conceived by an American writing about Italians, cannot help but be significantly different from "woman" as conceived by an Italian looking at Americans? Or again, an Italian woman may well, we must suppose, be an Italian patriot; but where, in the current vocabulary of feminists, is that dimension of her "woman-ness" allowed for? Let it be acknowledged only so as to be deplored; but let it in any event be acknowledged. At the moment, it isn't.

Said tells an affecting story which brings the issues home to us better than any argument can. When his Palestinian parents married, they had to register the marriage with the authorities of what was at that time a British mandate. The British officer, having registered the marriage, then and there tore up Mrs. Said's Palestinian passport, explaining that by doing so he made one more vacancy in the quota of permitted immigrants to Palestine from among the dispossessed of war-devastated Europe. The feminist response to this—"Aha, it was *the wife's* passport that was destroyed, not the husband's"—wholly fails to recognize the outrage that Mrs. Said felt, which her son now feels on her behalf. For if the law had been such that the husband took his bride's name, so that it was the man's passport that was destroyed, the outrage would have been just the same. Even further beside the point is the ready-made vocabulary about "colonialism." For the British officer's explanation was not that of the colonizer addressing the colonized but, on the contrary, was offered according to the utilitarian logic of "the greatest good of the greatest number." He spoke not the language of the master race but the language of international philanthropy, the language of "concerned" and enlightened liberalism, of social engineering. And that language, which is still by and large the language that we all use when speaking of these matters, has no words for the pang of ravishment that a person feels when his or her national identity is symbolically cancelled before his or her eyes. What was taken from the woman was her patria; and her sense of having been violated, though it may have been "irrational," was thoroughly reasonable. Anyone who cannot sympathize with her has become a slave to the terms of accepted discourse and has no access to the different vocabulary of literature, where the reality and rightness of such responses are continually asserted or taken for granted.

And yet, to make the point again, we should not jump to the conclusion that patiotism is a nobler, a more reliable, and more humane standard than others to which we find it easier to declare our allegiance. No one should need to be reminded of the wrongs done in the name of a debased patriotism by those who, for instance, hunt down and expose allegedly "un-American activities." And remembering Berkeley's "Irish" common sense, we should remember also from the Stalinist era the aberrations and obfuscations of "Soviet genetics" and "Soviet linguistics," not to speak of the dangerous myths peddled in all countries at all times by confessedly "patriotic" historians. Moreover, we clearly can't be drawn along the Woodrow Wilson path into national self-determination, to the point where we approve indiscriminately "free" Kurdistan and Armenia, "free" Croatia and Latvia and Ulster. At the outset I declared patriotism a puzzle, and I promised only to share my puzzlement about it. I contend only that it is more of a puzzle, and a more central puzzle, than most of us want to admit. May it not be the case, for instance, that those influential interpreters of events, our journalists, would be less puzzled (and puzzling) about what is going on in the Middle East if they were *more* puzzled about their own American-ness, and less confident that that condition of theirs did not colour their observations and judgments? Is not this, rather than any more conspiratorial theory, the most plausible explanation of what has been called "consensual determination" in this country about Iran both under the Shah and under Khomeini?

I have proposed as the firmest and most manageable focus for patriotism the mother tongue. (*Focus* in Latin means "hearth.") And I had in mind how Pasternak in *Doctor Zhivago* seems to rest his case against the October Revolution ultimately on the damage it has done to the Russian language, the language of Pushkin. But of course this notion too is full of puzzlements—in a way that we, as English speakers, are well placed to recognize. For Britons and Americans and New Zealanders all speak English; how, then, can a New Zealander's mother tongue be the badge and warranty of his nationhood, the focus of his allegiance to New Zealand as his patria? Must we assume that British English, American English, and New Zealand English are on the way to becoming distinct languages, as Romanian and Portuguese once became distinct languages by diverging differently from the parent stock of Roman Latin? The suggestion will seem bizarre except to those of us who study and try to practise translation as an exacting art, rather than as something which in the foreseeable future machines may do for us. Already there exist alternative translations of, for instance, the Russian poetry of Osip Mandelstam into American English and British English. Perhaps what we can expect and should hope for is not just a translation of Mandelstam into New Zealand English but (presumably at a later stage) also distinct translations into the several "Englishes" of prose, for instance of the French of Jacques Derrida.

If we want to be sure of distinguishing patriotism from the tub-thumping jingoism of the British Legion or the American Veterans of Foreign Wars, we can best do so by proposing that patriotism is an essentially tragic condition—not just for dispossessed nations like the Latvians and the Lebanese but for all of us. For what the sincere patriot feels most often is *shame*—shame for what his nation is, by contrast with what it might be, what he dreams of for it, what perhaps it once was. The pride and the shame are two faces of the one coin. Thus "shamefast" is a keen and bitter word, the edge of it lost when false etymology made it into "shamefaced." For what is most often and most painfully imposed on the patriot is silence. This too has its shadowy and disgraceful side, as when we speak of crimes and conspiracies of silence—the silence, for instance, of patriotic Germans about the Nazi "final solution." But I have in mind something altogether more commonplace, as when I confess that I have rather bitter criticisms to make of the present temper of British society, criticisms I would voice in London but prefer to keep silent about here, in Chicago. Silence, therefore. Or, if you will, silencing.

This may be imposed. We all know there are nation-states in which certain notions are held to be unthinkable, at all events unsayable—in which, accordingly, the state has reserved for itself powers to ensure that the unsayable shall not be said, at least in print. This is censorship; a power which, so far as I can see, every modern state has claimed for itself, though some exercise the power much more often and more light-heartedly than others. To legitimate this power, most such states claim to articulate the sentiments of the nation which the state represents; and the claim is not one which can be easily set aside—in a one-party state, when a specific ideology has been promulgated without competition through two generations, it is almost certainly true that the nation as a whole, on a count of heads, endorses with enthusiasm the censorship which the nation-state imposes on its dissidents. We are deluding ourselves if we suppose that when sorts of state censorship were imposed on Pasternak and Solzhenitsyn and Sakharov the consensus of the Soviet people was not behind such actions—on the contrary, ideological conditioning through the state-controlled communications media had almost certainly ensured that such a consensus existed. And if the Russian artist or scientist nevertheless bucks that consensus and claims patriotic motives for so doing, on what is his patriotism grounded? His patriotism is either unashamedly élitist or else (or as well) ideal: he must claim to speak for a Russian nation that *might have been* (if it had not been subjected to ideological conditioning) or else for a Russian nation defined in terms of its unrepresentative élite through the generations, from Aleksandr Radischev through Pushkin and Tolstoy. Either way—there is no getting away from it—his position is profoundly undemocratic, if by democracy we understand citizens' individual opinions registered either by a show of hands or through the ballot-box.

Such state-authorized silencing of artists and scholars can take many forms, some much more lenient than others. The dissident thinker, for instance, can be allowed to publicize his dissident opinions abroad and in a foreign language; he may even be allowed to publicize them at home and in his native language but through a publishing house from which state subsidies have been withheld so as to ensure that his opinions do not circulate widely. State censorship, if we consider the supposedly free world as well as the demonstrably unfree, can take many forms, some of which appear at first sight innocuous and unexceptionable.

However, far more interesting and moving than any instances of externally imposed silence are the cases of silence self-imposed. But how are such cases to be enumerated or documented? Silence is silence and by its nature registers no blips on any radar screen. We can only speculate how many scholars there are, and have been, who have arrived at interpretations or findings which they have judged too perilous to promulgate—not just too dangerous for them personally but too dangerously demoralizing or distracting for the nation of which they feel themselves a part, committed (it may well be) to a national short-term programme which calls for all citizens' efforts to be directed to a single unblinking end. It is easy, and perhaps it is even right, to condemn as unscholarly or worse any instance we come across of scholarly findings thus suppressed or postponed to a date when publication of them will cause less uproar. But it is not hard for any of us to imagine circumstances—for instance, of our nation at war and facing defeat—in which the issue would not be, for the solitary scholar, at all so clear-cut. Consider only the case of "the secret weapon," on whose secret deployment rested the only hope for one's nation of staving off military defeat. Is it true that, if one possessed the crucial secret, one would be duty bound to communicate it at once to the international scholarly community, at whatever cost?

An easier case, and one that can be documented, though only circumstantially, is the silence that poets at any rate have imposed on themselves through periods when, in their opinion, their nation was behaving shamefully—for instance (though here I speak subject to correction), the increasingly eloquent silence maintained from about 1948 through 1955 by the dean of Hungarian poets, Gyula Illyes. In the case of a poet like Illyes, whose rank has been widely acknowledged, silence—refusal to publish—can itself be eloquent: conspicuous inaction qualifies as momentous *action*. But of course for a writer or scholar whose reputation has yet to be made, that finesse is not available. And with self-imposed as with state-imposed silence, many gradations may be observed. Is one, for instance, eloquently keeping silence when one publishes indeed, but only translations from a foreign tongue? The Academies of many unfree states, including the Soviet Union, have tempted men of letters with that beguiling half-way house between speech and silence. The texts to be translated are prescribed of course, not left to the translator's whim or need. But if I, in such circumstances, were presented with such an innocuously bland and even seemingly enlightened alternative, I don't know how I would determine where my duty lay. Between fearlessly independent "speaking out" and craven "knuckling under," that issue which seems so clear-cut in the abstract, there are, in practice, innumerable twilit zones where the choice presented is not clear-cut at all; and that crepuscular atmosphere is the one where politicians and government functionaries of *all* states have learned to manoeuvre when they have to deal with artists and scholars. Solzhenitsyn's scorn for what he saw as Pasternak's "knuckling under" at the time of the award of the Nobel Prize shows how two men, both patriots, can differ on where their patriotic duty lies.

At this point I must turn to face a question which perhaps I should have confronted earlier. The title of this book is *The Politics of Interpretation,* and it must seem that I am begging a large question when I assume, as I have assumed, that artist can stand beside scholar under this rubric: that poet and painter are "interpreters," no less than the scholar-critic who subsequently undertakes to "interpret" their interpretations, their poems, or their paintings.[3] A great deal of the most exciting work now being done in theoretical and practical criticism proceeds on a quite different assumption: that, whatever a poem may be, it is not what Matthew Arnold called it—"a criticism of life." As has been said, irrefutably, a poem is as little a criticism of life as a burning brand is a criticism of fire. Much of the most searching interpretation of poems today has as its main objective the demonstration that even those poems which patently seem to interpret a reality outside of themselves in fact do no such thing; and equally there are produced daily poems and other literary texts which quite brazenly or boldly announce themselves as having no truck with any reality other than themselves, as compositions in language quite deliberately equivocal in their references to the extralinguistic reality which their words seem, but only *seem,* to name. This is not the appropriate occasion on which to embark on in-fighting on this fascinating issue. Instead, I have tried to bypass it by citing for the most part texts from Eastern Europe. For who will want to deny that, in at least one of their aspects, texts like Pasternak's *Doctor Zhivago* and Solzhenitsyn's *Cancer*

---

3. This is not to suppose, with Harold Bloom and others, that a critic-interpreter's activity is *of the same order as,* on a level with, that of the poet whose text he interprets. On the contrary, I agree with common sense in thinking that criticism is a second-order activity and that there is absurd, rather sinister presumption in the critic's claim that his text is on a level with the text that he offers to interpret.

Ward or, if you prefer verse, his *Prussian Nights* are interpretations of recent Russian history and therefore, by the plainest implication, criticisms of life—of the life that is lived in the Soviet Union? There may be, and indeed there are, dimensions of these massive compositions which go unnoticed when we attend exclusively to them as "interpretations." But it is on their character as critical interpretations that these works have fallen foul of the Soviet state. Are we to say that the Soviet state functionaries absurdly misconceived the nature of these texts, as of *all* artistically composed texts, and therefore we view the silencing of these voices as less wrong or reprehensible than simply foolish? It is possible to take that view, but few of the artists themselves are ready to do so. More than twenty years ago, at the time of the furor about Pasternak's *Doctor Zhivago,* Alberto Moravia came near to envying Pasternak for writing in a society where his work was taken seriously enough for it to be suppressed and silenced, whereas in Moravia's "free" Italy all writings were tolerated since none of them was thought to have any important bearing on public life. This is the phenomenon which got the name, in the 1960s, "repressive tolerance", and, for my part, the logic behind it is too devious to be trusted. All the same, there is a logic behind it; and the outcome can be stated in this way—a writer, given the alternative of having his text interpreted only in graduate seminars or also in the sequestered chambers of the CIA or the KGB, is not in every case going to opt for the first alternative.

The question that presents itself quite insistently at this point is: What is the political motivation (unconscious of course) which impels deconstructionist and other interpreters to insist that reliable interpretation of even apparently limpid texts can take place only in seminar rooms or in the pages of learned journals? Since the effect of such attitudes is certainly to shut off literary texts from circulating in the public domain generally, the assumption behind them can only be *either* that literary texts are too explosive and inflammable for their free circulation to be permitted *or else* (more probably) that they are so innocuous and so irrelevant to public life that they have no use except as raw material for an arcane priesthood of interpreters. Either way, artists like Moravia who see themselves as interpreters are going to feel emasculated and, effectively, silenced. Silencing can, as we have seen, take many forms; and this seems to be one form that it takes at the present time in the United States—the writer is effectively silenced by those who undertake to be his interpreters.

The point that I am making does not originate with me. Two years ago Said—who else?—made just this point with a sort of deliberate prolixity that I take it was called for by the occasion and by the sort of readers he most wanted to reach and to hurt. This was in an essay he called "Reflections on Recent American 'Left' Literary Criticism." There he said:

> To a very great extent culture, cultural formations and intellectuals
> (artists, writers, critics, producers of culture like teachers, adminis-
> trators and the like) exist and are made possible by virtue of a very
> interesting network of relationships with the State's commanding,
> almost absolute power. About this set of relationships I must say
> immediately that all contemporary "Left" criticism . . . is stunningly
> silent.[4]

There were, Said allowed, exceptions, and he named two: Michel
Foucault and Richard Ohmann. But with these honourable exceptions,
no one, so far as he could see, made any allowance in his interpretive
work "for the truth that all intellectual and/or cultural work occurs
somewhere, at some time, on some very precisely mapped-out, and per-
missible terrain, which is ultimately contained, if not actually regulated,
by the State." And he rammed the accusation home by at once sealing off
the all too obvious bolt-hole that in fact is a cul-de-sac:

> If it is true that, according to an art-for-art's sake theory, the world
> of culture and aesthetic production subsists on its own, away from
> the encroachments of the State and authority, then we must still be
> prepared to show how that independence was gained, and more
> important, how it is maintained, or if it was ever maintained. In
> other words, the relationship between aesthetics and State author-
> ity prevails in the cases both of direct dependence or the much less
> likely one of complete independence.[5]

When Said in the same essay remarked of the written style of such
interpreters that it revealed them as "deliberately aiming for
alienation—the critic from other critics, from his readers, from the work
he studies," he made another of the points that I have sought to make.
And the circle of my agreement with him is perfected when he protests
to his fellow-interpreters: "If the body of objects we study . . . belongs to,
gains coherence from, and in a sense emanates out of and reconfirms the
concepts of nation, nationality and even of race, there is very little in
contemporary critical discourse making these actualities possible as subjects of analysis or discussion."[6]

　　Why, if Said has made all the points I want to make, do I bother to
reiterate them here and now? For three reasons. First, I arrived at these
opinions quite independent of his statement, which came to me only as
confirmation after the fact; second, whereas such observations are

　　4. Edward Said, "Reflections on Recent American 'Left' Literary Criticism," *Boundary 2* 8 (Fall 1979): 21.
　　5. Ibid.
　　6. Ibid., pp. 25, 22.

thought to be the perquisite of those who are, or like to think that they are, on the Left, they present themselves just as urgently to those like me who are, or have been thought to be, on the Right; and third, those colleagues whom Said hoped to *hurt* rather plainly were not hurt but continue to practise their interpretations with buoyant good humour, often with a sort of glee that I am tempted to characterize as childish but instead (since an admixture of gallicisms seems expected in these contexts) will describe as insouciant.

Whence this insouciance, this glee? Why do our colleagues take such evident pleasure in conceiving of literature as self-cancelling, self-sealed from any reality other than a literary reality? After all it would be possible, and might even be thought likely, that we should concede their arguments indeed, but reluctantly, *with distress*. The illusion that good literature interprets for us a reality outside of itself, if it is an illusion, is one that we might be expected to relinquish with some pain. But not so; the tone in which this revelation is transmitted to us is frequently jaunty, laughing, *liberated*. What is it that these interpreters have been liberated from, and what is the liberation that they offer to us? Rather clearly it is liberation from authority, from the authority of the text and of the "classic" author of that text. But is there not also the illusion of liberation from other sorts of authority, more tangible ones? If so, we are offered liberation from civic and political responsibility, from citizenship and what citizenship entails. In fact, such interpreters cannot deliver on this promise, as Said points out. But even if they could, what sort of liberation is that for any adult to be gratified by? One begins to think that "childish" is the right word after all.

And yet one perceives that, when all is said and done, their high spirits are appropriate. For indeed their enterprise is frivolous, frivolous in the ways that Said has brought out. In particular it is frivolous because it never asks itself what the implications are of these gambols taking place within the confines of one nation-state—the French republic or the United States—rather than in another state where perhaps the state powers would view these diversions with less indulgence. To put it another way, the door to the seminar room can be burst open, whether by an organized mob or by a posse of cops or National Guardsmen. It is not more than twelve years ago, as many of us will poignantly remember, that in the United States, in France, in the U.K., and elsewhere the seminar room and the lecture hall and the scholar's study *were* invaded in these ways. How can we have forgotten this so soon and exchanged the complacency of "It can't happen here" for the less excusable assurance of "It can't happen here *again*"? After all, we know that the citizenry off campus, along with many on campus, have no great love for us and no great respect for what we are doing. And no wonder, since we take such evident and arrogant pleasure in the fact that what we are doing at no point touches on *their* concerns, meets none of their needs and desires.

Every day when our classes are *not* disrupted, there is some power at work to ensure that they aren't. Could it not be that that power has a vested interest in ensuring that we continue with our frivolity rather than (perhaps) question and criticize *through* literature what lies outside literature? Such unworried assurance as we have that our immunities are guaranteed forever is not necessarily patriotic pride in the strength of our national institutions. It may be something much less respectable. Is it not at least possible that some political power is interested in ensuring that we pass our time in this way rather than in anything more pointed, more urgent, and more consequential?

Postscript

A narrow but certainly interesting light was thrown upon these concerns by Stanley Fish when he responded to this paper orally, and also in a typescript that he circulated. The title of the latter, "The Case against Blind Submission," bears out one of my contentions in a way he can hardly have intended. "Blind submission"—the expression resounded in my ears with a Miltonic or Shakespearean, even Sophoclean, grandeur. But no, I was quite at fault: what was at issue was not submission to Fate or to inscrutable Providence. Fish meant by it no more than a disputed editorial procedure, on the part of one of our professional journals. Should papers be submitted to the *PMLA* without the name of the author appended? Samson blind in Gaza at the mill with slaves was not to the point at all. And yet should not the risible disparity have been noticed, between the grand and resonant gravity of the expression and the triviality of what it was expressing? That it was not noticed surely witnesses to the same gross insensitivity as tolerates "comprehensive graphs of affiliated disciplines in the epistème." One has long been inured to such grossness in the use of the mother tongue by scholars in other disciplines; what makes one weep is that such use of English is now not just tolerated but considered normal in the disciplines supposedly devoted to literature, that is to say, to language as a medium of *art*.

To what extent Fish is conscious of these disparities is not clear to me. I incline to think that he is aware of them but shrugs them off as inevitable once the study of literature has been professionalized. And for professionalism in literary studies he has a respectful tenderness that I cannot share, preferring for my own part the less easily institutionalized concept of "vocation," of "calling." At any rate we hear from him of "the profession of literary criticism," though also of "the profession of letters"—which I should have supposed to be an altogether ampler conception. Fish in any case takes "profession" quite literally; he as good as said at several points in his typescript what he took for granted in his response to my paper—that today no one reads Edmund Spenser or contemplates writing about him, unless he has first paid his dues to the Modern Language Association of America. Fish must know that at this very moment persons in foreign countries, including, for instance, the Soviet Union, are doubtless struggling to read Spenser either in translation or laboriously with constant application to a dictionary and a grammar book; but for him, I take it, such reading, such construal, such *interpretation,* since it is "unprofessional," is beneath his consideration. However, take another case: an Irish poet of the present day, who has not paid his dues to the MLA nor kept abreast of Spenser scholarship in the way the *PMLA* would require, who nonetheless interprets Spenser's *Faerie Queene* and publishes his interpretation—might not that interpretation have special value, precisely because an Irishman's patriotism would be engaged, as an American's wouldn't be, by the fact that Spenser was an English "planter" in Munster? Fish, if I understand him, might have to deny that possibility. For he goes so far as to say that the entity we call Edmund Spenser *has no identity except in terms of the questions that have been ruled admissible about him.* And that ruling, he makes clear, has been handed down by certain professional bodies like the Modern Language Association and the Spenser Society of America. My own sense of the matter is quite otherwise; it seems to me that I was educated chiefly by men and women who in their own time and place were "mavericks," insisting on addressing to an illustrious shade like Spenser just those questions which the professional bodies had declared inadmissible.

I am not clear how these matters are connected with the wider and more troubling questions that I had hoped my paper was mainly concerned with. The connection, no doubt, could be established by speculating or enquiring how what we may call the micro-politics of the MLA and similar professional bodies is sustained or underwritten by the macro-politics of the state. Doubtless such interrelations exist, and doubtless they can be exploited to sinister purposes. Rather than inveighing against this, or (with Fish) more or less blithely acquiescing in it, we can best spend our time bypassing the network altogether, as the truly independent and illuminating interpreters always have.

Freedom of Interpretation:
Bakhtin and the Challenge of Feminist Criticism

Wayne C. Booth

> My language is the sum total of myself.
> —CHARLES S. PEIRCE

Most critics today would see the "politics of interpretation" as beginning and ending not with freedom but with power. For them, the central task of a conference on the politics of interpretation would be to see how various forms of power, open or covert, enforce various kinds of interpretation or perhaps how a given interpretation serves a given established power. In that view, the search for freedom of interpretation becomes the problem of how to resist power—how to wrest it from those who have it or how to produce a text that will not be co-opted by it. Who has the power—which class, which ruler, which faction, which sex—to impose what can be said and not said? Whose language, because of the power of its users, imposes a given view of reality upon whoever fails to resist that language?

It is always easy to find examples showing that to control a language is to control everyone who uses that language; critics have found that analysis of power turns up astonishing and sometimes even persuasive transformations of our traditional views, both of our cultural history and of our picture of how we work together in discourse.[1] I am not interested in arguing that it is a mistake to travel this route. Power is one good starting point in thinking about any human problem. But of course

1. I am thinking most immediately of Michel Foucault and Edward Said, but I am also attempting to rule out in advance the reduction of feminist criticism to questions of power.

every starting point exacts a price, and when we start with power as our base term we tend to obscure certain distinctions,[2] especially if we do not quickly throw other ingredients into our blender. And we are almost certain to fall into a self-privileging discourse, the kind that provides a special exemption of itself from the analysis. Like B. F. Skinner's theories of conditioned behavior, such languages can explain the production of every text except the text that provides the explanation. Some of us think that we detect such self-privileging not only in the essays here by Edward Said and Hayden White but in the work of Stanley Fish and of—well, I must restrain myself lest I insult the whole world. Self-privileging is indeed an exercise of power, and thus it may fall under the politics of interpretation; still, it should probably be reserved for some other volume.[3]

In turning to the language of freedom, I am not automatically freed from the dangers of reduction and self-privileging. "Freedom" as a term is at least as ambiguous as "power" (or as "politics" or "interpretation"). When I say that for me all questions about the politics of interpretation begin with the question of freedom, I can either be saying a mouthful or saying nothing at all, depending on whether I am willing to complicate my key term, "freedom," by relating it to the language of power. The best way to do that is to get power in from the beginning, by making a distinction taken for granted by many earlier thinkers and too often ignored today: *freedom from* as contrasted with *freedom to; freedom from* external restraints and the power of others to inhibit our actions, and *freedom to* act effectively when restraints disappear.[4]

2. Said has charged Foucault with this kind of reduction in "Travelling Theory," *Raritan* 1 (Winter 1982): 41–67.

3. One of the best accounts of self-privileging is Jacques Derrida's "Cogito and the History of Madness," a discussion of Foucault's *Folie et déraison: Histoire de la folie à l'âge classique,* in *Writing and Difference* (Chicago, 1978), pp. 31–63. I recommend the essay to anyone tempted to think of deconstructionist criticism as in any simple sense anti-intentionalist.

4. For the best brief modern discussion of the distinction I know, see F. H. Bradley, *Ethical Studies,* 2d ed. (Oxford, 1927), pp. 55–57. As Bradley's discussion suggests, the distinction has consequences both for our thinking about causation in general (can we really get along, as so much of the modern world tries to, thinking only of "efficient causes"?) and our notions of what the person *is* who causes or is caused, who is freed *from* or freed *to.* After sending this article to press, I have discovered a feminist discussion that centers on freedom rather than power and that relies on the distinction between *freedom from* and *freedom to* (though in a somewhat different vocabulary): see Janet Radcliffe Richards, "Enquiries for Liberators," *The Skeptical Feminist: A Philosophical Enquiry* (Boston,

Wayne C. Booth's most recent work, *Critical Understanding: The Powers and Limits of Pluralism,* won the Laing Prize in 1982. He is working on a book about ethical and political criticism of narrative. A new edition of *The Rhetoric of Fiction* appeared earlier this year.

All the *freedom from* in the world will not free me *to* make an intellectual discovery or to paint a picture unless I have somehow freed myself *to* perform certain tasks. Such freedoms are gained only by those who surrender to disciplines and codes invented by others, giving up certain *freedoms from*. Nobody forbids my interpreting the original text of Confucius' *Analects* or the *Principia Mathematica*, yet I am not *free to* do so, lacking the disciplines—having not *been* disciplined—to do so. The distinction can lead to troublesome complexities, but in its simple form here it cuts through some of the problems that arise in power language.

Every critical revolution tends to speak more clearly about what it is against than about what it seeks. The historicists against impressionism, the New Critics against historicism, the new new critics against intentionalism and the authority of canons, the feminists against misogynous art and criticism—clearly one could write a history of modern criticism as a glorious casting off of errors. But it is rightly a commonplace among intellectual historians that all revolutionaries depend on their past far more than they know. Revolutionary critics are enslaved by a nasty law of nature: I can say only what I *can* say, and that will be largely what I have learned to say from the kings I would depose.[5]

Everyone who tries to forge any kind of ideological criticism must struggle with these complexities. Nobody ever knows just what powers have been rejected and what voices heard. But at the moment it seems clear that what follows here, both in its emerging clarities and remaining confusions, results from my somewhat surprised surrender to voices previously alien to me: the "Mikhail Bakhtin" who speaks to me, muffled by my ignorance of Russian, and the "feminist criticism" that in its vigor and diversity and challenge to canonic views has— belatedly, belatedly— forced me to begin listening.

2

My first step must be an attempt at *freeing from*, joining those who have questioned the incompatibility of concern for ideology and concern for art. The powers whose influence I would thus cast off were themselves busy at casting off. In their view, art, or at least the best art, was to

---

1980), esp. pp. 66–67. I cannot endorse every detail of Richards' mode of argument; she still believes, for example, that reason dictates an absolute separation of the "ought" from the "is." But her sorting out of issues faced by every feminist is the best I've seen; as a result of her clarity, she can provide what is to me an unanswerable argument showing why everyone in our time ought to be a feminist, *while* showing that many arguments for and against feminism are absurd.

5. See my " 'Preserving the Exemplar': or, How Not to Dig Our Own Graves," *Critical Inquiry* 3 (Spring 1977): 407–23, and *Critical Understanding: The Powers and Limits of Pluralism* (Chicago, 1979), esp. pp. 219–23, 341–45.

be achieved by rejecting all practical restraints, and the best criticism was to be written in the same spirit. Increasing numbers of modern critics have until recently found the chief enemy of artistic freedom to be any concern for ethical, political, social, religious, or philosophical validity. Faced with all sorts of obvious restraints imposed by the social and political spheres, threatened by political tyrannies on the one hand and by bourgeois pieties on the other, harangued by scientismists who can prove, so they say, that everything we do is "in principle" programmable, they have found that true art is to be found in opposition to *all that*. Art is the one last saving domain, the domain of aesthetics where alone freedom is untrammeled.

It is then but a small step to the assumption that criticism, like the art it feeds on and supports, should ban all efforts to judge the relative political or ethical powers of individual works of art. *Art* as the general domain of pure freedom thus becomes good per se, so long as it maintains its autonomy; whatever compromises that autonomy is bad, and judgments of relative political or ethical value obviously violate that autonomy. Poetry makes nothing happen. A poem should not mean but be. To judge what it means or does is a form of tyranny.

Such views have never gone uncontested. A history of ethical and political criticism of art through this century would include many distinguished names, from wide-ranging theorists like F. R. Leavis, Lionel Trilling, Yvor Winters, and Kenneth Burke to the hundreds of specialists who defend or attack the morality or political value of individual authors or texts or genres: *Ethical Perspective in the Novels of Thomas Hardy; George Gissing: Ideology and Fiction; The Moral Vision of Oscar Wilde; The Moral Imagination of Joseph Conrad.* The list would include a considerable number of Marxists of various persuasions; they were on principle largely untempted by the drive for aesthetic and critical autonomy, which they considered a foreordained bourgeois deflection (but not entirely so: witness Clement Greenberg's famous *Partisan Review* articles of 1939 and 1940, discussed by T. J. Clark in this volume). What is striking is that almost all of these critics have written with a sense of being the opposition. Academic liberals have in general cast them as outlaws, and as outlaws they have often performed their criticism in tones somewhat less than suave.

As an academic liberal myself—I resist the label, but that's what people call me—as a liberal who has reluctantly been driven to give up dogmas of autonomy, I perhaps exaggerate the degree of change in our climate. But I do see signs of a great shift, and not only in the very existence of a conference of the kind that initiated most of the essays in this volume—a conference, be it noted, organized by a journal founded by "Chicago formalists": a bursting open of sealed caskets. If I am right we can now question, without too much anxiety, the "natural" opposition of the aesthetic order and the political order. We can now look at the ethics and politics that were concealed in the professedly anti-ethical and apolitical stances of modern aesthetic movements. We can question the notion, implicit in certain of those movements, that art is more important than people; that artists not only can but should ignore their audiences; that didactic and rhetorical interests are essentially nonaesthetic; that concern with ideologies and with the truth or practical value of art is a sure mark of its enemies; that didactic intent is always a mark of impurity; that any true art work must be above politics. In short, we may soon be freed of that most debilitating of all inhibitions for the critic— the fear that if we find the artist's self-expressions spiritually empty or socially futile or politically destructive or otherwise repugnant, we should not say so, because to say so reveals us as philistines and bourgeois nincompoops.

As we here participate in that movement, we must all be haunted by the fear that I find expressed whenever I have talked about the possibility of a revived ethical and political criticism. "You are opening the door to censorship, to political suppression of artists. Have you forgotten about what happens to artists whenever the political order takes seriously your claim that artworks may be subjected to moral or political judgment?" The anguishing history of atrocities in the name of political authority over artists—the ever-growing accounts of arrest, exile, torture, and assassination—should be enough, we are sometimes told, to warn us away from even talking about such matters. And the dangers are not all external to criticism itself. Every kind of criticism can produce bad examples; but there is a special badness about the naive application of ready-made ideological standards to isolated elements of artworks reduced for the purpose to propositional simplicities. We can be sure that once the floodgates are opened, what flows will not be only pure spring water.

One way for an ideological critic to escape these dangers is to forego judgment and attempt only description, as some neo-Marxists have done. There are signs that some feminist critics, embarrassed by certain excesses and distortions of the sixties and seventies, are turning away from evaluation—especially the negative grading of sexist works. (See, for example, Elizabeth Abel's introduction to *Writing and Sexual Difference*, a special issue of *Critical Inquiry* on feminist criticism [Winter 1981].) But though it is no doubt important to extend ideological criticism far beyond the mere grading of works as sound or unsound, it is a serious mistake to give up the claim that the quality of an artwork's ideology affects its quality *as art*. Indeed when we use the term "ideology" in the general sense I intend here, it is clear that the struggle for an art freed from ideology was itself informed by an ideology. The "dehumanized," ideologically pure art pursued by so many through this century thus becomes subject to our ideological criticism;[6] it is as thoroughly tainted with choices among possible values as is *Paradise Lost*—if having an ideology is a taint.

I am consequently driven to seek some path—or rather paths, because in such matters no one way will ever say all we want to say—between obviously undesirable extremes. Freedom from past dogmas of autonomy can do nothing for me unless I can find a mode of ideological criticism that will avoid the faults of ideologues.[7]

3

No doubt that is why the work of Bakhtin seems so attractive to me now. Bakhtin was dissatisfied both with his formalist mentors of the twenties and with the simpleminded ideological labelings and gradings of too many Marxist colleagues. In a series of books, written often under great political pressure and published, many of them, only late in his life, Bakhtin undertook to develop a dialogue between two truths: our sharing of artworks offers forms and experiences found in no other activity; yet art is inherently, inescapably, loaded with—indeed made of—ideology. Art springs from and in turn influences systems of belief and human practice. It is true that one can, with a little tinkering, find in the great Western ideological critics, from Plato on, useful ways of harmonizing these two truths. Bakhtin seems to me to require less tinkering than most. Discovering a "dialogic imagination" at the heart of human life in all its forms, he can discuss its artistic expressions with no temptation to place isolated, simple ideological propositions into flat opposition. At the same time he provides clear, bold, yet flexible criteria for appraising ideological worth.

6. José Ortega y Gasset's *"The Dehumanization of Art," and Other Writings on Art and Culture* described a modern art that was programmatically against all "human" impurities: "Tears and laughter are, aesthetically, frauds" (trans. Willard R. Trask [Garden City, N.Y., 1956], p. 25). By the time I wrote my own first questioning of such views (in *The Rhetoric of Fiction* [Chicago, 1961]), they had long since been carried beyond anything Ortega could have dreamed of. And in the twenty years since, the effort to remove even the last vestiges of human reference from the words used in literary art has been so widespread that citation would be pointless.

7. In "The 'Second Self' in Novel Criticism" (*British Journal of Aesthetics* 6 [1966]: 272–90), John Killham suggested that *The Rhetoric of Fiction* was a mistaken effort to mediate between doctrines of autonomy and everyone's knowledge that works of fiction do, after all, express their author's commitments. He was wrong about the central thrust of that book; he would be closer to being right about my present project. But I do not see the problem as a simple dilemma, presenting me with the task of grasping or passing between two clearly pointed horns. As the afterword to the new edition of *The Rhetoric of Fiction* will make clear (Chicago, 1983), the question of who does what to whom in writing and reading fiction seems even more complicated to me now than it did in 1961, and the problems for any ideological criticism, ethical, political, religious, psychological, are even more complicated than the formal analysis of telling and listening to stories.

Even if space permitted, it would be a mistake to pretend to summarize Bakhtin's immensely varied and aggressively fluid views; for him all "monologue" is faulty, and flat summary is an especially destructive form of monologue. But for the purpose of thinking about freedom of interpretation, one can extract—somewhat brutally—two elements in the dialogic imagination that he both exemplifies and defends: his view of what people are made of and his view of how fictions are made.[8]

1. He conducts a steady polemic against atomized, narrowly formalist or individualistic views of selves. His targets here—all "monological" views—are shared with other Marxists and with many a social psychologist in the West: he demolishes the notion of the atomic self, authentic in its privacy only, clearly separable from other selves and identified as free to the degree that it has purged itself of "external influences."

For him, as for more orthodox Marxists, what I call my "self" is essentially social. Each of us is constituted not as an individual, private, atomic self but as a collective of the many selves we have taken in from birth. We encounter these selves as what he calls "languages," the "voices" spoken by others. Languages are of course made not only of words; they are whole systems of meaning, each language constituting an interrelated set of beliefs or norms. "Language" is often thus for him roughly synonymous with "ideology." Each person is constituted as a hierarchy of languages, each language being a kind of ideology-brought-into-speech.

In this view ideology cannot be conceived as something to be avoided at all cost; it is inescapable in every moment of human speech. We speak *with* our ideology—our collection of languages, of words-laden-with-values. And the speaking is always thus more or less polyglot—it *is* a collection. Though some speakers may aspire to the condition of monologue, we have all inherited languages from many different sources ("science, art, religion, class, etc."), and to attempt to rule out all voices but "my own" is at best an artificial pretense. We are constituted in polyphony.

8. I am unfortunately having to rely entirely on works in translation: see Bakhtin, *The Dialogic Imagination*, ed. Michael Holquist and trans. Holquist and Caryl Emerson, University of Texas Press Slavic Series, no. 1 (Austin, Tex., 1981); the better-known *Rabelais and His World*, trans. Helene Iswolsky (Cambridge, Mass., 1968); *Problems of Dostoevsky's Poetics*, trans. R. W. Rotsel (n.p., 1973); in manuscript, a new translation of the latter by Emerson (forthcoming from the Univ. of Minn. Press); and the work of disputed authorship, P. N. Medvedev/Bakhtin, *The Formal Method in Literary Scholarship: A Critical Introduction to Sociological Poetics*, trans. Albert J. Wehrle, Goucher College Series (Baltimore, 1978). For assistance in reading Bakhtin through the murk of translation, I am especially indebted to Tzvetan Todorov, *Mikhaïl Bakhtine: Le Principe dialogique* (Paris, 1981); to Julia Kristeva for her *"presentation"* to Bakhtin's *La Poétique de Dostoïevski*, trans. Isabelle Kolitcheff (Paris, 1970); and to Gary Saul Morson, *The Boundaries of Genre: Dostoevsky's "Diary of a Writer" and the Traditions of Literary Utopia* (Austin, Tex., 1981).

> Social man [and there is no other kind] is surrounded by ideological phenomena, by objects-signs [*veshch'-znak*] of various types and categories: by words in the multifarious forms of their realization (sounds, writing, and the others), by scientific statements, religious symbols and beliefs, works of art, and so on. All of these things in their totality comprise the ideological environment, which forms a solid ring around man. And man's consciousness lives and develops in this environment. Human consciousness does not come into contact with existence directly, but through the medium of the surrounding ideological world. . . . In fact, the individual consciousness can only become a consciousness by being realized in the forms of the ideological environment proper to it: in language, in conventionalized gesture, in artistic image, in myth, and so on.[9]

2. Such a view of the polyphonic self accords necessarily with a view of artworks as more or less adequate representations of polyphony. Throughout his wide-ranging histories and typologies of literary forms runs a consistent standard: since literary forms are in fact formed ideologies, and since those who make and receive them are in fact plural selves, those works that do most justice to polyphony, or "heteroglossia," are most praiseworthy. The formal critic must be an ideological critic, since ideologies, as embodied in "languages" or "voices," are what forms are made of. The path from this point to the conclusion that "the novel" is the highest literary form, and Dostoevsky the greatest of novelists, is too intricate to be traced here. What is important is his insistence on the supreme value, in art as in life, of resisting monologue: our essence and our value are found in whatever counters the temptation to treat human beings as "objects" reducible to their usefulness to us. People—and this includes the people who inhabit fictions—are essentially, irreducibly "subjects," voices rich beyond anyone's uses, performing in a chorus too grand for any participant's full comprehension.

Bakhtin sometimes makes the list of sources of ideology, whether in selves or in novels, seem deceptively short and simple: "scientific statements, religious symbols and beliefs, works of art, and so on." The "and so on" refers explicitly, in some contexts, only to ethics. But we can find scattered through his work a much longer list of particular languages that for any individual constitute the society of ideologies that will be either "authoritatively persuasive," if left uncriticized, or perhaps

9. Medvedev/Bakhtin, *The Formal Method*, p. 14. Obviously in this view whatever *freedom to* we possess will depend absolutely on the "languages" we have imbibed. I find it interesting—though not surprising in view of common Hegelian origins—that the same Bradley whom I cite for a discussion of *freedom to* versus *freedom from* should provide one of the best nineteenth-century critiques of individualism, in the name of an irreducibly social psyche; see his *Ethical Studies*, esp. "My Station and Its Duties," pp. 160–213.

"internally persuasive," if they survive the winnowing of a conscious critical review.

The list, and the subordination of items on it, will be somewhat different for each of us, even if we live in the same society; each of us has had different parents, read different books, met different people, conversed in different bars or dining rooms or truck stops. But what I—*call it "I"*—can utter will nevertheless always be some sort of complex amalgam of voices derived not only from my patria, as emphasized beautifully in Donald Davie's essay, but more particularly, within any one society, from my economic class; my profession (we at the conference shared certain special dialects, not to say jargons); my particular social circles (gourmet cooking clubs, chamber music societies, bowling leagues); my generation (*I* happen to know what it means to be "cooking with gas" or to "consider joining the CCC until I find a job," yet most younger people today do not); my epoch (no one in the nineteenth century organized a conference anything like "The Politics of Interpretation," and if anybody from that time attended ours, much of what we said would have been unintelligible—not just because of lexical difficulties but because our language places quite different values on the very words we inherit from that time); my political party; the special institutions I have belonged to (my college, my trade school, my church—Bakhtin seems to have been deeply and even "dangerously" religious[10]—my neighborhood ethnic group); my family, with its private jokes and ethnic echoes; even my particular political "day" (the way I talked during Watergate is different from how I talk during Reagan's Revolution).

> At any given moment of its historical existence, language [and of course my own resources of language] is heteroglot from top to bottom: it represents the co-existence of socio-ideological contradictions between the present and the past, between differing epochs of the past, between different socio-ideological groups in the present, between tendencies, schools, circles and so forth, all given a bodily form. These "languages" of heteroglossia intersect each other in a variety of ways, forming new socially typifying "languages."[11]

10. The claim that Bakhtin's own base is finally religious is not accepted by all Bakhtin scholars. It is sometimes said that the claims about his religious beliefs were invented by those who preferred to see him as in opposition to the regime. But there can be no question that he sees the effort to improve the possibilities of genuine critical understanding among undiminished voices as at the heart of all human endeavor. And his ultimate reason for this placement is obviously cosmic, not political or in any sense "merely personal." I am aware that to say that he is clearly religious in this sense gets us nowhere in resolving the debated question of his degree of orthodoxy. That question is touched on by several contributors to a forthcoming forum on Bakhtin in *Critical Inquiry*, ed. Morson.

11. Bakhtin, "Discourse in the Novel," *The Dialogic Imagination*, p. 291.

I run through all this in some detail to underline the omission that you will have noticed. Is it not remarkable to discover no hint in such a penetrating and exhaustive inquiry into how our various dialects are constituted, no shadow of a suggestion in the lists and the "and so forths" of the influence of sexual differences, no hint that women now talk or have ever talked in ways different from men's? The omission may not seem strange if we view Bakhtin in the light of Western literary criticism, which has seldom acknowledged separate female voices. And it is not strange, in the light of the almost exclusively male criticism in the Soviet Union during Bakhtin's lifetime. But surely it is strange discovered in a Bakhtin. The omission is so glaring that it makes one long for the skill to make up for it. If only we could have the work of a Bakhtin who had, in violation of all history, undergone a full "raising of consciousness" and decided to add one more source of our voices, perhaps the most important of all, to his contrapuntal chorus.[12]

4

Despite the many differences between Bakhtin's situation and our own, I see strong similarities that make his version of dialectical thinking peculiarly useful to us now. Various formalisms and scientific structuralisms offer themselves, each one promising to provide the language of languages, the one right way. In reaction, various antiscientific rebels recently have raided the scientific bastions, insisting on freedom from the restraints of system or the need for proof.[13] And among these we witness the conflict I have described between those who would find their freedom in an autonomous artistic domain (even while sneaking

12. There are obvious parallels between Bakhtin's dialogical enterprise and the work of prominent Western critics of positivism: Kenneth Burke, Michael Polanyi, Richard McKeon, Roland Barthes, John Dewey, George Herbert Mead and other founders of "social psychology," and cultural anthropologists like Clifford Geertz. But Bakhtin's claims seem most forceful about why the drive toward monologism is morally—or even metaphysically—wrong. I like to imagine a dialogue among such pluralizers. Among other topics I would assign them is the question of why, despite their rich underminings, dogmatic monologists still dominate our scene.

13. I'm thinking here not only of the many anti-intentionalists in literary criticism and the many new critics who happily violate the old "affective fallacy" and "didactic heresy" but of a new groundswell of impatience with methodical rigor: the Paul Feyerabends in the physical sciences, the Hayden Whites in history, the Richard Rortys in philosophy. The pragmatic moves that I make in *Critical Understanding* might be considered as part of the same explosion outward from "the text itself" (and its explication) and away from scientific or logical proof. But my pluralism is not "unlimited," and I insist that critical modes and conclusions can be judged as better or worse, tested both by special criteria within a given mode (for example, coherence, correspondence, and comprehensiveness) and by three transmodal values, justice, vitality, and understanding.

ideological judgments into their discourse)[14] and those who proclaim the saving power of this or that ideology.

In attempting to emulate Bakhtin's way of preserving ideological criticism from its characteristic dangers, we might pursue any ideology that any critic has seriously embraced. Every intrusion of "the good" into the domain of "the beautiful" will encounter the same problems and possibilities. But I have chosen the feminist challenge as perhaps the most important, if only because it is the only one that is presented directly to everybody who deals with any literature of any period or culture. As I offer a version of it now, I naturally hope that you will find it recognizably close to what you think about misogyny or androcentrism in literature, in any of their forms, open or disguised. But if you happen to find my version of a feminist standard offensive, then please slot *that* anti-ideology—itself an ideology—into my later argument. Or you may want to make explicit some other code, objecting to works that "feed the complacency of the sleepy bourgeoisie," or that "portray romantic love as the ultimate good," or that "show men as *not* superior to women." It is extremely difficult not to cheat in such matters. An astonishing number of critics have ruled out ideological criticism as always irrelevant—except of course when the ideology in question is one that they care about. If ideological intrusions are critical errors, it is as wrong to condemn a work for being "self-indulgent" or "puritanical" or "jingoist" as to reject it for undermining belief in God, Church, and Country.

Here, then, is my ideology for the day:

1. It is an act of injustice to treat women as members of a class inherently, inescapably inferior to men; it is a manifestation of this act to reduce individual women to objects, not persons, objects to be used or abused for the delectation of men. (On another occasion one could of course reverse the genders, with the happy consequence of decimating the available instances for study.)

2. To *talk* of women unjustly is to act unjustly. Talking in such matters is action. Though the *degree* of an injustice may vary immensely from overt rape to varying kinds of verbal rape to "harmless" jokes about dumb broads, hot chicks, and farmers' daughters, the *kind* of injustice remains for our purposes the same.

3. Therefore works of art that portray women as inherently inferior to men, as objects for use, commit unjust acts—unless, of course, the portrayal is somehow effectively criticized by the work itself. The injustice may be subtle; it may be gross. It can occur in works as sophisticated as *Don Giovanni* or Norman Mailer's *The Deer Park* or as crude as Mickey Spillane's *I, the Jury*. In blatant form it violates the poor fantasy

---

14. I trace some of these in a forthcoming paper, "The Language of Praise and Blame in the Arts," delivered at Columbia University's centenary celebration of the founding of the graduate school.

creatures who, for the delectation of the readers of *Penthouse* magazine, find themselves at first frightened and then overjoyed to be gang-raped.

It may seem politically absurd to pick at a possible flaw in a great imaginative author, François Rabelais, as I shall now do, instead of spending my energies on the gross injustices committed daily by the pornographic industry. *Penthouse: The International Magazine for Men* boasts 5,350,000 "average monthly sales," and there are scores of other such magazines, accounting, my neighborhood news vendor tells me, for far more than half of his total business. Yet if Rabelais finds fifty readers in America this month, I'll be surprised. The politics of sexism in America cries out for interpretation, and more of us should be engaged in it. But the consequences for critical theory, and for what we do as teachers, are raised more acutely when we face works that are not so easily dismissed as trashy regardless of ideology.

The question we now face, then, as believers in feminist (or any other) ideology, is this: Am I free, in interpreting and criticizing a work of art, to employ that ideology as one element in my appraisal of the artistic value of that work? Or is my freedom best served by casting off such concerns and letting art works behave in any way they please, so long as they do so "artistically"? To put the challenge at its best, the inquiry would require me to develop here a fully articulated attempt at feminist criticism. Instead I can only sketch a reply to Bakhtin's effort to exonerate Rabelais from the charge of antifeminism.[15]

What might it mean to say, as many have said before me, that Rabelais' great works, *Gargantua* and *Pantagruel,* are flawed by their sexism—or, in the earlier language, their antifeminism? The books were published at a time when the great *querelle des femmes,* begun in medieval times (or one could say in classical times), was still raging;[16] all of the

15. As I reported earlier, it is being said frequently now that the feminist effort to revalue masculinist classics has been outgrown. The movement in its early days, the claim goes, did indeed spend its energies showing how male chauvinism scarred many a work in the official canon, but women have by now gone beyond that rather immature stage— having been caught in unfortunate overstatements and simplified misreadings—and are working at the more mature task of interpreting work *by* women. The new moves are clearly important, as is illustrated throughout the Winter 1981 issue of *Critical Inquiry* on *Writing and Sexual Difference.* The authors provide the best single survey of where feminist criticism now is and a first-class selective bibliography (in footnotes) of where it has been.

16. A good brief summary of the state of the quarrel in Rabelais' time is given by Michael A. Screech in "The Rhetorical Dilemma: The Background to Rabelais's Thought," *The Rabelaisian Marriage* (London, 1958). A bibliography of nearly nine hundred primary Renaissance texts about women, many of them directly concerned with the quarrel, is given in Ruth Kelso's *Doctrine for the Lady of the Renaissance* (Urbana, Ill., 1956). A bibliography of both primary and secondary texts dealing with the question of feminism and Rabelais is given by Julianna Kitty Lerner in "Rabelais and Woman" (Ph.D. diss., The City University of New York, 1976). Every issue of *Etudes Rabelaisiennes* seems to add to the immense

topics of that quarrel receive explicit discussion, showing Rabelais to have been master of every topic of such a debate. From the beginning readers have disagreed about precisely where he stands on the issues: Was he *for* women or *against* them? What critics have not done is to face the immense technical problems raised when we try to ask such questions, or the consequences for criticism if we answer them in this or that way.

The technical problem is primarily that of deciding what it is that we are to judge. A surprising amount of worthless attack and defense has been conducted as if the problem is to determine what Rabelais *says* about women, collecting favorable and unfavorable propositions from the works and balancing them against each other. But surely what we shall want to grapple with is not words or propositions in isolation but the total "act of discourse" that the author commits. Rabelais cannot be blamed for an act of injustice unless we have some reason to believe that his work as a whole—the complete imaginative offering, the experience the work makes possible for us—is vulnerable to the charge,[17] In short, ideological criticism depends on discovering the ideology *of* the form.

Judging isolated parts is particularly pointless in a work as rich as Rabelais', offering as it does a marvelous encyclopedia of every conceivable crazy way of talking. An easy and useless case for the charge of sexism could be made—and indeed it has often been made—simply by listing the immense number of moments in which women are degraded, mocked, humiliated, or explicitly pronounced as inferior to men. One character, Rondibilis, argues for example that a woman is inherently, simply, biologically, a failed or botched man. He describes all of her grotesque flaws and concludes:

> I've thought it all over a hundred and five times, and I am sure I do not know what conclusion to come to, unless it is that, in turning out woman, Nature had more in mind the social delectation of man and the perpetuation of the human species than she did the perfecting of individual womankind.[18]

bibliography. It is no exaggeration to say that by now the literature on this one aspect of Rabelais' work alone is so extensive that no one can pretend to do more than select from it.

17. I deliberately avoid the term that hovers in the background here, "speech act." The connotations of that term, as used by most people, are much too narrowly verbal or propositional for my purposes. Though speech-act theory has to some degree corrected the desiccations of some earlier systems of linguistic analysis, it still tends to do scant justice to the richness of human action performed by any developed literary work. Questions about the rhetorical effectiveness of an interchange tend to be ignored; in the special jargon that has almost become public currency, the connection between the illocutionary and the perlocutionary act is in effect broken—not always, of course, and not programmatically, but see, for example, J. L. Austin, *How to Do Things with Words* (Oxford, 1962), the last half of lecture 9.

18. Rabelais, *Third Book, The Portable Rabelais*, trans. and ed. Samuel Putnam (1929; Harmondsworth, 1977), p. 477; chap. 32 in the original. It should be noted that the *Third*

It is really astonishing to see how many critics from the sixteenth century on have taken such statements as self-evidently coming from Rabelais himself, proving his sexism. Regardless of how offensive any such quotations may be, taken out of context they prove nothing until we can establish either how they are intended or—if we reject concern for intentions—how they are actually taken by sensitive readers. And the fact is that it has been equally easy for defenders of Rabelais to find many quotations showing a much different picture.

Consider the utopian Abbey of Thélème at the end of *Gargantua* (that is, of the *First Book,* written, or, at any rate, published, a couple of years after *Pantagruel,* the *Second Book*). In constructing what seems to be his ideal of a human community, Rabelais shows women in a light totally foreign to the vision of Rondibilis: they are admitted to the abbey equally with men; they are given, so the text directly states, equal rights in the daily conduct of the abbey; they are educated in full equality in the same gracious arts and sciences as the men. And they are given equal rights of free choice about how to spend their days. Obviously, Rondibilis could not have created that abbey.[19] Surely the fact that critical history has been able to compile *double* columns, and not just the sexist column that

---

Book was published many years after the first two; but I cannot discern any difference in tone that fundamentally affects our problem. Because it is the most up-to-date and accessible, I have used Putnam's translation for most quotations that follow, giving in the text, when relevant, first the book and chapter reference to the original and then the page number in Putnam. Unfortunately this edition of Putnam's translation is not complete, and he does not provide the original chapter divisions.

19. Another favorite of the defenders of Rabelais is the highly favorable description of the ideal wife given by Hippothadeus as advice to Panurge to help him avoid becoming a cuckold. The theologian first describes all of the qualities of the wife most to be recommended: "Commendable extraction, descended of honest parents, and instructed in all piety and virtue; . . . one loving and fearing God . . . ; and finally, one who, standing in awe of the divine majesty of the Most High, will be loth to offend Him and lose the favourable kindness of His grace, through any defect of faith or transgression against the ordinances of His holy law, wherein adultery is most rigorously forbidden, and a close adherence to her husband alone most strictly and severely enjoined; yea, in such sort, that she is to cherish, serve and love him above anything next to God, that meriteth to be beloved" (3, 3; the Thomas Urquhart–Peter Antony le Motteux trans., ed. Albert Jay Nock and Catherine Rose Wilson, 2 vols. [New York, 1931], 2:538. Putnam, whose translation is in general more reliable than the livelier Urquhart–le Motteux, does not include this chapter in his edition).

A modern feminist might well bridle at the explicitly submissive role assigned here, but what follows has impressed critics looking for evidence in defense of Rabelais:

"In the interim, for the better schooling of her in these instructions, and that the wholesome doctrine of a matrimonial duty may take the deeper root in her mind, you [Panurge] must needs carry yourself so on your part, and your behavior is to be such, that you are to go before her in a good example, by entertaining her unfeignedly with a conjugal amity, by continually approving yourself, in all your words and actions, a faithful and discreet husband, and by living not only at home and privately with your own household and family, but in the face also of all men and open view of the world, devoutly, virtuously and chastely, as you would have her on

the word "Rabelaisian" connotes, exonerates the author at least from simple charges that can be made based on what is said by his characters.

What's more, if surface attitudes count, we ought to do some counting of the attacks on *males*. Here we find hundreds of satirical pages with no references to women whatever. Indeed, *Gargantua* and *Pantagruel,* the two first books, are in no sense "about" women or even "about" men and women together. It is true that much of the *Third Book,* published fourteen years after *Pantagruel,* is ostensibly about Panurge's attempt to decide whether to marry and how, if he marries, to avoid being cuckolded. But anyone who pays attention to what is being satirized when women are discussed will recognize that the central subject is more often something like "zany reasoning" than "the nobility or baseness of women."

Propositions *about* women can tell us nothing, then, until we ask, Who utters them? In what circumstances? In what tone? With what qualification by other utterances? And, most important of all, What is the quality of our emotional response, point by point and overall? Unless we face such questions, we can at most establish that the *narrator,* Alcofribas, exhibits a leaning toward sexism. For all we yet know, Alcofribas could have been used by Rabelais to exhibit sexism ironically, just as Mark Twain sometimes used Huck Finn and others to expose racist language ironically. "Anybody hurt?" asks Aunt Sally. "No'm," Huck replies. "Killed a nigger."

There is no escape then from the task, difficult as it is, of appraising the quality of the response invited by the whole work: What will it do with or to us if we surrender our imaginations to its paths? It is to Bakhtin's credit that in his discussion of Rabelais he faces this question head-on. Generations of critics have accused Rabelais of a kind of moral fault, that of being "Rabelaisian." Standard critical practice has been to say, "Yes, of course: a great comic (or satiric) genius, but unfortunately he is coarse, gross, base; he asks us to laugh in ways that no civilized reader should laugh, at scenes that no civilized reader can enjoy." Bakhtin refuses to offer the easy reply: "Moral questions about comedy or satire represent an absurd confusion of the aesthetic and practical domains." Instead he accepts the charge: if Rabelais is in fact what is usually meant by Rabelaisian, if he asks us simply to snigger at dirty

---

her side to deport and demean herself towards you. . . . Just so should you be a pattern to your wife, in virtue, goodly zeal and true devotion." [Pp. 538–39]

Panurge dismisses this advice with a twist of his whiskers and a claim that he never saw such a woman: "Without all doubt she is dead, and truly, to my best remembrance, I never saw her—the Lord forgive me!" (p. 539). Does this conclusion mock mocking Panurge for his failure to hear what a man must do to deserve a good woman? Or does it mock the theologian for naive and preachy idealism? Readers have seen it both ways. But in either view the question still remains of how such bits are viewed by the work as a whole.

words scrawled on toilet walls, then the book is not by any means worthy of the praise it has received. But if the quality of the imaginative experience, and particularly of the *center* of that experience, our laughter, can be defended on ideological grounds, then Rabelais is redeemed. Thus, though the ideological test is subtle and complex, it is the final test. It cannot be applied in separation from inquiry into the work as a created form: the ideology is not something separable from the form, and the form is not something separable from our emotional engagement with it. (The question of whether judgments about it can be separated from historical placement is something else again; Bakhtin would seem to answer yes and no.)

If this is ideological or "sociological" criticism (the word Bakhtin himself applies to his work on Dostoevsky), it is also affective and historical and expressive. It is both author-criticism and reader-criticism. The laughter we appraise is not only what we infer in Rabelais himself but also what we find in his society as influencing the work and what we find in ourselves. Thus a great deal is at stake when we ask, with Bakhtin, What is the quality of that laughter? Generalized to include all qualities, the question will become, What is the quality of the imagination that wrought this book? And that will be no different from the question, What is the quality of the effects, in us as readers, of reading this book "in its own terms"?

From the beginning, many readers have been offended by the more extreme bits of scatology and bawdry in the book, especially those that seem to ask us to laugh at women *because* they are women and hence inferior. How are we to respond, for example, to the famous episode that almost everyone would consider as in itself sexist, the trick Panurge plays upon the Lady of Paris who refuses his advances? He sprinkles her gown, you will remember, with the ground-up pieces of the genitals of a bitch in heat and then withdraws to watch the sport, as all of the male dogs of Paris assemble to piss on her, head to toe ("la sentens et pissans. . . . C'estoyt la plus grande villanie du monde. . . . un grand levrier luy pissa sur la teste" [2, 22]). She flees through the streets of Paris, pursued and pissed on by more and more dogs, laughed at by all, her story later laughed at again when Panurge tells Pantagruel about it. And Pantagruel, who by this point is by no means clearly distanced from Rabelais, "trouva [le mystère] fort beau et nouveau."[20] Her offense, remember, is simply that she turned Panurge down and—I suppose—that she is a woman of high degree.[21]

20. The scene is often chosen by illustrators and is used for the cover of the paperback *Rabelais and His World.* The illustrators generally soften the harsh details: the dogs are shown scurrying about the great lady, with at most an occasional lifted leg over a slipper.
21. One friend has suggested that the whole scene is centered not on the lady as representative of her sex but as representative of the haughty upper classes. Another friend, closer to Bakhtin, sees it not as ridiculing women but as a healthy comment on our

Or what shall we say about Panurge's suggestion of how to build an impregnable wall? You should build it of women's "what-you-may-call-thems," he says. "What the devil could knock down a wall like that? There is no metal that is so resistant to blows. And then, when the culverins came to rub up against them, you'd damned soon see the blessed fruit of the old pox distilled in a fine rain." The only drawback he can see is that such a wall would attract flies that would "collect there and do their dung," and all the work would be spoiled. But then that difficulty might be obviated; one must wipe (*esmoucheter;* Putnam translates the verb as "fly-swat") them with "nice foxes' tails or a big ass's prick from Provence [gros vietz d'azes]" (2, 15; p. 301).

Bakhtin recognizes that any full defense of Rabelais must deal with the quality of the laughter sought in such moments. Though his main effort is to refute those who would call Rabelais' laughter base or destructive, he makes quite explicit the claim that though Rabelais was not, as many have claimed, on the side of the feminists in the great *querelle*, his laughter, so often using women as its center, is finally the expression of a healthy counter-ideology, an ideology invaluable in his time as in our own. (It is important to see that Bakhtin's lengthy discussion of Rabelais' *attitude toward* women does not contradict my earlier claim that the *voice* of women does not enter his dialogue.)

Bawdy, scatological laughter is for Bakhtin a great progressive force, the expression of an ideology that opposes the official and authoritarian languages that dominate our surfaces. Bakhtin sees Rabelais' period and his work as the last full expression of a folk wisdom that could enjoy a harmonious dialogue between the "lower" body and the "higher" and more official "spirit": the "voice" of the body transforms monologue into chorus. Carnival laughter, the intrusion of everything forbidden or slanderous or joyfully blasphemous into the purified domains of officialdom, expressed a complex sense that the material body was not unequivocally base: every death contains within it the meaning of rebirth, every birth comes from the same region of the body as does the excremental. And the excremental is itself a source of regeneration—it manures life just as the dogs' urine in Panurge's trick becomes the source of a well-known modern creek.

Rabelais in this view represents a possibility that the world later lost, the possibility for what Bakhtin calls "grotesque realism." When Rabelais and his predecessors made sexual and scatological jokes, they were not serving a sniggering laughter that divorced spirit from body, seeing the latter as merely dirty. References to the lower body were not simply

sexuality in general. Perhaps both elements are present; both might be encompassed in Bakhtin's notion of carnival laughter. But both seem to me too easy. The whole episode consists of a relatively sustained wooing by Panurge, with only a hint or two of the possibility that the lady's rejection may be hypocritical. The laughter it invites is surely informed with the feeling: *that's* exactly what those resistant bitches deserve.

naughty or degrading: they were used to produce a regenerative, an affirmative, a healing—finally a politically progressive—laughter. When the natural forces of joyful celebration of the lower body reached their peak, in time of carnival, mankind was healed with a laughter that was lost when, in later centuries, the body, and especially the lower body, came to be viewed as entirely negative and shameful.

Bakhtin distinguishes two strands in the "Gallic tradition" of portrayals of women. The ascetic Christian tradition opposed Platonist idealizing of women by showing them as "the incarnation of sin, the temptation of the flesh."[22] But the "popular comic tradition," he says, was in no way simply hostile to women, though it provides plenty of material that may look sexist when viewed out of context through modern eyes. It viewed women as representing "the material bodily lower stratum; she is the incarnation of this stratum that degrades and regenerates simultaneously. She is ambivalent. She debases, brings down to earth, lends a bodily substance to things, and destroys; but, first of all, she is the principle that gives birth. She is the womb. Such is woman's image in the popular comic tradition" (p. 240). Treating her as such, Bakhtin goes on, is by no means to be guilty of antifeminism. "We must note that the image of the woman in the 'Gallic tradition,' like other images in this tradition, is given on the level of ambivalent laughter, at once mocking, destructive, and joyfully reasserting. Can it be said that this tradition offers a negative, hostile attitude toward woman? Obviously not. The image is ambivalent" (p. 241).

It is the treatment of this ambiguous image in later centuries that for him debases it and trivializes it, turning woman into a merely "wayward, sensual, concupiscent character of falsehood, materialism, and baseness" (p. 240). As "considered by [both] the ascetic tendencies of Christianity and the moralistic abstract thought of modern satirists, the Gallic image loses its positive pole and becomes purely negative" (p. 241). Thus we have a double answer in Bakhtin to the question of whether Rabelais was ideologically defensible on the feminist issue. No, he did not support the feminist cause in the great quarrel—but then the feminist position was itself a simplified debasement of women in the misleading form of idealization. On the other hand, yes, he was essentially defensible on the woman question, when we place him in his true tradition, the tradition of the carnivalesque laughter of grotesque realism, the tradition of a true ambivalence about the destructive and energizing powers of the lower body. If we imagine the world that Rabelais imagined, and laugh as he would have us laugh, we are healed.

The defense is impressive, especially since it is buttressed by an immensely energetic and sympathetic reconstruction of Rabelais' histori-

---

22. Bakhtin, *Rabelais and His World,* p. 240; all further references to this work will be included in the text.

cal situation. Surely it is true that we moderns, freed as we have been from our Victorian prejudices, should be able to revel in Rabelais' comedy in something like the healthy spirit in which 'twas writ?

Unfortunately, "we" have all this while been ignoring a crucial question: Who are "we" who laugh, who are those to whom the defense is being written, who are those who are healed by this laughter? The questions raised with great force at the beginning of Said's essay, "Who writes? For whom is the writing being done?" have all this while gone begging. And as soon as we raise them, we see that just as the original *querelle des femmes* was conducted largely by men, accusers and champions, this exoneration of carnival laughter is conducted by and for men, ignoring or playing down the evidence that the book itself largely excludes women. A man of great genius wrote a book offering a rich imaginative experience to men of sensitive and liberal spirit, and a male critic of great genius wrote a defense of that great book, addressed to other men.

It is in the nature of the case that I cannot really demonstrate my claim. I can look you in the eye and assert that if you go read or reread Rabelais now, you will find both a surviving masterpiece and its serious flaw. I can ask you to question male and female readers and try to discover women who like the book *very* much or who like it as much as the many males who have written about it. Or I could take you through a further sampling of passages. What I cannot do is bring before us the very thing I am trying to talk about: the central imaginative experience offered by Rabelais to readers of his time or of ours. Even if given unlimited time, even if I were to read the whole thing aloud to you here and now, I could not demonstrate my case decisively, because what you imagined as you listened would not be precisely what I imagined as I read. It does seem to me extremely unlikely that you would deny my case at the end, but if you did, saying that you saw nothing flawed in all that, where would we turn?

I would be forced as I am forced now to look closely at fragmentary evidence showing who is included and who excluded. An examination of the actual language of almost any passage, whether it at first appears superficially pro- or anti-feminist, shows quite clearly who are the laughers, and how they laugh.

Consider the opening addresses to the readers of each successive book. Those readers are invariably "lads," "drinking comrades," "syphilitic blades," "gentlemen," "Lords," "paternal worships." The *Second Book* begins: "Most illustrious and most chivalrous champions, gentlemen and others, . . . you have already seen, read, and are familiar with . . . *Gargantua,* and, like true believers, have right gallantly given [it] credence; and more than once you have passed the time with the ladies—God bless 'em—and the young ladies, when you were out of any other conversation, by telling them fine long stories from those chronicles . . ." (p. 224).[23] Quite clearly those "honorables dames et damoyselles" are not invited to pick up the book on their own, though they were expected to enjoy their menfolks' retelling of the juicier narratives.[24]

Alerted by such clues we see immediately that though a great deal of the work is addressed to interests and responses we all might share, there is really no passage that counters the general address to males and implied exclusion of female readers. It is not only that there are no significant female characters;[25] it is that even the passages most favorable to women are spoken by and addressed to men who are the sole arbiters of the question.

23. Rabelais' *Gargantua* is not being referred to here but a popular anonymous story of giants: *Les Grandes et Inestimables Cronicques: Du grant et enorme geant Gargantua . . .* published in 1532, the same year as Rabelais' work.

24. A possible exception is the dedication of the *Third Book* to "the soul of Marguerite, Queen of Navarre," urging it to descend from the ecstatic heights of the queen's recently embraced mysticism in order to read "this third history / Of the joyous deeds of good Pantagruel" (p. 386). Since we know that the queen did in fact read his work (see *Oeuvres,* ed. Abel Lefranc, 6 vols. [Paris, 1931], 5:2, n.9), it seems probable that other educated women of the time did so too. But even if we knew that every literate woman read him cover to cover, the knowledge would not affect our conclusions about our question, any more than discovering that many women of our time read Fitzgerald and Faulkner with pleasure would settle whether Fitzgerald's and Faulkner's works are—as I would claim—often marred by sexism.

Many critics slightly alter their accounts, consciously or unconsciously, to soften the realities of Rabelais' views and procedures. Jean Plattard, perhaps the most respected critic and biographer in the first half of this century, changes the whole direction of the opening address. In his report, Alcofribas addresses *Pantagruel* to the "très chevaleureux champions, gentilshommes, honorables dames et damoiselles" (*La Vie et l'oeuvre de Rabelais* [Paris, 1939], p. 37). But in fact he addresses only the men and assumes that they will have recounted to the women some of the more interesting anecdotes of the *Cronicques.* While judging Rabelais to be antifeminist, Plattard barely mentions the episode of the Parisian lady; she is one victim among many, and he gives his reader little hint of what Panurge actually does. Anatole France retells the pissing anecdote like this: "Le lendemain, à l'église, il s'approche de la dame, lui prend son chapelet et lui fait gâter sa robe par des chiens. Indigne vengeance. Telles sont les amours de Panurge; elles ne sont point honnêtes" (*Rabelais* [1909; Paris, 1928], p. 88). That France, the passionate opponent of hypocrisy and deceit, felt it necessary in his praise for the great Rabelais to change "pissed on her head" to "defiled her dress" surely says something about a need to rescue the classic from what it in fact says.

25. There are only two possible exceptions, the giant mothers Gargamelle and Badebec. Gargantua's grief over the death of his beloved wife is sometimes cited, for example, as a sign that women *are* important in the work. But the whole passage is handled as a source of male laughter, as Gargantua balances the two male emotions, grief over losing a helpful wife and joy over gaining a son. The epitaph Gargantua composes concludes with a joke:

HERE LIES ONE NOT TOO REMISS,
WHO DIED THE DAY THAT SHE PASSED OUT. [P. 241]

CY GIST SON CORPS, LEQUEL VESQUIT SANS VICE,
ET MOURUT L'AN ET JOUR QUE TRESPASSA. [3, 3]

Consider again the Abbey of Thélème (1, 52–57; pp. 196–216), where Gargantua and Friar John set up no rules except one: "Fay ce que vouldras"; Do what thou wouldst. To make the rule work, Gargantua has provided that nobody can enter the convent except handsome healthy people who, because they were "free born and well born, well brought up, and used to decent society," possessed "by nature" the unfailing instinct to do right, that is, a sense of honor (p. 214). He explains that all are to be educated alike, male and female: "They were all so nobly educated that there was not, in their whole number, a single one, man or woman, who was not able to read, write, sing, play musical instruments, and speak five or six languages, composing in these languages both poetry and prose" (p. 215).

So far, so good. But now note the summary of who these people are: "In short, there never were seen knights so bold, so gallant, so clever on horse and on foot, more vigorous, or more adept at handling all kinds of weapons. . . . There never were seen ladies so well groomed, so pretty, less boring, or more skilled at hand and needlework and in every respectable feminine activity" (p. 215). The men bold, gallant, good at riding, hunting, and war; the women well groomed, pretty, not boring (not boring *to whom?*), and skilled in handwork and other respectable feminine activities.

Rabelais goes on to reveal—I confess, with considerable diffidence, that I think the revelation quite unconscious—just how equal the ladies really were. "For this reason [that is, because they were all such paragons], when the time came that any member of this abbey . . . wished to leave, he always took with him one of the ladies, the one who had taken him for her devoted follower, and the two of them were then married." And they "remained as ardent lovers at the end of their days, as they had been on the first day of their honeymoon" (p. 215). One must ask, What happens here to the *lady* who might decide on her own to leave the abbey? She is simply not mentioned, not thought about, and never missed, so far as I can determine, until this moment in 1982, though hundreds of pages have been written praising Rabelais for imagining a society providing total equality. Some may object that "it would have been unthinkable in Rabelais' time to go that far, to allow a *lady* that kind of freedom to leave Utopia and return to the real world, taking with her some anonymous will-less male who was her choice." To which I must answer, "Of course. But isn't that what we are talking about: human ideals, how they are created in art and thus implanted in readers and left uncriticized—even by the subtlest of critics who makes it his business to discover ideologies as revealed by language and to do justice to every genuine human voice?"

The truth is that nowhere in Rabelais does one find any hint of an effort to imagine any woman's point of view or to incorporate women into a dialogue. And nowhere in Bakhtin does one discover any sugges-

tion that he sees the importance of this kind of monologue, not even
when he discusses Rabelais' attitude toward women.[26]

5

I am suggesting, then, that Rabelais' work is unjust to women not
simply in the superficial ways that the traditions have claimed but, to
some degree, in its fundamental imaginative act. But I have not
established yet either the degree of his offense or the meaning of that
offense in our final view of Rabelais.

To undertake this inquiry requires, of course, that I try to exercise
my *freedom from* the restraints of certain contemporary dogmas teaching
that I should never attempt such a thing in the name of literary criticism.
But my *freedom to,* feeble as it may be, is earned by surrendering to
certain other contemporary voices, particularly those of feminist critics I
have admired, and to the voice of Bakhtin. Surrendering to these voices,
some of them providing ideology and one providing a method, I find
their ultimate conclusions in conflict, and I have chosen to speak with the
feminists, finding Bakhtin in this one respect entirely unpersuasive. I
know in advance, of course, that there must be booby traps along this
trail that I haven't even dreamed of yet. And I am aware that I have
largely bypassed the question of the source of my freedom to make that
choice among voices.

Where then, for me, does this, my first and belated effort at feminist
criticism, seem to lead? I can imagine someone answering:

> Nowhere, really, because your exercise could self-evidently be per-
> formed, with the same results, on a great majority of the classics
> written before our time. Rabelais was indeed a male-centered au-
> thor writing primarily for males and reinforcing their views that
> women are at best a delectation for the life of man and at worst a
> threat to it; let us admit as well that Bakhtin, otherwise a subtle
> critic of ideologies and pleader for a dialogic imagination, has
> largely excluded women from the dialogue. Nothing in that is
> either surprising or new. According to Bakhtin's own analysis all
> language is not only tainted with ideology—it actually exists *as*
> ideology. Every statement, every work of art, will be ridden with
> ideologies—which means that even the most polyphonic work must
> exclude, simply by its existence, some languages in order to do
> justice to others. We could not even have *Gargantua* and *Pantagruel*
> without the raucous bawdry that you have judged to be sexist. It
> doesn't matter to a serious criticism that a given work is built upon

26. If it were my purpose to pick at Bakhtin, I could cite many more signs of his casual
assumption that women are not present. See, e.g., his *Rabelais and His World,* pp. 420–21.

offenses to this or that group, since all works will commit offenses to *many* groups. Why can't we simply place Rabelais in his time, and Bakhtin in *his,* and accept them for what they are?

One reads many statements of this kind, particularly by male critics, in response to what they consider the excesses of feminist criticism.[27] Often the response is reinforced by reference to the widely accepted belief considered earlier, that ideological criticism is simply forbidden—uncritical, old-fashioned, by definition doctrinaire.

The response simply will not do. For one thing, both Rabelais and Bakhtin would view such neutrality with contempt. As Bakhtin says, "Rabelais has no neutral words; we always hear a mixture of praise and abuse. But this is the praise and abuse of the whole. . . . The point of view of the whole is far from being neutral and indifferent. It is not the dispassionate position of a third party, for there is no place for a third party in the world of becoming. The whole simultaneously praises and abuses" (pp. 415–16). In every part of Bakhtin's work it is clear that he hails Rabelais' simultaneous celebration and comic denigration of the lower body as a mark of an ideological—that is, artistic—superiority to those corrupted divorces of spirit from body that too often followed the move into modernism. He is eager to show, as part of the evidence for Rabelais' greatness, that "in the political conflicts of his time Rabelais took the most advanced and progressive positions" (p. 452). One cannot, in short, do justice to aggressively evaluative novelists and critics without daring to face evaluative questions of one's own.

But in the second place, the defense is itself sexist. It is based on a comfortable acceptance of the open misogyny and covert sexism in other

27. But not only male critics. The "apology by historical placement" plays a heavy role in Julianna Kitty Lerner's claim that Rabelais was a feminist: "Rabelais in many ways transcended his contemporaries in his feminist views" ("Rabelais and Woman," p. 217). Lerner is right that many of Rabelais' contemporaries were much harder on women than he. Reading some of their stuff does indeed provide a valid defense for the *man,* Rabelais, and surely that to some degree excuses the books. Since he wrote at a time when no one, meaning in effect no male, seems to have thought more than ten minutes about what equality for women might mean or about what the religious, literary, and political traditions had done to women, he could hardly be expected to leap suddenly into a different order of imagination entirely. Indeed I have already given evidence that with far less historical excuse I accepted without criticism, until well past middle age, something like the perspective he offers. A man who was able to write an entire dissertation on *Tristram Shandy* without once even thinking about, let alone mentioning, so far as I can remember, the problem of its sexism, can hardly feel any moral superiority in his critique of Rabelais. Only now does it occur to me to check such a matter as my youthful bibliography: How many women, do you suppose, had written on *Tristram Shandy,* in nearly two hundred years, with sufficient interest (for me) to include them in my highly selective fifty-item bibliography? Exactly two, both Germans, both writing in the 1930s, about questions of form and technique. I remember that I had *read* Virginia Woolf and others on Sterne, but they are not listed.

classics. The fact that Rabelais is far from unique is the very reason why a feminist critique is important. If Rabelais were alone, if the other classics of our tradition were addressed equally to men and women, portraying both with equality, implanting favorable or unfavorable stereotypes in full impartiality, then the tradition itself would criticize Rabelais for us, and we would have no worries. But of course the reverse is true. Many a classic that seems less offensive on its surface turns out on close reading to be more sexist than Rabelais' masterpiece. Indeed, many later canonic works, like *Tristram Shandy,* borrowed and cheapened Rabelais' materials and effects, as Bakhtin shows.[28] The tradition thus does not, on the whole, criticize his work and mitigate its possible effects in constituting readers' views of women. Rather, insofar as it may excuse Rabelais as one of many, it exacerbates our problems in thinking about this kind of fault, wherever it is found. If our goal is not to arrive at fixed labels but to find better ways of talking about ideological faults, we merely postpone our problem when we blame the absent cronies, not the thief who got caught.

Finally, the answer will not do, just because—and here is a scandal indeed—I find that my pleasure in some parts of this text has now been somewhat diminished by my critical act. This is not a theoretical matter. If it were, I could perhaps reject it or change my theory to fit my reading. The fact is that reading now, try as I may to "suspend my disbelief," reading *now* I don't laugh at this book quite as hard or quite as often as I used to.

When I read, as a young man, the account of how Panurge got his revenge on the Lady of Paris, I was transported with delighted laughter; and when I later read Rabelais aloud to my young wife, as she did the ironing(!), she could easily tell that I expected her to be as fully transported as I was. Of course she did find a lot of it funny; a great deal of it *is* very funny. But now, reading passages like that, when everything I know about the work as a whole suggests that my earlier response was closer to the spirit of the work itself, I draw back and start thinking rather than laughing, taking a different kind of pleasure with a *somewhat* diminished text. And neither Rabelais nor Bakhtin can be given the credit for vexing me out of laughter and into thought: it is feminist criticism that has done it.

It is not hard to predict what some will want to say to *that:* I've lost my sense of humor or I don't know how to read "aesthetically." But if you really want to take a neutralist position on such a matter, you must be ready to imagine, or to conceive of some woman's imagining, an alternative scene in which the lover is a woman, not Panurge, and the dogs are led to piss on a man as the comic butt.[29] If you can imagine

28. What I am saying can be said considerably more strongly about the most influential translation in English, that of Urquhart and le Motteux.

29. In an early draft of this paper I attempted to construct such a scene. The construction simply would not work. One woman friend said that it was in "impossibly bad

yourself finding such a scene *as* funny as male readers have traditionally found the actual scene, or if you think the masterpiece undiminished by the substitutions, then perhaps you are that perfect reader we are all advised to emulate: one who is freed of ideological biases, one who reads aesthetically. But of course I won't believe you. Bakhtin is right: none of us can be freed from ideological biases; what we can hope to be freed from is a kind of monologism that turns all ideologies into falsehoods.

6

Any critic, male or female, who tries to break through the hegemony of male voices is going to sound, as I have no doubt sounded here at least to some readers, a bit marginal, perhaps greatly so. Everyone who has attempted feminist criticism can tell you stories of how that kind of marginality feels.

But it is not the marginality that troubles me; what was extremely daring fifteen years ago is now only slightly marginal and tomorrow may be mainstream. What worries me rather are the two violations that I have committed along my way. I have said that Rabelais' work, though to me still a great classic, is flawed by its sexism. I could also have shown that it is flawed by other ideological limitations, such as the author's total obliviousness to the lot of the lower orders—those slaveys whose daily ministrations make possible the freedoms of the Abbey of Thélème.[30] I have spent my time on the ideological fault, not on the greatness, thus doing a disservice to Rabelais, especially for any reader who may come to my discussion without personal knowledge of his full genius. Similarly, I have said that Bakhtin is a great dialectical critic who provides a path we might follow. Yet I have dwelt more on a voice he leaves out than on the power of his achievement.

Two distortions, then, distortions built into my enterprise from the beginning. But if we take Bakhtin seriously in his pursuit of a polyphonic language that is rigorously critical, we find built into the project the proper form of correction. Whatever monologic distortions I have committed cannot be corrected by anything I might say in a parenthesis,

---

taste." That was hardly what was wrong with it, though, because the original is in impossibly bad taste, too.

30. One could wish that all of the modern spirits who have hailed the Abbey of Thélème and its free-spirited motto as a classic of liberalism had read what we might call the fine print about those plentiful servants, the "functionaries" who dress and feed and clean and barber the blessed monks and nuns. They live in houses nearby the abbey: "houses that were well lighted and well equipped, in which dwelt the goldsmiths, lapidaries, embroiderers, tailors, gold-thread-workers, velvet-makers, tapestry-makers, and upholsterers; and there each one labored at his trade and the whole product went for the monks and nuns of the abbey" (1, 52; p. 213).

but they can be corrected by anyone who returns to listen to the two masters themselves.

Rabelais, first, will survive gloriously, even if I were to strengthen my statement of feminist reservations. What has been most obviously missing from my account is the sheer pleasure of *his* text, the exuberance, the subversive, vitalizing laughter that survives the worst that can be said about its sources. If you do not return to Rabelais for that fun (or to other accounts like Erich Auerbach's that do it more justice), your freedom to add an alien voice to Rabelais' dialogue will have been dearly bought. At the same time, I am convinced, with no possibility of providing evidence, that Rabelais himself would have welcomed my effort at intruding a new voice into his chorus. As Auerbach says, "The revolutionary thing about his way of thinking is not his opposition to Christianity [or to any other single belief], but the freedom of vision, feeling, and thought which his perpetual playing with things produces, and which invites the reader to deal directly with the world and its wealth of phenomena."[31] The essential artistic drive of Rabelais will thus criticize both himself *and* me, no doubt with raucous laughter.

Similarly, Bakhtin, if given a chance, will respond triumphantly, and his response will be, as always, at least double. I hear him saying:

> None of the voices in your troubled dialogue-with-yourself can be taken as justified without the correction of other voices. To those who, like you, would join the effort to bring the long suppressed voices of women into critical dialogue, reviving as you do so an ethical and political criticism that risks putting art into some kind of subordinate place, I would warn against turning art into a simple message. Don't reduce fictions and the criticism of fictions to a simple conflict of doctrines or dogmas. Don't assume that an idea expressed in a great complex imaginative work is exactly the same as that "same" idea when it is extracted and restated in your critical work. Art can do what no other human activity can do, and you will not find freedom of interpretation by a simple rejection of what seemed to be said by it, and by its critics, in the past.
>
> But as for my own failure to invite women into the discussion [I hope he might go on], it illustrates perfectly my point about the dangers of monologue and the need for a deliberate drive for heteroglossia. It had not occurred to me that sexual difference might yield a further source of "hybridization." Now that I see the possibility, my task is to look more closely at what women writers have said and at what they are now saying. If I have committed the sin, in my discussion of Rabelais, of treating women not as subjects but as objects, objects of male laughter and male-dominated in-

---

31. Erich Auerbach, *Mimesis: The Representation of Reality in Western Literature,* trans. Willard Trask (1953; Garden City, N.Y., 1957), p. 242.

tellectual dispute, then their critique might be for me as important
as carnival laughter has been for others at other times.

But we need not rely on imagined words. Toward the end of
Rabelais and His World, Bakhtin offers the words to describe our situation:

> In the sphere of literary and artistic creation it is impossible to
> overcome through abstract thought alone, within the system of a
> unique language, that deep dogmatism hidden in all the forms of
> this system. The completely new, self-criticizing, absolutely sober,
> fearless, and gay life of the image can start only on linguistic con-
> fines [is that to say, perhaps, the borders between an older sexist
> "language" and a new feminist voice?].
>   In the system of one language, closed to all others, the image is
> too strictly imprisoned to allow . . . [a] "truly divine boldness and
> shamelessness." . . . We repeat, another language means another
> philosophy and another culture but in their concrete and not fully
> translatable form. The exceptional freedom and pitiless gaiety of
> the Rabelaisian image were possible only on the confines of [bor-
> ders between?] languages. [Pp. 472–73]

7

Even if we could hear Rabelais and Bakhtin brought back into full
voice, we would still be left with a multitude of questions, difficulties, and
objections. To me, the most troublesome objections are those based on
the appeal to historical placement. To wrench Rabelais and Bakhtin out
of their moments and then blame them for not seeing the world my way
is to risk violating not only their integrity but my own as well. Everything I
know about trying to understand someone requires me to suppress my
"local" biases and enter as intimately as possible into the alien moment.

The objection seems to me to hold, so long as I am thinking about
justice to the *men,* Rabelais and Bakhtin. It would be absurd to blame
them for faults that I would almost certainly have exhibited, living in
their time and place (see n. 27 above). Even the works themselves, so
long as we view them as objects to be understood, must surely be viewed
only in the light cast by their own historical setting.

But the objection has its own difficulties, difficulties that perhaps
reveal a permanent irreconcilability of a fully historical and a fully critical view. There is first the plain fact that nobody ever manages fully to
enter an alien period or culture. We bring ourselves with us wherever we
go; we cannot ever deliberately forget the voices that have become
"internally persuasive." I must always look skeptically at anyone's claim
to have judged authors entirely according to "the standards of their own

times." It will be an ideal that I constantly strive for, when I am attempting to discover what any work of art *is* (or, in another critical language,
what it is "attempting to do to me"). But it is a permanently elusive ideal,
and criticism should always be seeking ways of uncovering our failures to
understand and the grounds for such failures.

But there is a more serious problem with the historical objection.
Though it is true that Rabelais the man cannot be justly blamed for not
being someone else living at another time, it is also true that the
"Rabelais" *I* have is here and now. I do not possess Rabelais' works *then;*
I possess them, if at all, *now.* I read him as I read anyone: in my own
time. Whatever he does to me will be done in my time, not his. There is
thus a quite obvious truth to the once famous and often refuted claim by
T. S. Eliot in "Tradition and the Individual Talent"—that the whole
literary tradition exists simultaneously and is shifted somewhat
whenever a new work is added. For me, here and now, the power of any
classic to work on me and to reshape me, for good or ill, is in one sense
ahistorical. All works I rework speak to me where I am, and they speak,
more often than not, conflicting messages. To pretend that they all are
equally defensible, because when seen in their own time they are equally
explicable, is to dodge my own life with them. The only way I can do
justice to their history is to re-create that history in myself. Some of that
work is done for me simply by my inevitably imbibing whatever traditions are alive in my time. Some of it can be done by hard work and
thought. But even at best, I still have only the Rabelais I have and not the
Rabelais that any one of his contemporaries could have enjoyed.

A related problem lies in the selectivity of our ideological attention
and thus of our willingness to excuse on historical grounds. Our own
interests dictate concern about some ideological deflections and not
others. How many faults and of what kinds are we willing to forgive, and
why? Why is it that some ideological conflicts between myself and an
author seem like faults, and others, like my disagreement with Rabelais
about many religious doctrines, or about the casual and grotesque mis-
treatment of animals, or about the trustworthiness of Italianate lawyers,
or about the quality of scholarship at the Sorbonne, seem hardly worth
mentioning? And why, among the faulty views, do some seem to affect
the quality of the work while others do not matter?

I can only hint at an answer here, considering briefly another act of
injustice that on any abstract scale might seem much worse than
humiliating women: Rabelais' cruel indifference to the burning of heretics. Michael Screech points to jokes about such burnings and concludes
that in *Gargantua* Rabelais "positively incites Francis I to send the Principal of the Collège de Montaigu to the stake, together with his cronies."[32]

32. Screech, *Rabelais* (Ithaca, N.Y., 1979), p. 73; all further references to this work
will be included in the text.

Screech's defense is a historical placement: "Renaissance Christians were, on the whole, highly selective with their pity," and besides Jean de Caturce (if that is who the Principal was in fact) was a puritan who tried to substitute Christian prayers for the carnival buffoonery of Twelfth Night—"a sectarian extremist whose death would not call forth Rabelais' pity as a matter of course. All the great figures of the time seem impervious to the sufferings of those they fundamentally disagreed with" (pp. 72, 73).

To say that "everybody else was doing it" seems a rather feeble excuse for cruelty to heretics. Yet curiously enough it works better for laughter about heretic burning than for the ridicule of women *as* women. No doubt this is partly because the reasons for the two forms of ridicule are disproportionate: to mock individuals because of something they have done or might do to you and yours is really quite different from laughing at a person because she belongs to the wrong half of the race.

Not only are the reasons of a different kind, but the likely moral effects will trouble me in different ways and degrees. Whatever harm Rabelais might do in reinforcing his contemporaries' willingness to burn heretics or to witness the burning without pity is, viewed from our time and place, scarcely threatening. But there is no modern reader, however up-to-date, who is immune to the effects of reading about how men and women treat each other. The specific ideology on which Rabelais' laughter often depends is in 1982 still a dominant ideology of our culture: women are fair game; they are sillier than men, as nine out of ten television comedies proclaim; it is funnier to set pissing dogs onto their fine gowns than onto male finery. Unlike most other views that we might dispute, this one goes to the very heart of our picture of what it is to be human. And unlike most others, it involves everyone in its threat, not just some minority and not just unsophisticated readers. *If* a work may be harmful, it threatens us all.

The ideological differences that bite, then, are those that present alternatives still tempting in our own time—or in our own souls. For someone like myself, having changed my views, however slightly, about the greatness of a classic, the effect is something like that of losing a brother, or a part of my past, or a part of myself. My need to sharpen my statement of the differences is thus strengthened both by my regret at the loss and by my fear that others, my contemporaries, may still be taken in by what was once for me seductive. If this is so, it is another reason for saying that any ethical criticism we try to develop in a systematic way must take into account an ethics of the reader as well as an ethics of what is written. Works that might be ideologically worrisome for some readers in some times might later be excused. We might very well conclude that the same Homer who was feared and banned by Plato as a bad "core curriculum" for Greek youth should present no ideological problem for modern youth, who are not likely to change their notions of the gods very much as they read the *Iliad*.[33]

A third and even more difficult question concerns the import of all this for our judgments about literary traditions. If Rabelais and Bakhtin have revealed a failure of imagination, a failure that for both is in direct conflict with what they seem most strongly to stand for, we can never again listen to them uncritically. And if we say that of *them*, we are simultaneously saying it of most of the classics. I have heard men say—not often in the presence of women—that the feminist critique is absurd, because if you took it seriously you would have to repudiate almost the whole of Western literature and most of the rest of the world's literature, too. "Repudiate" is no doubt too strong a word, but it is quite true that if what I have been doing here has any legitimacy at all, then most of the world's classics are indeed placed into a controversy that will never be easily resolved. Not thrown out, not censored, not burned, but thrown into controversy. In short, I finally accept what many feminist critics have been saying all along: our various canons have been established by men, reading books written mostly by men for men, with women as eavesdroppers, and now is the time for men to join women in working at the vast project of reeducating our imaginations.

If we choose to listen, we will find no simple direction. As male critics are too fond of pointing out, feminist critics present no unified front; and it is probably at least as easy to write a bad feminist indictment as to write a bad *explication de texte* or historical study. The easy feminist way would be to think only in terms of *freedom from* all those wicked male voices of the past. But as Bakhtin would want to point out, the very language with which one does the casting off will be a collection of inherited languages.

8

In that collection we can always expect to find legitimate male voices asking whether after all feminist perspectives are not as biased as masculine perspectives. And are we then to have many canons, one for each legitimate ideological interest? Or should we hope for a time when all

33. My speculation here about the relative degree of offense was stimulated in part by criticism from my colleague, Gregory Colomb. Since the effort to do feminist criticism is entirely new to me, I have sought and received far more advice about this essay than I usually do. In addition to Colomb I wish to thank Elizabeth Abel, Phyllis Booth, James Chandler, Marcel Gutwirth, Robert von Hallberg, David Hanson, Françoise Meltzer, W. J. T. Mitchell, Robert Morrissey, Janel Mueller, Wendy Olmsted, Nancy Rabinowitz, Judith Sensibar, Michael Silverstein, Richard Strier, Frantisek Svejkovsky, Charles Wegener, and James White—not to mention many who offered criticism at the conference and some whose criticism must have been so devastating that memory has repressed the encounter.

readers will exercise imaginations so fully educated that only those works written *for* all will be enjoyed *by* all?

Nobody can answer such questions with much confidence. But my hunch is that we will always have—and need—alternative canons and controversy about our canons. As Hume says, concluding "Of the Standard of Taste," though standards are not merely a matter of individual preference, we cannot expect that all people of taste will on all occasions recognize the merits of all works of high quality. The poems I loved as a young man I may not respond to at all as an old man; the British reader will rightly admire some works that the French cannot even understand. What's more, he goes on, we all find ourselves disagreeing with the "manners" portrayed in some admired works, and each of us will be inclined to respond somewhat differently depending on whether the differences are great or small.

But Hume then makes an important distinction that I think applies directly to our problem here.

> Where any *innocent* peculiarities of manners are represented . . .
> they ought certainly to be admitted; and a man who is shocked with
> them, gives an evident proof of false delicacy and refinement. . . .
> But where the ideas of morality and decency alter from one age to
> another, and where *vicious* manners are described, without being
> marked with the proper characters of blame and disapprobation,
> this must be allowed to disfigure the poem, and to be a real de-
> formity. I cannot, nor is it proper I should, enter into such senti-
> ments; and however I may excuse the poet, on account of the
> manners of his age, I can never relish the composition. The want of
> humanity and of decency, so conspicuous in the characters drawn
> by several of the ancient poets . . . diminishes considerably the
> merit of their noble performances, and gives modern authors an
> advantage over them. [My italics]

Though the language of innocence and viciousness is not fashionable, I hope that we could all agree that some ideological faults, like debasement of women, must ever be taken seriously, while others may be merely "innocent peculiarities."

In all of his sensitive discrimination of the sources of prejudice, curable and incurable, Hume gives no hint (shall I say that *of course* Hume gives no hint?) that the "men" who may fail in their taste might suffer from sexual prejudice. The only females mentioned are certain characters in earlier literature who exhibit absurd manners that should not trouble us. But Hume's oversight should not obscure the usefulness of his way of accommodating irreducible differences of perspective. If old "men" and young "men" are different in their "passion," they will always exhibit some differences in responding to literature; to the extent that women and men *really* differ—nobody knows now and perhaps nobody ever will know the extent to which we do—they will respond differently to those works of art that engage with those differences.

   With this concession made to perspectivism, and with many other problems left in the air, a final word about freedom. Can we not say that if there is no freedom of interpretation, there is no significant freedom of any kind? If the critic of a given repressive regime and the *Gauleiter* who arrests and tortures that critic are expressing equally convention-bound preferences, and if, in *interpreting* their interpretations, I am simply playing a game according to unbreakable rules imposed on me by my culture or ideological perspective—if, in other words, there is never any real sense to the question, Which one of these two interpreters has produced a better reading of the dictator's words?—then of course all political questions are reduced to questions of power, and we are back in Thrasymachus' trap: Justice is whatever power says it is, and if you disagree with me, then of course I will seek ways of showing you, by all the means available, that I am right; I will bludgeon you with propaganda, or if that does not work, I'll use truncheons or prisons.
   But no reader of Bakhtin can conclude that we are in Thrasymachus' trap. He shows us that we are not freed merely by learning how to cast off the powers that made us; we are freed by taking in the many voices we have inherited and discovering, in our inescapably choral performance, which voices must be cast out of our choir. Each of the voices within is already itself such a chorus, and thus each voice was always at least partially free even as we took it in.
   Perhaps it remains true that the freedom to make new interpretations by exercising freedom from old methods and assumptions is more important in some epochs than in others. There may even have been past moments when freedom from established interpretations was not even possible, whether desirable or not. One can place oneself, Bakhtin says, "outside one's own language only when an essential historic change of language occurs. Such precisely was the time of Rabelais. And only in such a period was the artistic and ideological radicalism of Rabelaisian images made possible" (p. 471).
   We seem to be living in another such period. What would it mean to make it work for us as something other than a threatening chaos?

Psychoanalysis and the Polis

Julia Kristeva

Translated by Margaret Waller

> Up until now philosophers have only interpreted the world. The
> point now is to change it.
> —KARL MARX and FRIEDRICH ENGELS, *Theses on Feuerbach*

> The delusions [*Wahnbildungen*] of patients appear to me to be the
> equivalents of the [interpretive] constructions which we build up in
> the course of an analytic treatment—attempts at explanation and
> cure.
> —SIGMUND FREUD, "Constructions in Analysis"

The essays in this volume convince me of something which, until now,
was only a hypothesis of mine. Academic discourse, and perhaps American university discourse in particular, possesses an extraordinary ability
to absorb, digest, and neutralize all of the key, radical, or dramatic moments of thought, particularly, a fortiori, of contemporary thought.
Marxism in the United States, though marginalized, remains deafly
dominant and exercises a fascination that we have not seen in Europe
since the Russian *Proletkult* of the 1930s. Post-Heideggerian "de-
constructivism," though esoteric, is welcomed in the United States as an
antidote to analytic philosophy or, rather, as a way to valorize, through
contrast, that philosophy. Only one theoretical breakthrough seems
consistently to *mobilize* resistances, rejections, and deafness: psychoanalysis—not as the "plague" allowed by Freud to implant itself in

Translator's note.—I would like to thank Domna Stanton and Alice Jardine for their
help on an earlier version of this translation.

America as a "commerce in couches" but rather as that which, with Freud and after him, has led the psychoanalytic decentering of the speaking subject to the very foundations of language. It is this latter direction that I will be exploring here, with no other hope than to awaken the resistances and, perhaps, the attention of a concerned few, after the event *(après coup).*

For I have the impression that the "professionalism" discussed throughout the "Politics of Interpretation" conference is never as strong as when professionals denounce it. In fact, the same preanalytic rationality unites them all, "conservatives" and "revolutionaries"—in all cases, jealous guardians of their academic "chairs" whose very existence, I am sure, is thrown into question and put into jeopardy by psychoanalytic discourse. I would therefore schematically summarize what is to follow in this way:

1. There are political implications inherent in the act of interpretation itself, whatever meaning that interpretation bestows. What is the meaning, interest, and benefit of the interpretive position itself, a position from which I wish to give meaning to an enigma? To give a political meaning to something is perhaps only the ultimate consequence of the epistemological attitude which consists, simply, of the desire *to give meaning.* This attitude is not innocent but, rather, is rooted in the speaking subject's need to reassure himself of his image and his identity faced with an object. Political interpretation is thus the apogee of the obsessive quest for A Meaning.

2. The psychoanalytic intervention within Western knowledge has a fundamentally deceptive effect. Psychoanalysis, critical and dissolvant, cuts through political illusions, fantasies, and beliefs to the extent that they consist in providing only one meaning, an uncriticizable ultimate Meaning, to human behavior. If such a situation can lead to despair within the polis, we must not forget that it is also a source of lucidity and ethics. The psychoanalytic intervention is, from this point of view, a counterweight, an antidote, to political discourse which, without it, is free to become our modern religion: the final explanation.

3. The political interpretations of our century have produced two powerful and totalitarian results: fascism and Stalinism. Parallel to the socioeconomic reasons for these phenomena, there exists as well another, more intrinsic reason: the simple desire to give a meaning, to

Julia Kristeva, professor of linguistics at the University of Paris VII and a regular visiting professor at Columbia University, is the author of *Desire in Language: A Semiotic Approach to Literature and Art* and *About Chinese Women.* **Margaret Waller,** a doctoral candidate in French at Columbia University, is currently translating Kristeva's *Revolution du langage poétique.*

explain, to provide the answer, to interpret. In that context I will briefly discuss Louis Ferdinand Céline's texts insofar as the ideological inter-pretations given by him are an example of political delirium in avant-garde writing.

I would say that interpretation as an epistemological and ethical attitude began with the Stoics. In other words, it should not be confused with *theory* in the Platonic sense, which assumes a prior knowledge of the ideal Forms to which all action or creation is subordinate. Man, says Epictetus, is "born to contemplate God and his works, and not only to contemplate them but also to interpret them [kai ou monon teatin, ala kai exegetin auton]." "To interpret" in this context, and I think always, means "to make a connection." Thus the birth of interpretation is con-sidered the birth of semiology, since the semiological sciences relate a sign (an event-sign) to a signified in order to *act* accordingly, consistently, consequently.[1]

Much has been made of the circularity of this connection which, throughout the history of interpretive disciplines up to hermeneutics, consists in enclosing the enigmatic (interpretable) object within the interpretive theory's preexistent system. Instead of creating an object, however, this process merely produces what the interpretive theory had preselected as an object within the enclosure of its own system. Thus it seems that one does not interpret something outside theory but rather that theory harbors its object within its own logic. Theory merely pro-jects that object onto a theoretical place at a distance, outside its grasp, thereby eliciting the very possibility of interrogation (Heidegger's *Sach-verhalt*).

We could argue at length about whether interpretation is a circle or a spiral: in other words, whether the interpretable object it assigns itself is simply constituted by the interpretation's own logic or whether it is recreated, enriched, and thus raised to a higher level of knowledge through the unfolding of interpretive discourse. Prestigious work in philosophy and logic is engaged in this investigation. I will not pursue it here. Such a question, finally, seems to me closer to a Platonic idea of interpretation (i.e., theorization) than it does to the true innovation of the Stoics' undertaking. This innovation is the reduction, indeed the elimination, of the distance between theory and action as well as between model and copy. What permits this elimination of the distance between nature (which the Stoics considered interpretable) and the interpreter is the extraordinary opening of the field of subjectivity. The person who does the interpretation, the subject who makes the connection between the sign and the signified, is the Stoic sage displaying, on the one hand,

1. See Victor Goldschmidt, *Le Système stoïcien et l'idée de temps* (Paris, 1953).

the extraordinary architectonics of his *will* and, on the other, his mastery of *time* (both momentary and infinite).

I merely want to allude to this Stoic notion of the primordial interdependence of *interpretation,* subjective *will,* and mastery of *time.* For my own interest is in contemporary thought which has rediscovered, in its own way, that even if interpretation does no more than establish a simple logical connection, it is nevertheless played out on the scene of speaking subjectivity and the moment of speech. Two great intellectual ventures of our time, those of Marx and Freud, have broken through the hermeneutic tautology to make of it a *revolution* in one instance and, in the other, a *cure.* We must recognize that all contemporary political thought which does not deal with technocratic administration—although technocratic purity is perhaps only a dream—uses interpretation in Marx's and Freud's sense: as transformation and as cure. Whatever *object* one selects (a patient's discourse, a literary or journalistic text, or certain sociopolitical behavior), its interpretation reaches its full power, so as to tip the object toward the *unknown* of the interpretive theory or, more simply, toward the theory's *intentions,* only when the interpreter *confronts* the interpretable object.

It is within this field of confrontation between the object and the subject of interpretation that I want to pursue my investigation. I assume that at its resolution there are two major outcomes. First, the object may succumb to the interpretive intentions of the interpreter, and then we have the whole range of domination from suggestion to propaganda to revolution. Or second, the object may reveal to the interpreter the unknown of his theory and permit the constitution of a new theory. Discourse in this case is renewed; it can begin again: it forms a new object and a new interpretation in this reciprocal transference.

Before going any further, however, I would like to suggest that another path, posthermeneutic and perhaps even postinterpretive, opens up for us within the lucidity of contemporary discourse. Not satisfied to stay within the interpretive place which is, essentially, that of the Stoic sage, the contemporary interpreter renounces the game of *indebtedness, proximity,* and *presence* hidden within the connotations of the concept of interpretation. (*Interpretare* means "to be mutually indebted"; *prêt:* from popular Latin *praestus,* from the classical adverb *praesto,* meaning "close at hand," "nearby"; *praesto esse:* "to be present, attend"; *praestare:* "to furnish, to present [as an object, e.g., money].") The modern interpreter avoids the presentness of subjects to themselves and to things. For in this presentness a strange object appears to speaking subjects, a kind of currency they grant themselves—interpretation—to make certain that they are really there, close by, within reach. Breaking out of the enclosure of the presentness of meaning, the *new* "interpreter" no longer interprets: he speaks, he "associates," because there is no longer an object to interpret; there is, instead, the setting off of semantic, logical, phantasmatic, and indeterminable sequences. As a result, a fiction, an uncentered discourse, a subjective polytopia come about, canceling the metalinguistic status of the discourses currently governing the post-analytic fate of interpretation.

The Freudian position on interpretation has the immense advantage of being midway between a classic interpretive attitude—that of providing meaning through the connection of two terms from a stable place and theory—and the questioning of the subjective and theoretical stability of the interpretant which, in the act of interpretation itself, establishes the theory and the interpreter himself as interpretable objects. The dimension of *desire,* appearing for the first time in the citadel of interpretive will, steals the platform from the Stoic sage, but at the same time it opens up time, suspends Stoic suicide, and confers not only an interpretive power but also a transforming power to these new, unpredictable signifying effects which must be called *an imaginary.* I would suggest that the wise interpreter give way to delirium so that, out of his desire, the imaginary may join interpretive closure, thus producing a perpetual interpretive creative force.

1. What Is Delirium?

Delirium is a discourse which has supposedly strayed from a presumed reality. The speaking subject is presumed to have known an object, a relationship, an experience that he is henceforth incapable of reconstituting accurately. Why? Because the knowing subject is also a *desiring* subject, and the paths of desire ensnarl the paths of knowledge.

Repressed desire pushes against the repression barrier in order to impose its contents on consciousness. Yet the resistance offered by consciousness, on the one hand, and the pressure of desire, on the other, leads to a displacement and deformation of that which otherwise could be reconstituted unaltered. This dynamic of delirium recalls the constitution of the dream or the phantasm. Two of its most important moments are especially noteworthy here.

First, we normally assume the opposite of delirium to be an objective reality, objectively perceptible and objectively knowable, as if the speaking subject were only a simple knowing subject. Yet we must admit that, given the cleavage of the subject (conscious/unconscious) and given that the subject is also a subject of desire, perceptual and knowing apprehension of the original object is only a theoretical, albeit undoubtedly indispensable, hypothesis. More importantly, the system Freud calls perception-knowledge (subsequently an object of interpretation or delirium) is always already marked by a *lack:* for it shelters within its very being the nonsignifiable, the nonsymbolized. This "minus factor," by which, even in perception-knowledge, the subject signifies himself as subject of the desire of the Other, is what provokes, through its insistence on acceding to further significations, those deformations and displacements which characterize delirium. Within the nucleus of delirious construction, we must retain this hollow, this void, this "minus 1," as the instinctual drive's insistence, as the unsymbolizable condition of the desire to speak and to know.

Yet delirium holds; it asserts itself to the point of procuring for the subject both *jouissance* and stability which, without that adhesive of delirium, would disintegrate rapidly into a somatic symptom, indeed, into the unleashing of the death drive. It can do so, however, only because the discourse of delirium "owes its convincing power to the element of historical truth which it inserts in the place of the rejected reality."[2] In other words, delirium masks reality or spares itself from a reality while at the same time saying a truth about it. More true? Less true? Does delirium know a truth which is true in a different way than objective reality because it speaks a certain subjective truth, instead of a presumed objective truth? Because it presents the state of the subject's desire? This "mad truth" (*folle vérité*) of delirium is not evoked here to introduce some kind of relativism or epistemological skepticism.[3] I am insisting on the part played by truth in delirium to indicate, rather, that since the displacement and deformation peculiar to delirium are moved by desire, they are not foreign to the passion for knowledge, that is, the subject's subjugation to the desire to know. Desire and the desire to know are not strangers to each other, up to a certain point. What is that point?

Desire, the discourse of desire, moves toward its object through a connection, by displacement and deformation. The discourse of desire becomes a discourse of delirium when it forecloses its object, which is always already marked by that "minus factor" mentioned earlier, and when it establishes itself as the complete locus of *jouissance* (full and without exteriority). In other words, no other exists, no object survives in its irreducible alterity. On the contrary, he who speaks, Daniel Schreber, for example, identifies himself with the very place of alterity, he merges with the Other, experiencing *jouissance* in and through the place of otherness. Thus in delirium the subject himself is so to speak the Phallus, which implies that he has obliterated the primordial object of desire—the mother—either because he has foreclosed the mother, whom he finds lacking, or because he has submerged himself in her, exaggerating the totality thus formed, as if it were the Phallus. Delirium's structure thus constitutes the foreclosure of the paternal func-

2. Sigmund Freud, "Constructions in Analysis," *The Standard Edition of the Complete Psychological Works of Sigmund Freud,* trans. and ed. James Strachey, 24 vols. (London, 1953–74), 23:268.
3. See in my *Folle vérité* (Paris, 1979) the texts presented in my seminar at l'Hôpital de la Cité Universitaire, Service de psychiatrie.

tion because of the place it reserves for the maternal—but also feminine—object which serves to exclude, moreover, any other consideration of objectality.

By contrast, if it is true that the discourse of knowledge leads its enigmatic preobject, that which solicits interpretation—its *Sachverhalt*—inside its own circle and as such brings about a certain hesitation of objectness, it does not take itself for the Phallus but rather places the Phallus outside itself in what is to be known: object, nature, destiny. That is why the person through whom knowledge comes about is not mad, but (as the Stoics have indicated) he is (subject to) death. The time of accurate interpretation, that is, an interpretation in accordance with destiny (or the Other's Phallus), is a moment that includes and completes eternity; interpretation is consequently both happiness and death of time and of the subject: suicide. The transformation of sexual desire into the desire to know an object deprives the subject of this desire and abandons him or reveals him as subject to death. Interpretation, in its felicitous accuracy, expurgating passion and desire, reveals the interpreter as master of his will but at the same time as slave of death. Stoicism is, and I'll return to this point, the last great pagan ideology, tributary of nature as mother, raised to the phallic rank of Destiny to be interpreted.

2. Analytic Interpretation

Like the delirious subject, the psychoanalyst builds, by way of interpretation, a construction which is true only if it triggers other associations on the part of the analysand, thus expanding the boundaries of the analyzable. In other words, this analytic interpretation is only, in the best of cases, *partially true*, and its truth, even though it operates with the past, is demonstrable only by its *effects in the present*.

In a strictly Stoic sense, analytic interpretation aims to correspond to a (repressed) event or sign in order to *act*. In the same sense, it is a *connection* between disparate terms of the patient's discourse, thereby reestablishing the causes and effects of desire; but it is especially a connection of the signifiers peculiar to the analyst with those of the analysand. This second circulation, dependent on the analyst's desire and operative only with him, departs from interpretive mastery and opens the field to suggestion as well as to projection and indeterminable drifts. In this way, the analyst approaches the vertigo of delirium and, with it, the phallic *jouissance* of a subject subsumed in the dyadic, narcissistic construction of a discourse in which the *Same* mistakes itself for the *Other*. It is, however, only by detaching himself from such a vertigo that the analyst derives both his *jouissance* and his efficacy.

Thus far, we have seen that analytic interpretation resembles delirium in that it introduces desire into discourse. It does so by giving narcissistic satisfaction to the subject (the analyst or the analysand), who, at the risk of foreclosing any true object, derives phallic jubilation from being the author/actor of a connection that leaves room for desire or for death in discourse.

Yet the analytic position also has counterweights that make delirium work on behalf of analytic truth. The most obvious, the most often cited, of these is the *suspension* of interpretation: silence as frustration of meaning reveals the ex-centricity of desire with regard to meaning. Madness/meaninglessness *exists*—this is what interpretive silence suggests. Second, the analyst, constantly tracking his own desire, never stops analyzing not only his patients' discourse but also his own attitude toward it which is his own countertransference. He is not fixed in the position of the classical interpreter, who interprets by virtue of stable meanings derived from a solid system or morality or who at least tries to restrict the range of his delirium through a stable theoretical counterweight. This is not to say that analytic theory does not exist but rather that, all things considered, its consistency is rudimentary when compared to the countertransferential operation which is always specific and which sets the interpretive machine in motion differently every time. If I know that my desire can make me delirious in my interpretive constructions, my return to this delirium allows me to dissolve its meaning, to displace by one or more notches the quest for meaning which I suppose to be *one* and *one only* but which I can *only* indefinitely approach. *There is meaning, and I am supposed to know it to the extent that it escapes me.*

Finally, there is what I will call the *unnameable:* that which is necessarily enclosed in every questionable, interpretable, enigmatic object. The analyst does not exclude the unnameable. He knows that every interpretation will float over that shadowy point which Freud in *The Interpretation of Dreams* calls the dreams' "umbilical." The analyst knows that delirium, in its phallic ambition, consists precisely in the belief that light can rule everywhere, without a shadow. Yet the analyst can sight and hear the unnameable, which he preserves as the condition of interpretation, *only if he sees it as a phantasm.* As origin and condition of the interpretable, the unnameable is, perhaps, the primordial phantasm. What analysis reveals is that the human being does not speak and that, a fortiori, he does not interpret *without* the phantasm of a return to the origin, without the hypothesis of an unnameable, of a *Sachverhalt.*

Furthermore, analysis reveals that interpretive speech, like all speech which is concerned with an object, is acted upon by the desire to return to the archaic mother who is resistant to meaning. Interpretive speech does this so as to place the archaic mother within the order of language—where the subject of desire, insofar as he is a speaking subject, is immediately displaced and yet, henceforth, situated. The return to the unnameable mother may take the form of narcissistic and masochistic delirium, in which the subject merely confronts an idealized petrification of himself in the form of an interpretive Verb, interpretation becoming, in this case, Everything, subject and object. This is what analytic interpretation confronts, undergoes, and, also, displaces.

For, in short, the analyst-interpreter or the interpreter turned analyst derives the originality of his position from his capacity for displacement, from his mobility, from his polytopia. From past to present, from frustration to desire, from the parameter of pleasure to the parameter of death, and so on—he dazes the analysand with the unexpectedness of his interpretation; even so, however, the unexpectedness of the analysis is in any case sustained by a constant: the desire for the Other. ("If you want me to interpret, you are bound in my desire.")

Since Edward Glover's *Technique of Psychoanalysis* (1928), a highly regarded work in its time, analytic theory has appreciably refined its notion of interpretation.[4] The criteria for sound interpretation may undoubtedly vary: "good adaptation" of the analysand, "progress," appearance of remote childhood memories, encounter with the analyst's transference, and so on. Or criteria for a sound interpretation may even disappear, leaving only the need for a temporary sanction (which may be on the order of the parameters already outlined) within an essentially open interpretive process. In this process, *one* meaning and *one meaning alone* is always specifiable for a particular moment of transference; but, given the vast storehouse of the unknown from which analytic interpretation proceeds, this meaning must be transformed.

If it seems that analytic interpretation, like all interpretation in the strong sense of the word, is therefore an action, can we say that this interpretation aims to change the analysand? Two extreme practices exist. In one, the analysis suggests interpretations; in the other, it assumes a purist attitude: by refusing to interpret, the analysis leaves the patient, faced with the absolute silence of the interpreter, dependent on his own capacity for listening, interpreting, and eventually changing. Faced with these excesses, one could argue that in the vast majority of analyses a psychotherapeutic moment occurs which consists in compensating for previous traumatic situations and allowing the analysand to construct another transference, another meaning of his relationship to the Other, the analyst. In the analytic interpretation, however, such a therapeutic moment has, ultimately, no other function than to effect a transference which would otherwise remain doubtful. Only from that moment does true analytic work (i.e., *dissolving*) begin. Basically, this work involves removing obvious, immediate, realistic meaning from discourse so that the meaninglessness/madness of desire may appear and,

4. See esp. Jacques Lacan, "De l'interpretation au transfert," *Le Séminaire de Jacques Lacan*, vol. 11, *Les Quatre Concepts fondamentaux de la psychanalyse* (Paris, 1973), pp. 221 ff.

beyond that, so that every phantasm is revealed as an attempt to return to the unnameable.

I interpret, the analyst seems to say, because Meaning exists. But my interpretation is infinite because Meaning is made infinite by desire. I am not therefore a dead subject, a wise interpreter, happy and self-annihilated in a uniform totality. I am subject to Meaning, a non-Total Meaning, which escapes me.

Analytic interpretation finally leads the analyst to a fundamental problem which I believe underlies all theory and practice of interpretation: the heterogeneous in meaning, the limitation of meaning, its incompleteness. Psychoanalysis, the only modern interpretive theory to hypothesize the heterogeneous in meaning, nevertheless makes that heterogeneity so interdependent with language and thought as to be its very condition, indeed, its driving force. Furthermore, psychoanalysis gives heterogeneity an operative and analyzable status by designating it as sexual desire and/or as death wish.

3. Can Political Interpretation Be True?

The efficacy of interpretation is a function of its transferential truth: this is what political man learns from the analyst, or in any case shares with him. Consider, for example, those political discourses which are said to reflect the desires of a social group or even of large masses. There is always a moment in history when those discourses obtain a general consensus not so much because they interpret the situation correctly (i.e., in accordance with the exigencies of the moment and developments dictated by the needs of the majority) but rather because they correspond to the essentially utopian desires of that majority. Such political interpretation interprets *desires;* even if it lacks reality, it contains the truth of desires. It is, for that very reason, utopian and ideological.

Yet, as in analysis, such an interpretation can be a powerful factor in the mobilization of energies that can lead social groups and masses beyond a sadomasochistic ascesis to change real conditions. Such a mobilizing interpretation can be called revolution or demagogy. By contrast, a more objective, neutral, and technocratic interpretation would only solidify or very slowly modify the real conditions.

All political discourse that wants to be and is efficacious shares that dynamic. Unlike the analytic dynamic, however, the dynamic of political interpretation does not lead its subjects to an elucidation of their own (and its own) truth. For, as I pointed out earlier, analytic interpretation uses desire and transference, but only to lead the subject, faced with the erosion of meaning, to the economy of his own speaking. It does so by deflating the subject's phantasms and by showing that all phantasms, like any attempt to give meaning, come from the phallic *jouissance* obtained by usurping that unnameable object, that *Sachverhalt,* which is the archaic mother.

Of course, no political discourse can pass into nonmeaning. Its goal, Marx stated explicitly, is to reach the goal of interpretation: interpreting the world in order to transform it according to our needs and desires. Now, from the position of the post-Freudian, post-phenomenological analyst—a position which is really an untenable locus of rationality, a close proximity of meaning and nonmeaning—it is clear that there is no World (or that the World is not all there is) and that *to transform* it is only one of the circles of the interpretation—be it Marxist—which refuses to perceive that it winds around a *void.*

Given this constant factor of the human psyche confirmed by the semiotician and the psychoanalyst when they analyze that ordeal of discourse which is the discourse of delirium, what becomes of interpretive discourse? Indeed, what happens to interpretive discourse in view of the void which is integral to meaning and which we find, for example, in the "arbitrariness of the sign" (the unmotivated relation between signifier and signified in Saussure), in the "mirror stage" (where the subject perceives his own image as essentially split, foreign, other), or in the various forms of psychic alienation? Clearly, interpretive discourse cannot be merely a hermeneutics or a politics. Different variants of sacred discourse assume the function of interpretation at this point.

Our cultural orb is centered around the axiom that "the Word became flesh." Two thousand years after a tireless exploration of the comings and goings between discourse and the object to be named or interpreted, an object which is the solicitor of interrogation, we have finally achieved a discourse on discourse, an interpretation of interpretation. For the psychoanalyst, this vertigo in abstraction is, nevertheless, a means of protecting us from a masochistic and jubilatory fall into nature, into the full and pagan mother, a fall which is a tempting and crushing enigma for anyone who has not gained some distance from it with the help of an interpretive device. However, and this is the second step post-phenomenological analytic rationality has taken, we have also perceived the incompleteness of interpretation itself, the incompleteness characteristic of all language, sign, discourse. This perception prevents the closure of our interpretation as a self-sufficient totality, which resembles delirium, and at the same time this perception of interpretation constitutes the true life of interpretations (in the plural).

4. Literature as Interpretation: The Text

Philosophical interpretation as well as literary criticism therefore and henceforth both have a tendency to be written as *text*s. They openly assume their status as fiction without, however, abandoning their goal of stating One meaning, The True Meaning, of the discourse they interpret.

The fate of interpretation has allowed it to leave behind the protective enclosure of a metalanguage and to approach the imaginary, without necessarily confusing the two. I would now like to evoke some specifics and some dangers of openly fictional interpretation in literary discourse itself. So as not to simplify the task, I will take as my example a modern French novelist, Louis Ferdinand Céline (1894–1961), whose popular and musical style represents the height of twentieth-century French literature and whose anti-Semitic and para-Nazi pamphlets reveal one of the blackest aspects of contemporary history.

I consider all fiction (poetic language or narrative) already an interpretation in the broad sense of the speaking subject's implication in a transposition (connection) of a presupposed object. If it is impossible to assign to a literary text a preexisting "objective reality," the critic (the interpreter) can nevertheless find the mark of the interpretive function of writing in the transformation which that writing inflicts on the language of everyday communication. In other words, *style* is the mark of interpretation in literature. To quote Céline, "I am not a man of ideas. I am a man of style. . . . This involves taking sentences, I was telling you, and unhinging them."[5] Such an interpretive strategy is clearly an enunciative strategy, and, in Célinian language, it uses two fundamental techniques: *segmentation* of the sentence, characteristic of the first novels; and the more or less recuperable *syntactical ellipses* which appear in the late novels.

The peculiar segmentation of the Célinian phrase, which is considered colloquial, is a cutting up of the syntactic unit by the projected or rejected displacement of one of its components. As a result, the normally descending modulation of the phrasal melody becomes an intonation with two centers. Thus: "I had just discovered war in its entirety. . . . Have to be almost in front of it, like I was then, to really see it, the bitch, face on and in profile."[6]

An analysis of this utterance, not as a syntactic structure but as a *message* in the process of enunciation between a speaking subject and his addressee, would show that the aim of this ejection is to *thematize* the displaced element, which then acquires the status not merely of a theme but of an emphatic theme. "La vache" ("the bitch") is the vehicle for the primary information, the essential message which the speaker emphasizes. From this perspective, the ejected element is desyntacticized, but it

---

5. Louis Ferdinand Céline, "Louis Ferdinand Céline vous parle," *Oeuvres complètes*, 2 vols. (Paris, 1966–69), 2:934.

6. "Je venais de découvrir la guerre toute entière. . . . Faut être à peu près devant elle comme je l'étais à ce moment-là pour bien la voir, *la vache*, en face et de profil" (Céline, *Voyage au bout de la nuit, Oeuvres complètes*, 1:8).

is charged with supplementary semantic value, bearing the speaker's emotive attitude and his moral judgment. Thus, the ejection emphasizes the informative kernel at the expense of the syntactic structure and makes the logic of the message (theme/rheme, support/apport, topic/comment, presupposed/posed) dominate over the logic of syntax (verb-object); in other words, the logic of enunciation dominates over that of the enunciated. In fact, the terminal intonational contour of the rheme (along two modalities: assertive and interrogative) indicates the very point at which the modality of enunciation is most profoundly revealed. The notable preponderance of this contour with the bipartition theme/rheme in children's acquisition of syntax or in the emotive or relaxed speech of popular or everyday discourse is added proof that it is a *deeper* organizer of the utterance than syntactic structures.

This "binary shape" in Céline's first novels has been interpreted as an indication of his uncertainty about self-narration in front of the Other. Awareness of the Other's existence would be what determines the phenomena of recall and excessive clarity, which then produces segmentation. In this type of sentence, then, the speaking subject would occupy two places: that of his own identity (when he goes straight to the information, to the rheme) and that of objective expression, for the Other (when he goes back, recalls, clarifies). Given the prevalence of this type of construction in the first phases of children's acquisition of syntax, we can state that this binomial, which is both intonational and logical, coincides with a fundamental stage in the constitution of the speaking subject: his autonomization with respect to the Other, the constitution of his own identity.

To Freud's and René Spitz's insistence that "no" is the mark of man's access to the symbolic and the founding of a distinction between the pleasure principle and the reality principle, one could add that the "binarism" of the message (theme/rheme and vice versa) is another step, a fundamental step, in the symbolic integration of negativism, rejection, and the death drive. It is even a decisive step: with the binarism of the message and before the constitution of syntax, the subject not only differentiates pleasure from reality—a painful and ultimately impossible distinction—but he also distinguishes between the statements: "I say by presupposing" and "I say by making explicit," that is, "I say what matters to me" versus "I say to be clear" or even, "I say what I like" versus "I say for you, for us, so that we can understand each other." In this way, the binary message effects a slippage from the *I* as the pole of pleasure to the *you* as addressee and to the impersonal *one*, he, which is necessary to establish a true universal syntax. This is how the subject of enunciation is born. And it is in remembering this path that the subject rediscovers, if not his origin, at least his originality. The "spoken" writing of Céline achieves just such a remembering.

In addition, in Céline's last novels, *D'un château l'autre, Nord,* and

Rigodon, he repeatedly uses the famous "three dots" (suspension points) and the exclamations which sometimes indicate an ellipsis in the clause but serve more fundamentally to make the clause overflow into the larger whole of the message. This technique produces a kind of long syntactic period, covering a half-page, a full page, or more. In contrast to Proustian fluctuation, it avoids subordinations, is not given as a logical-syntactic unit, and proceeds by brief utterances: clauses pronounceable in one breath which cut, chop, and give rhythm. Laconism (nominal sentences), exclamations, and the predominance of intonation over syntax reecho (like segmentation but in another way) the archaic phases of the subject of enunciation. On the one hand, these techniques, because of the influx of nonmeaning, arouse the nonsemanticized emotion of the reader. On the other hand, they give an infrasyntactical, intonational inscription of that same emotion which transverses syntax but integrates the message (theme/rheme and subject-addressee).[7]

From this brief linguistico-stylistic discussion, I would like to stress the following: style is interpretation in the sense that it is a connection between the logic of utterance and the logic of enunciation, between syntax and message and their two corresponding subjective structures. The unobjectifiable, unnameable "object" which is thereby caught in the text is what Céline calls an *emotion.* "Drive," and its most radical component, the death drive, is perhaps an even better term for it. "You know, in Scriptures, it is written: 'In the beginning was the Word.' No! In the beginning was emotion. The Word came afterwards to replace emotion as the trot replaced the gallop."[8] And again: "Slang is a language of hatred that knocks the reader over for you . . . annihilates him! . . . at your mercy! . . . he sits there like an ass."[9]

It is as if Céline's stylistic adventure were an aspect of the eternal return to a place which escapes naming and which can be named only if one plays on the whole register of language (syntax, but also message, intonation, etc.). This locus of emotion, of instinctual drive, of non-semanticized hatred, resistant to logico-syntactic naming, appears in Céline's work, as in other great literary texts, as a locus of the ab-ject. The abject, not yet object, is anterior to the distinction between subject and object in normative language. But the abject is also the nonobjectality of the archaic mother, the locus of needs, of attraction and repulsion, from which an object of forbidden desire arises. And finally, abject can be understood in the sense of the horrible and fascinating abomination which is connoted in all cultures by the feminine or, more indirectly, by every partial object which is related to the state of abjection (in the sense of the nonseparation subject/object). It becomes what culture, the *sacred,*

7. For a lengthier discussion of Céline's style and its interpretation, see my *Pouvoirs de l'horreur: Essai sur l'abjection* (Paris, 1980).

8. Céline, "Céline vous parle," p. 933.

9. Céline, *Entretiens avec le professeur Y* (1955; Paris, 1976), p. 72.

must purge, separate, and banish so that it may establish itself as such in the universal logic of catharsis.

Is the abject, the ultimate object of style, the archetype of the *Sach-verhalt,* of what solicits interpretation? Is it the archi-interpretable? This is, as I said earlier, something analytic interpretation can argue. Meaning, and the interpretation which both posits and lives off meaning, are sustained by that *elsewhere* which goes beyond them and which fiction, style (other variants of interpretation), never stops approaching—and dissolving.

For this is in fact the central issue in Céline as in the great writers of all times. By their themes (evil, idiocy, infamy, the feminine, etc.) and their styles, they immerse us in the ab-ject (the unnameable, the *Sach-verhalt*), not in order to name, reify, or objectify them once and for all but to dissolve them and to displace us. In what direction? Into the harmony of the Word and into the fundamental incompleteness of discourse constituted by a cleavage, a void: an effervescent and dangerous beauty, the fragile obverse of a radical nihilism that can only fade away in "those sparkling depths which [say] that nothing exists any more."[10]

Yet this pulverization of the abject, the ultimate case of interpretation by style, remains fragile. Because it does not always satisfy desire, the writer is tempted to give one interpretation and one only to the outer limit of the nameable. The *Sachverhalt,* the abject, is then embodied in the figure of a maleficent agent, both feminine and phallic, miserable and all-powerful, victim and satrap, idiot and genius, bestial and wily. What once defied discourse now becomes the ultimate object of one and only one interpretation, the source and acme of a polymorphous *jouis-sance* in which the interpreter, this time in his delirium, is finally reunited with what denies, exceeds, and excites him. He blends into this abject and its feminine-maternal resonance which threatens identity itself. This interpretive delirium—writing's weak moment—found in Céline the Jew as its privileged object in the context of Hitlerism. The historical and social causes of Céline's anti-Semitism can be sought in monotheism, or, rather, in its denials, and in the history of France and the reality of the Second World War. His anti-Semitism also has a more subtle foundation, more intrinsically linked to the psychic instability of the writer and the speaking subject in general: it is the fascination with the wandering and elusive other, who attracts, repels, puts one literally beside oneself. This other, before being another subject, is an object of discourse, a nonob-ject, an abject. This abject awakens in the one who speaks archaic con-flicts with his own improper objects, his ab-jects, at the edge of meaning, at the limits of the interpretable. And it arouses the paranoid rage to dominate those objects, to transform them, to exterminate them.

I do not presume to elucidate in this brief presentation the many

10. Céline, *Rigodon, Oeuvres complètes,* 2:927.

causes and aspects of Céline's anti-Semitism. A lengthier consideration of the subject can be found in my *Pouvoirs de l'horreur*. I have broached this difficult and complex subject here to indicate by a *paroxysm*, which we could take as a *hyperbole*, the dangerous paths of interpretive passion, fascinated by an enigma that is beyond discourse. For the psychoanalyst, it recalls a desiring indebtedness to the maternal continent.

I would like the above remarks to be taken both as a "free association" and as the consequence of a certain position. I would want them to be considered not only an epistemological discussion but also a personal involvement (need I say one of desire?) in the dramas of thought, personality, and contemporary politics. Such a vast theme ("the politics of interpretation") cannot help but involve a multiplicity of questions. If their conjunction in my paper seems chaotic, inelegant, and nonscientific to a positivist rationality, this conjunction is precisely what defines for me the originality and the difficulty of psychoanalytic interpretation. The task is not to make an interpretive summa in the name of a system of truths—for that attitude has always made interpretation a rather poor cousin of theology. The task is, instead, to record the *crisis* of modern interpretive systems without smoothing it over, to affirm that this crisis is inherent in the symbolic function itself, and to perceive as symptoms all constructions, including totalizing interpretation, which try to deny this crisis: to dissolve, to displace indefinitely, in Kafka's words, "temporarily and for a lifetime."

Perhaps nothing of the wise Stoic interpreter remains in the analyst except his function as *actor:* he accepts the text and puts all his effort and desire, his passion and personal virtuosity, into reciting it, while remaining indifferent to the events that he enacts. This "indifference," called "benevolent neutrality," is the modest toga with which we cover our interpretive desire. Yet by shedding it, by implicating ourselves, we bring to life, to meaning, the dead discourses of patients which summon us. The ambiguity of such an interpretive position is both untenable and pleasurable. Knowing this, knowing that he is constantly in abjection and in neutrality, in desire and in indifference, the analyst builds a strong ethics, not normative but directed, which no transcendence guarantees. That is where, it seems to me, the modern version of liberty is being played out, threatened as much by a single, total, and totalitarian Meaning as it is by delirium.

The Construal of Reality:
Criticism in Modern and Postmodern Science

Stephen Toulmin

Introduction and Summary

I shall attempt to demonstrate here that the general categories of hermeneutics can be applied just as well to the natural sciences as to the humanities, and I shall explore the implications of this demonstration for both types of disciplines. In doing so, it will be necessary for me to raise some unfashionable issues about the objectivity and rationality of critical interpretations, and, as a result, I may appear to be cast in the role of *advocatus diaboli*. The value of lowering the critical barriers that have been set up between the human and natural sciences, however, will outweigh any incidental paradoxes that may crop up en route.

The hermeneutic movement in philosophy and criticism has done us a service by directing our attention to the role of critical interpretation in understanding the humanities. But it has done us a disservice also because it does not recognize any comparable role for interpretation in the natural sciences and in this way sharply separates the two fields of scholarship and experience.[1] Consequently, I shall argue, the central

1. Some will respond that Edmund Husserl, for one, spoke of the natural sciences as being, in their own way, "interpretive"; but the role allotted to natural science by the phenomenologists and their successors—I have in mind Hans Georg Gadamer and Jürgen Habermas as much as Martin Heidegger and Husserl—is an impoverished and unhistorical one. The hermeneutic philosophers have not, in this respect, fully recognized either the plurality or the historical variability of the interpretive modes adopted in one or another of the natural sciences for different intellectual purposes and at different stages in their historical development.

truths and virtues of hermeneutics have become encumbered with a whole string of false inferences and misleading dichotomies.

These distortions have had two effects. On the one hand, they have led readers to misunderstand the true character of that objectivity and rationality which are crucial goals of the natural sciences; and, on the other hand, they have encouraged an exaggerated idea of the extent to which differences in personal and/or cultural standpoint rule out any such goal for the humanities. Once we recognize that the natural sciences too are in the business of "construing" reality, we shall be better able to preserve the central insights of the hermeneutic method, without succumbing to the misleading implications of its rhetorical misuse.

Physics, in particular, has always required its participants to adopt an interpretive standpoint, and this standpoint has changed more than once during the historical development of that science. Yet this variable standpoint has done nothing to undercut the commitment of physicists to rationality and objectivity: on the contrary, they have made it one of their chief aims to discover just what aspects of reality, or nature, *lend themselves to* interpretation and understanding as considered from any particular standpoint. If we can drive this wedge between scientific objectivity and hermeneutic relativity in the case of physics, we are free to return to the humanities and apply the same distinction there too. It has too often, and too readily, been assumed that whatever needs to be interpreted in order to be understood will, to that extent, become a matter of taste or subjectivity; and, as a result, any claims to rationality and objectivity in the critical realms—whether moral or aesthetic, political or intellectual—have been too hastily surrendered.

The current sharp distinction between scientific explanation and hermeneutic interpretation was launched by Wilhelm Dilthey nearly a century ago; and, in justice to Dilthey, we need to bear in mind that the interpretive element in natural science was far less evident then than it is today. Scientists nowadays view the world from a new and less rigid standpoint. This period, which Frederick Ferre calls "postmodern science," differs from the older one of "modern science" in just those respects that enable us to reconcile the rational claims that have always been central to the natural sciences with a new hermeneutic richness and variability.

Stephen Toulmin is a professor in the committee on social thought, the department of philosophy, and the Divinity School at the University of Chicago. He is author of, among other works, *Foresight and Understanding, Human Understanding,* and *Knowing and Acting* and is currently at work on volume 2 of *Human Understanding.*

It is a pity then for scholars working in the humanities to continue shaping their critical attitudes and theories by relying on a contrast with a modern science that—among scientists themselves—no longer even *seems* to exist. (In this respect, both Gadamer and Habermas share Heidegger's instrumentalist misreading of science and technology as "value neutral" enterprises without their own intrinsic goals or ideals and, in so doing, involve themselves in a curious alliance with the positivists whom they otherwise despise.)[2] Instead, we should ask scholars to pay more attention to the elements of interpretation—even of hermeneutics—that have nowadays become essential to both the natural and human sciences and to base their comparisons between the sciences and the humanities not on the assumed *absence* of hermeneutic interpretation from natural science but rather on the different *modes* of interpretation characteristic of the two general fields.

The Way Down

1. The doctrines of the natural sciences are critical interpretations of their subject matter, no less than those of the humanities.

Among the spokesmen for the new "mathematical and experimental philosophy" of the seventeenth century, there were some who claimed to rest their scientific conclusions on simple deductions and/or generalizations from the "facts" of observation. This claim, from time to time, has been revived by enthusiastic scientists interested in affirming a unique kind of rationality or objectivity for their results as well as by empiricist philosophers interested in using science to support a positivist theory of knowledge. This positivist view of scientific argument is, however, deceptive: scientists always approach their investigations with specific problems in mind and view the phenomena or processes that they study with the hope of shedding light on those problems. As a result, scientific discoveries are typically arrived at not by generalizing from preexisting *facts* but by providing answers to preexisting *questions*.[3]

2. Significant changes have occurred in the current styles of interpretation as the natural sciences have moved from one stage of historical development to another.

The interpretive standpoint characteristic of the physical sciences in

2. For a fuller discussion, see my "Can Science and Ethics Be Reconnected?," *Hastings Center Report* (June 1979): 27–34.

3. The limitations of the "orthodox" philosophy of science are discussed from a variety of viewpoints in *The Legacy of Logical Positivism*, ed. Peter Achinstein and Stephen F. Barker (Baltimore, 1969), and in *The Structure of Scientific Theories*, ed. Frederick Suppe (Urbana, Ill., 1974).

the "classical" period, which lasted from the mid–seventeenth century until around 1920, required scientists to approach the world as pure *spectators*. In theory, at least, the ideal viewpoint for observing the processes of nature was one that permitted scientists to look on at them and describe them without significantly influencing them. Whereas the alchemists had been continually open to the worry that their own states of mind might be altering the very phenomena they were hoping to control, the "new philosophers" thought they had hit on a method for obtaining truly objective knowledge of nature which was in no way affected by their own motives and prejudices. Thus the intellectual program and strategy of modern science was established, and this dominated the thinking of physical scientists until well into the twentieth century. It was nicely captured in Pierre Simon Laplace's image of the Omniscient Calculator, who looked on at the universe *from outside* and predicted its entire future course as a straightforward exercise in Newtonian mechanics.[4]

During the heyday of the modern scientific program, the inherent limits to the scope of this method were not, however, borne in mind as carefully as they might have been. It was too often assumed that the particular ideal of objective, scientific knowledge on which it was based could, in principle, be extended without limit to embrace natural systems and phenomena of all kinds. This method could be applied without difficulty—not surprisingly—to inert physical or material *objects* and also to other natural happenings that follow the same course, regardless of whether they were observed or not. But once the scope of investigation was extended to include systems and subjects whose behavior may be changed by the very fact that they are being investigated, it could no longer play the same exclusive part.

At first this meant only that modern science provided an unsuitable method and an irrelevant ideal of objectivity for the *human* sciences. (Human beings—qua research subjects—are normally aware when their behavior is being studied and are capable of reacting countersuggestibly.) That is to say, at first this limitation served merely to reinforce the contrast between the passivity and objectivity of material nature, on the one hand, and the activity and subjectivity of human beings, on the other. During the first thirty years of the twentieth century, however, these difficulties began to cut deeper. All along, it now appeared, the standpoint of the detached onlooker, from which—in theory at least—classical scientists had observed and speculated about the world, was no more than an abstraction.

It was convenient to *assume* that such detachment was possible, for

---

4. For a discussion of the role of Laplace's image of the Omniscient Calculator in the history of the classical standpoint in physical theory, see my *The Return to Cosmology* (forthcoming).

the purposes of interpretation, but that assumption misrepresented the actual situation. As we now realize, the interaction between scientists and their objects of study is always a *two-way* affair. There is no way in which scientists can continue to reduce the effects of their observations on those objects without limit. Even in fundamental physics, for instance, the fact that subatomic particles are under observation will make the influence of the physicists' instruments a significant element in the phenomena themselves. As a result, during the twentieth century scientists have had to change their interpretive standpoint not merely in the human sciences but elsewhere. In quantum mechanics as much as in psychiatry, in ecology as much as in anthropology, the scientific observer is now—willy-nilly—also a *participant.* The scientists of the mid–twentieth century, then, have entered the period of postmodern science. For natural scientists today, the classical posture of pure spectator is no longer available even on the level of pure theory; and the objectivity of scientific knowledge can no longer rely on the passivity of the scientists' objects of knowledge alone. In the physical sciences, objectivity can now be achieved only in the way it is in the human sciences: the scientist must acknowledge and discount his own reactions to and influence on that which he seeks to understand.

In this respect, the problems facing physicists today turn out to be like those which psychologists have always faced—which are typified, for example, by countertransference problems in psychoanalysis. As a direct consequence, the intellectual basis on which Dilthey had relied to distinguish the natural from the moral sciences is called into question. For Dilthey had, pardonably, taken it for granted that the difference between the objectivity of material objects and the subjectivity of states of mind was absolute: in the human sciences we did not pretend to explain one another's actions objectively but rather learned to interpret each other's subjective states of mind. Yet it now appears that these two cases lie, rather, at the opposite ends of a spectrum. At one extreme, there are objects that respond to us only minimally when we observe them; at the other, there are people who interact with us in a highly responsive manner. In between, there are all kinds of more or less complex and subtle processes and organisms, and these are, correspondingly, more or less unresponsive to being studied. In its own way, accordingly, the contrast between *Natur* and *Geist* has served as a twentieth-century restatement of the traditional Cartesian matter/mind dichotomy, and, as such, it is as vulnerable as its predecessors to changes in our scientific understanding of mentality.

This shift within the physical sciences—from the detached point of view of the uninfluencing spectator to the interactive point of view of the participant-observer—is only one (though perhaps the most radical) illustration of the multiplicity of interpretive standpoints that twentieth-century scientists have occasion to adopt. In the biological sciences, there is a similar (though longer-standing) multiplicity, about which J. B. S. Haldane and C. H. Waddington have written interesting commentaries.[5]

As Haldane and Waddington point out, no biological event can ever be viewed as a phenomenon of one and only one kind. On the contrary, every such event has at least four distinct aspects, and biologists ask at least four kinds of questions about it. On one level, it has biochemical or biophysical aspects, involving small-scale physicochemical processes that occupy minutes, seconds, or even fractions of a second; on another level, it typically has physiological aspects, involving functional processes in the major organs of the body that occupy minutes, hours, or perhaps days; on another level, it has a morphogenetic or developmental significance, which is exemplified in changes that occupy months, years, and decades; while, on a final level, it has a fourth significance, as it relates to species' adaptation and evolution. No one of the resulting accounts of the event will be biologically exhaustive. But, taken together, biochemical, physiological, developmental, and evolutionary accounts give us complementary interpretations which between them show us what biology has to teach us about the event in question; and any would-be biologist will normally have to master all four branches of biology, so learning to take up the points of view appropriate to each of them.

With this biological example in mind, we can see that the dividing line between the biological and psychological sciences is no longer a hard and fast one. In the mental or behavioral sciences, we can always take up *at least* the four different standpoints of biology, and we are now free to add other points of view, each with its own correspondingly different type of account. In psychology, therefore, we may reasonably expect to find a considerably greater number of standpoints than exists even in biology; and this could well lead us to accept the conclusion that Aristotle reaches in the *Categories*—namely, that there are, at a minimum, *nineteen* distinct kinds of things to be said about a human being at any given time.

3. The apprentice scientist masters the current interpretive standpoint of a science in the course of being enculturated into the professional community of that science.

In order to grasp fully the disciplines of the natural sciences, it is necessary to become a natural scientist oneself. Thus one would master all the tacit elements of interpretation that stand between, say, a mathematical formula, such as $E = mc^2$, and the actual features of the physical world which this formula is currently used to explain. To that extent, the newer methods of historiography within the history of science are right

5. See J. B. S. Haldane, Herbert Spencer Lecture, given at Oxford University, 1955, and rpt. as "Time in Biology" (*Science Progress* 44 [July 1956]: 385–402), and C. H. Waddington, *The Nature of Life* (London, 1961).

to treat the history of disciplines and the history of professions as two faces of a single coin.[6]

The intellectual styles of interpretation and the particular interpretive standpoints characteristic of any given science are, in these respects, "carried by" the community of scientists who are professionally committed to cultivating that discipline. And the manner in which those scientists customarily *interpret* the doctrines and propositions of the science plays an inescapable part in determining the *meaning* of those statements.

4. Any scientist, then, who is fully "inside" a particular discipline belongs to a special "polis," and his work has a corresponding "collective" aspect.

That being so, the thesis from which this symposium begins— namely, that "interpretation . . . seems inseparable from questions of private and public ethics, questions, in the broadest sense, of politics"—is not without some color of a foundation, even in the natural sciences. At this point, however, it is essential to be quite clear just how much and how little foundation that thesis really possesses; and beyond this point, my argument turns a corner. For it is here that talking about the interpretive element in science as implicitly "political" may tempt us to gloss over some important distinctions.

To cite just one of these: there is an important difference between (1), those postmodern fields of science, such as ecology and psychiatry, in which the topics of inquiry involve the interactions between human beings (or between humans and their immediate environment) and whose *content* is therefore liable to have direct social or political implications, and (2), the traditional fields of modern science, in which most of the scientist's professional activities continue to have little or no socially or politically significant impact on his or her objects of study. In the latter case, the "exigencies of the [immediate] subject matter," to borrow Edward Said's phrase, are the determinative factor, both intellectually and politically; in the former case, by contrast, the very manner in which the problems to be studied are formulated reflects both intellectual and political considerations.

We can perhaps stretch the sense of the term "politics" far enough to include the scientist's involvement with his own colleagues as a political fact about science.[7] We can, for instance, study the institutional prac-

6. For a discussion of this thesis, see the first half of my *Human Understanding* (Princeton, N.J., 1972), esp. pt. 1, chap. 4. By now this is one of the commonplaces of the newer work in the history and sociology of science.

7. See Ludwik Fleck, *Genesis and Development of a Scientific Fact* (1935), trans. Fred Bradley and Thaddeus J. Trenn and ed. Trenn and Robert K. Merton (Chicago, 1979); this fascinating book anticipated so many of the themes of the more recent debate in the history of science.

tices of any science—its journals, societies, awards, and the rest—with an eye to how far those practices are fully warranted by the needs and purposes of the discipline concerned, and how far the power and solidarity of the profession are utilized in pursuit of *frankly* political goals. (In any science, the institutional instruments and influence that are created initially for disciplinary purposes are liable to be utilized also for other, sectarian ends.) But if we fail to keep the difference between these two kinds of "scientific politics" in mind, we may well destroy the very sense and elasticity of the term "politics" itself and so leave ourselves with no way of marking the difference between those scientific disciplines which have an *essentially* political content and those which can be spoken of as political only as a *façon de parler*.

The Way Up

1. In any well-defined (or "compact") discipline, interpretation is never merely personal or arbitrary.

In the core natural sciences, the choice between available interpretations (or interpretive standpoints) is never a matter of individual taste or preference alone. Rather, it turns on all the *experience* that has been accumulated in that discipline: in particular, on how far the subject matter of the discipline has turned out to *lend itself to* interpretations of one kind rather than another. (Sticks and stones lend themselves naturally to study by the detached methods of modern science, while human research subjects require a more interactive, postmodern style of investigation.) The mere presence, then, of an interpretive element in the natural sciences does nothing to detract from the objectivity of scientific results. On the contrary, the question Which style of interpretation would it be appropriate to adopt in dealing with this particular kind of subject matter? itself calls for an answer based on actual experience—and so an objective answer.

There is nothing especially new about this insight. At the very beginning of the modern scientific movement, in fact, Galileo himself acknowledged the *interpretive* aspect of science when he described the Book of Nature as "written in mathematical symbols" which the scientist had to decipher. His warm admirer, René Descartes, recognized the same point at the end of his *Principia philosophiae,* where he compared the methods of natural philosophy to those of cryptography. The scientist's task, he argued, is to *break the code of nature* and so to interpret the theoretical significance of the natural phenomena he investigates. If he can do so, he can hope to arrive at "objective truths" about the world; but, in doing so, he can never achieve more than a *moral* certainty that his particular reading is in fact correct, as his successful decipherments—or explanations—accumulate and support one another.

As Descartes' and Galileo's analogies remind us, the art of interpretation had its original home in the field of linguistics; and there, too, one interpretation can perfectly well prove to be "correct," another "incorrect." For instance, in the debate over the deciphering of the Linear Minoan B inscriptions recovered from preclassical archeological sites in Crete and the Peloponnese, the choice between reading these signs as "proto Greek" with Michael Ventris or as Phoenician with Cyrus Gordon was well balanced and open to individual judgment for so long as the quantity of the material involved remained small. But, as time went on, the sheer bulk of the texts that lent themselves naturally to the Ventris reading was so impressive that it became hard to deny the basic correctness of his interpretation.

Meanwhile, all attempts to read the central *content* of the core natural sciences as purely, or even primarily, political continue to fall on their faces. Even those historians of science who follow the newer fashions in historiography acknowledge the power that "proven" methods of investigation retain over the intellectual allegiance of those professionals. So, interpretations of the core sciences such as that which John Desmond Bernal gave of the theory of natural selection—as rooted in Darwin's assumptions about parliamentary democracy—remain as strained and artificial as ever.[8] This is not to deny that in natural science, as in the humanities, there is room for peripheral differences of interpretation between different professional communities: for example, between Europeans and Americans, Japanese and Russian geneticists, or even between behaviorist psychologists at Harvard and Columbia. At the core of the natural sciences, however, there are bodies of well-established interpretations whose "moral certainty" is at least as great as that of a well-established decipherment.

In some cases, of course, the scientists who collaborate in a particular profession may believe—mistakenly—that the body of interpretations which they are currently justified in agreeing upon is more extensive than it truly is; and the reasons underlying this belief may have a genuinely political aspect. In late seventeenth-century England, for example, all of the "new scientists" took it for granted that matter is essentially inert and so intrinsically incapable of initiating genuine "actions"; and they clearly believed that this assumption was supported by the results obtained in recent scientific investigations. Yet, as Joseph Priestley was later to demonstrate, nothing in the actual content of Newtonian mechanics enforced that assumption. On the contrary, it was

8. See, e.g., John Desmond Bernal, *Science in History* (London and Cambridge, Mass., 1969).

possible, without inconsistency, to interpret all of Newton's theory as a dynamical account of the effects of "active" particles, or "point sources" of action.[9] Why, then, had the *passivity* of matter remained an axiom of the new physics for so long? The answer to that question becomes clearer (it has been argued recently) if you ask *just who* in the England of the Commonwealth had publicly taught the opposite doctrine, namely, that matter is essentially *active*.[10] Certainly the respectable divines, who were Newton's chief supporters at the court of Charles II, did not care to class themselves with an anarchistic rabble of Shakers, Ranters, and the like. The Newtonian choice for passive over active matter seems, thus, to have turned as much on issues of social imagery—God being seen to "inspire" matter and confer motion on it, just as the king was seen to be the final source of political agency—as it did on genuine matters of scientific interpretation and explanation.

That last distinction, between issues of imagery and matters of interpretation, is easier to draw in physics than it is, say, in psychology; as a result, there is more temptation to present *all* interpretations in the human sciences as being essentially political in character than there is in the physical sciences. Still, it is a temptation that we ought to resist. In the long run, much of human behavior and mentality should come within the reach of the core sciences; and the fact that, in such cases, the present distinction is *difficult* to draw does not mean that it is irrelevant to the human sciences or not worth *attempting* to draw.

2. Alternative styles of interpretation within an established scientific discipline reflect the fact that alternative interpretive standpoints are available within the science, each with its own scope and justification.

A variety of parallel interpretations does not reflect the personal preferences or characteristics—their personalities, political views, or cultural backgrounds—of the individual scientists who adopt them. It reflects, rather, the fact that alternative investigative postures and interpretive standpoints *have been found* productive in dealing with different aspects of the discipline's subject matter. My choice of the phrase "have been found" underlines our concern with genuine *matters of experience*. (Faced with the question whether the systems we are studying are simple "objects" and so unresponsive to our investigation or whether they are "agents" and thus to be dealt with in a more interactive manner, we cannot afford to make premature or hasty assumptions and can proceed only in the light of all our practical experience.)

9. See, e.g., Joseph Priestley's "Disquisitions Relating to Matter and Spirit" (1777), *Priestley's Writings on Philosophy, Science, and Politics,* ed. John A. Passmore (New York, 1965).

10. See Steven Shapin, "Of Gods and Kings: Natural Philosophy and Politics in the Leibniz-Clarke Disputes," *Isis* 72 (February 1981): 187–215.

To assume without examination that *all* internally consistent interpretations of any scientifically significant event were equally possible would be as gratuitous and unjustifiable as assuming without examination that such an event can lend itself to *only one* interpretation. We cannot hope to decide in advance how far and in what respects the aspects of the natural world that concern us in any particular investigation can fruitfully be studied from alternative standpoints and so lend themselves to multiple interpretations, or how far and in what respects they demand a unique standpoint and style of interpretation. As yet, the answers to those questions remain to be seen. (The fact that electromagnetic phenomena demand *two* alternative "wave" and "particle" interpretations was a genuine discovery within physics; the fact that biologically significant events lend themselves to interpretation on *four* parallel levels was the outcome of a whole series of biological discoveries; and so on in other cases.)

3. The same is true, equally, of interpretation in the critical disciplines of the humanities.

Just as, in the natural sciences, the choice between interpretive styles and standpoints is not a matter of personal taste or preference but rather the outcome of experience and discrimination, so too it is in the humanities. When different critics approach the same text, artifact, or situation from varied standpoints and find different things worth drawing attention to and commenting on, those differences need no more reflect the varied personal characteristics of those critics than they would in the sciences. Once again, it is a mistake to assume that the multiplicity of standpoints in the humanities implies that our choice of a critical standpoint has an inevitable subjectivity, which is absent in the case of the natural sciences.

Certainly we all know of critical writers who, from time to time, let their personalities, political views, or cultural backgrounds distort their discriminations and who, as a result, take up critical standpoints which other perceptive, experienced observers (critics/readers, etc.) find idiosyncratic or worse. But that case neither is, nor should be, paradigmatic or typical. The more fundamental distinction separates central, legitimate, and acceptable standpoints for criticism and interpretation from those that are eccentric, inadmissible, or merely bizarre. One does not need to be Matthew Arnold to understand what power "the central tone" adds to the cogency of a critical argument.

In the humanities, we know that a number of different critical standpoints may be relevant to the same work, whether or not they are truly central to understanding that work. To that extent, it is rarely possible to identify *one single* standpoint as the uniquely correct one for critics or observers to adopt. But this does not imply that we cannot

recognize truly incorrect, impossible, or even frankly outrageous interpretations when we meet them. Still less does it imply that there are no
genuinely *incorrect* standpoints, only idiosyncratic, ideologically biased,
or otherwise unusual ones.

The situation that faces us in the critical disciplines is like that which
we face, for example, when we write letters of reference. Often enough,
we can properly write from any of a number of points of view, and we
can truthfully say rather different things, depending on the exact nature
of both the occasion and the audience; yet that fact does not open up a
complete "free-for-all." Alongside these *possible* points of view and
statements, there are also countless others which would be irresponsible,
libelous, or otherwise impermissible. Here again variety in no way implies subjectivity, let alone warranting political or ideological bias. In
itself, it reminds us only that different occasions and topics, subjects and
contexts, may give us *good reasons* for adopting one standpoint rather
than another and for emphasizing one aspect of a work rather than
another. (In this respect, Hayden White lets himself be carried away
when he reads the multiplicity of historical interpretations as implying
that our choice between them is free of external constraints.)

*4. The traditional claims of the critical judgment to its own kind of "rationality"
and "objectivity" therefore deserve to be reconsidered.*

The dichotomy between the sciences and the humanities that has
developed in the years since philosophers and critics elevated the
threefold distinction underlying the program of hermeneutics—
between *Natur* and *Geist,* explanation and interpretation, the "value free"
and the "value laden"—into a methodological axiom has distracted us
from the justice of those claims. Dilthey was right to assert that the
humanities necessarily involve interpretation; but he was misled when he
took the claims of positivistically minded scientists at their face value and
denied a similar role to interpretation in the sciences. In sciences and
humanities alike, we must be prepared to consider the products of
human imagination and creation—whether ideas or artifacts, poems or
theories—from a variety of different points of view, some of them internal to the immediate content and professional goal, others reflecting
more the influence of external factors. That is to say, in critical analysis
as in the history of science, we need to address both the technical issues
that arise within any well-established professional enterprise—whether
scientific or artistic—and also those broader issues that have to do with
the manner in which the technical concerns of the enterprise interact
with the larger political or cultural contexts.

In dealing with the technical issues, we are centrally concerned with
the considerations that carry weight (and so count as *reasons*) for anyone

who is professionally engaged in the enterprise, as well as with any peripheral factors that may influence their work, without being seen as reasons. In dealing with the broader issues, we are centrally concerned with a larger and more turbulent world of *causes,* for example, the interactions between the professionals and their human contexts, as well as with any consequential influences that contextual factors may exert on the professional argument itself.

This whole spectrum of considerations, from the purely causal to the fully rational, is available for reflective interpretation in all fields of creative and professional work equally. Prosody and portraiture, character drawing and fugal composition involve their own technicalities and innovations, quite as much as physics and biology. And those who change the accepted methods of creation and criticism in the arts and the humanities will do so for good or convincing reasons, whether of sonority, balance, or whatever, while at the same time putting those techniques to work to serve goals whose novelty may well reflect the influence of outside causes.

Seen against this background, the supposed contrast between the scientists' claim to rational objectivity (which requires no interpretation) and the humanists' rival claim to subjective sensibility (in which interpretation is all) shows *on its face* its essential irrelevance to the actual work of art and science. At most, there is a difference of balance or emphasis reflecting the different occasions that arts and sciences provide for the public discussion of professional and critical issues.

Commentary

1. The crucial change distinguishing the postmodern sciences of the present from their immediate precursors, the modern sciences, lies in their ideas about the nature of objectivity. The importance of this change is best seen if we recall the stress that philosophers like Heidegger and Habermas have put on the perils of "objectification": for example, on the supposed tendency of science and technology to treat things and people alike as objects and so to *dehumanize* people by disregarding their subjective interests, values, and feelings.

From their point of view, the sciences remain *by definition,* even today, value free, and we must deny the possibility of finding a genuinely hermeneutic element in any properly so-called natural science. On this view, hermeneutic interpretation is possible only where two genuine *minds* are involved: the mind of the agent whose acts or intentions are interpreted and the mind of the commentator who does the interpreting. So the typical hermeneutic situation *differs in kind* from any situation in which a scientist observes, or a technologist acts upon, a material object or an "objectified" person. By their very nature, science and technology—so defined—operate without regard to "inner," intentional, or mental considerations.

This way of stating the difference between the sciences and the humanities, as we can now see, begs the crucial questions, since it takes for granted an *absolute* contrast between material processes and mental activities, objects and people, or (in general) the material and the mental. Yet, in recent decades, the whole basis for this contrast has been largely eroded. With the recognition that all scientific observation involves two-way interactions between the observer and the system being observed, we are no longer entitled even to treat material objects in a purely objectified manner. That being so, there is, a fortiori, no longer any reason to assume that studying human beings from a scientific point of view necessarily involves dehumanizing them.

To say this is not, of course, to imply that electrons, for instance, react to being observed as they do because they, too, have minds; nor is it to deny that there are genuine differences between the kinds of understanding we have of physical phenomena and human experience, respectively. (Where differences in degree are extreme enough, we scarcely *need* to relabel them as "differences in kind.") But it does imply that the kind of objectivity involved in the natural sciences is less drastic than most philosophers have been assuming, and it does deny that the scientist's eye necessarily devalues, to say nothing of dehumanizing, its subject matter. The truth of the matter is in fact the other way around. The new view of objectivity to which postmodern scientists are accustoming themselves means that the older, absolute division between human and natural sciences has dismantled itself, and there is no longer any obstacle to prevent interactive fields of study such as psychiatry and human ecology from being numbered among the natural sciences.

So, we may say, in postmodern science *nature is no longer held at arm's length*. The objectivity of the sciences today is no different from the objectivity aimed at in other fields of judgment—the objectivity, for example, at which a judge must aim in trying a case or to which a parent should aspire when mediating a quarrel between children. In all these cases, to be objective does not require us to be *un*interested, that is, devoid of interests or feelings; it requires us only to acknowledge those interests and feelings, to discount any resulting biases and prejudices, and to do our best to act in a *dis*interested way.

The postmodern scientist may, thus, still be something of a spectator, but he need no longer be a purely *detached* spectator. The human ecologist, for instance, has the task of studying the modes of interaction between human agents or communities and the natural environment and explaining the effects of, for example, land use or agriculture on the lives of other species. But, in doing so, he is not required to pretend that he has no interests of his own in water supply and food production. At most, he is required to discount his own needs and hopes in this work and to analyze the manner in which the activities of human beings and other species influence each other in terms that "do equal justice" to all of the species involved. At times, the resulting accounts may surprise the lay public as much as the older-style explanations of the modern scientists did: many Americans found it hard to view snail darters with the required degree of piety and equity. But it is important to recognize how, through the shift from the modern to the postmodern standpoint, questions of justice have taken a place in the forum of scientific judgment alongside questions of truth.

In the course of this shift, the very concept of "scientific truth" has itself been clarified. The truth of theories turns out to resemble the truth of plain, factual statements, which aim at being straightforward, veracious, and undistorted reports, less than it does the truth of portraits, which aim at being faithful, just, or "unmisleading" likenesses. What puzzles a scientist about any phenomenon is less the question What is *true* about this? than the question What can we *make* of this?; and there the interpretive element is quite explicit. What P. F. Strawson calls a "conceptual framework," and Bakhtin—a little misleadingly—an "ideology," the theoretical physicist thus calls a "treatment." The question to be faced in quantum electrodynamics, say, will be, Can we find a *treatment* for the radiation effects of moving electrons which assumes a consistent value for the radius of the electron? In fact, the empirical content of any science comes less from checking the straightforward "factual truth" of all its theoretical statements than it does from discovering the range and scope of the interpretive standpoints that have won a place within it. As a result, the task of seeing just how far some theoretical treatment will take us in science has much in common with the task that Ronald Dworkin described here in the law: the problem will often be to discover just how far a particular representation of light as, for example, particulate in nature can be taken in the interest of explaining the phenomena of optics, or just how far a particular reading of, for example, the constitutional theory of "protected speech" can be taken in the interest of protecting political demonstrators.

2. In judging where to draw the line between admissible and inadmissible (or true and false) interpretations, the central question for us to address is: In what respects, and to what extent, are our choices of interpretation imposed on us by the exigencies of our subject matter? In what respects, and to what extent, are we free to make those choices on some other basis, or for reasons of other kinds? That question arises in the same general form in disciplines and enterprises of many kinds, whether scientific or humanistic, legal or critical; and it is not always easy to see just how far "the exigencies of our subject matter" can actually take us.

We encountered the question earlier on, when we looked at the idea of matter in seventeenth-century Newtonian physics. There, the choice whether to view matter as active or passive turns out to have been underdetermined by the subject matter; and, as the Leibniz-Clarke correspondence testifies, it was taken in favor of passivity partly, also, for reasons of theological doctrine, if not downright political prejudice.[11] But the same question arises in psychology as well as in physics, and there it may be harder to see just how far the subject matter imposes an interpretation on us or at just what point the choice is up to us. Still, to repeat, the fact that a distinction may not be easily drawn in actual cases does not imply that it cannot be drawn or that it is not worth drawing. Though the phenomena of psychotherapy may lend themselves to a great variety of theoretical interpretations, between which we cannot at present choose on the basis of sufficient evidence alone, it does not follow that our choice of an interpretation becomes, at this point, entirely subjective.

Here, the difficulties involved in White's position can be made clearer. He would not allow us to begin talking about "interpretation" until all the "external constraints" have run out: that is, until all the "exigencies of our subject matter" have been respected and our hands are free, so that we can go on to choose whatever interpretation we please or whatever we may have other motives for preferring. This position, however, is a kind of positivism-in-reverse: one which keeps the positivists' original sharp line, between the objective testimony of empirical facts and subjective issues of taste or preference, but welcomes that very subjectivism over questions of interpretation which the positivists themselves deplore. Yet if we take this route, treating all interpretation as idiosyncratic, the effect of doing so will be to rob the whole topic of interpretation of its intellectual significance. Since all interpretive choices then become, *by definition,* matters of preference unrelated to the demands of the problem—if not matters of mere personal taste—those choices are no longer ones to be made under any genuinely *intellectual* constraint.

3. Finally, let me place this whole discussion back into an older context. The twentieth-century opposition between *Natur* and *Geist* (science and the humanities) involves some of the same oversimplifications as the Platonic opposition between *epistēmē* and *doxa;* and it too easily reinforces the resulting opposition between "logic," considered as the science of the demonstrable, and "rhetoric," regarded as the art of persuasion. Yet, as Aristotle himself was quick to insist, in sciences that deal with particular, concrete situations and problems, such as medicine and ethics, we cannot hope to find the "essences" we should need in order to guarantee the relevance of formal syllogistic arguments to actual prac-

11. See ibid.

tice; as a result, we need to understand how the subject matter we deal with in different situations affects the nature of the *sound arguments* that are relevant to it in practice. (Hence, Aristotle thought of *logic* as embracing not merely the formal arguments that he discussed in the *Prior and Posterior Analytics* but also the substantive and functional arguments that were his concern in the *Topics* and the *Ethics.*)

Accordingly, in both today's postmodern natural and human sciences and the critical disciplines of the humanities, we are concerned with a mix, or blend, of explanation and interpretation. All of our scientific explanations and critical readings start from, embody, and imply some interpretive standpoint, conceptual framework, or theoretical perspective. The relevance and adequacy of our explanations can never be demonstrated with Platonic rigor or geometrical necessity. (Not to mince matters, *epistēmē* was always too much to ask.) Instead, the operative question is, Which of our positions are rationally warranted, reasonable, or defensible– that is, well-founded rather than groundless opinions, sound *doxai* rather than shaky ones?

The controversy over interpretation with which this conference was concerned flows, more directly than is at first apparent, from the narrowing of the field of logic that took place at the hands of Gottlob Frege and his successors, between the years 1880 and 1914. Frege, Bertrand Russell, and their colleagues confined logic to the study of *formally valid* arguments, as discussed in Aristotle's *Analytics,* and, by the same decision, expelled from logic all consideration of *substantively sound* arguments, as discussed, for example, in the *Topics.* At the very beginning of the present century, some of the most influential logicians and philosophers thus put back into circulation the old Platonic prejudice against *doxa,* and in favor of *epistēmē;* and they did so, perhaps, without wholly understanding what the effects of their action would be.

In doing so, however, they overlooked and set aside the other half of Aristotle's logic; and, before very long, this whole field of discussion was actually banned from the philosophy departments at most English-speaking universities and colleges. Yet, naturam expellas furca, tamen usque recurret. Thrown out by the front door, the critical analysis of substantive argumentation came in again at the back; and by now it is established, under a variety of names, in departments of speech communication, journalism, English literature, and elsewhere.[12]

The essential point is not to quarrel about jargon—to debate, for example, the exact connotation and denotation of the term "logic" or to argue whether the validity of scientific explanations can be analyzed in

12. Wayne Booth and I have both made excursions into this field. See, e.g., his *Modern Dogma and the Rhetoric of Assent* (Chicago, 1974), and *Critical Understanding: The Powers and Limits of Pluralism* (Chicago, 1979); see also my *The Uses of Argument* (Cambridge, 1958), and (with Richard Rieke and Allan Janik) *An Introduction to Reasoning* (New York, 1977).

logical terms alone. The essential points to recognize are:

> *a*) that all critical analysis and explanation, whether in the sci-
> ences or the humanities, begin only at a point where some inter-
> pretive (theoretical, conceptual) standpoint has already been
> adopted—so that the question, whether any specific analysis or ex-
> planation is well founded, takes for granted the prior question,
> whether the particular standpoint from which it is offered is in
> general an acceptable one;
> *b*) that our need to choose an interpretive standpoint at the
> outset of any specific piece of humanistic investigation or criticism
> does not condemn the results to the second-class status of mere
> subjective opinions but leaves open all sorts of questions about the
> objective considerations that are available as rational support for
> those opinions.

Those who overlook the first point are tempted to demand more
formal and geometrical arguments from the natural sciences than the
nature of the case permits—as in the logical empiricists' attempt to transform scientific explanation into a species of pure demonstrative deduc-
tion. Those who overlook the second point are tempted to claim for
humanistic disciplines a freedom from objective standards of judgment
that removes them from the sphere of rational criticism—as in the more
recent tendency to allow all psychologists and anthropologists to choose
their own paradigms and argue in the resulting idiosyncratic terms.
Thus, the Platonic confusion, of equating *rational adequacy* with *formal
validity,* has generated the two opposing misconceptions embodied in the
current *Natur/Geist* dichotomy: that which demands an unrealistic and
interpretationless objectivity of the natural sciences and that which
exaggerates the role of interpretation and subjectivity in the humanities.

Properly understood, however, the sciences and the humanities
both require a middle way. The choice of a basic theory or conceptual
scheme—a choice made *in the light of* experience, to be sure, but never
imposed by it—precedes the formulation of those scientific questions to
which any specific explanation is a possible answer; and the soundness of
a particular explanation depends both on the validity of the specific
arguments in its favor and on the proven scope and relevance of the
general theory which it exemplifies. An acceptable scientific explanation
must be both relevant in its general features and correct in its details.

But the same is surely true of critical interpretations in the
humanities. The initial choice of an interpretive point of view that is
idiosyncratic, distorting, or plainly silly cannot subsequently be redeemed by the accumulation of rich and complex details. Unless the
critical standpoint from which a particular interpretation is offered represents a *possible* approach to the work in question, it can hardly lead the
critic to any worthwhile comments or aperçus.

Critical judgment in the natural sciences, then, is not geometrical, and critical interpretation in the humanities is not whimsical. In both spheres, the proper aims should be the same—that is, to be perceptive, illuminating, and reasonable. In the sciences, formal rigor is not the same as rational soundness; in the humanities, idiosyncrasy is not the same as originality. In either case, a successful interpretation will combine *soundness and centrality* in its general approach with *relevance and sensitivity* in its specific details, and the task of judging any such interpretation requires us to pay attention to its claims in both respects.

The Politics of Historical Interpretation: Discipline and De-Sublimation

Hayden White

The politics of interpretation should not be confused with interpretive practices such as political theory, political commentary, or histories of political institutions, parties, and conflicts that have politics itself as a specific object of interest. In these other interpretive practices, the politics that informs or motivates them—"politics" in the sense of political values or ideology—is relatively easily perceived and no particular meta-interpretive analysis is required. The politics *of* interpretation, on the other hand, arises in those interpretive practices which are ostensibly most remote from overtly political concerns, practices which are carried out under the aegis of a purely disinterested search for the truth or inquiry into the natures of things which appear to have no political relevance at all. This "politics" has to do with the kind of *authority* the interpreter claims vis-à-vis the established political authorities of his society, on the one side, and vis-à-vis other interpreters in his own field of study or investigation, on the other, as the basis of whatever *rights* he conceives himself to possess and whatever *duties* he feels obliged to discharge as a *professional* seeker of truth. This politics which presides over interpretive conflicts is difficult to identify because traditionally, in our culture at least, interpretation is thought to operate properly only as long as the interpreter does not have recourse to the one instrument which the politician *per vocationem* utilizes as a matter of course in his practice—the appeal to force as a means of resolving disputes and conflicts.[1]

---

1. I have followed the lead of Max Weber in defining the phrase "politics of interpretation." In "Politics as a Vocation," Weber wrote that " 'politics' means for us striving to

Interpretive conflicts reach a limit as specifically *interpretive* ones when political power or authority is invoked to resolve them. This suggests that interpretation is an activity which, in principle, stands over against political activity in much the same way that contemplation is seen to stand over against action or theory against practice.[2] But in the same way that contemplation presupposes action and theory presupposes practice, so, too, interpretation presupposes politics as a condition of its possibility as a social activity. "Pure" interpretation, the disinterested inquiry into anything whatsoever, is unthinkable as an ideal without the presupposition of the kind of activity which politics represents. The purity of any interpretation can be measured only by the extent to which it succeeds in repressing any impulse to appeal to political authority.

---

share power or striving to influence the distribution of power, either among states or among groups within a state" (*From Max Weber: Essays in Sociology,* ed. and trans. H. H. Gerth and C. W. Mills [New York, 1958], p. 78). Rather than discuss the age-old problem of the professional interpreter's political responsibilities, I will consider that politics which is endemic to the pursuit of truth—the striving to share power amongst interpreters themselves. The activity of interpreting becomes political at the point where a given interpreter claims authority over rival interpreters. As long as this claim is not reinforced by appeal to the power of the state to compel conformity of belief or conviction, it is "political" only in a metaphorical sense. Of course, interpretation becomes political when a given point of view or finding is taken as orthodoxy of belief by those holding political power, as in the Soviet Union, Germany under Hitler, or any number of religiously puritanical regimes. But these are the easy cases. It is much more difficult to determine the political nature of interpretive practices which, as in literary criticism or antiquarian scholarship, appear to have no bearing upon political policies or practices.

2. In modern Western culture, the relationship between the activity of interpretation and politics has been construed in four ways: Hobbes insisted on the absolute subordination of interpretation to the demands of the state; Kant viewed the interpreter's social function as that of mediator between the people and the sovereign; Nietzsche subordinated politics to interpretation, conceived as the form which the will to power took in its intellectual or artistic manifestation; and Weber held that interpretation and politics occupied different and essentially mutually exclusive domains of culture—"science" for him was a "vocation" with aims and values quite other than those of politics. See Thomas Hobbes, *Leviathan* (Oxford, 1929), pt. 2, chaps. 26 and 29; Immanuel Kant, "The Strife of the Faculties" (pt. 2), trans. Robert E. Anchor, and *On History,* ed. Lewis White Beck (New York, 1963), sec. 8, pp. 148–50; Friedrich Nietzsche, *The Genealogy of Morals,* trans. Francis Golffing (New York, 1956), preface, "First Essay," and "Second Essay," secs. 1–3; and Weber, "Science as a Vocation," *From Max Weber,* pp. 145–56.

Hayden White is a professor and director of the program in the history of consciousness at the University of California, Santa Cruz. He is coeditor of *Representing Kenneth Burke* and is currently working on a book on the rhetoric of realism.

This means that the politics of interpretation must find the means *either* to effect this repression *or* to so sublimate the impulse to appeal to political authority as to transform it into an instrument of interpretation itself.[3]

This may seem an inordinately circuitous and abstract entry into our subject, but it is necessary for my purpose, which is to consider the question of the politics of interpretation within the context of the general topic of the "disciplinization" of fields of study in the human and social sciences. The question is, What is involved in the transformation of a field of studies into a "discipline," especially in the context of *modern* social institutions designed for the regulation of knowledge production, where the physical sciences function as a paradigm for all cognitive disciplines? The question has special importance for understanding the social function of institutionalized forms of study in the human and social sciences; for all of them have been promoted to the status of disciplines without having developed the theoretical and methodological regimentation characteristic of the physical sciences.[4]

It is often argued that the human and social sciences are precluded from developing into true sciences due to the nature of their objects of study (man, society, culture), which differ from natural objects in their interiority, their autonomy vis-à-vis their environments, and their capacity to change social processes through the exercise of a certain freedom of will. For some theorists, the human possession of this interiority, autonomy, and freedom of will makes it not only impossible but also undesirable even to aspire to the creation of full-blown sciences of man, culture, and society.[5] In fact, one tradition of theory and philosophy of science has it that such an aspiration is *politically* undesirable. For this tradition, if man, society, and culture are to be objects of disciplined

3. Here I am extending René Girard's notion of "the sacrificial crisis" to include the kinds of crises that arise in situations of radical doubt as to the *kind* of science that should be used for interpreting social and cultural phenomena. See Girard's remarks about "impartiality" in *Violence and the Sacred*, trans. Patrick Gregory (Baltimore, 1977), chap. 2.

4. See Michel Foucault, *The Order of Things: An Archaeology of the Human Sciences* (New York, 1970), chap. 10. Cf. Thomas S. Kuhn, *The Structure of Scientific Revolutions*, 2d ed. (Chicago, 1970), a work which, on its appearance in 1962, effectively defined the terms within which the whole question of the difference between "professionalization" in the physical sciences and in the social sciences would be debated for the next twenty years. On the debate itself, see Imre Lakatos and Alan Musgrave, eds., *Criticism and the Growth of Knowledge* (Cambridge, 1970), and J. P. Nettl, "Ideas, Intellectuals, and Structures of Dissent," in *On Intellectuals: Theoretical and Case Studies*, ed. Phillip Rieff (New York, 1969), pp. 53–122.

5. This is the neoidealist tradition deriving from Hegel by way of Wilhelm Dilthey and Wilhelm Windelband and any number of "vitalists" and humanists in the twentieth century. On Dilthey, see Michael Earmarth, *Wilhelm Dilthey: The Critique of Historical Reason* (Chicago, 1978), esp. pp. 95–108, and for a survey of the modern development of the question of a specifically *human* science, see Lucien Goldmann, *The Human Sciences and Philosophy*, trans. White and Anchor (London, 1969).

inquiry, the disciplines should aim at "understanding" these objects, not at explaining them, as in the physical sciences.[6]

The field of historical studies may be taken as exemplary of those disciplines in the human and social sciences which rest content with the understanding of the matters with which they deal in place of aspiring to explain them. This is not to say that historians do not purport to explain certain aspects either of "the past" or of the "historical process." It is rather that they do not in general claim to have discovered the kinds of causal laws that would permit them to explain phenomena by viewing them as instantiations of the operations of such laws, in the way that physical scientists do in their explanations. Historians also often claim to explain their objects of study by providing a proper understanding of them. The means by which this understanding is provided is "interpretation." "Narration" is both the way in which a historical interpretation is achieved and the mode of discourse in which a successful understanding of matters historical is represented.[7]

The connection between interpretation, narration, and understanding provides the theoretical rationale for considering historical studies as a special kind of discipline, on the one side, and for resisting the demand (made by positivists and Marxists) for the transformation of historical studies into a science, on the other. The *ideological* nature of both these claims is indicated by the politics which each is imagined to serve. In general, the demand that historical studies be transformed into a science is advanced in the interest of promoting a politics thought to be progressive—liberal in the case of positivists, radical in the case of Marxists. The resistance to this demand, per contra, is usually justified by appeal to political or ethical values that are manifestly conservative or reactionary.[8] Since the constitution of historical studies as a discipline

6. This is the position represented by Karl R. Popper, on the neopositivist side of the question, and by Hannah Arendt, on the more humanistic side. Both thought that pretensions to the scientific in the human and social sciences contributed to the creation of totalitarian political philosophies. For their positions on social and political philosophy in general and its relation to philosophy of history in the "scientistic" vein, see Popper, *The Poverty of Historicism* (London, 1960), and Arendt, *Between Past and Future* (London, 1961).

7. On the problem of narration and its relation to historical understanding, see my "The Value of Narrativity in the Representation of Reality," *Critical Inquiry* 7 (Autumn 1980): 5–28; cf. in the same issue Paul Ricoeur, "Narrative Time," pp. 169–90. For a consideration of philosophers' recent handling of the question, see my "The Politics of Contemporary Philosophy of History," *Clio* 3 (October 1973): 35–53, and "Historicism, History, and the Figurative Imagination," *History and Theory* 14 (1975): 48–67.

8. This kind of division over the political implications of any attempt to transform historical studies into a science is as old as the debate between Edmund Burke and Thomas Paine over the possibilities of a rationalist approach to the study of society. And it appears even within Marxism from time to time. See, e.g., Perry Anderson, *Arguments within English Marxism* (London, 1980), pp. 194–207, and *History and Theory* 17 (1978), a special issue on *Historical Consciousness and Political Action*.

was carried out in the modern period in the service of political values and regimes that were in general antirevolutionary and conservative, the burden for establishing the feasibility and desirability of treating history as the object of a possible science falls upon those who would so treat it. This means that the politics of interpretation in modern historical studies turns upon the question of the political uses to which a knowledge thought to be specifically "historical" can or ought conceivably to be put.

My approach here requires that I specify what was involved in the transformation of historical studies into a discipline which applied rules for construing and studying their objects of interest different from the rules of investigation prevailing in the physical sciences. The social function of a properly disciplined study of history and the political interests which it served at its inception in the early nineteenth century, the period of the consolidation of the (bourgeois) nation-state, are well known and hardly in need of documentation. We do not have to impute dark ideological motives to those who endowed history with the authority of a discipline in order to recognize the ideological benefits to new social classes and political constituencies which professional, academic historiography served and which, mutatis mutandis, it continues to serve down to our own time.

The desirability of transforming historical studies into a discipline could be urged on grounds more purely theoretical and epistemological. It made eminently good sense to constitute a discipline in an age characterized by conflicts between representatives of a host of political positions, each of which came attended by a "philosophy of history" or master narrative of the historical process, on the basis of which their claims to "realism" were in part authorized. The purpose of such a discipline would be simply to determine the "facts" of history, by which to assess the objectivity, veridicality, and realism of the philosophies of history which authorized the different political programs. Under the auspices of the philosophy of history, programs of social and political reconstruction shared an ideology with utopian visions of man, culture, and society. This linkage of ideology justified both and made a study of history, considered as a recovery of the facts of the past, a social desideratum at once epistemologically necessary and politically relevant. To analyze the elements of this linkage, epistemological criticism proceeded by opposing a properly disciplined historical method conceived as *empirical* to a philosophy of history conceived as inherently *metaphysical*. The political aspect of this analytical effort consisted in the opposition of a properly disciplined historical consciousness to utopian thinking in all its forms (religious, social, and, above all, political). The combination of these two aspects of history's disciplinization had the effect of permitting the kind of "historical knowledge" produced by professional historians to serve as the standard of "realism" in political thought and action in general.[9]

What politics of interpretation is involved in this transformation of historical studies into a discipline which purports to serve as custodian of realism in political and social thinking? I take issue with a view of the relationship between historical and political thinking that has become a commonplace of modern theories of totalitarian ideologies. This view has been forcefully represented by the late Hannah Arendt, and it is shared by many, especially humanistically oriented theorists of totalitarianism who attribute the degeneration of classical politics and its attendant theory to the rise of modern philosophy of history of the sort associated with the names of Hegel, Marx, Nietzsche, Spengler, and so forth.

In "The Concept of History," Arendt put the matter in the following terms: "In any consideration of the modern concept of history one of the crucial problems is to explain its sudden rise during the last third of the eighteenth century *and the concomitant decrease* of interest in purely political thinking" (my emphasis).[10] Leaving aside the question of whether there has actually been a general "decrease of interest in purely political thinking" (not to mention the difficulty of distinguishing between a "thinking" that is "purely political" and one that is not), we may accept as generally valid Arendt's linkage of history and politics in those ideologies which took shape in the wake of the French Revolution and continue, in one form or another, to contaminate even the most chaste efforts to contrive a theory of politics which would be free of the charge of being "ideological" either in motivation or in effect.

Arendt leads us astray, however, in identifying "the modern concept of history" with those philosophies of history which take their rise in Hegel's effort to use historical knowledge as a basis for a metaphysics adequate to the aims and interests of the modern secular state. For while it is true that, as Arendt says, Marx went even further than Hegel and sought to give direction to "the aims of political action," it was not his "influence" alone (or even primarily) which "politicalized" both "the historian and the philosopher of history," thereby causing the "decrease of interest in purely political thinking" which she laments.[11] The politicalization of historical thinking was a virtual precondition of its own professionalization, the basis of its promotion to the status of a discipline worthy of being taught in the universities, and a prerequisite of whatever "constructive" social function historical knowledge was thought to serve. This was true especially of professional, academic, institutionalized, or (to use Nietzsche's term) "incorporated" historical studies, that approach

9. On historical knowledge as a basis for political realism, see my *Metahistory: The Historical Imagination in Nineteenth Century Europe* (Baltimore, 1973), pt. 2.

10. Arendt, *Between Past and Future*, pp. 76–77.

11. Ibid., pp. 77–78.

to the study of history which defined its aims *in opposition* to those of philosophy of history, that discipline which limited itself to unearthing facts relevant to finite domains of the past, contented itself with the narration of "true stories," and eschewed any temptation to construct grandiose "metahistorical" theories, to find the key to the secret of the whole historical process, to prophesy the future, and to dictate what was both best and necessary for the present.

The politics of this disciplinization, conceived, as all disciplinization must be, as a set of negations, consists in what it marks out for *repression* for those who wish to claim the authority of discipline itself for their learning. What it marks out for repression in general is utopian thinking—the kind of thinking without which revolutionary politics, whether of the Left or the Right, becomes unthinkable (insofar, of course, as such thinking is based on a claim to authority by virtue of the knowledge of history that informs it). To be sure, positivists and Marxists claimed to transcend the opposition of historical thinking and utopian thinking by virtue of their claims to have provided the basis of a genuinely *scientific* study of history capable of revealing the laws of historical process. From the standpoint of a properly disciplined historical consciousness, however, such claims simply evidenced the presence of the philosophy of history in positivism and Marxism, which a properly disciplined historical consciousness was supposed to guard against. The fact that Marxism especially claimed to be a science of history which justified the hope for and would help to bring about the revolution of bourgeois society only attested to the utopian nature of both Marxism and its putative science of history.

Now, I am against revolutions, whether launched from "above" or "below" in the social hierarchy and whether directed by leaders who profess a science of society and history or by celebrators of political "spontaneity."[12] Like Arendt, I would wish that in political and social matters both politicians and political thinkers were guided by the kind of realism to which a disciplined historical knowledge conduces. But on the level of interpretive theory, where the matter under contention is the politics inherent in alternative conceptions of what historical discipline itself consists of, one cannot seek to resolve differences of opinion by an appeal either to political values or to some criterion of what a properly disciplined historical knowledge consists of. For it is political values and what constitutes historical discipline that are at issue. The problem, however, does not lie with philosophy of history, which is at least *openly* political, but rather lies with a conception of historical studies that pur-

12. It seemed necessary to register this item of personal belief because the relativism with which I am usually charged is conceived by many theorists to imply the kind of nihilism which invites revolutionary activism of a particularly irresponsible sort. In my view, relativism is the moral equivalent of epistemological skepticism; moreover, I conceive relativism to be the basis of social tolerance, not a license to "do as you please."

ports to be above politics and at the same time rules out as "unrealistic" any political program or thought in the least tinged with utopianism. And it does so, moreover, by so disciplining historical consciousness as to make realism effectively identical with anti-utopianism. One is at least obliged to try to clarify the nature of the politics implicit in the disciplinization of a field of studies which was undertaken with the express purpose of recuperating its objects of study from the "distortions" of political ideology in general.

It may seem perverse, however, to characterize as a politics of interpretation the project of disengaging historical thought from utopian thinking, the de-ideologization of its discipline which modern historical studies values most highly. Those who value the kind of works that professional historians typically produce must regard the philosophy of history (à la Hegel, Marx, etc.) as a pernicious, when not deluded, activity—even if, unlike many modern humanists, they do not regard philosophy of history as a mainstay of totalitarian ideologies. But the fight between historians and philosophers of history is really more in the nature of a family feud than a conflict between practitioners of different disciplines or between a discipline properly practiced and one improperly practiced. For historians and philosophers of history do have the same objects of study in common, and the fight between them is over what a properly disciplined study of those objects *should* consist of. Since this dispute cannot be arbitrated on the grounds of any appeal to "what history teaches" (since this is what is at issue), it becomes incumbent upon us to attempt to characterize what constitutes the notion of *disciplined* historical reflection itself, the general belief in the possibility of which both parties share. The problem can be narrowed to characterizing the positive content of the historical object for which philosophy of history is conceived to be the "undisciplined" (or what amounts to the same thing, the "overdisciplined") counterpart. And this problem can be approached by asking, What is *ruled out* by conceiving the historical object in such a way that *not* to conceive it in that way would constitute prima facie evidence of want of "discipline"?

In order to get a handle on this question, we must recall what was considered undisciplined about historical studies prior to the nineteenth century. Throughout the eighteenth century, historical studies had no discipline proper to itself. It was for the most part an activity of amateurs. Scholars *per vocationem* were trained in ancient and modern languages, in how to study different kinds of documents (a discipline known as "diplomatic"), and in mastering the techniques of rhetorical composition. Historical writing, in fact, was regarded as a branch of the art of rhetoric. These constituted the methods of the historian.[13]

13. On the relationship between rhetoric and history, see my "Rhetoric and History" (with Frank E. Manuel), *Theories of History: Papers of the Clark Library Seminar* (Los Angeles,

The eighteenth-century historian's field of phenomena was simply "the past," conceived as the source and repository of tradition, moral exemplars, and admonitory lessons to be investigated by one of the modes of interpretation into which Aristotle divided the kinds of rhetorical discourse: ceremonial, forensic, and political.[14] The preliminary ordering of this field of phenomena was consigned to the "disciplines" of chronology and the techniques of ordering documents for study in the form of "annals." As for the uses to which historical reflection was to be put, this was as wide as rhetorical practice, political partisanship, and confessional variation admitted. And as for what "history," considered as a record of human development, told about human society, this either fell under the charge of Christian myth or its secular, Enlightenment counterpart, the myth of Progress, or displayed a panorama of failure, duplicity, fraud, deceit, and stupidity.

When Kant turned to the consideration of what could be *known* from the study of history, so as to be able to determine what mankind could legitimately *hope* on the basis of that knowledge, he identified three kinds of equally pertinent conclusions. These were that (1), the human race was progressing continually; (2), the human race was degenerating continually; and (3), the human race remained at the same general level of development continually. He called these three notions of historical development "eudaemonism," "terrorism," and "farce," respectively, and they might just as well be called "comedy," "tragedy," and "irony" (if considered from the standpoint of the plot structures which they impose upon the historical panorama) or "idealism," "cynicism," and "skepticism" (if considered from the standpoint of the world views they authorize).[15]

Whatever names we attach to them as labels, Kant's three conceptualizations of the process of historical development indicate that all of the types of philosophy of history subsequently developed in the nineteenth century were not distinctively "modern" (as Arendt suggests) but were already conceptually present in historical thinking of the premodern period. Moreover, far from being a modern innovation, the

1978), pp. 1–25. See also Lionel Gossman, "History and Literature," in *The Writing of History: Literary Form and Historical Understanding*, ed. Robert H. Canary and Henry Kozicki (Madison, Wis., 1978).

14. See Aristotle *Rhetoric* 1. 3.

15. Kant, "Strife of the Faculties," p. 139. Actually, Kant calls the third type of historical conceptualization "abderitism," after the city of Abdera, where the Atomic School of philosophy was centered in the ancient world. I have substituted "farce" because, as Beck indicates in a note, abderitism was generally regarded as a synonym for "silliness"; moreover, Kant says: "It is a vain affair to have good so alternate with evil that the whole traffic of our species with itself on this globe would have to be considered as a mere farcical comedy [als ein blosses Possenspiel]" (p. 141).

"politicalization" of the historian and the philosopher of history was the rule in pre-modern thinking rather than the exception. The important point is that the variety of uses to which written history's subordination to rhetoric permitted it to be put exposed historical thinking to the threat of being conceived solely in terms of Kant's third type, the farcical: as long as history was subordinated to rhetoric, the historical *field* itself (i.e., the past or the historical process) had to be viewed as a *chaos* that made no sense at all or one that could be made to bear as many senses as wit and rhetorical talent could impose upon it. Accordingly, the disciplining of historical thinking that had to be undertaken, if history considered as a kind of *knowledge* was to be established as arbitrator of the realism of contending political programs, each attended by its own philosophy of history, had to consist first of all in its de-rhetoricization.

The de-rhetoricization of historical thinking was an effort to distinguish history from fiction, especially from the kind of prose fiction represented by the romance and the novel. This effort was, of course, a rhetorical move in its own right, the kind of rhetorical move which Paolo Valesio calls "the rhetoric of anti-rhetoric."[16] It consisted of little more than a *reaffirmation* of the Aristotelian distinction between history and poetry—the study of events that had actually occurred as distinguished from the imagining of events that might have occurred, or could possibly occur—and the *affirmation* of the fiction that the "stories" historians tell are *found* in the evidence rather than invented. Thus the whole question of the *composition* of the historian's discourse was moot: it appeared to be solely a function of the rigorous application of "rules of evidence" to the examination of the "historical record." In point of fact, the narratives produced by historians lend themselves to analysis in terms of their rhetorical topoi, which in general have been canonized in the classical notion of the so-called middle style of declamation.

The subordination of historical narrative to the deliberative mode of the middle style entails stylistic exclusions, and this has implications for the *kind of events* which can be represented in a narrative. What is excluded are the kind of events traditionally conceived to be the stuff of religious belief and ritual (miracles, magical events, godly events), on the one side, and the kind of "grotesque" events which are the stuff of farce, satire, and calumny, on the other. Above all, these two orders of exclusion consign to historical thinking the kind of events that lend themselves to the understanding of whatever currently passes for educated common sense. They effect a disciplining of the imagination, in this case, the *historical imagination,* and they set limits on what constitutes a specifically *historical event.* Moreover, since these exclusions effectively set limits on rules of description (or descriptive protocols) and since a "fact"

16. See Paolo Valesio, *Novantiqua: Rhetorics as a Contemporary Theory* (Bloomington, Ind., 1980), pp. 41–60.

must be regarded as "an event under a description," it follows that they constitute what can count as a specifically *historical fact.*[17]

Because history, unlike fiction, is supposed to represent real events and therefore contribute to knowledge of the real world, imagination (or "fancy") is a faculty particularly in need of disciplinization in historical studies. Political partisanship and moral prejudice may lead the historian to misread or misrepresent documents and thus to construct events which never took place. On the conscious level of the historian's investigative operations, he can guard against such errors by the judicious employment of "the rules of evidence." The imagination, however, operates on a different level of the historian's consciousness. It is present above all in the effort, peculiar to the modern concept of the historian's task, to enter sympathetically into the minds or consciousnesses of human agents long dead, to empathize with the intentions and motivations of actors impelled by beliefs and values which may differ totally from anything the historian might himself honor in his own life, and to understand, even when he cannot condone, the most bizarre social and cultural practices. This is often described as putting oneself in the place of past agents, seeing things from their point of view, and so forth, all of which leads to a notion of "objectivity" that is quite different from anything that might be meant by that term in the physical sciences.[18]

This notion is quite specific to modern historical theory, and it is typically thought of as being imaginative rather than rational. For it is one thing to try to *be* rational, in the sense of being on guard against unwarranted inferences or one's own prejudices, and quite another to think one's way into the minds and consciousnesses of past actors whose "historicity" consists in part in the fact that they acted under the impulsion of beliefs and values peculiar to their own times, places, and cultural presuppositions. But imagination is dangerous for the historian because he cannot know that what he has imagined was actually the case, that it is not a product of his "imagination" in the sense in which that term is used to characterize the activity of the poet or writer of fiction. Here of course the imagination is disciplined by its subordination to the rules of evidence which require that whatever is imagined be consistent with what the evidence permits one to assert as a "matter of fact." Yet imagination, precisely in the sense in which it is used to characterize the activity of the poet or novelist, is operative in the work of the historian at the last stage of his labors, when it becomes necessary to compose a discourse or nar-

17. See Louis O. Mink, "Narrative Form as a Cognitive Instrument," in *The Writing of History,* p. 132.

18. This position found its most forceful representation in the work of R. G. Collingwood, *The Idea of History* (Oxford, 1956), pt. 5, secs. 2 and 4. See also Mink, *Mind, History and Dialectic: The Philosophy of R. G. Collingwood* (Bloomington, Ind., 1969), pp. 162–94.

rative in which to represent his findings, that is, his notion of "what really happened" in the past. It is at this point that what some theorists call "the style" of the historian, considered now as a writer of prose, takes over and that an operation considered to be exactly like that of the novelist supervenes, an operation that is openly admitted to be *literary*.[19] And since it is literary, the disciplinization of this aspect of the historian's work entails an aesthetic regulation. What is the nature of a *disciplined* historical style?

Here again we must recall that discipline consists less of prescriptions of what must be done than of exclusions or proscriptions of certain ways of *imaging* historical reality. This is where the late eighteenth-century debate over what Edmund Burke called "our ideas of the sublime and the beautiful" becomes relevant to our understanding of what was involved in the disciplinization of historical sensibility.[20] For our purposes, the crucial turn in this discussion has to do with the progressive demotion of the sublime in favor of the beautiful as a solution to the problems of "taste" and imagination. For the most part, these problems were construed in terms of the imagination's response to different kinds of *natural* phenomena: those that possessed the capacity to "charm," on the one side, and those that "terrified" (by their grandeur, extent, awesomeness, etc.), on the other.[21] Burke did not explicitly address the question of the sublime and the beautiful with respect to historical or social phenomena (though he likened the feeling of the sublime to that which the subject must feel in the presence of political majesty), but he condemned the French Revolution as a "strange chaos of levity and ferocity" and a "monstrous tragi-comic scene" that could only fill its observers with "scorn and horror" rather than with that feeling of "astonishment" that the sublime in nature inspired or that feeling of respect for sheer "power" that he took to be the essence of religious awe.[22] Viewed as a contribution to the aesthetics (or what

19. No more vexed—and mystifying—notion appears in the theory of historical writing than that of the historian's "style." It is a problem because insofar as the historian's discourse is conceived to *have style*, it is also conceived to *be literary*. But insofar as a historian's discourse is literary, it seems to *be* rhetorical, which is anathema for those who wish to claim the status of objective representation for historical discourse. On the whole question, see Roland Barthes, "Historical Discourse," in *Structuralism: A Reader*, ed. Michael Lane (London, 1970), pp. 145–55; Peter Gay, *Style in History* (New York, 1974); and Stephen Bann, "Towards a Critical Historiography: Recent Work in Philosophy of History," *Philosophy* 56 (July 1981): 365–85.

20. See Thomas Weiskel, *The Romantic Sublime: Studies in the Structure and Psychology of Transcendence* (Baltimore, 1976), pp. 78–103.

21. See Burke, *A Philosophical Inquiry into the Origin of Our Ideas of the Sublime and Beautiful* (New York, 1909), pt. 1, sec. 8, p. 36 and sec. 10, p. 39. I exclude from this discussion certain rhetoricians who continued to invoke the notion of the sublime to designate a specific style of oratory or poetic mode.

22. Burke, *Reflections on the Revolution in France* (New York, 1961), pp. 21–22; *Sublime and Beautiful*, pt. 4, sec. 8, p. 114 (see also pt. 2, sec. 5, p. 59, where Burke dilates on

amounts to the same thing, the psychology) of historical consciousness, Burke's *Reflections on the Revolution in France* can be seen as one of many efforts to exorcise the notion of the sublime from any apprehension of the historical process, so that the "beauty" of its "proper" development, which for him was given in the example of the "English constitution," could be adequately comprehended.[23]

It was quite otherwise with Schiller, who, in his theory of the imagination, equated the attraction of the "bizarre savagery in physical creation" to the "delight" one might feel in contemplating "the uncertain anarchy of the moral world."[24] Meditation on the "confusion" which the "spectacle" of history displayed could produce a sense of a specifically human "freedom," and insofar as it did, "world history" appeared to him "a sublime object" (pp. 204, 206). The feeling of the sublime, Schiller believed, could transform the "pure daemon" in humankind into the ground for belief in a "dignity" unique to man. The sublime, then, was a necessary "complement" to the beautiful if "aesthetic education" were to be made into a "complete whole." Because the beautiful ruled over the "ceaseless quarrel between our natural and rational vocations," it took precedence over the sublime in this education, constantly returning us to "our *spiritual* mission" which has its sphere in "the world of sense" and "action to which we are after all committed" (pp. 210–11).

Schiller's linkage of the beautiful with the sphere of "sense" and "action" anticipated what was to become a commonplace of nineteenth-century aesthetics and had important consequences for both historical thought and political theory, radical as well as conservative. The gradual displacement of the sublime by the beautiful in a generally accredited aesthetic theory, as uncritically accepted by Marxists as by their conservative and liberal opponents, had the effect of restricting speculation on any ideal social order to some variant of *pastoralism* in which freedom was apprehended less as an exercise of individual will than as a release of beautiful "feelings." Yet Schiller himself joined the notion of the historical sublime to the kind of response to it that would authorize a totally different politics. In a passage that could have been written by Nietzsche he declares:

> Then away with falsely construed forebearance and vapidly effeminate taste which cast a veil over the solemn face of necessity and, in order to curry favor with the senses, *counterfeit* a har-

---

religious awe in a passage immediately following a description of the "dread majesty" of sovereigns).

23. See Burke, *Reflections,* pp. 43–47.

24. *Two Essays by Friedrich von Schiller: "Naive and Sentimental Poetry" and "On the Sublime,"* trans. Julius A. Elias (New York, 1966), p. 205; all further references to Elias' translation will be included in the text.

mony between good fortune and good behavior of which not a
trace is to be found in the actual world. . . . We are aided in [the
attainment of this point of view] by the terrifying and magnificent
spectacle of change which destroys everything and creates it anew,
and destroys again. . . . We are aided by the pathetic spectacle of
mankind wrestling with fate, the irresistible elusiveness of happiness, confidence betrayed, unrighteousness triumphant and innocence laid low; of these history supplies ample instances, and
tragic art imitates them before our eyes. [Pp. 209–10]

Hegel saw the dangers in such a conception of history, and in the
introduction to his *Philosophy of History* he subjects it to scathing criticism
on both cognitive and moral grounds.[25] Cognitively, such a conception
remains on the level of appearances and fails to subject phenomena to
the critical analysis that would reveal the laws governing their articulation. Morally, such a conception could lead not to human freedom and
dignity but to pessimism, lassitude, and submission to fate. The sublimity
of the spectacle of history had to be transcended if it was to serve as an
object of knowledge and deprived of the terror it induced as a
"panorama of sin and suffering."[26]
    Kant's "analytic of the sublime," in the *Critique of Judgment*, had
related the apprehension of anything merely "powerful" (which belonged to what he called "the dynamical sublime") to our feeling of
possessing a freedom and dignity uniquely human, but he grounds this
feeling in the faculty of reason alone.[27] Seen thus, the sublime is effectively cut free from the aesthetic faculty, which remains under the sway
of judgments appropriate to the "beautiful," in order to be relegated to
the rule of the cognitive and moral faculties.[28] And this for obvious

25. According to Hegel, any merely "objective" view of historical phenomena would
suggest that the "most effective springs of [human] action" are nothing other than "passions, private aims, and the satisfaction of selfish desires." Any "simply truthful combination of the miseries that have overwhelmed the noblest of nations and polities, and the
finest exemplars of private virtue" forms a picture of most fearful aspect [furchtbarsten
Gemälde] that we are inclined to take refuge in fatalism and to withdraw in disgust "into the
more agreeable environment of our individual life—the Present formed by our private
aims and interests" (G. W. F. Hegel, *The Philosophy of History*, trans. J. Sibree [New York,
1956], pp. 20–21).
    26. Ibid., p. 22. I analyze this passage in *Metahistory*, pp. 105–8.
    27. See Kant, *Critique of Judgement*, trans. J. H. Bernard (New York, 1951), bk. 2
("Analytic of the Sublime"): "Now we may see from this that, in general, we express
ourselves incorrectly if we call any *object of nature* sublime, although we can quite correctly
call many objects of nature beautiful" (p. 83).
    28. "Sublimity, therefore, does not reside in anything of nature, but only in our mind,
in so far as we can become conscious that we are superior to nature within, and therefore
also to nature without us (so far as it influences us)." And again: "Properly speaking, the
word [sublime] should only be applied to a state of mind, or rather to its foundation in
human nature" (ibid., pp. 104, 121).

reasons: Kant had no faith in the capacity of reflection on history to teach anything that could not be learned—and learned better—from reflection on present human existence or, indeed, on the experience of a single socialized individual.

Although Hegel took up the question of the sublime, both explicitly in his *Aesthetics* and implicitly in the *Philosophy of History,* he subordinated it to the notion of the beautiful in the former and to the notion of the rational in the latter. It was this demotion of the sublime in favor of the beautiful that constituted the heritage from German idealism to both radical and conservative thought about the kind of utopian existence mankind could justifiably envisage as the ideal aim or goal of any putatively *progressive* historical process. Here is a prime example of a certain kind of "politics of interpretation" which produces an "interpretation of politics" with distinct ideological implications. It is the aesthetics of the beautiful which, as Thomas Weiskel suggests, undercuts the radical impulse of this tradition.[29] This undercutting may account in part for the weak psychological appeal of "the beautiful life" as a project to be realized in political struggles and, more importantly, for the apparent incapacity of political regimes founded on Marxist principles to sustain their professed programs for the radical transformation of society in anything but the most banal ways.

What must be recognized, however, is that for both the Left and the Right this same aesthetics of the beautiful presides over the process in which historical studies are constituted as an autonomous scholarly discipline. It takes little reflection to perceive that *aestheticism* is endemic to what is regarded as a proper attitude toward objects of historical study in a certain tradition, deriving from Leopold von Ranke and his epigones, which represents the nearest thing to an orthodoxy that the profession possesses. For this tradition, whatever "confusion" is displayed by the historical record is only a surface phenomenon: a product of lacunae in the documentary sources, of mistakes in ordering the archives, or of previous inattention or scholarly errors. If this confusion is not reducible to the kind of order that a science of laws might impose upon it, it can still be dispelled by historians endowed with the proper kind of understanding. And when this understanding is subjected to analysis, it is always revealed to be of an essentially aesthetic nature. This aestheticism permits the historian to see some beauty, if not good, in everything human and to assume an Olympian calm in the face of any current social situation, however terrifying it may appear to anyone who lacks historical perspective. It renders him receptive to a genial pluralism in matters epistemological, suspicious of anything smacking of reductionism, irritated with theory, disdainful of technical terminology or jargon, and

29. See Weiskel, *Romantic Sublime,* p. 48.

contemptuous of any effort to discern the direction that the future development of his own society might take.

Historical facts are politically domesticated precisely insofar as they
are effectively removed from displaying any aspect of the sublime that
Schiller attributed to them. That is, insofar as historical events and processes become understandable, as conservatives maintain, or explainable, as radicals believe them to be, they can never serve as a basis for a
visionary politics more concerned to endow social life with meaning than
with beauty. In my view, the theorists of the sublime had correctly divined that whatever dignity and freedom human beings could lay claim
to could come only by way of what Freud called a "reaction-formation"
to an apperception of history's meaninglessness.

Let me try to put this somewhat more clearly. It seems to me that the
kind of politics that is based on a vision of a perfected society can compel
devotion to it only by virtue of the contrast it offers to a past that is
understood in the way that Schiller conceived it, that is to say, as a
"spectacle" of "confusion," "uncertainty," and "moral anarchy." Surely
this is the appeal of those eschatological religions which envision a "rule
of the saints" that is the very antithesis of the spectacle of sin and corruption which the history of a fallen humanity displays to the eye of the
faithful. But modern ideologies seem to me to differ crucially from
eschatological religious myths in that they impute a meaning to history
that renders its manifest confusion comprehensible either to reason,
understanding, or aesthetic sensibility. To the extent to which they succeed in doing so, these ideologies deprive history of the kind of
meaninglessness which alone can goad the moral sense of living human
beings to make their lives different for themselves and their children,
which is to say, to endow their lives with a meaning for which they alone
are fully responsible. One can never move with any politically effective
confidence from an apprehension of "the way things actually are or have
been" to the kind of moral insistence that they "should be otherwise"
without passing through a feeling of repugnance for and negative
judgment of the condition that is to be superseded. And precisely insofar
as historical reflection is disciplined to understand history in such a way
that it can forgive everything or at best to practice a kind of "disinterested interest" of the sort that Kant imagined to inform every properly aesthetic perception, it is removed from any connection with a
visionary politics and consigned to a service that will always be anti-
utopian in nature. Indeed, this is as true of a Marxist view of the way
things are or have been in the past as it is of the bourgeois historian's
concern with the study of the past "for itself alone."

It is bound to seem paradoxical to suggest that Marxism is inherently anti-utopian as a philosophy of history, especially inasmuch as
professional academic historiography in the West derives much of its

political prestige from its proven capacity to counter the kind of utopian thinking which Marxism is supposed to exemplify. But Marxism is anti-utopian insofar as it shares with its bourgeois counterpart the conviction that history is not a sublime spectacle but a comprehensible process, the various parts, stages, epochs, and even individual events of which are transparent to a consciousness endowed with the means to make sense of it in one way or another.

I am not suggesting that Marxists have got history wrong while their bourgeois opponents have it right, or vice versa. Nor am I suggesting that the claim merely to understand history rather than to explain it, which non-Marxist humanist historians make, is a more appropriate way to approach the study of history than that recommended by Marxists and that, therefore, Marxism can be dismissed as either tactless or arrogant. Everyone recognizes that the way one makes sense of history is important in determining what politics one will credit as realistic, practicable, and socially responsible. But it is often overlooked that the conviction that one *can* make sense of history stands on the same level of epistemic plausibility as the conviction that it makes no sense whatsoever. My point is that the kind of politics that one can justify by an appeal to history will differ according to whether one proceeds on the basis of the former or the latter conviction. I am inclined to think that a visionary politics can proceed only on the latter conviction. And I conclude that, however radical Marxism may be as a social philosophy and especially as a critique of capitalism, in its aspect as a philosophy of history it is no more visionary than its bourgeois counterpart.

We have seen that, prior to the nineteenth century, history had been conceived as a spectacle of crimes, superstitions, errors, duplicities, and terrorisms that justified visionary recommendations for a politics that would place social processes on a new ground. Philosophies of history, like those of Voltaire and Condorcet, constituted the basis of the Enlightenment's contribution to a progressive political theory. Romanticism represented the last attempt in the West to generate a visionary politics on the basis of a sublime conception of the historical process. But what Schiller called the "shudder to the grim law of necessity" occasioned by reflection on the historical spectacle and the "fastening on the eternal" which it was supposed instinctively to call up were progressively consigned to the class of errors to which the Romantics in general and Romanticist historians in particular—Michelet and Carlyle above all—were singularly prone (p. 210). In fact, the extent to which historical studies were disciplinized can be measured by the extent to which professional practitioners on both sides of the political barricades succeeded in identifying as errors the attitudes with which the Romantics approached history. The domestication of historical thinking required that Romanticism be consigned to the category of well-meaning but ultimately irresponsible cultural movements which used history for only literary or poetic purposes.[30]

In the politics of contemporary discussions of historical interpretation, the kind of perspective on history which I have been implicitly praising is conventionally associated with the ideologies of fascist regimes. Something like Schiller's notion of the historical sublime or Nietzsche's version of it is certainly present in the thought of such philosophers as Heidegger and Gentile as well as in the intuitions of Hitler and Mussolini. But having granted as much, we must guard against a sentimentalism that would lead us to write off such a conception of history simply because it has been associated with fascist ideologies. One must face the fact that, when it comes to the historical record, there are no grounds to be found in the record itself for preferring one way of construing its meaning rather than another. Nor can such grounds be found in any putative science of man, society, or culture because such sciences are compelled simply to presuppose some conception of historical reality in order to get on with their program of constituting themselves as sciences. Far from providing us with grounds for choosing among different conceptions of history, the human and social sciences merely beg the question of history's meaning which, in one sense, they were created to resolve. Therefore, to appeal to sociology, anthropology, or psychology for some basis for determining an appropriate perspective on history is rather like basing one's notion of the soundness of a building's foundations on the structural properties of its second or third story. The human and social sciences, insofar as they are based on or presuppose a specific conception of historical reality, are just as blind to the sublimity of the historical process and to the visionary politics which it authorizes as is the disciplinized historical consciousness that informs their investigative procedures.

The domestication of history effected by the suppression of the historical sublime may well be the sole basis for the proud claim to *social responsibility* in modern capitalist as well as in communist societies. While this pride derives in part from the claim to see through the distortions and duplicities of fascist ideologies, it is possible that fascist politics is in part the price paid for the very domestication of historical consciousness that is supposed to stand against it. Fascist social and political policies are undeniably horrible, and they may well be a function of a vision of history that sees no meaning in it and therefore imposes a meaning where none is to be found. But the appeal of fascism not only to the masses but to any number of intellectuals who had certainly been exposed to a culture of history that explained and understood the past to

30. I have in mind such judgments as that of Hugh Trevor-Roper, who, in a recent essay, remarks of Carlyle: "Perhaps it is the surest sign of Carlyle's genius that we read him still, and are interested in him still, although his ideas are totally discredited" ("Thomas Carlyle's Historical Philosophy," *Times Literary Supplement,* 26 June 1981, p. 734).

the very depths of all possibility leaves us with the necessity of trying to understand why this culture provided so weak an impediment to fascism's appeal.

The problem of fascism's appeal to modern political constituencies is certainly not to be solved by intellectual historical inquiry, the history of ideas, or, if what I have suggested thus far regarding the politics of interpretation in the human and social sciences is correct, by historical inquiry in general. The events that comprise fascism's history occupy a domain of human experience far removed from the kinds of theoretical questions that we are addressing here. But fascism in its Nazi incarnation and especially in its aspect as a politics of genocide constitutes a crucial test case for determining the ways in which any human or social science may construe its social responsibilities as a discipline productive of a certain kind of "knowledge."

It is often alleged that "formalists" such as myself, who hold that any historical object can sustain a number of equally plausible descriptions or narratives of its processes, effectively deny the reality of the referent, promote a debilitating relativism which permits any manipulation of the evidence as long as the account produced is structurally coherent, and thereby allow the kind of perspectivism that permits even a Nazi version of Nazism's history to claim a certain minimal credibility. Such formalists are typically confronted with questions like these: Do you mean to say that the occurrence and nature of the Holocaust is only a matter of opinion and that one can write its history however one pleases? Do you imply that any account of that event is as valid as any other account, so long as it meets certain formal requirements of discursive practices, and that one has no responsibility to the victims to tell the truth about the indignities and cruelties they suffered? Are there not certain historical events that tolerate none of that mere cleverness which allows criminals or their admirers to feign accounts of their crimes which effectively relieve them of their guilt or responsibility or even, in the worst instances, allows them to maintain that the crimes they committed never happened? In such questions we come to the bottom line of the politics of interpretation which informs not only historical studies but the human and social sciences in general.

I do not have to tell you, I am sure, that these questions have been given a new urgency by the appearance in recent years of a group of "revisionist" historians of the Holocaust who indeed argue that this event never occurred.[31] The claim is as morally offensive as it is intellectually

31. On the "revisionist" group of historians of the Holocaust, see Lucy S. Dawidowicz, "Lies about the Holocaust," *Commentary* 70 (December 1980): 31–37. Dawidowicz surveys the entire literature on the Holocaust in *The Holocaust and the Historians* (Cambridge, Mass., 1981), an invaluable work for anyone interested in the subject and also in the ethics of historical interpretation. Arno J. Mayer summarizes the issues of "revisionism" in "A Note on Vidal-Naquet," his introduction to the English translation of Pierre Vidal-Naquet's "A Paper Eichmann?," *Democracy* (April 1981): 67–95.

bewildering. It is not of course bewildering to most Jews who have no difficulty recognizing in it another instance of the kind of thinking that led to the implementation of the "final solution" in Germany in the first place. But it has proven bewildering to some Jewish scholars who had thought that fidelity to a rigorous "historical method" could not possibly result in a conclusion so monstrous. For indeed, as Pierre Vidal-Naquet has recently written, the revisionist case features as an important element of its brief that massive research in the archives and pursuit of documentary and oral testimony that are the mainstays of this "method."[32]

Vidal-Naquet takes it as a matter requiring nothing more than its assertion that the "research" that has gone into the putative search for anyone or anything that could "prove" that the Holocaust actually "happened" is not genuinely "historical" but is rather "ideological." The aim of this research "is to deprive a community of what is represented by its historic memory." But he is confident that "on the terrain of positive history . . . true opposes false quite simply, independent of any kind of interpretation," and that when it is a matter of the *occurrence* of events (he cites the taking of the Bastille on 14 July 1789 as an example), there is no question of alternative interpretations or "revisionist" hypotheses. Such an occurrence is simply a matter of fact, and therefore a positive historiography can always set a limit on its interpretation which permits of no transgression and distinguishes well enough between a genuinely

32. It is precisely the issue of "historical method" that I wish to bring under question in this essay. Vidal-Naquet views this method as the best ensurance against the kind of ideological distortion of which the revisionists are justly accused: see "Paper Eichmann," p. 74; all further references will be included in the text. So, too, Dawidowicz in *The Holocaust* conflates the problem of that "fairness and objectivity" for which historians strive with adherence "to methodological rules concerning the use of historical evidence" (p. 26). Yet, in her survey of the work of professional historians who have dealt with the Holocaust since World War II, she finds them all wanting in the kind of "conscientious" approach to history commended by Lord Acton as the sole possible basis of a genuinely "objective history" (p. 144). It does not occur to her, it seems, that her study indicts the very "professionalism" which she prescribes as the necessary precondition of objectivity. Indeed, one could conclude from her study that the failure of historians to come to terms with the Holocaust in a morally responsible way is a result of this professionalism.

As for the question of "historical method," one can legitimately and responsibly ask what it consists of. It is a commonplace of current social scientific theory that there is no "method" specific to historical research. Claude Lévi-Strauss is only the most prominent of social theorists holding this view. In "History and Dialectic," his famous conclusion to *The Savage Mind* (London, 1962), he denies that history is either object- or method-specific. The whole issue was debated in a conference organized by Alan Bullock and Raymond Aron (Venice, 1971), on the relationship between historical, sociological, and anthropological inquiry. Here Peter Wiles pilloried "historical method" by dismissing it as simply "measurement without theory" and stating bluntly: "There is no such thing as a historical explanation." See the account of the proceedings of the conference, *The Historian between the Ethnologist and the Futurologist,* ed. Jerome Dumoulin and Dominique Moisi (Paris and The Hague, 1973), and my review of this book, "The Historian at the Bridge of Sighs," *Reviews in European History* 1 (March 1975): 437–45.

historical account and a fictive or mythic deformation of "reality." Vidal-Naquet extends his criticism of such deformations to include a Zionism which "exploits this terrible massacre in a way that is at times quite scandalous." "Finally," he writes, "it is the duty of historians to take historical facts out of the hands of ideologists who exploit them" and set limits on "this permanent rewriting of history that characterizes ideological speech." For him, these limits are approached when one encounters the kind of manifest "total lie" produced by the revisionists (pp. 75, 90–91).

This is clear enough, although the distinction between a lie and an error or mistake in interpretation may be more difficult to draw with respect to historical events less amply documented than the Holocaust. What is less clear is the relative validity of an interpretation of the Holocaust which, according to Vidal-Naquet, has been produced by "the Israelis, or rather their ideologists," for whom "Auschwitz was the ineluctable, logical outcome of life lived in the Diaspora, and all the victims of the death camps were destined to become Israeli citizens," which he labels less a lie than an "untruth" (p. 90). Here the distinction seems to turn, for Vidal-Naquet at least, on the difference between an interpretation which would "have profoundly transformed the *reality* of the massacre" and one that would not. The Israeli interpretation leaves the "reality" of the event intact, whereas the revisionist interpretation derealizes it by redescribing it in such a way as to make it something other than what the victims know the Holocaust to have been. The phenomenon in question is rather like A. J. P. Taylor's controversial interpretation of Hitler as your run-of-the-mill European statesman whose methods were a bit excessive but whose ends were respectable enough, given the conventions of European politics in his time.[33] The theoretical point to be taken, however, is that an interpretation falls into the category of a lie when it denies the reality of the events of which it treats and into the category of an untruth when it draws false conclusions from reflection on events whose reality remains attestable on the level of "positive" historical inquiry.

There is a question of interpretive tact that should be raised at this point. It must seem unconscionably pedantic, arguably eristic, and conceivably tasteless to be fiddling with what appear to be points of method in the context of a question having to do with an event so horrendous that those who experienced it and their relatives and descendants can hardly bear to hear it spoken of, much less turned into an occasion for a purely scholarly discussion of the politics of interpretation. But if this question is not a crucial example of how the politics of interpretation arises from an interpretation of politics, especially in matters historical,

33. See A. J. P. Taylor, *The Origins of the Second World War* (New York, 1964). See also W. H. Dray, "Concepts of Causation in A. J. P. Taylor's *The Origins of the Second World War*," *History and Theory* 17 (1978): 149–74.

how could we imagine a better one? The cause of taste and sensitivity to the feelings of those who have a living investment in the memory of this event could be served by taking an example more remote in time—the French Revolution, the American Civil War, the Wars of Religion, the Crusades, the Inquisition—events remote enough in time to permit us to disengage whatever emotional weight they might have had for the people who experienced *them* from our purely intellectual "interest" in what they were or how they happened. But this very temptation to discuss the problem of the politics of interpretation in historical studies in the context of a consideration of events remote in time should itself enliven us to the morally domesticating effects of consigning an event definitively to "history."

Vidal-Naquet eloquently dilates on the poignant moment at which a people or group is forced, by the death of its members, to transfer an experience, existentially determinative of its own image of the nature of its existence as a historical entity, from the domain of *memory* to that of *history*. The resolution of the Holocaust question, he says, does not lie in the direction of simply exposing the "fraudulence" of the revisionists' "version" of history:

> For whatever the circumstances, today we are witnessing the trans-
> formation of memory into history. . . . My generation, people of
> about fifty, is probably the last one for whom Hitler's crimes are still
> a memory. That both disappearance and, worse still, depreciation
> of this memory must be combatted seems to me obvious. Neither
> prescription nor pardon seems conceivable. . . . But what are we
> going to do with this memory that, while it is our memory, is not
> that of everybody? [Pp. 93–94]

What indeed? In the answer that a historian gives to that question is contained an entire politics of interpretation—and not only for historical studies. Vidal-Naquet's own efforts to answer it are instructive and illuminate some of the points that I have been trying to make here. His remarks warrant full quotation, for they return us to the relevance of the historical sublime, to the larger questions of historical interpretation:

> It is hard for me to explain myself on this point. I was brought up
> with an elevated—some might say megalomaniacal—conception of
> the task of the historian, and it was during the war that my father
> made me read Chateaubriand's famous article in the *Mercure* of
> July 4, 1807:
>
> > In the silence of abjection, when the only sounds to be heard are
> > the chains of the slave and the voice of the informer; when every-
> > thing trembles before the tyrant and it is as dangerous to incur his
> > favor as to deserve his disfavor, this is when the historian appears,
> > charged with avenging the people.

I still believe in the need to remember and, in my way, I try to be a man of memory; but I no longer believe that historians are "charged with avenging the people." We must accept the fact that "the war is over," that the tragedy has become, in a way, secularized, even if this carries with it for us, I mean for we who are Jewish, the loss of a certain privilege of speech that has largely been ours since Europe discovered the great massacre. And this, in itself, is not a bad thing; for what can be more intolerable than the pose of certain personages draped in the sash of the Order of Extermination, who believe that in this way they can avoid the everyday pettiness and baseness that are our human lot? [P. 94]

I find these words moving, not least because, over and above the humaneness to which they attest, they attest to the politically domesticating effects of a historical attitude which is always much too prone to equate the consignment of an event to history with the end of a war. In point of fact, for French anti-Semites the war was far from over, as the attack on the synagogue in the rue Copernic in October 1980, which postdated the composition of Vidal-Naquet's article, amply indicated. It is less easy to neutralize human memory by the consignment of an event or experience of it to history than Vidal-Naquet suggests. What he condemns as ideology may be nothing other than the treatment of a historical event *as if* it were still a memory of living men; but a memory, whether real or only *felt* to be so, cannot be deprived of its emotional charge and the action it seems to justify by presenting an historical-real that has remembrance as its only purpose.

Vidal-Naquet is inclined, too hastily I think, to consign the Zionist interpretation of the Holocaust (or his version of that interpretation) to the category of untruth. In fact, its truth, as a historical interpretation, consists precisely in its effectiveness in justifying a wide range of current Israeli political policies which, from the standpoint of those who articulate them, are crucial to the security and indeed the very existence of the Jewish people. Whether one supports these policies or condemns them, they are undeniably a product, at least in part, of a conception of Jewish history that is conceived to be meaningless to Jews insofar as this history was dominated by agencies, processes, and groups who encouraged or permitted policies that led to the "final solution" of the "Jewish Question." The totalitarian, not to say fascist, aspects of Israeli treatment of the Palestinians on the West Bank may be attributable primarily to a Zionist ideology that is detestable to anti-Zionists, Jewish and non-Jewish alike. But who is to say that this ideology is a product of a *distorted* conception of history in general and of the history of Jews in the Diaspora specifically? It is, in fact, fully comprehensible as a morally responsible response to the meaninglessness of a certain history, that spectacle of "moral anarchy" which Schiller perceived in "world history" and which he specified as a "sublime object." The Israeli political response to this spectacle is fully consonant with the aspiration to human freedom and dignity which Schiller took to be the necessary consequence of sustained reflection on it. So far as I can see, the effort of the Palestinian people to mount a politically effective response to Israeli policies entails the production of a similarly effective ideology, complete with an interpretation of their history capable of endowing it with a meaning that it has hitherto lacked (a project to which Edward Said wishes to contribute).

Does this imply that historical knowledge, or, rather, the kind of discourses produced by historians, finds the measure of its validity in its status as an instrument of a political program or of an ideology which rationalizes, when it does not inspire, such a program? And if so, what does this tell us about the kind of historical knowledge that comes attended by a claim to have foregone service to any specific political cause and simply purports to tell the truth about the past as an end in itself and *sine ira et studio,* to provide "understanding" of what cannot be perfectly "explained," and to lead to tolerance and forebearance rather than reverence or a spirit of vengefulness?

In answer to the first question, one must grant that, while it is possible to produce a kind of knowledge that is not *explicitly* linked to any specific political program, all knowledge produced in the human and social sciences lends itself to use by some ideology better than it does to some others. This is especially true of historical knowledge of the conceptually underdetermined sort that appears in the form of a conventional narrative. This brings us back to the question of the political or ideological implications of narrativity itself as a modality of historical representation, of the sort that Roland Barthes associates with nineteenth-century bourgeois notions of realism.[34] Is narrativity itself an ideological instrument? It is sufficient here to indicate the extent to which a number of contemporary analysts of narratology, among whom must be numbered Julia Kristeva, think it to be so.[35] If, by contrast, it is possible to imagine a conception of history which would signal its resistance to the bourgeois ideology of realism by its refusal to attempt a narrativist mode for the representation of its truth, is it possible that this refusal itself signals a recovery of the historical sublime which bourgeois historiography repressed in the process of its disciplinization? And if this is or might be the case, is this recovery of the historical sublime a necessary precondition for the production of a historiography of the sort that Chateaubriand conceived to be desirable in times of "abjection"? A historiography "charged with avenging the people"? This seems plausible to me.

34. See Barthes, "Historical Discourse," pp. 145–55 (n. 19 above).
35. See Julia Kristeva, "The Novel of Polylogue," *Desire in Language: A Semiotic Approach to Literature and Art,* ed. Leon S. Roudiez, trans. Roudiez, Thomas Gora, and Alice Jardine (New York, 1980), esp. pp. 201–8.

As for the second question, namely, what all of this might imply for any effort to comprehend that politics of interpretation in historical studies which instructs us to recognize that "the war is over" and to forego the attractions of a desire for revenge, it seems obvious to me that such instruction is the kind that always emanates from centers of established political power and social authority and that this kind of tolerance is a luxury which only devotees of dominant groups can afford. For subordinant, emergent, or resisting social groups, this recommendation, that they view history with the kind of "objectivity," "modesty," "realism," and "social responsibility" that has characterized historical studies since its establishment as a professional discipline, can only appear as another aspect of the ideology they are indentured to oppose. They cannot effectively oppose such an ideology while only offering their own versions, Marxist or otherwise, of the "objectivity" and so forth that the established discipline claims. This opposition can be carried forward only on the basis of a conception of the historical record as being not a window through which the past "as it really was" can be apprehended but rather a wall that must be broken through if the "terror of history" is to be directly confronted and the fear it induces dispelled.

Santayana said that "those who neglect the study of the past are condemned to repeat it." It is not so much the study of the past itself that assures against its repetition but how you study it, to what aim, interest, or purpose. Nothing is better suited to lead to a repetition of the past than a study of it that is either reverential or convincingly objective in the way that conventional historical studies tend to be. Hegel opined that "the only thing anyone ever learned from the study of history is that no one ever learned anything from the study of history." But he was convinced, and demonstrated to the satisfaction of a number of students of history more sapient than I am, that you could learn a great deal, of both practical and theoretical worth, from the study of the study of history. And one of the things you learn from the study of the study of history is that such study is never innocent, ideologically or otherwise, whether launched from the political perspective of the Left, Right, or Center. This is because our very notion of the possibility of discriminating among the Left, Right, and Center is in part a function of the disciplinization of historical studies which ruled out the possibility—a possibility that should never be ruled out of any area of inquiry—that history may be as meaningless "in itself" as the theorists of the historical sublime thought it to be.

The Pseudo-Politics of Interpretation

Gerald Graff

A good deal of theorizing about literature makes use of political arguments. By "political arguments," I mean those reasons given for or against a theory of literature or criticism which refer to the theory's alleged political motivations or consequences. My concern here is chiefly with arguments about consequences rather than arguments about motivations, but the problems posed by both kinds are much the same. Typically, an argument about political consequences takes the form, "We should ascribe (or not ascribe) characteristic x to literature or criticism, since if we do (or don't) social consequence y will tend to result." No critic puts the matter quite so bluntly as that, to be sure, yet the implied logic of much critical argument often follows that line. Thus it's suggested that certain notions of the referentiality of literature should be favored or opposed since these notions have beneficial or retrograde social consequences. Or it's suggested that if certain theories of the determinacy of textual meaning are maintained or overthrown, such and such political effects will ensue.

A recent critic, for example, writes that "if we deny the existence of objective texts," and "indeed the possibility of objectivity altogether," then "the net result of this epistemological revolution is to repoliticize literature and criticism," presumably to repoliticize them in a desirable way.[1] A second critic writes of a "growing reactionary movement in the

---

1. Jane P. Tompkins, "An Introduction to Reader-Response Criticism," in *Reader-Response Criticism: From Formalism to Post-Structuralism*, ed. Tompkins (Baltimore, 1980), p. xxv.

academy to recover the ideals of logic, reason, and determinate meaning
and to repudiate the radicalism of the sixties and early seventies."[2] A
third states that E. D. Hirsch's theory of interpretive validity is "unsuited
to a modern democracy," is "the intellectual equivalent of aggressiveness
and a wish to dominate," and "is part of an ideology of society that is
authoritarian and hierarchical."[3] A fourth invokes the view that "the
attempt to establish an objective or scientific hermeneutics is an act of
defensive mastery" and that this attempted mastery "involves technocratic violence."[4] A fifth writes of M. H. Abrams' "normative system of
stable meanings" that "there is something of the police state in Abrams's
vision, complete with posted rules and boundaries, watchdogs to enforce
them, procedures for identifying their violators as criminals."[5] And a
sixth writes of John Searle's theories of the context-related nature of
meaning that "there is always a police and a tribunal ready to intervene
each time that a rule . . . is invoked in a case involving signatures, events, or
contexts. . . . If the police is always waiting in the wings, it is because
conventions are by essence violable and precarious, *in themselves* and by
the fictionality that constitutes them, even before there has been any
overt transgression."[6]

Each of the above quotations comes from an advocate of some form
of "new" hermeneutical theory. Several of them draw a connection between hostility to such theory and hostility to radical politics. Opponents
of new hermeneutical theories, however, often make use of the same

2. Michael Sprinker, "Criticism as Reaction," *Diacritics* 10 (Fall 1980): 2–14. Sprinker's essay, a review of my *Literature against Itself: Literary Ideas in Modern Society* (Chicago,
1979), maintains that my work is symptomatic of the reactionary trend in the university as
well as the country.

3. Richard Crosman, "Do Readers Make Meaning?" in *The Reader in the Text: Essays on
Audience and Interpretation,* ed. Susan Suleiman and Inge Crosman (Princeton, N.J., 1980),
p. 154.

4. Geoffrey Hartman, "Literary Criticism and Its Discontents," *Critical Inquiry* 3
(Winter 1976): 218, 217. Hartman is summarizing Heidegger's views here, but he gives no
indication that he dissents from them.

5. Stanley Fish, *Is There a Text in This Class?* (Cambridge, Mass., 1980), p. 337. Since
Fish himself, if I read his final chapters correctly, believes in "rules and boundaries," does
this make his vision a police-state one as well?

6. Jacques Derrida, "Limited Inc abc . . . ," *Glyph* 2 (1977): 250. In grouping together
the above quotations, I don't mean to suggest that there aren't important differences
between the views of their authors. What interests me here, however, is not these authors'
individual theories but a certain form of literary-political "discourse," the idioms of which
are found in critics of very diverse views.

Gerald Graff, professor and chairman of the English department at
Northwestern University, is the author of *Literature against Itself: Literary
Ideas in Modern Society.*

kinds of political arguments. Thus it's argued that revisionist modes of interpretation represent a kind of built-in critical obsolescence, their chief effect being not to change the criticism industry but to keep its productive wheels rolling: "the new wave of paracritical and metacritical improvisation in criticism, sometimes to the point of transforming explication into prose poetry, may be a necessary spur to industrial growth at a time when the conventional modes of professional publication have worn thin."[7] Or it's argued that deconstruction doesn't threaten professorial authority so much as transfer it to other hands: "I shall say that what can be seen [in Derrida] so visibly is a historically well-determined little pedagogy . . . a pedagogy which gives . . . to the master's voice the limitless sovereignty which allows it to restate the text indefinitely."[8]

Whether they are deployed for or against new hermeneutic theories, these political arguments pose a number of problems. I want to isolate three of these problems in particular, which for convenience I'll call the problems of *relevance*, of *specificity*, and of *adequacy*. They can be stated briefly as follows: (1) Are political arguments relevant in literary theory and, if so, under what conditions? (2) To what extent can literary theories be identified—as they are by several of the above critics—with a specific politics, such as radicalism, conservatism, leftism, reactionism, and so forth? (3) Do literary theorists have an adequate sociological basis for their political arguments?

1. The problem of *relevance* can be easily described: the fact that a literary theory may result in good or bad social consequences is logically irrelevant to its cogency as a theory. Suppose, for example, it's true that a theory of textual determinacy is "part of an ideology of society that is authoritarian and hierarchical," that its motivation or effect is to defeat "the radicalism of the sixties and early seventies." It still doesn't follow that the theory is *wrong* about the determinate nature of meaning. Or suppose it's true that "the police is always waiting in the wings" to enforce the contextual rules governing the interpretation of speech acts. This fact doesn't discredit whatever logical justification those rules may claim. Or, finally, suppose Foucault is right that Derrida's pedagogy plays into the hands of the sovereign teacher. This does not invalidate that pedagogy as a theoretical project. That an idea has certain political consequences is irrelevant when adduced as an argument against (or for) the idea. Nor is an idea discredited because the motives that led to its formulation are suspect.

But in much recent critical discourse, the assertion that theories are forms of discursive power, that they are used for certain political purposes, is put forth as if it were not only an argument against the truth of

7. Graff, *Literature against Itself*, p. 97.

8. Michel Foucault, "My Body, This Paper, This Fire," trans. Geoff Bennington, *Oxford Literary Review* 4 (Autumn 1979): 27. Foucault is responding to Derrida's criticisms in *Writing and Difference* of *Madness and Civilization*.

certain theories but a devastating argument. It is considered sufficient to disprove the claims of objectivism, empiricism, essentialism, logocentrism, and other currently disapproved -*isms* to point out that they are not "innocent" but function within disciplinary regimes. Opposing this line of argument is rather like hitting a tennis ball against a brick wall. The harder you smash the ball, hoping to come up with a theoretical (or factual) proposition not "always already" encoded in a system of power, the faster it is returned to you with the words "institutionally determined" stamped upon it. It must be obvious that one can't hope to defeat this hermeneutics of power at its own game, since its chief tactic, the repetitive assertion of the omnipresence of power, is a tautology. What one ought to reply to this assertion is not "No, you're wrong to maintain that all theories are a function of politics and power" but rather "Yes, you're right to maintain that all theories are a function of politics and power, but *so what?* What can that fact tell us about whether we should accept any theory or not? Your point is true as far as it goes but without specific consequences theoretically, since the political motivations and effects of a theory are irrelevant to its truth."

The retort to this argument, however, is likely to be that "truth" is itself a politically determined concept, and therefore one can't simply invoke it as a way of making political effects irrelevant. Truth isn't an independent standard apart from politics and power, so this argument runs, but is itself a political effect, a product of politics and power. What counts as true within any community—the "criteriology" which determines what questions are pertinent, what is accepted as a relevant fact or argument, as valid reasoning, as proper evidence, and so forth—is necessarily a function of institutional convention, that is, of power. Therefore to argue that the political motivations and effects of a theory are irrelevant to its truth is to forget that truth itself is politically motivated and implicated.

Like the famous paradox of the liar, this line of argument suffers from a built-in tendency to self-destruct. Presumably the proposition that truth is a function of power is itself asserted as true; yet presumably, by its own declaration, the proposition too is a function of power. How then is the proposition to be taken? If the truth of the proposition that truth is a function of power is compromised by the fact that the proposition itself is a function of power, then there ceases to be any reason to take the proposition seriously as an argument. If the truth of this proposition (that truth is a function of power) *isn't* compromised by the fact that the proposition is a function of power, then the proposition becomes trivial—the fact that truth is a function of power doesn't compromise the status of truth. We have, then, two possibilities: either the argument that truth is a function of power contradicts and thus neutralizes itself, or else it's trivially true, true but without theoretical consequences.

This isn't to say that we have to accept all concepts of truth un-critically. We can question the canons of truth embodied in any system of discourse, but only by invoking other canons of truth not themselves assumed to be compromised by their historically and institutionally produced status. The project of demystifying the ideology of any system commits the demystifier to an alternate set of concepts which can't themselves be regarded as "ideological" in the compromising sense without appearing incoherent. These alternate concepts needn't (perhaps can't) be claimed to be independent of power and history, but it has to be assumed that their dependence on power and history doesn't discredit them. Again, one can object that these arguments are persuasive only so long as one goes along with Western notions of coherence and contradiction, notions themselves ethnocentrically produced and enforced. But again, even to make this complaint is to be caught up in the very notions one is seeking to criticize as ethnocentric. There's not much one can say to the person who complains that for all we know *all* our notions of truth might be politically biased, except to ask, "Biased as compared with what?" The critique of any body of ideas as biased is coherent only in terms of an implied comparison with ideas alleged to be *less* biased. If everything is biased, including the perception of the omnipresence of bias, critical discourse becomes absurd. The critique of ideology presupposes a standpoint not necessarily outside of history but also not necessarily discredited by its historical status.

Of course, sexist, racist, imperialist, orientalist, and other ideologies of domination *do* frequently hide behind spurious claims of truth. But what makes these claims spurious is not that the concept of truth is spurious but that *the ideologies making the claims are untrue*. When we employ the sociology of knowledge to explain the motivation or success of these claims in terms of social interest, we are already assuming that these philosophies are untrue. That is, what causes us to seek the motivation of these philosophies is our previous decision that their motivation isn't to be found in reality. Take, for example, the research which is sometimes adduced as demonstrating the inferiority of blacks or of other races. The claims of such research are probably both false and ideologically motivated. But *whether* such claims are false or not doesn't depend on the nature of their ideological motive or effect. It's true that when an argument seems obviously motivated by personal or group interest, we tend to scrutinize it more warily than we might otherwise. But this scrutiny itself operates on canons of reasons and evidence assumed to be independent of ideological considerations. To argue that theories of racial inferiority are ideological projections is already to assume that these theories are not justified by the evidence, quite apart from their motives and effects.

Nevertheless, the fact that the social consequences (or motivations) of a theory are irrelevant to determining its truth or falsity doesn't make these consequences any less real or significant. We feel there is something unsatisfactory about any invocation of the objectivity of knowledge that stops short of inquiring into knowledge's social effects. In this respect, one might liken the suspicion lately directed against objectivist literary theories to the protests against war-related research in universities. In both cases what's at issue are the political consequences which follow from certain forms of inquiry. Here again, however, it seems necessary to distinguish between the truth of some inquiry and the practical consequences that ensue from it. Those who protest against war-related research don't claim that the research is epistemologically invalidated by the political uses to which it is put, that is, they wouldn't claim that the principles of ballistics or of nuclear fission are somehow rendered less true when they are used for destructive ends. What underlies such protests is not a *theoretical* objection to the research in question but a *practical* objection to the way that research is used—and perhaps must tend to be used, given a certain context. Given an international situation of a certain sort, it is argued, certain forms of inquiry *can't help* being used for destructive purposes.

2. But this poses a problem concerning the political *specificity* of various kinds of inquiry. (I pass over here the distinctions that need to be made between "knowledge," "research," "theories," "ideas," etc., with the broad term "inquiry.") Assuming that any theory will necessarily have *some* political consequences merely by virtue of the fact that it exists in the world, how does one determine specifically what those political consequences will be? How specific can one be about the political tendency of a theory? How does one test the claims critics are making now about such political tendencies? Take the claim quoted above that Hirsch's theory of interpretive validity is "part of an ideology of society that is authoritarian and hierarchical" or the claim that objective hermeneutics is tied to a police-state vision of society or to technocratic violence. Even if these political charges are irrelevant to the truth of the theories they attack, they are still significant. What does one say about them?

One of the difficulties these charges encounter is that any theory can evidently be used in a variety of different ways. Therefore, it's not clear to what degree a theorist can be held politically responsible for the use that is made of his ideas. History suggests that the same theory is often used for different and sometimes sharply antithetical political purposes or has sharply antithetical political effects.[9] There is left Hegelianism

9. This proposition encounters an immediate objection from post-structuralist theory, namely, that the notion of *the same* is "problematic." Derrida writes that "once inserted into another network, the 'same' philosopheme is no longer the same, and besides it never had an identity external to its functioning" ("Economimesis," trans. R. Klein, *Diacritics* 11 [Summer 1981]: 3). Taken literally, this argument would have it that the principles of physics cease to be the same principles when used by a Socialist and Fascist. I don't

and right Hegelianism, left and right Christianity, and even left and right deconstruction. Whereas some of Stanley Fish's current followers seek to deploy his theories of "interpretive communities" in a politically radical way, Fish himself seems to see these theories as a vindication of established professional usages. It appears, then, that theories—again, rather like the principles of ballistics or nuclear fission—are politically *ambidextrous;* they can be appropriated by the Right, Left, or Center, and, indeed, they come to be fought over by these factions once they reach a certain point of acceptance in a scholarly community. This is not to say that such theories are politically neutral—they invariably have *some* political consequence—but *what that consequence is* in a specific instance can't be deduced a priori from the theory itself. Again, we come back to the true but theoretically trivial nature of the assumption that all ideas are political. It's true *in general* that all ideas are political; but since what their politics is in a specific case can't be deduced or predicted from the ideas themselves, this truth doesn't tell us very much.

Critics, then, who label theories such as objectivism or deconstructionism as "authoritarian" or "subversive" are committing a fallacy of overspecificity. To call Hirsch's theory authoritarian is to assume that such a theory lends itself to one and only one kind of political use and that that use can be determined a priori. To refute such an assumption, one need only stand back from the present in order to recall that today's authoritarian ideology is often yesterday's progressive one, and vice versa. Indeed, there's considerable historical irony in the fact that objectivism has now acquired the status of a right-wing idea, while Nietzsche and Heidegger have emerged as heroes of literary leftism. As recently as a few decades ago, these alignments were different. George Orwell, for instance, thought that the tendency to deny the possibility of objective truth reflected a totalitarian mentality. "Totalitarianism," he wrote, "in the long run probably demands a disbelief in the existence of objective truth." He added that "the friends of totalitarianism in this country tend to argue that since absolute truth is not attainable, a big lie

---

propose to try to grapple with this argument here except to say that I see little difference between it and the Heraclitean maxim that one never steps into the same river twice—or, indeed, once. (I'm aware that I'm begging the question all the more by suggesting that Derrida and Heraclitus are propounding "the same" "philosopheme.") From this viewpoint, the very notions of identity and continuity are suspect; nothing can be distinguished from its "context," and there are no privileged or stable contexts (except presumably those imposed arbitrarily by the police who are behind John Searle). But as Derrida well knows, since the simplest procedures of logic and grammar depend on the assumption of identity, to seek to maintain this Heraclitean view consistently would mean abandoning all coherent discourse as we know it. To this extreme, neither Derrida nor others, so far, choose to go—though Jorge Luis Borges has imagined a whole planet, the Tlön of his "Tlön, Uqbar, Orbis Tertius," in which Heraclitean thinking is normal common sense. Like the argument that all statements are logically biased, including this one, Derrida's point ends either in paradox or triviality.

is no worse than a little lie. It is pointed out that all historical records are biased and inaccurate, or, on the other hand, that modern physics has proved that what seems to us the real world is an illusion, so that to believe in the evidence of the senses is simply vulgar philistinism."[10]

It's not that it hadn't occurred to Orwell that the notion of objective truth could easily be used to justify the actions of tyrants and oppressors. But Orwell's experience of Fascist and Communist falsification of history showed how the denial of the possibility of objectivity could also justify oppressive actions, perhaps in a more disarming way. For various historical reasons, Orwell's insight is easily lost today. His is one of those Enlightenment concepts of truth which have been compromised in usage. As the Enlightenment has come to be associated not with progress, democracy, and equality but with the ideological exploitation of those concepts in the interests of social control, a great moral and political transvaluation of the epistemological vocabulary has occurred. Enlightenment thinking is frequently associated with the bourgeois complacency or the menacing technology of Western democracies or is identified with the totalitarian regimentation of the Soviet Union. Thus the concepts of objective truth, nature, essence, identity, and teleology have come to be viewed as conservative or reactionary ideas, as if these ideas had never operated, and never could operate, in quite other ways.[11]

If one wished, a plausible case could be made for the view that the interpretive objectivists are the real heirs of the radical tradition which has sought to secularize and demystify the concept of meaning, and that the deconstructionists are carrying on a rearguard attempt to preserve some element of linguistic mystery from secularization. But it's not my purpose to argue that deconstruction has been classed falsely as an ideology of the Left and ought from now on be classed as an ideology of the Right. The point is not merely to reverse the current political valences but to get beyond the whole dubious project of attaching specific political implications to theories independent of the way they operate in concrete social practice. A theory such as interpretive objectivism doesn't "imply" any single politics. Of course to deal with this question fully I should have to go more deeply than I can here into the things which might be meant by "objectivism" and "objectivity," distinguishing, for

10. George Orwell, "The Prevention of Literature," *The Collected Essays, Journalism, and Letters of George Orwell,* ed. Sonia Orwell and Ian Angus, 4 vols. (London, 1968), 4: 63–64.

11. As Fredric Jameson has noted, "it is certainly the case that a belief in the natural is ideological and that much of bourgeois art has worked to perpetuate such a belief. . . . Yet in different historical circumstances the idea of nature was once a subversive concept with a genuinely revolutionary function, and only the analysis of the concrete historical and cultural conjuncture can tell us whether, in the post-natural world of late capitalism, the categories of nature may not have acquired such a critical charge again" ("Conclusion," *Aesthetics and Politics* [London, 1977], p. 207).

instance, between flexible and dogmatic versions of objectivity. Even then, however, it would be necessary to go beyond the a priori way of treating the political question by investigating the way concepts of objectivity have operated in particular social contexts. What this suggests is that the politics of any theory is as much a matter of empirical investigation as of logical analysis. To determine the politics of any theory, we must look at the way it functions in particular social circumstances.

3. But this poses a third problem, that of sociological *adequacy*. If the politics of a literary theory depend on the way that theory operates in social practice, then making political judgments and classifications of theories requires an adequate analysis of social practices. Is there reason to think current literary critics possess such an analysis? When one of the above-quoted critics draws a connection between objectivist hermeneutics and "technocratic violence," for example, it's noteworthy that he leaves it to the reader to guess what theory of technocracy he may have in mind. When another mentions the police waiting in the wings to enforce speech-act rules, he leaves equally unclear what theory of modern authority he is employing. Most of the statements quoted advance sociological theses of considerable weight and comprehensiveness as if there were no need to defend or elaborate on them; yet a little scrutiny suggests that these theses are little more than commonplaces about technology or authority. It might of course be objected that philosophers and literary critics can't reasonably be expected to go beyond the commonplaces of sociology since their main business is elsewhere. This objection would have more force if it weren't that the theories of these critics and philosophers are often strongly conditioned, if not strictly determined, by their sociological premises.

Thus without denying the force of Derrida's rigorously philosophical interrogations of language, one can still wonder if these interrogations would have achieved anything approximating their current celebrity if it were not widely felt that our cultural institutions rest on the sort of logocentric thinking which Derrida wishes to oppose. It seems fair to say that a good part of the success of radical interpretation theory stems from its capturing the authority of the iconoclastic; and it has captured that authority by appealing to the conviction that established society, and the university within it, depends ideologically on traditional centrist hierarchies. It's only on this assumption—that American culture is bound to centrist ideology—that the claim of radical political efficacy for strategies of textual dissemination and free play makes sense. To put this another way, it's only if modern power structures depend on a sort of metaphysical gold standard, in which notions like "nature," "reality," and "essence" underwrite their discourses, that it can be claimed that by undoing the logic of language a critic is helping to undo established social ideology.

To be sure, it's not hard to find enough examples of essentialist thinking in support of racist, sexist, or imperialist attitudes to vindicate this diagnosis. The upsurge of the Moral Majority and other religious fundamentalisms would alone be sufficient proof of the survival of the logocentric thinking that political deconstructionists seek to unmask. But isn't there another side to this picture? Despite such manifestations as the Moral Majority, couldn't it be argued that modern authority tends to operate not by ideologies of centrism, hierarchy, and constraint but rather by a permissiveness that encourages a great variety of ideologies, confident that the very proliferation of these ideologies will not only diffuse any threat to existing economic foundations but will promote a vital consumerism? Isn't it at least possible that nature, essence, immanence, and other logocentric concepts are less of a live issue than they once were, that these and other hierarchical concepts were rendered negligible long ago by a more powerful "deconstructive" force than that of any school of philosophy or criticism, namely, the force of consumer capitalism itself? Aren't strategies of textual dissemination of questionable effectiveness if the culture they seek to strike against is already more like a disseminated text than an organically unified one?[12]

As for the police which are said to be waiting in the wings to enforce the juridico-political contracts of language—perhaps the more disturbing possibility is that the police *aren't* waiting in the wings, that modern authority, in its attitude toward the radicalisms of culture and literature, is more indifferent than repressive. The notion that modern authority *needs* the support of the culture with which humanities professors deal may be self-flattering as well as optimistic. If modern authority has freed itself from dependency on traditional forms of philosophy, religion, and high literature, it does little good to attack modern authority by attacking those agencies. The Moral Majority notwithstanding—and the Moral Majority has its own considerable ax to grind against the "secular humanism" of consumer society—it's far from clear that the dominant drift of present authority isn't *anti*-authoritarian, partly perhaps because it has discovered less wasteful methods of management.

One might object at this point that the "co-optation" of dissident culture by modern authority—Marcuse called it "repressive desublimation"—is well understood by radical literary theorists. What is deconstruction, after all, but a strategy for making texts immune to

12. Susan Jeffords has pointed out to me that Herbert I. Schiller's *The Mind Managers* (New York, 1968) supports some of these generalizations. Schiller's study suggests that, in modern mass communications, the very discontinuity and ephemerality of the flux of information and pseudoinformation disarms the critical faculty of the audience more effectively than would overt indoctrination. "The importance of tomorrow's newspaper," Schiller comments concisely, "is that it makes perishable what happened today. . . . Total preoccupation with the moment destroys necessary links with the past"—and thus with any contrastive perspective against which the present might be measured (p. 28). Orwell is again highly relevant here: the ultimate illustration of how destruction of the past can lead to passivity rather than revolt is his *Nineteen Eighty-Four*.

appropriation by the consumer. By insisting on the element of un-containable excess that attends any chain of signification, decon-structionists see to it that no text can be reduced to a mere commod-ity. If this is the deconstructive strategy, then the response would have to be that it is at once ineffective and too effective. On the one hand, the very procedures by which texts are made to seem unmanageable rather easily become a critical commodity fetish—that is, the styles of resisting commodification themselves become commodities. On the other hand, the texts which have been revealed to be unmanageable may indeed cease to be consumable commodities, but only because in that form they no longer interest anyone but a coterie of professors and their students. As noted above, such sociological observations don't refute the philo-sophical claims of deconstruction. They do, however, challenge its strategic political claims.

What needs to be underscored is that the views of society which critical theorists entertain have an influence on their theories which is easily overlooked, and if these views aren't handled with care they can result in distortions. Thus theorists come to derive the nature of inter-pretation or of literature from hypotheses about society: if society is diagnosed as characterized by repressive closure, interpretation or liter-ature is defined as undecidable or open. The nature of interpretation or of literature comes to be whatever we think it ought to be if certain social evils are to be counteracted. Such a procedure is obviously illogical because the nature of interpretation or of literature doesn't depend on the features of society that may need alteration; and it's erroneous in-sofar as the diagnosis of those social features is simplistic. But it should not be supposed that contemporary theory holds a monopoly on this process of negative dialectic. Many of our modern definitions of litera-ture have been arrived at by reckoning up the more sordid or unattrac-tive features of industrial society and turning them on their heads. Liter-ature in its essence becomes the repository of those qualities of thought, feeling, and perception for which industrial society allegedly has no use or to which it's allegedly hostile.

The trouble is, industrial society being what it is, the number of negative characteristics that can be attributed to it is likely to be very large, not to say mutually contradictory. Insofar as the features ascribed to literature are negatively determined by these characteristics, theories not only proliferate confusingly but collide in ways that resist arbitration. Take, for example, the many theories of literature as a vehicle of *order* in a society perceived to be overrun with anarchy and disorder. On the other side, place the equally numerous theories of literature as disrup-tion, defamiliarization, high-energy discharge, erotic release, and cogni-tive dissonance—in a society perceived as *all too* orderly, regimented, dominated by stock perceptions and categories. When theorists holding these antithetical views of literature enter into disputes, one can see why they usually have difficulty advancing beyond assertion and counter-assertion. In the first place, these theorists may be arguing not, as they suppose, about the nature of literature so much as about what conception of the nature of literature (or what type of literature) is most pertinent to the condition of society as they see it. In the second place, since the condition of society is arguably *both* too orderly and too disorderly, any dispute in which we have to choose between one or the other diagnosis is likely to be confused. Unless the disputants recognize the way the sociological issue has displaced the literary one, they are likely to go on talking at cross-purposes.

In similar disputes over the referentiality or nonreferentiality of literature there is often a tendency on both sides to let the debate hinge on the social consequences that can be claimed for one theory or the other. Much of the opposition to referential theories has rested on the feeling that it's not a good thing for society if literature is taken as a form of referential discourse, since that promotes philistinism, narrow moralism, and, for some critics, retrograde politics. On the other side, such political arguments are simply reversed, so that literature's referentiality is defended on the ground that it's not a good thing for society if literature is *not* permitted to make reference to reality. Formalist theories are then attacked not because they are theoretically indefensible as accounts of literary communication (which they may or may not be) but because they have a trivializing educational or cultural effect. Having made much capital myself of this "trivialization" argument against formalism, I hasten to add that the argument may be perfectly legitimate in the relevant context. Where it falls short is where it claims to refute the truth of formalist theory. Then attempts at debate tend to founder, since what has come to be at issue is no longer the nature of literature but rather the kinds of educational or cultural values that literature ought to help encourage.

Perhaps no account of literary communication can have the neutrality of a scientific analysis. But it seems possible to distinguish between a more or less descriptive understanding of literary conventions (perhaps in their changing historical configurations) and a polemical defense of the convention that is arguably most pertinent to a particular cultural situation. That we use the term "literary theory" to cover these very different projects points up an ambiguity. Historically, literary theory has vacillated between academic detachment and cultural engagement. Its contemporary forms have evolved partly from a tradition of philosophical aesthetics, which seeks disinterestedly to extract the general principles of literature and the arts, and partly from a tradition of cultural criticism, which seeks diagnoses and prescriptions for the urgent problems of modernity. Describing this latter impulse, Irving Howe observes:

> In a secular age literary criticism carries a heavy burden of intention, becoming a surrogate mode of speech for people blocked in public life. Unable to fulfill directly their visions of politics, morality, and religion, critics transfer these to the seemingly narrower channels of literary criticism. Precisely this spilling over of thought and passion has made criticism so interesting in our time—so perilous, too. The dominant formal claim of modern criticism has been an insistence upon treating literature as autonomous; the main actual circumstance for writing criticism has been a pressure for extraliterary connections. Ever since Arnold found that reflecting upon the place of poetry in an industrial society led him to worry about "a girl named Wragg," the most valuable critics have often doubled as cultural spokesmen, moral prophets, political insurgents.[13]

This drive toward prophecy and insurgency produces a criticism that wants to affect and alter the way literature is written and received—by contrast with the academic tradition which professes to describe from the sidelines and to let the chips fall where they may. An academic avant-gardism arises which makes perpetual revision of the definition of literature a criterion of value, so that no writer (and, by extension, no critic) can claim serious attention who doesn't reinvent the very idea of literature with every new work. What result from this mix of academic detachment and avant-garde passion are theories which present themselves as empirical accounts of the nature of literature yet clearly aim to save or change the world. This is heady mix, but one whose elements need some sorting out if there is to be more instructive controversy than has been produced so far.

It's not a question of purifying literary discourse of politics. Even if that could be done—which is doubtful—it would only result in eliminating the very aspect of our recent theoretical disputes which makes them vital and absorbing. When literary criticism and other forms of professionalism became so introverted that they ceased to take stock of their relations to society, rude political questions became salutary. The critics of the forties and fifties, in their reaction against the vulgar Marxism of the thirties, often went so far as to divorce literature and criticism from all social concerns. The current tendency to totalize the concepts of power and politics represents a swing of the pendulum toward the opposite extreme. Given a choice between an apolitical criticism that refuses to permit the questions of politics to arise (or relegates them to the status

13. Irving Howe, *A Margin of Hope: An Intellectual Autobiography* (New York, 1982), p. 147.

of the "extraliterary") and a pseudo-political criticism that poses these questions in misleading ways, one would have to choose the latter. At least the questions are kept alive, and corrections in the ways of dealing with them can be made.

But the conditions which have bred the impulse to totalize politics and power are deeper and more permanent than talk of pendulum-swings implies. Professional work in the humanities, the vocational setting in which most criticism is now done, has come to feel more desperately private and devoid of apparent social context than ever before. Even when they are couched in highly esoteric terminology, current attempts to politicize criticism express a longing to recover a public function for critical work at a moment when that function has become abstract and attenuated. There *was* a "literary culture" once, and if its members were not central to their society they at least were bound together by the sense that what they had to say about that society had a chance to be listened to, if not put into practice. That critics no longer feel that this is so may explain the excesses of current ways of politicizing criticism. It also may explain why these excesses may be difficult to overcome.

Critical Inquiry (*Kritik*) in Clausewitz

Garry Wills

1. Wechselwirkung

Suppose that A is standing at a bar with his friend B and tells B, "I'll give you a dollar to fight the man on the other side of you" (C). B, naturally, answers: "Are you crazy? Even if I win, I'll probably tear my clothes, or mess them up. A dollar wouldn't even cover the dry-cleaning bill." B is very sensible.

But then C starts to pick up B's change on the bar—about a dollar's worth. "You can't do that," B assures him, emphatically. C says, "Who says?" "Oh yeah?"'s get traded, then shoulders pushed in rotation—and, before you know it, B is fighting for a dollar after all.

But now, B will assure us, the money does not matter, it's the principle of the thing. What principle? "That no one can steal from me, no matter what the amount." But the man picking up the change thought it was his; no principle about stealing existed in his mind. "Well, I don't want the idea to get around that anyone can take things from me." So C is suffering proleptically for all the people who might feel tempted to engage in C-like activities (the deterrence theory of punishment). But what if C's calamity does not get around to all the bars? What, that is, if future Cs do not know about the educational improvements B has effected on C's nose? "They might not know, but I would." B, it appears, can have no pride in himself unless he fights over one-dollar misunderstandings.

But all B's principle mongering does not convince us, the onlookers, who saw the flush on his face, the fire in his eyes, by the third or fourth shoulder pushing. The cash didn't matter, and the principle didn't matter, at that moment—just the vivid memory of C's last shove. We have observed in action what Carl von Clausewitz, in *On War,* called the dynamics of warfare considered in itself, the interplay of opponents that drives them mutually toward a maximum effort, regardless of the initial motive for fighting or the ultimate object.[1] If one could control one's own actions, keep emotions subject to reason, war could be guided without waste effort or self-defeating excess. But the process of war is not simply a transaction with oneself, a war of one's passions with one's reason. The process is reciprocal, a *mutual* altering, one of the other (*Wechselwirkung*), which works each side up, ratchet by ratchet, toward the absolute in violence (*zum Äussersten*). The shoulder pushings become their own reason for existing, and of their nature they escalate.

Clausewitz gives three examples of this *Wechselwirkung* in *On War* (1.1.3). In the first, hostile emotion (*Gefühl*) continually outruns hostile intent (*Ansicht*). This is not an accident or side effect of war but part of its essence. Popular hostility (*Hass*) is the necessary fuel for the dangerous work of war: *Hass* is as much the people's contribution as maneuver is the field commander's and strategy is the statesman-general's.[2] Without all these, the vast apparatus of war could not be heaved into motion. But these factors are at odds with each other. Hatred outruns the nice calculations of maneuver, as immediate tactical advantage tugs against the overall demands of strategy. Clausewitz continually mocks any effort to make of war "a kind of algebra" (1.1, p. 76). He would make short work of all modern game theory that depends on the assumption of rational actors calculating their next step for cold advantage. War is, first of all, at war with the rationality of its own

1. See Carl von Clausewitz, *On War,* ed. and trans. Michael Howard and Peter Paret (Princeton, N.J., 1976), based on the 1st ed. (Berlin, 1832) of *Vom Kriege;* all further references to this translation will be included in the text, with book, chapter, section (where available), and page numbers in parentheses. I rely heavily on Paret's *Yorck and the Era of Prussian Reform* (Princeton, N.J., 1966) and *Clausewitz and the State* (Oxford, 1976).
2. For a Clausewitzian analysis of America's effort in Vietnam, which blames defeat on the failure to engage Americans' *Hass,* see Harry G. Summers, Jr., *On Strategy: A Critical Analysis of the Vietnam War* (Novato, Calif., 1982).

Garry Wills, a prize-winning author and journalist, is Henry R. Luce Professor of American Culture and Public Policy at Northwestern University. Among his many books are *Nixon Agonistes* (1970), *Inventing America* (1978), *Explaining America* (1981), and *The Kennedy Imprisonment* (1982). His *Cincinnatus: George Washington in the Enlightenment* is forthcoming.

participants. One is led to substitute the immediate for the ultimate, the personal for the social, the target for the goal, the means for the end. In this way, the least responsible enemy becomes the most actively hated.

> Even where there is no national hatred and no animosity to start with, the fighting itself will stir up hostile feelings: violence committed on superior orders will stir up the desire for revenge and retaliation against the perpetrator rather than against the powers that ordered the action. That is only human (or animal, if you like), but it is a fact. Theorists are apt to look on fighting in the abstract as a trial of strength without emotion entering into it. [2.2, p. 138]

The lowliest soldier on the other side is the immediate target of the fighting man's hatred, even though that soldier is just as surprised and resentful at being on the front line as his enemy is. But he (or someone beside him or just like him) killed one's friend, took a village, raped a woman, tortured a captive. So one reciprocates those outrages, even at the cost of one's own long-term advantage. Captives are tortured in retaliation, though this breaks down the convention that protects one's own people when taken prisoner.

Hatred assimilates each side to the other, the *Wechselwirkung* becomes an oscillation as well as a mutuality, each side *becoming* the other as the sides work each other up to a resemblance in extremism. There is even an altruism of hatred, in which the other becomes more important than the self. One is willing to give one's own life in order to take the foe's. This is the selflessness that gives war its weird and inverted nobility. It is, in Clausewitz's view, a necessary mark of fighting men. But it is hardly rational; and it offers the most spectacular example of the way one's immediate target in war (*Ziel*), the hurting of the foe, tends to displace the larger social purpose (*Zweck*) for which the nation mobilized itself in the first place. The former intrudes itself (*vertrit*) and extrudes (*verdränkt*) the latter (1.1.2). The paradoxical result is that when we are most exalted by hostility and have the greatest sense of wielding war to serve our purposes, war is wielding us, carrying us away from ourselves in the nobility of self-sacrifice inspired by hate. Shoulder shoving, on the largest scale, has become an end in itself.

Clausewitz suggests a second way in which the mutual stimulation to a maximum effort takes place automatically. Where a state of hostility exists, "deterrence" becomes provocation. Each side's defensive measures become offensive to the other side. Any move taken to keep oneself invulnerable is perceived by the foe as removing power from him, an act that must be redressed. Perfect security for one side makes the other feel insecure. To place myself outside your power is to rob you of power, until I am placed back within your power:

> So long as I have not overthrown my opponent I am bound to fear

he may overthrow me. Thus I am not in control: he dictates to me as much as I dictate to him. This is the *second case of interaction and it leads to the second "extreme."* [1.1.4, p. 77]

Any attempt to justify to oneself the *purely* defensive nature of one's arms implicitly denies the *Wechselwirkung* that war involves by its very nature. The history of the cold war and the arms race is summed up in this second instance from Clausewitz. Both the official and the revisionist interpretations of the cold war were flawed insofar as they tried to blame just one side for the escalating hostilities. Each side wrought upon the other, turn by turn, in an interplay of two irrationalities.

A third way war works itself up toward the absolute use of force is the calculation of enemy intent from enemy means. One can estimate quantitatively the resources of a foe. "But the strength of his will is much less easy to determine and can only be gauged approximately by the strength of the motive animating it" (1.1.5, p. 77). Even the judging of resources is affected by emotion, since "men are always more inclined to pitch their estimate of the enemy's strength too high than too low, such is human nature" (1.1.18, p. 85). In this way we construct "missile gaps" faster than the enemy can construct missiles. And, naturally, the enemy's intent and willpower are less visible than his resources; so we over-estimate them in much larger degree—this is called the "worst-case" scenario. If we must presume the worst in order to be prepared for anything, then the slightest increase in enemy resources must be read as part of a larger design being implemented. Even a cutback in one area will be read as an economy called for by greater expenditure elsewhere. The worst-case scenario adopted by one side leads to countermeasures on the other side, and by this interplay the opponents *effect* the worst they were trying to deflect. *Wechselwirkung* means that each side infects the other with suspicion and then hastens to confirm what is suspected. In this way disarmament proposals themselves become aggressions, their "real" intent to be deciphered through lenses of mutual suspicion.

So far we have been considering, under Clausewitz's guidance, the internal dynamics of war considered in itself, abstracted from the obstructive conditions which it must rub up against in actual operation. For it is typical of Clausewitz that he does not think the rational *goal* can reassert itself against the intruding *target* without the help of conflicting irrational forces. As each opponent ratchets himself higher on the scale of violence, notch by notch, an attritive rub up against difficulties slows the process. And the longer the succession of escalations, the greater becomes the contrary drag of friction. One simply cannot mobilize all one's forces instantly, at one spot, to give the absolute blow that will obliterate an enemy. Time and space militate against the abstract unity of war considered in itself.

Here is a corollary of the paradox of power we have already considered: to conduct war successfully, a commander must often fight his own side's fighting spirit, wrestle it back into constructive channels. He is aided in this by the very difficulties that impede his way. He must cooperate with his own problems in order to make his men succeed and at the same time thwart those same men. This seems anomalous, but it is a commonplace. A commander must check rash aggression as well as cowardly panic—must, for instance, insure proper treatment of prisoners if his own side is to profit by the conventions of war.

The conflict with one's own troops has been a staple of our cold war. President Harry Truman was told by Senator Arthur Vandenberg that he could get support for the Truman Doctrine only by scaring the hell out of the country. This aroused the *Hass* of warfare in a time of peace, to make possible the infringement of civil rights and the Constitution (e.g., the Attorney General's List and the secretly funded covert activities of the CIA) which is permitted in time of war but frowned on in more peaceful days. Yet once Truman had put in place the machinery for fighting communism *his* way, he found he had created the instruments for Joseph McCarthy to fight it *his* way. Then, like Dr. Frankenstein, Truman had to denounce the use of procedures he had himself established. His war against communism became, of necessity, a war against anti-Communists of too inflamed a hatred. He had to *unscare* the hell out of the country; but he realized that too late.

Ben Bradlee, asked why his friend John Kennedy could not openly trade our obsolete missiles in Turkey to remove Russian missiles from Cuba, said that had the president done so, "the country would have thought him yellow." Robert Kennedy agreed; he thought his brother would have been impeached. The *Hass* of war had outrun the intentions of those who first unleashed it. John Kennedy had denounced Dwight D. Eisenhower for losing Cuba and had called for support of freedom fighters in that country. Eugene Rostow argued in *New Yorker* interviews that the missiles had to be removed or the American people would have reacted in an even more violent way. The leader must be *therapeutically* bellicose, as a first step toward reducing the fevers of the disordered popular mind.

But this is often a self-defeating task. Preemptive bellicosity, instead of putting out the popular fires, fans them. The history of the cold war in America is largely a matter of Democrats taking a hard line against communism in order to undercut Republican claims to be the true anti-Communists. But instead the Democrats have only legitimized all the stances and procedures taken against the "internal threat." The Americans for Democratic Action (ADA) created an informal blacklist to purge the Democratic party of Henry Wallace's supporters. Far from precluding similar Republican blacklists, the action stimulated them.

Henry Kissinger liked to say that his efforts in Vietnam were meant to head off a new McCarthyism, more virulent than the first, which would emerge from any "defeat" in Indochina. *Who lost Vietnam?* was the cry that haunted his nightmares. The war made no sense in terms of permanent results achievable in Asia. But it *had* to go on, to pacify the warriors at home.

The danger inherent in the need to control one's own troops is that one will make *them* an enemy. If that happens, the *Wechselwirkung* of war will take place internally, working up both sides automatically to an ever more bellicose stand. Anticommunism becomes a prize to be wrested from the other side domestically, and accusations escalate as the foes become more divided by becoming more similar—the ADA and the Republican party each claiming *it* nurtured *true* anticommunism, while the other side traitorously gave the Communists an advantage.

A perfect example of such internal *Wechselwirkung* is the way Richard Nixon's administration had to keep the public in the dark over the bombing of Cambodia. The official explanation for this was a rather touching regard for Prince Sihanouk's sensibilities (touching because Nixon and Kissinger showed so little concern for Sihanouk before that time). But Kissinger's first volume of memoirs makes it apparent that the real threat came from the American populace, which would have indulged in troublesome demonstrations against such a development.[3] But when knowledge of the bombing became public, the anticipated resentment was actually increased—the offense of bombing had been exacerbated by the deception. So, ratchet by ratchet, the war within the war increased, the opposition between the leaders and their balking followers. According to Clausewitz, the very simplicity of war considered in itself leads to endless contradiction and paradox when this rational unleashing of irrational forces takes place in real time and space.

2. Friktion

My father was, for a while, a college boxing coach; and he liked to impress people with the ordeal of simply being in a boxing ring, even before an opponent's assault, by asking them to dance around, throwing fake punches off and on, for three minutes. That is enough to exhaust most nonathletes. He mercifully did not ask them to repeat the exercise

3. The secret bombing was made to substitute for the first choice, a public bombing of North Vietnam, which was rejected for fear of demonstrations. See Henry Kissinger, *The White House Years* (Boston, 1979), p. 245: "On March 4 I passed on to the President without comment a Laird memo recommending against proposals by the Joint Chiefs to attack North Vietnam. Laird was far from a 'dove'; in normal circumstances his instincts were rather on the bellicose side. He would have preferred to aim for victory. But he was also a careful student of the public and Congressional mood."

three times, or ten, or fifteen, as fighters must. Merely "doing the time" wears one down.

Even that was not a fair demonstration of the demands on a boxer. Before any blow is struck, energy is consumed in concentration, wariness, anticipation of the foe's moves. Danger, of itself, takes a toll, in apprehension or despair, in heightened alertness or the racing of one's pulse. And danger, says Clausewitz, is the very air one breathes in war. It charges the atmosphere, giddying a person, unsettling judgment. "It is an exceptional man who keeps his powers of quick decision intact if he has never been through this experience before" (1.4, p. 113). Admittedly, one can become accustomed to danger and grow steadier under assault; but this takes place over time, and time exacts its own price: the mind being cleared of fear is increasingly beset by fatigue. In the thirteenth or fourteenth round of a fight, the boxer has proved his powers of endurance but expended in the process some of his powers of concentration and quick response: "If no one had the right to give his views on military operations except when he is frozen, or faint from heat and thirst, or depressed from privation and fatigue, objective and accurate views would be even rarer than they are. But they would at least be subjectively valid, for the speaker's experience would precisely determine his judgment" (1.5, p. 115).

All of these considerations come into play before an opponent has the chance to strike a blow. Even if one *could* dance for fifteen three-minute rounds, throwing arms that get increasingly sluggish, it is hard to imagine what that effort would entail if the arms had been catching blows and meeting a resistant target; if one's breathing, labored already, had been interfered with by pummeling about the lungs and ribs; if one's eyes, veiled with sweat, were puffed as well; if one's concentration were rattled by occasional explosive contacts around the head and face. If one has been winning over the longer part of the fighting, even that achievement eats at one. Muhammad Ali understood this when he adopted his "rope-a-dope" strategy of letting a foe punch himself out. Given a set of conditions controllable as Ali controlled them, it can hurt a fighter more to hit than to be hit.

More than anyone, perhaps, but Tolstoy, Clausewitz understood that the very *conditions* of war tend to break down the effective *conduct* of war.[4] Movement, coordination, intelligence, and supply grind up the

---

4. There is a striking similarity between Tolstoy's description of Pierre on the field at Borodino in *War and Peace* and this passage from *On War:*

> Let us accompany a novice to the battlefield. As we approach, the rumble of guns grows louder and alternates with the whir of cannonballs, which begin to attract his attention. Shots begin to strike close around us. We hurry up the slope where the commanding general is stationed with his large staff. Here cannonballs and bursting shells are frequent, and life begins to seem more serious than the young man had imagined. Suddenly someone you know is wounded; then a shell falls among the staff. You notice that some of the officers act a little oddly; you

machinery even before it comes into contact with an enemy. Danger, uncertainty, error—lapses at one point tangling affairs all down the line—all these take a toll on the *way* to battle and then double or triple that toll *in* battle. "Everything in war is very simple, but the simplest thing is difficult. The difficulties accumulate and end by producing a kind of friction that is inconceivable unless one has experienced war." Even the effort to *overcome* the friction of motion *increases* that friction, by a kind of Catch-22: "Iron will-power can overcome this friction; it pulverizes every obstacle, but of course *it wears down the machine as well*" (italics mine). Friction must be anticipated by the wise commander, who never expects a paper maneuver to be replicated on the battlefield. That, says Clausewitz, would be like expecting to "walk through" an exercise on land—and then perform the same motions, rapidly and well, under water. "Action in war is like movement in a resistant element. Just as the simplest and most natural of movements, walking, cannot easily be performed in water, so in war it is difficult for normal efforts to achieve even moderate results" (1.7, pp. 119, 120).[5]

But the commander should also take friction into account as an *ally* against the internal dynamics of warfare, which lead to unwanted extremes. If *Wechselwirkung* works opponents up to an extreme pitch in three ways, there are three contrary forces of gravitation that tug the "ideal" of destruction back toward a less obliterative reality. Although hostile feeling tends to outrun hostile intent, it takes time for the emotions to become inflamed. There is the preliminary shoulder pushing to be done; and at this early stage the rational goal is not sufficient to make people fight (it is only a dollar on the bar, after all): "In the fiery climate of war, ordinary natures tend to move more ponderously; stronger and

---

yourself are not as steady and collected as you were: even the bravest can become slightly distracted. Now we enter the battle raging before us, still almost like a spectacle, and join the nearest divisional commander. Shot is falling like hail, and the thunder of our own guns adds to the din. Forward to the brigadier, a soldier of acknowledged bravery, but he is careful to take cover behind a rise, a house or a clump of trees. A noise is heard that is a certain indication of increasing danger—the rattling of grapeshot on roofs and on the ground. Cannonballs tear past, whizzing in all directions, and musketballs begin to whistle around us. A little further we reach the firing line, where the infantry endures the hammering for hours with incredible steadfastness. The air is filled with hissing bullets that sound like a sharp crack if they pass close to one's head. For a final shock, the sight of men being killed and mutilated moves our pounding hearts to awe and pity.

The novice cannot pass through these layers of increasing intensity of danger without sensing that here ideas are governed by other factors, that the light of reason is refracted in a manner quite different from that which is normal in academic speculation. [1.4, p. 113]

5. Though Clausewitz rejects *"jargon, technicalities and metaphors"* (2.5, p. 168), some of his most important concepts are enforced by unforgettable similes or metaphors, like this image of *Friktion* as walking through water. His most frequent metaphors are taken from economic transactions (see n. 15 below). In bk. 5, chap. 7 he compares an army's range of fire to a man's arms and its advance guard to his eyes—the simile gives us, at one stroke, his whole teaching on the uses of the advance guard.

more frequent stimuli are therefore needed to ensure that momentum is maintained. To understand why the war is being fought [its *Zweck*] is seldom sufficient in itself to overcome this ponderousness" (3.16, p. 217). Even to accomplish his *Zweck,* the commander must stimulate a hostility toward the *Ziel* that may threaten, further down the road, his larger purpose. There is an interplay of two momentums here, one stationary, one mobile. Each can be invoked only at the other's peril. The commander who launches the mechanical effort needed to overcome friction, to put the machinery into motion, may be dismayed when mechanics gives way to chemistry and the moving force ignites:

> The same political object can elicit *differing* reactions from different peoples, and even from the same people at different times. We can therefore take the political object as a standard only if we think of *the influence it can exert upon the forces it is meant to move.* The nature of those forces therefore calls for study. Depending on whether their characteristics increase or diminish the drive toward a particular action, the outcome will vary. Between two peoples and two states there can be such tensions, such a mass of inflammable material, that the slightest quarrel can produce a wholly disproportionate effect—a real explosion. [1.1.11, p. 81][6]

In such a case a commander will welcome any drag of friction that slows down the explosion outward of his forces.

Clausewitz's second example of an escalating *Wechselwirkung* is the way defensive moves are apprehended as offensive by the other side. This very suspicion brings with it a caution about the unknown. Fearing a blow, one pauses to parry it, and the action is slowed: "We hardly know accurately our own situation at any particular moment, while the enemy's, which is concealed from us, must be deduced from very little evidence" (3.16, p. 217).

The third form of escalation described by Clausewitz is based on the overestimation of hostile intent from enemy resources; but that, too, tends to throw a combatant on the defensive. Each side would like the advantage of a battle on its own turf. The result is a period of standoff: "It therefore happens that both sides at the same time not only feel too weak for an offensive, but that they really are too weak" (3.16, p. 218).

Strategic thinking in modern America seems based on an almost deliberate denial of all those factors making up what Clausewitz calls friction. Perhaps the most spectacular assault on that concept was mounted by John Kennedy, whose inaugural address proclaimed that America could "pay *any* price, bear any burden, meet any hardship, support any friend, oppose *any* foe" (italics mine), if, in each troubled

---

6. This passage combines two of the most important kinds of metaphor in the book: mechanical (e.g., the image involved in *Friktion*) and chemical (see 3.18 on explosions underground and in the air).

spot, we used just enough force and never too much. It was Robert McNamara's task to calibrate, with his fine tools, just the proper minimal response to any challenge. If we were to do everything, we must not do anything wastefully. Against the profligate doctrine of massive retaliation, the economical doctrine of flexible response was advanced. We were henceforth to play from our strength, our technology, our sophisticated communications, our new devices of "psywar," the paramilitary, the CIA, counterinsurgent forces, guerrillas, and the Green Berets.

Clausewitz treated the whole idea of minimal force as a delusion: "The first rule, therefore, should be: put the largest possible army into the field. This may sound like a platitude, but in reality it is not" (3.8, p. 195). There may be a *successive* engagement of forces at the tactical level, and reserves should be maintained, so long as they are *intended to be used,* but the real meaning of economy in war is to make sure *everything* gets used. In strategic terms "we can never use too great a force" (3.12, p. 207). Massive superiority will end the engagement more rapidly, costing less in the long run. The idea of success with minimum forces leads to local breakdowns, because of friction, which need larger efforts to retrieve one's first losses. Battle, Clausewitz makes clear, is such an important investment of any society's resources that *it cannot be allowed to fail.* This is what makes Clausewitz say that, at the tactical level, "battle exists for its own sake alone" (4.9, p. 248). It is a life-or-death struggle for those involved, and no relevant supporting power is felt to be "too much."[7]

The outright defiance of such considerations led immediately to the Bay of Pigs, where the CIA—forswearing the normal coordination of large forces of the army, navy, and air force—ran by itself an amphibious invasion, the kind of maneuver that must allow the widest margins for friction, for difficulties of navigation, communication, landing, and assembly. Then, to top it all, the president himself demanded a *night* landing, which thus multiplied the difficulties: "Conditions rarely provide a night attack with much promise of success," even on land (4.7, p. 241).[8] Friction began grinding up the Bay of Pigs operation even before it could reach the shore. Ships crashed on unseen reefs; air cover was neutralized by unforeseen enemy craft; and all the heavy communications equipment went down in a single ship. The operation was run with such little prevision of accident that there was no plan for taking the defeated troops off the beach.

---

7. Nuclear weapons, supposedly designed as deterrents that will never be used in battle, conflict with Clausewitz's notion that all forces should be used. Whether one reflects on this conflict to indict Clausewitz or to indict deterrence theory depends on arguments outside my immediate train of thought.

8. See the entirety of bk. 4, chap. 14, stressing this conclusion: "In a night operation, then, the attacker seldom if ever knows enough about the defense to make up for his lack of visual observation" (p. 273).

The illusion that one can undertake large tasks with small forces persisted into the Vietnam War, where "surgical" strikes and "innovative" techniques were meant to make up for the difficulties of combat in an alien setting ten thousand miles from home. If the gritty realities of the scene resisted such efforts, then modern science would just have to remake the scene. Did forests give the enemy cover? Defoliate them. Were hamlets hard to hold? Relocate them. Troops continued to pour down from North Vietnam? Try to build an electronic barrier to stop them. Move our troops around in rapid helicopter maneuvers. Give them rapid-firing M-16s. The grit got in the gears, and did so more effectively the more gears there were to be plagued by friction.

The attempt to perform a large military assignment with minimal tools reached a sadly hilarious climax in Jimmy Carter's raid to rescue the Americans held captive in Iran. Luckily, the helicopters broke down early enough so that all the *other* things bound to go wrong with that raid did not get a chance to occur. Friction very literally ground up the only-marginally-sufficient helicopter force, so the rest of the only-marginally-sufficient parts of that plan were happily canceled.

Clausewitz argued that a commander can sometimes put friction to use in reordering war toward its rightful goals. Nixon, of all people, offered an example of that in the controversy over the American plane shot down by North Koreans early in his first term. Kissinger advised a bellicose response; but Nixon argued that the difficulties involved in the concurrent war with Vietnam made such action unprofitable. Despite his own criticism of Lyndon Johnson's inaction during the Pueblo incident, Nixon used the argument from friction to achieve restraint.

By contrast, Gerald Ford *did* heed Kissinger's pleas for rapid action when Cambodians captured the U.S.S. *Mayaguez*. Though release of the prisoners through negotiation had every prospect of success, our thirty-nine men were hastily recovered (at the risk of their lives during combat) while forty-one men perished through the friction of battle and an air accident.

When President Kennedy discovered the presence of Russian land-to-land missiles in Cuba, he wanted to launch a surprise attack on their sites—what his own brother called a Pearl Harbor. The air force told the president they could not guarantee the destruction of all missiles in a single raid. Kennedy could have used this estimate of war's uncertainties to justify a negotiated settlement of the crisis involving a trade for our obsolete missiles in Turkey. Instead he issued an ultimatum that was reckless, one he fortunately did not have to deliver on because of the Russians' restraint.

The denial of friction has led to a regular underestimate of the cost for our postwar policy of global arbitrament. In Vietnam the military early on came up with large estimates of the tools necessary for protecting the Saigon regime—massive manpower and bombing and mining. Advocates of the "civilian solution" pooh-poohed this and tried to do the job with advisers and experts. Their failure involved, by the end, all the horrors the military had envisaged and still did not meet with success. It is obvious that Americans would not have supported entry into the Vietnam War if they had known the scale of military effort this would eventually entail. But we could not foresee it because of our denial of friction in military engagements. By the paradox that friction helps as well as hurts, our problems could have been our allies if we had recognized them as such. Instead, we dismissed them, for a time, till they returned to exact redoubled payment from us.

3. Kritik

Tactics, according to Clausewitz, relate to the conduct of an engagement. Strategy looks to the *use* of the engagement. The instrument for judging such uses is *Kritik,* the subject of one of Clausewitz's most carefully wrought and important chapters, book 2 chapter 5. *Kritik* is not dogma (*Lhere*). Nor is it theory, though it uses and tests the theories considered most workable up to the point of actual analysis. *Kritik* moves simultaneously in two directions, down into the actual details of the engagement and up to ever higher levels for judging that single clash. This rise to an ever higher *Standpunkt* is not an ascent into theory. Rather, it is the search for a vantage point from which to view larger *areas* of the actual. It does not desert particularity but takes in more of it. The metaphor implicit all through this chapter is that of seeking "higher ground" to see the army's engagement in its total context.[9] One rises above the particular battlefield to see the field in its theater, the theater in its campaign, the campaign in the war, and the war in the overall statecraft of the warring nation. In an elegant demonstration of the way *Kritik* changes as it rises, and must therefore keep rising until no higher vantage point is reachable, Clausewitz analyzes the events leading up to the Treaty of Campo Formio in 1797. Why, with the Austrians on the run, did Napoleon stop his pursuit and sign the cease-fire of Leoben? On the tactical level, says Clausewitz, this made no sense; and Napoleon was at first determined to force the Austrians back through the Alps so he could join the French armies on the Rhine. But the French Directory,

9. The critic's knowledge of the whole scene is an extension of the commander's grasp of topical particularities.

> A hussar or scout leading a patrol must find his way easily among the roads and tracks. All he needs are a few landmarks and some modest powers of observation and imagination. A commander-in-chief, on the other hand, must aim at acquiring an overall knowledge of the configuration of a province, of an entire country. His mind must hold a vivid picture of the road-network, the river-lines and the mountain ranges, without ever losing a sense of his immediate surroundings. [1.3, p. 110]

says Clausewitz, was taking a wider view. It knew the French at the Rhine would not be up to fighting force for another six weeks. Napoleon, chasing the Austrians toward the river, would be driving them into the arms of their fellows, joined with whom they could have destroyed the army of Italy. Napoleon came to see this, and that is why he signed the cease-fire.

But "if the critic takes a still wider view," he sees that Napoleon did not have to move toward the Rhine once he had crossed the Alps. He could have taken Vienna, which lay exposed to his advance. With that for prize, he might have imposed peace on his terms. From this third standpoint, Napoleon had reason to continue his campaign.

But what if the Austrians had surrendered their capital, like the Russians fifteen years later, and withdrawn into Austria's vast countryside? Could Napoleon, with help from the (presumably) victorious French forces on the Rhine, defeat the Austrian force as it evanesced over distances? If the French, drawn that far in, failed to bring about the total collapse of Austria, "the mere attempt to do so would have reversed the situation and even the conquest and occupation . . . would have placed the French in a strategic situation with which their forces could hardly have coped" (2.5, p. 160). So, having achieved this fourth and final standpoint, Napoleon moved from the cease-fire of Leoben to the Treaty of Campo Formio.[10] He did not exact all that he might from the Austrians; he did not want to harden their resistance. He negotiated not so much from strength as from his consideration of the balance of weaknesses that a prolonged campaign would bring about. In all this, Clausewitz implies, Napoleon showed a wisdom he no longer possessed by the time of the Russian campaign.[11]

Clausewitz has, clearly, chosen his example to demonstrate that *Kritik* not only alters judgments made "at ground level" but can *reverse* them. As he rises from the first judgment to the fourth in this discussion of Campo Formio, each higher judgment reverses the one made at the immediately lower level. In the most important decision (not to take Vienna), Clausewitz argues against conquest for its own sake. A tactical advantage that cannot be used for the state's larger purposes is a strategic setback. A strategist must judge conquest in terms of control. To take what one cannot put to use is wasteful, if not self-defeating.

Measuring the ratio between conquest and control is important to the realists of power, as opposed to the romanticists. Victory must never

10. Clausewitz seems not to have known about the bargaining for tenure of Venice that went into the Treaty of Campo Formio. His principle would be the same, however—that *Kritik* goes on so long as one can reach a standpoint that brings into view more relevant particulars.

11. Clausewitz devotes a whole chapter of *On War* to the errors of Napoleon's Russian campaign (6.25) and mentions it frequently throughout: see, e.g., pp. 166, 208, 220, 266, 269, 283, 324, 340, 365, 385, 460, 466, 467, 518–19, and 582.

exist for its own sake at the strategic (as opposed to the tactical) level. Machiavelli maintained that ease of conquest and ease of control are often in inverse relationship: "Comparing one state with the other, one would find it very hard to acquire the Turkish realm, yet easy to rule it after conquest. . . . But the contrary is true of realms like France."[12] Where efforts at control drain strength from the state, one can lose by winning—a truth Clayton Fritchey tried to convey to President Kennedy after the Bay of Pigs disaster: "It could have been worse. It could have succeeded."[13]

To judge when victories are really useful and which ones are most useful, one must understand "linkage" in Clausewitz's sense (very different from Kissinger's):

> It follows that in addition to theoretical insight into the subject, natural talent will greatly enhance the value of critical analysis: for it will primarily depend on such talent to illuminate the connections which link things together [der Zusammenhang der Dinge] and to determine which among the countless concatenations [Verknüpfungen] of events are the essential ones. [2.5, p. 161]

This calls for a discrimination between what is important and what not; what really connects, what merely distracts. Kritik sees through apparent gain or loss to real gains or losses. For Kissinger, by contrast, "linkage" was the calibration of all acts along a single scale of judgment: Did they show more or less of hostility in response to Russian shows of hostility? This policy was based on the perception of our relations as a zero-sum game—whatever Russia loses, we win, and vice versa. We "lost" China when Russia "gained" it. We "lost" Vietnam, which had to be contended for simply because Russia would otherwise be seen as "gaining" it. Anything Russia wants, we must want. If Russia goes into Angola, through its Cuban surrogates, we must go into Angola. In the same way, we are to choose our allies by measurement on a single scale: their willingness to side with Russia or oppose Russia. It is utopian to consider any other norm. Opposition to Russia is sufficient qualification for our support.

For the same reason, we must oppose all movements the Russians, even indirectly, support; oppose, that is, many anticolonial or nationalist movements, from Indochina to the Philippines to El Salvador to South Africa. Linkage in this sense becomes a kind of simpleminded game: "If you're fit for it, I'm agin' it." Far from discriminating the countless Verknüpfungen, it flattens differences and erases distinctions.

Clausewitz attacked zero-sum theory, under the name Polarität, in his very first chapter, sections 15 through 18. He says such a theory rests

12. Machiavelli, Il Principe, ed. L. Arthur Burd (Oxford, 1891), pp. 201–2.
13. Clayton Fritchey, quoted in Harris Woffard, Of Kennedys and Kings (New York, 1980), p. 363.

on the fallacy of treating all military power as a single currency. Actually, advantages to one side are not convertible by trade into advantages for the other side—especially when one side is pursuing a policy of defense and the other of offense. Napoleon's taking Moscow was not the same thing as Kutuzov's taking Paris would have been. For the defensive strategy adopted by the Russians against Napoleon, the loss of Moscow, though sad, made little *military* difference. If anything, it hurt Napoleon by luring him deeper into the countryside that was his real enemy. If an opponent takes from me something I did not plan to use anyway, he is "stealing" coins of an obsolete currency. *Kritik* looks to real gains or losses.

Kissinger argued in 1968 that we must stay in Vietnam, regardless of our initial engagement's folly or wisdom, because we could not be *seen* as losing. That would destroy our "credibility." Logically, that means one can never withdraw from a venture, no matter how ill considered. Having shot oneself in the foot, one must take careful aim at the other foot to prove one cannot be intimidated. Our credibility grows as we keep alternating shots into our feet. Such "toughness" will "deter." Kissinger was applying on the national level the norms of another member of the Nixon administration, G. Gordon Liddy, who roasted his hand in a flame to prove how strong was his will.

In military terms, the Kissinger doctrine means that an army must always advance and never retire—though artful retreat can win a war as surely as foolish advance can lose it. Psychologically, the doctrine means that one must always assert one's power, even where such assertion is irrelevant or embarrassing (as when some argued that we must hold on to the Panama Canal *because* other people have resented our doing so, to prove they could not affect us). Conversely, we must not admit to weaknesses, even the universal and necessary limitations on all nations: unlike others, *we* can bear *any* burden, and will take on special burdens to prove that fact.

There is a loss of freedom as well as of critical discrimination in this code. If we have to be tough everywhere, we are not free to pick our targets. We have to stay in Vietnam. We can never cut our losses. We have to go into Angola. We can never forgo an opportunity to show our power. Napoleon, in Clausewitz's example, would have *had* to take Vienna. He could not consider that move from a higher viewpoint and then reject it. The loss of freedom through the assertion of power is a fascinating paradox, one implicit in Clausewitz's whole discussion of *Kritik*. The victor is turned into a victim by his own conquest over things he cannot control to useful purpose. He takes a city and loses the war. Even more striking is the loss of *freedom* in the assertion of power, the inability to turn away from challenge. President Kennedy was not free to be "yellow" over the Cuban missiles, so he "won" through the loss of his freedom to maneuver.

Consider an exasperated parent who issues an ultimatum to a child: "If you do not make your bed, you are not leaving this house." The child is stubborn and will not make the bed—even the next day when time comes for school. The parent, by asserting the power to confine a child physically, has frozen his or her will in the ultimatum and left the outcome up to the child. If the parent cannot lose credibility by backing down, the child is in effective command of future events. That is precisely the kind of ultimatum John Kennedy issued to the Russians. For the first time in our history, an American leader's act left the fate of our nation to another country's decision. The outcome was for Russia to decide. If its leaders had been stubborn or had gambled wrong, we would have been forced to respond, at great risk to ourselves and the world. It was for this "victory" that Kennedy forswore a negotiated settlement. Even while denouncing the Russians, Kennedy was gambling on their good sense, which alone saved the situation—an odd way to establish one's control over events.

Clausewitz's *Kritik* is at odds with Kissinger's views on the balance of power as much as with his view of linkage—and for the same reason: one man distinguishes, the other erases distinctions. The balance in Kissinger's terms is usually stated as the relationship of one superpower to the other, in terms of specific measurements like the number of nuclear warheads in each state's possession. The interplay of multiple factors affecting many nations is not looked at as a whole. Here is Clausewitz's statement of the balance of power as an abiding consideration among nations:

> If we consider the community of states in Europe today, we do not find a systematically regulated balance of power and of spheres of influence, which does not exist and whose existence has often been justifiably denied; but we certainly do find major and minor interests of states and peoples interwoven in the most varied and changeable manner. Each point of intersection [*Kreuzpunkt*] binds and serves to balance one set of interests against the other. The broad effect of all these fixed points [*Knoten*] is obviously to give a certain amount of cohesion [*Zusammenhang*] to the whole. Any change will necessarily weaken this cohesion to some degree. The sum total of relations between states thus serves to maintain the stability of the whole rather than to promote change; at least, that *tendency* will generally be present. [6.6, p. 373]

The image Clausewitz suggests is not so much that of a seesaw (the Kissinger image, with the Russians on one end and us on the other), or even of measuring pans on a balancing beam, but of many people in an unstable boat: when the weight shifts toward one side, various people, not necessarily acting in conjunction, will lean in the other direction, to steady the whole for one's own purposes. Thus, if one state seems to be growing too powerful, a ruler may follow Machiavelli's advice to side with other powers, weaker in themselves, who can mitigate the dominance of a single master. In this sense, supremacy tends to undo itself, to frighten others into resisting coalitions. Americans during our postwar period of ascendancy could not understand why the rest of the world did not dance to our tune. We had the power, didn't we? It did not occur to us that this might be the problem, that the very possession of so much power constricted its use. Instead, we decided that recalcitrant parts of the world were dancing to a rival tune, that of the worldwide Communist conspiracy. We feared we were losing an *ideological* war ("the war for men's minds") to a foe who was weaker economically and militarily. Third World and other nations were acting against their own interests (which we could foster) out of a fanatical creed that bound them to the Soviet Union.

The belief that people act out of a single "ism," not from a complex of national interests, leads to bizarre strategic acts. The British, for instance, were willing to invest many lives and great sums of money in the essentially valueless and untenable Falkland Islands to preserve the principle that aggressors should not get away with their acts. The enunciators of this position must imagine that evil nations, desirous of annexing property, sit around passively until they can say, "Ah, at last someone has established the principle of aggression, so we can act on it." According to this view, aggressors may have bad manners in other respects, but they are marvelously punctilious about precedent. They never attack until the *principle* of attack has been vindicated somewhere.

In reality, nations get away with whatever they feel they can, principle or no.[14] They shift when they feel that doing so tilts the whole boat in some way advantageous to them. If, by asserting a "principle" in the South Atlantic, England weakens NATO, losing military equipment designed for that alliance's use, it has, de facto, strengthened anti-NATO forces, no matter what principle was "established" on the Falklands. Our credibility in Vietnam did not deter other countries from "adventurism" (in Kissinger's phrase) so much as it weakened American willingness to intervene in foreign wars. Nations maneuver and fight for complex reasons of interest, not in response to a single principle or link or ism.

The usefulness of Clausewitz's tools of analysis can be demonstrated by looking at a contemporary construct like the "window of vulnerability" to see how vulnerable *it* is to the concepts refined in *On War*. The belief in a window of vulnerability involves the assumptions that (*a*),

14. This view of things, which might be called Machiavellian in the pejorative sense, has as much right to be called Washingtonian. In his own draft of the Farewell Address, George Washington wrote: "Whatever may be their professions, be assured fellow citizens—and the event will (as it always has) invariably prove—that nations, as well as individuals, act for their own benefit and not for the benefit of others, unless both interests happen to be assimilated" (*Washington's Farewell Address*, ed. V. H. Paltsits [New York, 1935], p. 169).

Russia would launch a ground strike at our ICBMs that could destroy them all; after which (*b*), we would not use our submarines and bombers to deliver the majority of our warheads that they carry; because (*c*), Russia would still have enough ICBMs to hit our cities in a second strike; so (*d*), we would be forced to do Russia's will, since we had "lost."

The three main concepts I discuss in this paper show how questionable are the assumptions of the "window" theory. The assumption that Russians can "take out" all our ICBMs with one strike, directed over the North Pole under conditions never tested, will be denied by any student of *Friktion* in war. It would take a miraculous freedom from error for all those missiles to be launched successfully and perform perfectly. Not even our space shots have performed perfectly, and they were single efforts on which all kinds of expertise and continuing attention were lavished. One rocket exploded on its pad and killed the astronauts inside. Would no Russian rockets, released by the hundreds, explode in their silos or veer from their course? Our air force could not even assure President Kennedy that the few missiles in Cuba were vulnerable to a single strike. Why would the Russians gamble the existence of their country on a plan where everything must work perfectly or nothing works at all? How could the Russians be sure there would not be some form of warning, allowing for an advance launch on our part or a launch while their missiles were still in flight? The Russians would have to assume not only a freedom from *Friktion* in their actions but a freedom from it on our side—assume, that is, that our commanders would not only respond with restraint but could get their orders heard and obeyed in a time of confusion and breakdown; assume that no accident or defiance would result in the use of our air or sea missiles.

But why, for that matter, should the Russians count on restraint? With thousands of Americans killed and radioactive clouds drifting across our continent, we would be the victims of the most violent shoulder push in history. What makes us so saintly that the normal *Wechselwirkung* of war would not make us respond with vindictive hatred rather than as rational actors? Why would we, in this position, trust the Russians who had just performed an act of savagery? That is, if the Russian "blackmail" demand were "Do *x* or we shall release our missiles," why should we suppose that, *x* having been done, the Russians would not release their missiles anyway? The level of *Hass* would at this point be so great that the Russians must assume we would be working toward a future in which our air and sea missiles could be used.

But what if the Russians' first demand was, precisely, to disarm the air and sea missiles? How would the Russians enforce such a demand? Would they take our word for it that we had complied? If not, would they send investigating teams to verify our response? Any remaining Americans would love to have such teams come within their grasp. Told to disarm their missiles, Americans would have to assume that the Russians would destroy the rest of the country once our missiles were removed, so why not launch them anyway? The threat to our cities *could* not be greater than it would be after the disarming. From the Russian point of view, such hatred would have to be obliterated before it could rebuild its means of vengeance, or team up with any other nuclear power left in place. *America delenda est* would be the only policy Russia could pursue, for its own good; but American recognition of that situation would prevent any "bargaining" of the sort imagined by window theorists.

In terms of *Kritik* and the balance of power, what *use* could the Soviet Union make of an ICBM strike? Would it make other nations docile to conventional repression and exploitation (when the Russians have trouble controlling the satellites within their immediate physical sphere)? If not, would the Russians proceed to annihilate country after country? In terms of the real balance of power, so destructive a nation on one side of the boat would nudge every other power toward the other side. The hypothetical ICBM strike would not even destroy all the American nuclear weapons. What would happen to the Chinese and French and British and Indian and Israeli weapons? Would the Russians be able to save enough missiles from its actual and threatened strikes at the United States to cope with some or all of these nations? Even if the Soviets could presume success in this complex and fragile sequence of moves, what advantage would they reap from poisoning the atmosphere of half the world, disrupting the economy of every remaining state (including those in its sphere)? Even to think in the surreal categories of the window theory is to separate conquest from control in the most absolute fashion. In this whole area, a return to sanity is only likely if we abandon the concepts of men like Kissinger and learn to think with refined analytical tools like those of Clausewitz.

4. Kritik *versus* Theorie

Clausewitz fashioned one of the most important post-Enlightenment critical methods. The eighteenth-century desire to create a science of human behavior, meeting with the Napoleonic wars, led Heinrich von Bülow to create a *geometry* of war (all based on points and angles) and led Antoine Jomini to create a *mechanics* of war (based on the movement of masses). Clausewitz, oddly, culminated this scientific movement by destroying its very bases. From the Enlightenment he inherited his empiricism, skepticism, and taxonomic ingenuity. But he was totally opposed to the ideal of creating a *theory* of war. In his eyes, the Napoleonic theorists had replaced Frederician dogma with new dogmas, ones whose general use was just as invalid as Frederick's had proved.

Though Clausewitz liked to compare war to the young science of economics, to politics, and to litigation, he resisted the equation of war with any art or science.[15] The beginning of wisdom was, for him, the recognition of war's unique mixture of the rational and the irrational, of the controlled and the uncontrollable, the interplay of calculation with danger. The great commander must combine qualities not only at odds with each other but not appropriate for most other tasks. He must have a fighting spirit verging on recklessness, joined with restraint and sobriety. He must both love and hate war, keep his confidence while recognizing all the things to be feared. He must allow, always, for *Friktion,* almost foreseeing the unforeseen. His great gift is the *coup d'oeil,* the calm survey of each new development, the quick abandonment of preconceptions under the bombardment of events, without losing a sense of purpose and direction. He must, in Napoleon's dictum, often leap, *then* look: "On s'engage, puis on voit."

All this sounds like standard early Romanticism, the cult of the genius with his mysterious powers. Such a reading of Clausewitz seems confirmed when we ask him what the rules of war are and he answers: "*What genius does* is the best rule" (2.2, p. 136; italics mine). That is the language of Napoleon's cultists, who filled the early part of the nineteenth century with their raptures.

Yet Clausewitz was not a cultist where Napoleon was concerned. He is often critical of Napoleon's decisions, not only those reached late in his career but from the Italian campaign on. And we must finish the sentence about genius and rules to see what role Clausewitz assigns to theory: "What genius does is the best rule, and theory can do no better than show how and why this should be the case." Theory is retrospective and descriptive—not a tool of prediction, and certainly not of prescription. It creates the terms for useful discussion of what has gone on in war:

> Theory will have fulfilled its main task when it is used to analyze the constituent elements of war, to distinguish precisely what at first sight seems fused, to explain in full the properties of the means employed and to show their probable effects, to define clearly the nature of the ends in view, and to illuminate all phases of warfare in a thorough critical inquiry [*kritische Betrachtung*]. [2.2, p. 141]

That last clause annexes to *Theorie* what, four chapters later, Clausewitz will be careful to distinguish from it. *Kritik* uses theory without ever becoming subordinate to it. Theory is just one provisional tool of the higher activity. *Kritik* does not apply theory, any more than it looks to

---

15. Engels was especially struck by Clausewitz's comparison of war to "cash payment in commerce" (quoted in Paret, *Clausewitz and the State,* p. 90). For other uses of an economic model, see *On War,* pp. 97, 149, 182, 207, 230, 242, 244, 252, 259, 267, 269, 288, and 501.

perfecting theory: "The function of criticism would be missed entirely if criticism were to degenerate into a mechanical application of theory" (2.5, p. 157). It is true that Clausewitz speaks, once, of *Kritik* as "the application [*Anwendung*] of theoretical truths to actual events" (2.5, p. 156). But his larger treatment of this process shows that theory has no standing as Truth for him. It is not, properly, a separate kind of knowledge at all. It is a provisional aid to *Kritik, derived from earlier acts of criticism.* Theory is the currently acceptable generalization made from other acts of the critical faculty, not superior in kind to those acts and not determinative of any critical inquiry being made at the moment.[16] "Theory exists so that one need not start afresh each time sorting out the material and plowing through it" (2.2, p. 141). Such theory is not properly *applied* to reality. It poses certain *questions* that *Kritik* alone can answer. No abstraction can cover all the anfractuosities of the real. In war, detail is everything. Proof (*Beweis*), for Clausewitz, affects only particular situations; it is reached when no higher *Standpunkt* can be found for judging the methods used at one time.

Since theory is not prescriptive and *Kritik* is confined to the particular, how is one to generalize, to teach any methods in war? Clausewitz says several times that the best training for war is war itself. Only from experience does one appreciate the constant menace to one's analytic abilities in the midst of danger, learn how to cope with the unexpected, how to test assumptions under fire. But war only teaches in this way if one is disciplined enough to be analyzing *as* one acts. It is not so much war that teaches as *Kritik* undertaken in the midst of war. Yet the exercise of *Kritik* there implies a prior acquaintance with the practice and its past results (i.e., with theory). And *Kritik* does not end with the silencing of guns. The ongoing reflection on particulars equips one to deal with analogous if particular situations. And the critic can participate in this process even outside the actual engagement. In fact, a strategic leader must always be disassociating himself from the tactical engagement to fit it into its strategic use. Just as the commander strives to get above and outside the action, the critic presses to enter it.

Clausewitz suggests that one must *wage* criticism not so much alongside a commander as in competition with him. This is what freed him from an abject submission to Napoleon such as Jomini evidenced.

> If the critic points out that a Frederick or a Bonaparte made mistakes, it does not mean that he would not have made them too. He may even admit that in the general's place he might have made

16. Paret (*Clausewitz and the State*, p. 154) notes that some of Clausewitz's formulations resemble the application of Kantian reason to the material world though "we have no evidence that he read such works as the Kantian critiques" (p. 150). In *On War*, at least, theory does not represent a *higher* or different *kind* of knowledge than *Kritik*. His argument rejects all a priori knowledge of the Kantian sort.

far greater errors. What it does mean is that he can recognize
these mistakes from the pattern of events and feels that the commander's sagacity should have seen them as well. [2.5, p. 166]

What gives the critic his advantage, even in judging genius, is the greater
knowledge available to him, enabling him to assume a higher *Standpunkt*
in judging the interconnection of particulars during this or that campaign. Even the general would have to revise his judgments in the light
of this greater knowledge, sealed off from him at the time by the *Friktion*
of untrustworthy intelligence. Thus even genius must submit to *Kritik*.
Clausewitz does not encourage the Romantic submission to mystery;
rather, he proclaims the knowability of the particular when freed from
the false claims of theory. Theory that strives to be absolute must, for the
purposes of criticism, lose its universality by that very claim: "All the
positive results of theoretical investigation—all the principles, rules, and
methods—will increasingly lack universality and absolute truth the closer
they come to being positive doctrine" (2.5, pp. 157–58). Clausewitz's
important teachings on war—for example, on *Wechselwirkung* or
Friktion—allow one to understand war without giving any prescriptive
rules for its conduct. Clausewitz encourages the student to wage a war in
the mind as the only preparation for waging it in fact. As every general
must be a *Kritiker,* so every *Kritiker* must look to the better waging of
future wars, if not in his own person then in the state or the military he
helps to educate. Only in this way can war be "taught" according to
Clausewitz.

It is a critical method with many political uses—indeed, strategy in
the full sense always embraces, for Clausewitz, the entire statecraft of
any nation. His teachings on power can be used in practical psychology.
His opposition to theory suggests interesting approaches to various fields
of practical criticism. As all generals must be critics, though not all critics
are generals, so each poet must judge his work from without, while the
critic is striving to enter into the work. Both *wage* a criticism in fruitful
rivalry with each other. In poetry, too, the best rules are what genius
does, though even genius must submit to *Kritik*. But modern critics
might not like to hear that war waged in the mind or on paper is never
the equal or substitute for the real thing.

Politics as Opposed to What?

Stanley Cavell

If the politics of interpretation studies the public conditions of one's discourse, the forces it musters against the forces against it, where the victory of discourse consists in bringing those conditions to light, an early essay of mine on the philosophy of J. L. Austin, "Austin at Criticism," is meant as such a study.[1] This is worth my saying for two reasons. First, since I am still not ready to try a systematic account of what I understand either politics or interpretation to be, what profit I can be here, to myself and others, will come from a certain willingness for the autobiographical, both by way of meditating on some themes and instances that I would wish a systematic study to treat and by way of specifying some of the conditions of my discourse that I can recognize as political. These conditions will mostly, or at first, be institutional or professional forces. Second, in the early sixties, when I wrote my essay on Austin and for the dozen years before that, during which I went through graduate studies and began teaching for a living, about the only political questions I heard voiced in professional philosophical circles were about whether Hegel and Nietzsche were proto-Nazis and whether ordinary language philosophy was politically conservative. It will serve to orient these autobiographical notes if I spend my opening comments tracing my course from that essay to this.

No one in my earlier years would have thought that ordinary language philosophy had done the kind of public harm attributed to Ger-

---

1. See my "Austin at Criticism," *The Philosophical Review* 74 (April 1965): 204–19; rpt. in my *Must We Mean What We Say?* (Cambridge, Mass., 1976).

man philosophy, but on an institutional basis ordinary language philosophy was received as, and took itself to represent, a revolution in philosophy. Certainly it caused changes in the look and the sound of the subject and differences in who was attracted to the subject and who fled from it, who was rewarded by it and who deprived. Austin's claim against past philosophy, what we allowed ourselves to call the tradition, was not that it was wrong in this or that respect but that it was radically insufficient, childishly oversimple, as a mode of discourse altogether. Which is to say that ordinary language philosophy is a mode of interpretation and inherently involved in the politics of interpretation. The way I put this in my early essay on Austin was to say that it is an unmasking philosophy, as analytical philosophy generally is bound to be. (More so than Plato or Kant or Hume or Rousseau or Bentham—i.e., more than any philosophy? Well, let us just say this is its claim to philosophy.) Diagnosis of one's enemies calls forth counterdiagnosis as surely as anger calls forth anger. The counterdiagnosis or unmasking of Austin as politically conservative was shaped, it seemed to me, by a sense of him as socially and intellectually conservative, an impression I attributed in turn to his apparent indifference to speculation and his cultivation, in his prose, of common room wit and superficiality. My defense in turn against this unmasking of him was that it was itself taken in by Austin's use of his mask, that what looked like social manner was internal to what I would like now to call a politics of superficiality, directed accordingly against what Austin would have seen as a politics of profundity and mystification (associated primarily, I suppose, with a perception of German philosophy). (The profundity he was combatting was, I claim, also something he felt tempted to by the depth of his own thoughts—but I won't press that further here.)

Austin's favorite gesture in preparing or justifying his philosophical attacks is to appeal to the idea that the best way to stop a bad thing from happening is to prevent it from starting to happen. If I do not share Austin's confidence that self-mystification can always so be prevented, confident instead that it requires a perpetual undoing, and an undoing of the one who does it, I nevertheless value the gesture and am glad to accept it as an element of what I understand the ordinary to be in ordinary language philosophy.

In speaking of Austin's critical practice here as a gesture, I would

Stanley Cavell, professor of philosophy at Harvard University, is the author of, among other works, *Must We Mean What We Say?*, *The Senses of Walden, The Claim of Reason,* and most recently *Pursuits of Happiness.*

studiously avoid letting the political and the psychological possibilities of interpreting the gesture preempt one another. I think of it as a matter of character, of what you might call a writer's worldly character. Austin was committed to the manners, even the mannerisms, of an English professor the way a French intellectual is committed to seeming brilliant. It is the level at which an American thinker or artist is likely to play dumb, I mean undertake to seem like a hick, uncultivated. These are all characters in which authority is assumed, variations I suppose of the thinker's use—as unmasked by Nietzsche—of the character of the sage.

Wittgenstein is always prepared for the undoing that self-mystification calls for, and if I still find him insufficiently clear and explicit on the subject, I am guided by the uncanny beauty of some of his observations concerning it.

> Where does our investigation get its importance from, since it seems only to destroy everything interesting, that is, all that is great and important? . . . What we are destroying is nothing but houses of cards [literally: structures of air] and we are clearing up the ground of language on which they stand.[2]

What I mean by uncanniness in these words is their Zen master–ish assurance that every theoretical attachment to words (structures of air) is an attachment to illusion and the assurance that we have some mode of inhabitation outside such structures, or else that we can live without inhabitation. Wittgenstein is painting his quest for the ordinary and the everyday as a profound thing—a Romantic gesture that Austin must disapprove of. (He never, I think, wrote Wittgenstein's name in anything he published; and in my hearing he spoke it only once, and then after having for a moment expressed difficulty in remembering it.) So that when Austin voices his similar view of the interest and the importance of his investigation of the ordinary, he reaches for no further power, apparently, than his ordinary character of sociable wit. In the last two paragraphs of the last of the twelve lectures that constitute *How to Do Things with Words,* he announces, hailing us in farewell: "I have as usual failed to leave enough time in which to say why what I have said is interesting." And in the next sentence he instances a topic he says philosophers have been interested in. It is sufficiently obvious that he takes it as unarguable that the philosophers' interest, set beside the twelve hours of fascinating detail he has offered, is boredom itself. Austin says the lectures were bound to be a little dry and boring; but he was saying it mostly to the wrong parties. His first lecture had attracted several hundred people; by the last half-dozen we were down to a core of some twelve to fifteen souls, and not all of these few were happy. But this only

2. Ludwig Wittgenstein, *Philosophical Investigations,* trans. G. E. M. Anscombe (London, 1958), par. 118, p. 48e.

means that not everyone is interested in the need for revolution. Put his appeals to interest and boredom together with his having begun his lectures by locating his work on the line of those philosophers who have shown many traditional philosophical perplexities to have arisen through mistaking the form of one's language, which is the thing he claims as without doubt producing a revolution in philosophy. Since the only event in Austin's lectures that could satisfy the concept of a revolution is the shift of interest with respect to traditional philosophical problems, I find that a double implication is to be drawn: first, that the challenge of philosophy is the challenge of our interests as they stand, including our interests in philosophy itself, specifically in the present case a challenge to show that what is called a philosophical problem is in fact humanly interesting; second, that philosophy has no special or privileged discourse in which to level its challenge. I take these implications as two further specifications of the claims recorded in the title "ordinary language philosophy."

In my essay on Austin I did not specify what I took the politics of my own discourse to be, but the institutional pressures on it, in particular the pressures of the professionalization of American philosophy, were in outline clear enough. I was more and more galled by the mutual shunning of the continental and the Anglo-American traditions of philosophizing, and I was finding more and more oppressive the mutual indifference of philosophy and literature to one another, especially, I suppose, of American philosophy and American literature, and especially philosophy's indifference to the literary conditions of its own existence. (I understand this to imply not an interdisciplinary wish but rather a wish for philosophy to take a further step toward itself.) I was still near the beginning of what is turning out to be a lifelong quarrel with the profession of philosophy. One of its recent manifestations has been the question put to me by certain professional colleagues whether I do not take satisfaction from the newer literary theory and criticism, especially as that has been inspired by developments over the past fifteen or so years in French intellectual life. This would seem to answer my plea at one stroke for both continental philosophy and for an understanding with literary matters. The fact is that my ambivalence toward these developments has been so strong, or anyway periodic, that I have found it difficult to study in any very orderly way.

The reason for my difficulty is contained in what I mean by my quarrel with the profession of philosophy. That this is a quarrel means that I recognize the profession to be the genuine present of the impulse and the history of philosophy, so far as that present takes its place in our (English-speaking) public intellectual life. This is what makes my quarrel with it a part of what I take my intellectual adventure to be. My point in the quarrel is that I can recognize no expression of mine to be philosophical which simply thinks to escape my profession's paradigms of comprehensibility; so that the invocations of the name of philosophy in current literary debate are frequently not comprehensible to me as calls upon philosophy. It may be that I should care less about this than I do, even less than my ambivalence asks. I mean to bear this in mind as I go on to spend the bulk of my time here considering in a practical way some passages from the writing of two literary theorists who have recourse to the work of Austin. In the case of the passages from Stanley Fish, it may be that my efforts will just amount to clearing up some unnecessarily confusing terminology; some passages from Paul de Man I find more troubling.

As one further preparation for considering these passages I might indicate how hard it has become for me to conduct my quarrel with the profession, to find common ground for it. This difficulty is epitomized by my growing insistence on receiving Emerson and Thoreau as philosophers, figures who from the beginning of the professionalization of American philosophy have been regarded as philosophical amateurs. (Bruce Kuklick's book *American Philosophy* in effect tells the story of the establishment of academic philosophy proper in America, at Harvard, in such a way that it begins, achieves its first accreditation, so to speak, by declaring Emerson an amateur thinker, quite as if repressing Emerson's thought were an essential responsibility of professional philosophy; and if essential then, then still. Kuklick tells the story as a proud one for American philosophy.) The cause of my growing insistence is the work I have been doing that convinces me that Emerson and Thoreau underwrite the emphasis I have placed over the years on ordinary language philosophy. I felt from the beginning of my absorption in its confrontation with skepticism that the ordinariness in question spoke of an intimacy with existence, or an intimacy lost, that matched skepticism's despair of the world. After publishing *The Claim of Reason* a couple of years ago, much of which revolves around this confrontation, I was prepared to see that something I have meant by the ordinary is something Emerson and Thoreau mean in their devotion to the thing they call the common, the familiar, the everyday, the low, the near. Making this connection explicit felt to me like bringing pieces of my mind together, yet I know that to most of my colleagues the underwriting of ordinary language philosophy by transcendentalism would be about as promising as enlivening the passé by the extinct.[3]

3. In suggesting that these colleagues cannot be certain that they are right in this prediction, no more certain, at any rate, than they can be that philosophy is a science, I am appealing to this difference between the sciences and the humanities, that with the latter the past may at any time come to life, not merely as the recovery of certain neglected problems within the field but as a recovery of the field's originating, or preserving, authority. Along such lines the authority of philosophy is a guiding preoccupation of the essays in *Must We Mean What We Say?* as a whole, most explicitly, or consecutively, in the foreword to the volume, "An Audience for Philosophy."

This suggests, by the way, the right level of philosophical response to the old charge against Austin as politically conservative. The charge is fed by the idea that ordinary language philosophy is meant to be a defense of ordinary beliefs—say the belief that there are material objects. It may be that certain philosophers are so characterized fairly: G. E. Moore, for example. But for Austin and Wittgenstein, this description is itself an instance of the philosophical prejudices their work is made to bring to light, because it is a departure from ordinary language to say either that I do or that I do not believe there are material objects; so to that extent, it would be incoherent to provide a "defense" of such a "belief." Of course a story can be given that will take up the slack of this departure and realign the idea of belief here—the skeptical story according to which I might come to think of myself as doubting that there are material objects. It is true that Austin was intent on preventing such a story from getting off the ground, but while I regard this as a grave limitation in his philosophizing—a refusal, in effect, to consider why it looked as if he were defending common beliefs—it is something else again to charge that he was in fact defending those beliefs.

Wittgenstein speaks of his philosophical procedures as bringing words back from their metaphysical to their everyday use—as if our words are *away*, not at home, and as if it takes the best efforts of philosophy to recognize when and where our words have strayed into metaphysics. I have interpreted this task many ways over the years, but it was not until I was able to emerge from *The Claim of Reason* that I felt I had said something consecutive and of a reasonable depth about how words get away and lost, about the intuition I had taken away from my first useful encounter with the *Philosophical Investigations* that the repudiation of the world is as internal to what ordinary language is as its revelation of the world; or put otherwise, that skepticism would not be possible unless ordinary language is such that it can, sometimes must, repudiate itself, put its own naturalness into question. But to care about this, one must, I suppose, have sometimes found in oneself the burden of its revelation, that we had been away in our words, a burden within which Austin and Wittgenstein may be received with the power of a conversion of interest. This is still worth mentioning because those of us who have claimed responsibility for ordinary language procedures, or profit from them, have not to my mind satisfactorily described their performance. I do not mean, it goes without saying, that someone cannot perform them without being able to describe their performance. But to the extent that these procedures are philosophically undescribed, or underdescribed, ordinary language philosophy remains an esoteric practice.

This is not the aspect of ordinary language philosophy that is taken up in what I have been reading of the work of Fish and of de Man. The work of Austin's they cite primarily is *How to Do Things with Words,* that is, roughly, his doctrine of performative utterances, which I might call his most exoteric work. Or I might say it is his most traditionally political work. I mean: here there is comparatively little effort to work out structures within the ordinariness of language, which I regard as his best power; his goal is less to illuminate a system of what you might call natural—or naturally interesting—concepts (which may then have untold consequences for traditional so-called philosophical problems) than to undermine two philosophical theories or tendencies among his competitors within analytical philosophy (which will then allow his more genuine questions to find their own consequences). One tendency was the overattention to the statement of fact among the speech acts studied by philosophers (most recently associated with the work of the logical positivists); the other tendency was the recent emphasis on the uses, instead of the meanings, of words (an emphasis associated with the later Wittgenstein). Useful and surprising things emerge as Austin works through his tests for distinguishing kinds of speech acts, but the philosophical yield should not be exaggerated. Perhaps most important, it does not for Austin yield a theory of language; on the contrary, he takes this work to show how far we are from anything he would regard as a serious theory of language. This is cause enough for me to applaud Fish's deploring the efforts of "literary people . . . using speech-act theory to arrive at definitions of literature and/or fiction."[4] But Fish's case rests on a view of the question of the ordinary that is at odds with my understanding of it and which I believe may mislead further efforts to use Austin in thinking about language and literature.

For all his approval of certain ideas of ordinary language philosophy, Fish objects to its distinguishing so-called ordinary discourse from some other kind, say literary, and doing so on grounds that it itself, in the view of language taken in its theory of performative utterances, repudiates. Fish summarizes this repudiation by saying: "What philosophical semantics and the philosophy of speech acts are telling us is that ordinary language is extraordinary because at its heart is precisely that realm of values, intentions, and purposes which is often assumed to be the exclusive property of literature."[5] The wit in making ordinary language philosophy say that ordinary language is extraordinary may, I believe, cover up a series of misunderstandings, ironic, sometimes for me disheartening, misunderstandings.

To begin with, Fish does not mean by "ordinary" what Austin means. He assimilates Austin's term to a long chain of more or less established distinctions, including that of I. A. Richards between emotive

4. Stanley F. Fish, "How to Do Things with Austin and Searle," *Is There a Text in This Class? The Authority of Interpretive Communities* (Cambridge, Mass., 1980), p. 231; all further references to this essay, abbreviated "Austin and Searle," will be included in the text.
5. Fish, "How Ordinary Is Ordinary Language?," *Is There a Text?,* p. 108.

and scientific meaning. Philosophers generally spoke of essentially this distinction as one between emotive and cognitive meaning, a distinction one of whose initial ironies is that it reversed Richards' efforts to give to poetry some function of communication that was intellectually viable even if not scientific and instead ground aesthetic, moral, and religious discourses together as something whose essential character was that they were noncognitive. This distinction, together with its companion distinction between descriptive and normative utterance or discourse, is fundamental to two of the most influential books, or most often cited, in analytical philosophy throughout the years of my graduate studies: A. J. Ayer's *Language, Truth, and Logic* and Charles Stevenson's *Ethics and Language*. It would take considerable novelistic skills to recapture the mood of philosophical debate on such issues in those years, in which these distinctions struck some as being as unassailable as the difference between science and religion and struck others as jeopardizing everything they prized.

Now I think it is correct to say that the single most telling blow *against* the tyranny of this distinction between cognitive and emotive meaning came with Austin's counterdistinction between constative and performative utterances, one major effect of which was to defeat the credibility of the crude distinction between one form of discourse (call it cognitive) as responsible to facts or to reality and another form (call it noncognitive) as not in the same way responsible. I do not say Austin refuted this positivist theory, only that his theory (along with certain other major developments, critically that which attacked the distinction between analytic and synthetic judgments) removed or replaced interest in it. It is possible, of course, that he suffers from the disease he cured, but that is not exactly what Fish accuses him of. If in literary studies people have fastened on to the rubric "ordinary language" as something they take as opposed to literary language, that may or may not be unfortunate depending on what distinction they have in mind; but it must certainly be unfortunate to add to their problems by supposing this distinction either to be enforced or debarred by Austin's work.

What Austin did mean by "ordinary" is not, I hope I have begun to suggest, and cannot be, easy to say. Consider that it has no standing, or obvious, contrast. Ordinary as opposed to what—if not to scientific or religious or ethical or literary? In my reading of Austin's practice, the contrast is with the philosophical (what Wittgenstein calls the metaphysical). (Reasonably direct evidence for this is provided by assessing what I call the terms of criticism in Austin's diagnosis of his antagonists.) The errors or discrepancies or follies his appeals to ordinary language immediately counter are ones that philosophizing is apt to produce. Austin is not particularly interested to say so because, I think, he does not wish to give the impression that what is in question are two modes or realms of discourse, the ordinary and the philosophical. His claim, largely implicit, is that the philosophical is not a special mode of discourse at all; it has no interests of its own (as, say, science or religion or sports or trades have), or it ought not to have. So its departures from the ordinary are not into specialties but, let me say, into emptiness. Compared with Wittgenstein, Austin has no account of this emptiness, beyond perhaps various casual suggestions about distinguishing species of nonsense, in itself important enough. While his avoidance here is part of my sense of the limitation of his philosophizing, it is still reasonably clear to me that with modes of discourse other than the supposedly philosophical Austin takes no particular issue.

Then why does Fish suppose otherwise? In what I have read of his work so far, there seem to be two causes. The first, perhaps of no significance beyond its curiosity, concerns Fish's use of the term "normative." When speech-act theory is used to arrive at definitions of literature and/or fiction, the enterprise, according to Fish, "necessarily begins with an attempt to specify what is *not* literature and fiction, or, in a word, what is normative. According to most of those who have worked on this problem, what is normative is language that intends to be or is held to be responsible to the real world" ("Austin and Searle," pp. 231–32). The ensuing quotations Fish presents from three such workers do not themselves contain the term "normative," and indeed I thought I had invented the idea of speaking of the normative in this connection, and, until I began reading Fish's recent collection of essays, I believed that I had remained alone. When in the title essay of *Must We Mean What We Say?* I come out with the assertion that "what is normative is exactly ordinary use itself," it is with a certain air of triumph, and what I felt (still feel) I was triumphing in was not the affirmation of a distinction between ordinary and some other mode of discourse; on the contrary, I felt I was winning a measure of freedom from exactly such a distinction, namely, that between the normative and the descriptive that we were just talking about. The triumphant air was an expression of my relief in having discovered for myself what it was about the distinction that for ten years had had the power to make my flesh creep (I dare say a political emotion). Most probably my use of the term "normative" is irrelevant to the present coincidence of terms; but on the chance that it is not, my reversal or recapturing of the term seems to have defeated itself, seems to affirm precisely what it denies, and I do not understand why.

The second cause I mention for Fish to take Austin as opposing ordinary to literary language is that Austin all but says he does, in so many words. All but; but I think not really. Fish quotes what he calls Austin's classic formulation as follows:

> "A performative utterance will, for example, be *in a peculiar way* hollow or void if said by an actor on the stage, or if introduced in a poem. . . . Language in such circumstances is in special ways—

> intelligibly—used not seriously, but in ways *parasitic* upon its nor-
> mal use—ways which fall under the doctrine of the *etiolations* of
> language. All this we are *excluding* from consideration. Our per-
> formative utterances, felicitous or not, are to be understood as
> issued in ordinary circumstances." ["Austin and Searle," p. 233]

But why take a passage that says it is excluding something, as if guarding
against being misunderstood here, to be presenting a classic formulation
of a theory of that excluded thing, a thing about which the book has next
to nothing to say? Moreover, in the examples Austin adduces here, he is
egregiously, compared with his usual care about examples, his Austinian
care, careless; he seems to have some wires crossed. When he says that a
performative utterance will be in a peculiar way hollow or void if said by
an actor on the stage, this is either false or too poorly described to assess.
It is false to say, for example, that Horatio and Marcellus do not really or
felicitously swear by Hamlet's sword never to speak of what they have
seen and heard; and to say that the actors playing those roles have not
really sworn would be as useful as to say that those actors are not really,
except *per accidens,* in Denmark. Say that what actors do is imitate actions.
Then the conditions of any act you can specify can be imitated. So you
can imitate any way in which one of these conditions might fail and
hence perfectly imitate an infelicitous act of speech. If Hamlet had no
sword or if Horatio had crossed his fingers or winked aside to the audience, then he would not exactly have sworn on Hamlet's sword. But if
Austin had in mind an actor speaking not to other actors but rather to us
in the audience, then the case has to be imagined as one in which we or
the other actors do not know that the actor speaking is on the stage or
that we are members of an audience. And whatever it is to know this and
however we might be imagined to fail to know it are matters that have
nothing special to do with performative utterances. The question raised
by Austin's passage is why he should be prompted at all to attempt such
exclusions, what misunderstanding it is he takes himself to be guarding
against.

    I do not deny that Austin's speaking of roughly theatrical or
fictional uses of language as nonserious and as parasitic on normal use is
symptomatic of his cast of mind (as is the fact that he got some wires
crossed in exemplifying it). But is this basis enough on which to build a
confident description of this cast of mind? Is he, for example, contrasting the realm of the serious with the realm of play? Yet he more than
once accuses philosophers of having robbed philosophy of its fun. No
doubt he is suggesting that matters like promising and marrying and
warning (as of fire in a theater) require restrictions on the realm of play.
Don't they?

    Most immediately, it seems to me, what he is guarding against is
being taken as giving conditions for what he calls the seriousness of

assertion, as if he supposed that seriousness were something added on, as it were, to what is said. (Wittgenstein discusses this philosophical temptation in considering Frege's sign of assertion.)[6] The difference between assertion and fiction is not going to be settled by any such signs. The difference as Austin puts it, in the sentence omitted from the citation of what Fish calls Austin's classic formulation, is the result of a "sea-change" of language, which is to say, a metamorphosis of the whole of a discourse, as into another mode. This is hardly clear, but it is surely not meant to do much more than mark the merest suggestion of an idea worth pursuing. (One way to pursue it might be to compare it with Fish's suggestion of ordinary language as undergoing "framing" in literature.) So another danger I see in Fish's summary of the philosophy of speech acts as telling us that ordinary language is extraordinary is that it takes Austin's theory of speech acts to express Austin's vision of language, a vision Fish sketches this way: "When we communicate, it is because we are parties to a set of discourse agreements which are in effect decisions as to what can be stipulated as a fact" ("Austin and Searle," p. 242). I share a sense of agreement underlying communication, or community. But Fish's words here make this agreement seem much more, let me say, sheerly conventional than would seem plausible if one were considering other regions of Austin's work, for example, the region of excuses, where the differences, for one small instance, between doing something mistakenly, accidentally, heedlessly, carelessly, inadvertently, automatically, thoughtlessly, inconsiderately, and so on are worked out with unanticipated clarity and completeness but where the more convinced you are by the results, the less you will feel like attributing them to agreements that are expressible as decisions. How could we have agreed to consequences of our words that we are forever in the process of unearthing, consequences that with each turn seem further to unearth the world? (I don't say there is no way.) I suggest in *The Claim of Reason* that it is skepticism that produces as a reaction to itself the idea of language as essentially conventional. But skepticism, as I have conceived it, is a repudiation of the naturalness of language (by means of the power of this naturalness itself), not a theoretical observation about it.

I would expect these dissatisfactions with certain of Fish's remarks to find various measures of accommodation in further discussion. I am less confident of this in my study to date of de Man's *Allegories of Reading*. In this work the claim to philosophical rigor is repeatedly made, but the work's discourse is one that pretty well, to my ear, ignores the paradigms of comprehensibility established in Anglo-American philosophy. Perhaps they should be ignored; it has occurred to me more than once over the years that they should. But I have said that I remain, instead, in

6. See Wittgenstein, *Investigations,* par. 22, p. 10e.

quarrel with them; to that extent I cannot accept de Man's carelessness of them.

Take his prominent and recurrent invocation of a distinction between the constative and the performative. He sometimes, not always, associates Austin's name with these words, but so far as I understand his sense of what he wants the distinction to do, it contradicts Austin's. A hint of this occurs in his last chapter, when he describes an excuse as a performative utterance on the ground that its purpose is not to state but to convince.[7] But to say "I convince you" is not (except by chance) to convince you, and so it is trivially not a performative utterance. In Austin's more general theory, convincingness and persuasiveness are not illocutionary forces of utterances. They are perhaps the quintessential examples of what is not illocutionary, since one of Austin's philosophical motives is to deny that the alternative to stating something is to persuade someone of something (a motive bearing on what is to be called rhetoric and specifically on the claim that moral discourse is essentially persuasive).

More generally, de Man wishes, I believe, to align the constative-performative distinction with what he says about distinctions between grammar and rhetoric, or between the intraverbal and the extraverbal, or between referentiality and nonreferentiality, or between assertion and action. He appears to take the distinction to turn on whether a use of language refers to something outside language, something in the world, and on whether a use of language has some actual effect on others. But to defeat the idea that constative and performative utterances differ in their responsibilities, or responsiveness, to facts and to distinguish among ways in which words may have "effects" or "forces" just are Austin's purposes in arguing against positivism and the later Wittgenstein. Perhaps de Man will be defended on the ground that he is really denying the distinction, not endorsing it, or rather really arguing, as he puts it, that there is an "aporia between performative and constative language" (p. 131). Then I might offer the following as a parallel argument. Someone says that the difference between knives and forks is that you cut with a knife and spear with a fork; a second objects that you can also cut with a fork and spear with a knife; whereupon a third concludes that there is an aporia between knives and forks, that there is no stable distinction we can draw between them. Of course de Man may use the words "constative" and "performative" for any purpose he defines, and maybe he has; but it must not be assumed that the distinction Austin goes to such lengths to clarify lends clarity to that purpose.

This is something that those who are interested in both Austin and de Man will work out for themselves. There are much simpler matters

---

7. See Paul de Man, *Allegories of Reading: Figural Language in Rousseau, Nietzsche, Rilke, and Proust* (New Haven, Conn., 1979), p. 281; all further references to this work will be included in the text.

that discourage me from going on to work at what de Man says. I would like to be able to because I find in his book wonderful and sympathetic moments of insight, and about the texts he discusses at length it would, I think, be folly to deliver oneself without considering what he has to say. It is in this spirit that I go on to take up two of the principal examples he uses in his opening chapter, "Semiology and Rhetoric," "to illustrate the tension between grammar and rhetoric," a tension which will flower into his theory of reading as deconstruction (p. 9). The examples illustrate that conjunction of grammatical and rhetorical constraints called the rhetorical question.

The first example is an exceptionally elaborate gag about Archie Bunker, the character in the popular television series "All in the Family." I cite only the preparatory part of the gag, which is probably unfair and ungrateful of me; but since the gag is meant, I take it, to soften me up, it seems to me worth explaining why it hardens me. De Man writes:

> Asked by his wife whether he wants to have his bowling shoes laced over or laced under, Archie Bunker answers with a question: "What's the difference?" Being a reader of sublime simplicity, his wife replies by patiently explaining the difference between lacing over and lacing under, whatever this may be, but provokes only ire. "What's the difference" did not ask for difference but means instead "I don't give a damn what the difference is." The same grammatical pattern engenders two meanings that are mutually exclusive: the literal meaning asks for the concept (difference) whose existence is denied by the figurative meaning. [P. 9]

To discover one and the same grammatical pattern used for different rhetorical effects was the stock-in-trade of ordinary language philosophers. (This is to be contrasted with the program of earlier analytical philosophy, associated with the names of Frege and Russell, in which the grammatical pattern of a proposition is shown in certain cases to falsify what was called its logical form.) Wittgenstein, for example, observes that "we could imagine a language in which *all* statements had the form and tone of rhetorical questions," like "Isn't the weather glorious today?," which is grammatically a question but rhetorically a statement.[8] I assume that this is what Austin's constative-performative distinction is about, that certain utterances that are grammatically statements are rhetorically something else. Shall we say that their rhetoric deconstructs their grammar, or is in tension with it, or that their grammatical pattern or their rhetorical function is somehow aberrant? If not, then the question "What's the difference?" is not sufficiently analyzed.

Let us to begin with be sure we remember that there are definite, practical differences between ways of lacing shoes, say between lacing

8. Wittgenstein, *Investigations,* par. 21, p. 10e.

them so that they crisscross and lacing them so that they are parallel. The former might be called lacing over, the latter lacing under. Apart from neatness of appearance, lacing under butts the edges better but takes a longer lace. If Archie knows this difference, then he is saying that he doesn't care how the laces on his bowling shoes are tied (which is a fair-sized assumption), and he is angry because he's being told what he already knows. If he does not know there is a difference, then he is saying that his wife therefore cannot know a difference, tell him a difference that could matter to him, and he is angry that she should think otherwise (which is something like a political position). In neither case does "I don't give a damn what the difference is" seem a fair paraphrase. This form of words is likely to be used either to mean "I'm not interested in the difference" (which in this case may be quite false) or else to mean "The difference won't change my plans" (which would make good sense if, say, Mrs. Bunker were trying to *prevail* on Archie to wear the shoes). And in both cases the rhetorical question remains why he expressed what he meant *this* way. But isn't that what literary critics and theorists have always asked themselves? In the present case, to determine the point of the expression "What's the difference?" we would do well to compare it with expressions such as "Who knows?" "Who cares?" "Who's to say?" "What did I tell you?" "Isn't it awful?" Like them, Archie's question is a hedge against assertion, and like "Isn't the weather glorious?" it is a statement that asks for a response. But while the difference between asking "What's the difference?" and saying, for example, "It doesn't matter" is that the question asks for a response, it may be that Archie at the same time does not want a response from his wife. This would show an ambivalence that many would take as the commonest characteristic of marriage, or of a comic marriage. But that is a fact about some Archie, not about the inevitable relation between grammar and rhetoric. The moral of the example seems to me to be that there is no inevitable relation between them. This seems to me the moral of ordinary language philosophy as well, and of the practice of art. Put it this way: Grammar cannot, or ought not, of itself dictate what you mean, what it is up to you to say.

The second example de Man uses to illustrate the rhetorical question is William Butler Yeats' perhaps too-famous "How can we know the dancer from the dance?" De Man says, surely correctly, that this should not, not simply, be taken as conventionally rhetorical, as if it implied that obviously there is no difference between the dancer and the dance but only an exquisite unity realized; and he goes on to say that taken as literal "How *can* we know . . . ?" urgently denounces, or turns upside down, the error of the rhetorical confidence. But de Man is assuming that what the question "How can we know . . . ?" asks, or means to ask, is how we can tell, tell something apart from something, tell the difference between them. If this were the question here, the literal version would become fairly incomprehensible; it is not clear what would count as literally telling the difference between a dancer and a dance, like asking for the difference between a knife and a cut. This makes the question into a kind of riddle, and certainly an important feature of the question "What's the difference?" is that one of its conventional rhetorical functions is to introduce a riddle. In this function it simultaneously gives great range to the inventiveness of possible answers and places severe conditions on anything that is to count as an answer, for example, that it must be witty. ("What's the difference between a schoolteacher and a railroad conductor?" The teacher trains the mind, the conductor minds the train.) Let us suppose that this piece of rhetoric is irrelevant here.

The cause of taking Yeats' question about knowledge to be asking about telling a difference is evidently that knowing and telling are intimately related epistemological concepts, indeed they share a significant grammatical doubleness: telling something from something either may mean telling things apart that are similar or on a par or it may specify how, by what signs or on what basis, you tell them apart. You can perhaps tell a goldfinch (distinguish it) from a goldcrest, and you can perhaps tell this from (by means of) the tailfeathers. *Knowing* something from something shares this doubleness, but it does not claim to go by differences; to know a hawk from a handsaw you simply have to know what is before your eyes, and from your own experience—it would be suggestive of madness not to know them apart, to take one for the other. But knowing from, in Yeats' line, goes altogether beyond telling. The line asks how we know the dancer from, meaning by means of, the dance; how it is that the dance can reveal the dancer. (If the dance and the dancer were, as it were, the same thing, then this would be no question. As things are, the question is simultaneously one of epistemology and of aesthetics.) But the line equally asks how we can know from, meaning know apart from, the dance; meaning know the dancer *away* from the dance. The doubleness, or ambiguity, persists still here, for who is imagined to be away from the dance, hence to have been dancing—we, or some other? I suppose both. Apart from the other's passion in the dance, the other is no longer transfigured: Is this the one who was there? Apart from my passion in the dance, my perception is no longer transfigured: Who am I (are we) to take such perception as valid? And now we have to consider afresh who or what the dancer is and who or what the dance. If the dance is the poetry, then the dancer is the poet and/or the reader, on the one hand, and, on the other, the world. Here the rhetorical reading courts doubt and despair (there is no reliable connection to or from the dance, hence none with the dancer), but the unrhetorical holds out hope (there must be some ground for our conviction, however shaken, that there is a connection). I suppose one may say that the reading of despair and the reading of hope are denounced by one another or turn one another upside down. But these seem to me overly melodramatic, or may I say overly literary, ways of characterizing what Yeats' line offers, the enactment of the poise between hope and despair, a fair portrayal of a human life.[9]

The readings seem to me equally allegorical, equally (so far as I understand the matter) referential and nonreferential, equally consistent, equally partial. I like the sort of move de Man makes when, noting that Rousseau has had some silly things to say on a subject, he adds parenthetically that silliness is deeply associated with reference (see p. 209). I am more partial to this sort of thing from Wittgenstein's *Nachlass:* "Always climb from the heights of cleverness into the green valleys of silliness." It depends no doubt on what one wants from reading.

The importance to me of preserving in Yeats' words the asserting and the questioning of knowing is that I am interested in the possibility of art as a possibility of knowing, or of acknowledging. This means to me an interest in its confrontation with the threat of skepticism, with the possibility that the world we claim to know is not the world there is. It may be that the issue of what I call the threat of skepticism, the threat that perhaps our claims do not, let me say, penetrate a world of things and of others apart from me, is the issue de Man is raising in speaking of referentiality. I will just remark here that the access of skepticism and poetry to one another means to me that a theory of referentiality or textuality designed to explain, say, our relation to Wallace Stevens' jar in Tennessee or to Heidegger's jug in the Black Forest is of no use to me if it fails to explain my relation to the chipped mug from which I drank my coffee this morning, I mean explain its vulnerability to doubt, or say to imagination. It does not help to picture language as being turned from the world (say troped) unless you know how to picture it as owed to the world and given to it. I do not expect de Man disagrees with this.

Now we are back to what I called the underwriting of Austin and Wittgenstein by Emerson and Thoreau, in their ideas of the nearness to

9. I have registered my sense that my criticism of de Man's use of examples may be unfair and ungrateful; notwithstanding, in one discussion of my remarks I was told, in effect, that I mistook the spirit of the examples altogether. This is a serious matter. It may, for example, point to the correct charge against Austin's attack on Ayer in *Sense and Sensibilia* which, for all its brilliance in producing and in criticizing examples, seems persistently, even perversely, to miss the drift of the philosophy (say skepticism) that it attacks. The particular defense of de Man offered me, directed specifically to the case of Archie Bunker, was that its point just was the joke it prepared about arché-debunking. But I find (I hope without undue solemnity) that the examples I cite from de Man are cases of inaccuracy, and I am assuming that for a critic to choose between accuracy and wit is as fateful as for a poet to choose between reason and rhythm. It gives up the game, or stacks it. I add this observation here as a way of stating my sense that the underlying subject of what I take criticism to be is the subject of examples. I suppose it is the underlying subject of what I take philosophy as such to be.

us, hence distance from us, of the world. To accept this underwriting incurs a political liability of a kind I have so far not mentioned. Before recording it, I should make explicit that I have also not mentioned what has struck me as the most obvious tension between the sort of view represented by de Man and that represented in what I do. This is caused by the claim, most familiarly associated with the name of Jacques Derrida and endorsed by de Man, that an appreciation of textuality, of its literariness, or rather of the originariness (or equi-originariness) of its writtenness, constitutes, or requires, a deconstruction of philosophy's bondage to a metaphysics of presence.

Such a claim sets up at once an intimacy and an abyss between the ambitions of the Anglo-American analytical settlement and the new French upheavals. The intimacy is that both define themselves as critiques of metaphysics, which just says that we are all children of Kant. The abyss I might express by saying that the continentals rather regard metaphysics as having come to the wrong conclusions where the Anglo-Americans (so to speak) think of it as having come to nothing at all, nothing philosophical (at least not yet—they may still long for it). A symptom of this intimacy and abyss is Derrida's sense, or intuition, that the bondage to metaphysics is a function of the promotion of something called voice over something called writing; whereas for me it is evident that the reign of repressive philosophical systematizing—sometimes called metaphysics, sometimes called logical analysis—has depended upon the suppression of the human voice. It is as the recovery of this voice (as from an illness) that ordinary language philosophy is, as I have understood and written about it, before all to be understood. I am prepared, or prepared to get prepared, to regard this sorting out of the issue of the voice as a further stage of intellectual adventure, for certainly I do not claim that it is amply clear *why* the procedures of ordinary language philosophy strike me (not me alone, I believe) as functions of voice, nor clear what voice is felt in contrast with; nor do I claim that this function cannot be interpreted as an effect of what might be seen as writing. What I claim is that no such interpretation will be of the right thing from my point of view unless it accounts for the *fact* that the appeal to the ordinary, as an indictment of metaphysics, strikes one, and should strike one, as an appeal to the voice.

In speaking of the point of intellectual adventure, I hope I will be forgiven a certain impatience at being repeatedly told—quite apart from assertions about phonocentrism—that Western metaphysics is a metaphysics of presence, without being told very much, if a word, about how one might usefully understand and responsibly make such a claim. If it is Heidegger from whom this claim has been taken, then I would not know how to assess it apart from some place in a long line of companion assessments, for example, of Heidegger's own enterprise in overcoming metaphysics, represented, say, in his *What Is Called Thinking?*, his effort to replace philosophy by what he calls thinking; and apart from an assessment of any philosophy's efforts to end philosophy, a task in the absence of which I would hardly understand an intellectual enterprise to add up to a work of philosophy; and apart from an assessment of what would constitute understanding Heidegger without a conversion to his way of thinking. Since he stakes his claim to his extraordinary understanding of sentences from Parmenides or Hölderlin or Nietzsche on his authority as a thinker, which means on his being drawn to thinking, which means on his claim to have inherited, for example, those sentences, then presumably we are to claim, if we wish to claim his inheritance, authority as thinkers. (Is this politics, or religion, or pedagogy, or terrorism, or therapy, or perhaps philosophy?) What authority I could claim—or what I claim instead of his inheritance—is the inheritance of Emerson and Thoreau, whose affinity with Heidegger I have elsewhere maintained.

This takes me to the further political liability I said I incur in my acceptance of Emerson and Thoreau, namely, their interpretation of what you might call the politics of philosophical interpretation as a withdrawal or rejection of politics, even of society, as such.

For Emerson and for Thoreau, what requires justification is not the form of philosophical discourse so much as the intention to achieve what you might call philosophical discourse altogether. The perception of the necessity for this justification will force a serious thinker into uncomfortable postures, as for example when Emerson remarks in "Self-Reliance," as he pictures himself going off to write, "Do not tell me, as a good man did to-day, of my obligation to put all poor men in good situations. Are they *my* poor?" Why raise this issue if you have nothing more or better to say about it? Because Emerson has already shown his writing to be something that, so to speak, replaces religion ("I shun father and mother and wife and brother when my genius calls me"), and because it was always the only reason a good man could give for seeking the kingdom of heaven that the poor you have always with you; that is, the knowledge that there is always humanly a reason to postpone salvation. But it is part of Emerson's gesture to claim that his genius is redemptive beyond himself. The implication is that if you are not willing to make such claims for your work, do not call it philosophy. And has he said so little? When he asks whether the poor are his, he is claiming that it is not he who keeps them poor; that is to say, that he would be willing to undergo whatever costs to himself to end their poverty and that going off to write as he does is his best way of contributing to ending it, and first by interpreting it. It is a tremendous claim, expressing tremendous faith in himself. It makes his going off an indictment of his fellow countrymen.

Thoreau's withdrawal is more elaborately dramatized, its rebuke more continuous. In my book on *Walden,* I find that the writer who inhabits it asserts the priority in value of writing over speaking (at least

for the present) in order to maintain silence, where this means first of all
to withhold his voice, his consent, from his society. Hence the entire
book is an act of civil disobedience, a confrontation which takes the form
of a withdrawal. But his silence has many forces, as in such a sentence as
this: "You only need sit still long enough in some attractive spot in the
woods that all its inhabitants may exhibit themselves to you by turns."
This is a fair summation of the point of the book as a whole. At the
moment I focus on Thoreau's way of saying that reading his book is
redemptive. I take it for granted that the scene is one of interpretation,
of reading and being read. The inhabitants exhibiting themselves "by
turns" means many things, among them of course taking turns (readers
come to a book one at a time), and turning pages, and revealing themselves completely (convicting themselves, Thoreau elsewhere describes
it); and "by turns" also means by verses (that is, since this is not poetry, by
portions) and also by conversions. So the writer's silence (that is, this
writer's writing) declares itself redemptive religiously, aesthetically, and
politically.

For most of us, I believe, the idea of redemption or redemptive
reading and interpretation will not be credible apart from a plausible
model or picture of how a text can be therapeutic, that is, apart from an
idea of the redemptive as psychological. (Here Fish's admirable essay in
Is There a Text in This Class?, "Literature in the Reader: Affective Stylistics," and the first chapter of his *Self-Consuming Artifacts*, "The Aesthetic
of the Good Physician," are exactly to the point. I find a therapeutic wish
in de Man as well, though he might not appreciate the description.) I will
conclude these remarks by racing through a sketch of what I think such a
picture would have to look like. (Of all the problems that beckon and
seem to me worth following from the sketch, the one that is perhaps
paramount in terms of my work on skepticism that I have
mentioned—the work for which the transcendentalists underwrite the
ordinary language philosophers—is one I only mention here, namely,
why or how the same silence, or rather the stillness of the text, the
achievement of which perhaps constitutes textuality, or a text's self-
containedness, should be interpretable politically as rebuke and confrontation and be interpretable epistemologically as the withholding of
assertion, on which I have found the defeat of skepticism, and of whatever metaphysics is designed to overcome skepticism, to depend—as if
the withholding of assertion, the containing of the voice, amounts to the
forgoing of domination. Of course there are withholdings that are
manipulative. These are not silent. I expect this process will come to an
understanding of philosophy's own involvement in therapy, one of its
obligations that Plato did not banish from his republic. This understanding would be required of someone who has been helped as much as
I have by Wittgenstein, who speaks of his methods not as bringing solu-
tions to problems but as treatments of them, like therapies, for whom

accordingly philosophy is always a recovery from, and of, itself. My thought here is that this conceives of philosophy as a kind of reading.)

I imagine that the credible psychological model of redemption will have to be psychoanalytic in character; yet psychoanalytic interpretations of texts have seemed typically to tell us something we more or less already knew, to leave us pretty much where we were before we read. It ought to help to see that from the point of view of psychoanalytic therapy the situation of reading has typically been turned around, that it is not first of all the text that is subject to interpretation but we in the gaze or hearing of the text. I think good readers, or a certain kind of reader, have always known and acted on this, as in Thoreau's picture of reading by exposure to being read. But it is my impression that those who emphasize the psychoanalytic possibilities here tend to forget what a text is, the matter of its autonomy; while those who shun psychoanalysis tend not to offer a practice of reading that I can understand as having the consequence of therapy.

The practice suggested to me by turning the picture of interpreting a text into one of being interpreted by it would I think be guided by three principal ideas: first, access to the text is provided not by the mechanism of projection but by that of transference (which is why the accusation that in one's extended interpretations one is turning a work of art into a Rorschach test is desperately wrong but precisely significant and deserving of careful response); second, the pleasures of appreciation are succeeded by the risks of seduction; and third, the risks are worth running because the goal of the encounter is not consummation but freedom. Freedom from what, to do what? In the picture of psychoanalytic therapy, casting ourselves as its patient, its sufferer, its victim (according to the likes of Emerson and of Heidegger, this is the true form of philosophical thinking), the goal is freedom from the person of the author. (So we might see our model in Emerson's "Divinity School Address," which seeks to free us from our attachment to the person of the one who brings the message, an attachment in effect according to Emerson, of idolatry. So what I am producing here, or proposing, might be thought of as a theology of reading.) Presumably we would not require a therapy whose structure partakes of seduction, to undo seduction, unless we were already seduced. (I imagine that reading, so motivated, will not readily lend itself to classroom instruction. Would this be because of the nature of teaching or because of the nature of classrooms?)

But what is a text that it has this power of overcoming the person of its author? We can learn this, many of us have been forever saying, only by letting ourselves be instructed by texts we care about. For someone who thinks this way, there lies in wait what you might call the paradox of reading: I was just saying in effect that you cannot understand a text before you know what the text says about itself; but obviously you cannot understand what the text says about itself before you understand the text. One way of investigating this is to ask whether "before" bears meaning in this formulation, and if not, whether there is a paradox here. Another is to say that what you really want to know is what a text knows about itself, because you cannot know more than it does about this; and then to ask what the fantasy is of the text's knowledge of itself.

The sentence I cited from *Walden* about sitting still long enough knows, for example, all about the seductions of this writing—its writer is sitting still, maintaining silence, in what he calls an "*attractive* spot in the woods" ("woods" being one of his words for "words," hence for his book, and [hence] for America). The text he is producing, for our conversion, is based, along with some other things, on an equation between morning (as dawning) and mourning (as grieving). The general idea is that we crave change (say therapy) but we are appalled by the prospect; that in our capacity for loss there is the chance of ecstasy. What bears here on the idea of a text as therapeutic is the structure of what I call in my book on *Walden* its "immense repetitiveness," something you might think of as a capacity for boredom, which I say Thoreau learned from the Old Testament prophets, together with his notation of endless detail. Now the repetition of each fact in one's attachment to an object gone, an effort to undo or release the ties of association strand by strand, is part of the work of realization of loss that Freud and principally after him Melanie Klein recognize as the work of mourning. They call it reality-testing, a subjection to the verdict of reality that one's attachment to an object is to undergo severing. For *Walden*'s writer I understand the morning of mourning, the dawning of grieving, to be the proposed alternative, the only alternative, to what he calls "our present constitution," which he says must end. He means our political constitution, with its slaves, but he means more than this; he means what permits this constitution in our souls. He means that mourning is the only alternative to our nostalgias, in which we will otherwise despair and die. He completes the building of his house by showing how to leave it.

Listen again to the book's parting line: "The sun is but a morning star." Surely this means that our prospects are brighter than we know. But this must be taken as part of the news that the sun is a grieving star, presiding over a world of mourning, in which we are in mourning for the loss of the earth and for the loss of the sun's old cosmic station. It is an image of skepticism. (This is reinforced by the old pun of "sun" with "Son," which in this context signifies an identification, or confusion, of Christ with Lucifer, as though we still have not grasped the difference between heaven and hell.) If the sun is an old symbol of the metaphysics of presence, of a concentric centeredness of our orienting polarities (say between heaven and earth, and past and present, and culture and nature), an American is apt to be perplexed in being told that this metaphysics is to be undone, since he or she will conceive of his literature and his philosophy as having begun with the knowledge and the tasks of its passing. If deconstruction, as in de Man's recommendation of it, is to disillusion us, it is a noble promise and to be given welcome. Disillusion is what fits us for reality, whether in Plato's terms or D. W. Winnicott's. But then we must be assured that this promise is based on a true knowledge of what our illusions are.

Critical Exchange I:

The Politics of Modernism

Clement Greenberg's Theory of Art

T. J. Clark

In the issue of *Partisan Review* for Fall 1939 appeared an article by Clement Greenberg entitled "Avant-Garde and Kitsch." It was followed four issues later, in July-August 1940, by another wide-ranging essay on modern art, "Towards a Newer Laocoon."[1] These two articles, I believe, stake out the ground for Greenberg's later practice as a critic and set down the main lines of a theory and history of culture since 1850—since, shall we say, Courbet and Baudelaire. Greenberg reprinted "Avant-Garde and Kitsch," making no attempt to tone down its mordant hostility to capitalism, as the opening item of his collection of critical essays, *Art and Culture*, in 1961. "Towards a Newer Laocoon" was not reprinted, perhaps because the author felt that its arguments were made more effectively in some of his later, more particular pieces included in *Art and Culture*—the essays on "Collage" or "Cézanne," for example, or the brief paragraphs on "Abstract, Representational, and So Forth." I am not sure that the author was right to omit the piece: it is noble, lucid, and extraordinarily balanced, it seems to me, in its defense of abstract art and avant-garde culture; and certainly its arguments are taken up directly, sometimes almost verbatim, in the more famous theoretical study which appeared in *Art and Literature* (Spring 1965) with the balder title "Modernist Painting."

1. See Clement Greenberg, "Avant-Garde and Kitsch," *Partisan Review* 6 (Fall 1939): 34–49, and "Towards a Newer Laocoon," *Partisan Review* 7 (July August 1940): 296–310; all further references to these essays, abbreviated "AK" and "NL" respectively, will be included in the text.

The essays of 1939 and 1940 argue already for what were to become Greenberg's main preoccupations and commitments as a critic. And the arguments adduced, as the author himself admits at the end of "Towards a Newer Laocoon," are largely historical. "I find," Greenberg writes there, "that I have offered no other explanation for the present superiority of abstract art than its historical justification. So what I have written has turned out to be an historical apology for abstract art" ("NL," p. 310). The author's proffered half-surprise at having thus "turned out" to be composing an apology in the historical manner should not of course be taken literally. For it was historical consciousness, Greenberg had argued in "Avant-Garde and Kitsch," which was the key to the avant-garde's achievement—its ability, that is, to salvage something from the collapse of the bourgeois cultural order. "A part of Western bourgeois society," Greenberg writes, "has produced something unheard of heretofore:—avant-garde culture. A superior consciousness of history—more precisely, the appearance of a new kind of criticism of society, an historical criticism—made this possible. . . . It was no accident, therefore, that the birth of the avant-garde coincided chronologically—and geographically, too—with the first bold development of scientific revolutionary thought in Europe" ("AK," p. 35). By this last he means, need I say it, preeminently the thought of Marx, to whom the reader is grimly directed at the end of the essay, after a miserable and just description of fascism's skill at providing "art for the people," with the words: "Here, as in every other question today, it becomes necessary to quote Marx word for word. Today we no longer look toward socialism for a new culture—as inevitably as one will appear, once we do have socialism. Today we look to socialism *simply* for the preservation of whatever living culture we have right now" ("AK," p. 49).

It is not intended as some sort of revelation on my part that Greenberg's cultural theory was originally Marxist in its stresses and, indeed, in its attitude to what constituted explanation in such matters. I point out the Marxist and historical mode of proceeding as emphatically as I do partly because it may make my own procedure later in this paper seem a little less arbitrary. For I shall fall to arguing in the end with these essays' Marxism and their history, and I want it understood that I think that to do so *is* to take issue with their strengths and their main drift.

But I have to admit there are difficulties here. The essays in question are quite brief. They are, I think, extremely well written: it was not for nothing that *Partisan Review* described Clement Greenberg, when he

T. J. Clark, professor of fine arts at Harvard University, is the author of *The Absolute Bourgeois: Artists and Politics in France, 1848–1851* and *Image of the People: Gustave Courbet and the 1848 Revolution.* His book on impressionist painting and Paris is forthcoming.

first contributed to the journal early in 1939, as "a young writer who works in the New York customs house"—fine, redolent avant-garde pedigree, that! The language of these articles is forceful and easy, always straightforward, blessedly free from Marxist conundrums. Yet the price paid for such lucidity, here as so often, is a degree of inexplicitness— a certain amount of elegant skirting round the difficult issues, where one might otherwise be obliged to call out the ponderous armory of Marx's concepts and somewhat spoil the flow of the prose from one firm statement to another. The Marxism, in other words, is quite largely implicit; it is stated on occasion, with brittle and pugnacious finality, *as* the essays' frame of reference, but it remains to the reader to determine just how it works in the history and theory presented—what that history and theory depend on, in the way of Marxist assumptions about class and capital or even base and superstructure. That is what I intend to do in this paper: to interpret and extrapolate from the texts, even at the risk of making their Marxism declare itself more stridently than the "young writer" seems to have wished. And I should admit straight away that there are several points in what follows where I am genuinely uncertain as to whether I am diverging from Greenberg's argument or explaining it more fully. This does not worry me overmuch, as long as we are alerted to the special danger in this case, dealing with such transparent yet guarded prose, and as long as we can agree that the project in general—pressing home a Marxist reading of texts which situate themselves within the Marxist tradition—is a reasonable one.[2]

I should therefore add a word or two to conjure up the connotations of "Marxism" for a writer in 1939 in *Partisan Review*. I do not need to labour the point, I hope, that there *was* a considerable and various Marxist culture in New York at this time; it was not robust, not profound, but not frivolous or flimsy either, in the way of England in the same years; and it is worth spelling out how well the pages of *Partisan Review* in 1939 and 1940 mirrored its distinction and variety and its sense of impending doom. The issue in which the "Newer Laocoon" was pub-

2. This carelessness distinguishes the present paper from two recent studies of Greenberg's early writings, Serge Guilbaut's "The New Adventures of the Avant-Garde in America," *October* 15 (Winter 1980), and Fred Orton and Griselda Pollock's *"Avant-Gardes and Partisans Reviewed,"* *Art History* 3 (September 1981). I am indebted to both these essays and am sure that their strictures on the superficiality—not to say the opportunism—of Greenberg's Marxism are largely right. (Certainly Mr. Greenberg would not now disagree with them.) But I am nonetheless interested in the challenge offered to most Marxist, and non-Marxist, accounts of modern history by what I take to be a justified, though extreme, pessimism as to the nature of established culture since 1870. That pessimism is characteristic, I suppose, of what Marxists call an ultraleftist point of view. I believe, as I say, that a version of some such view is correct and would therefore wish to treat Greenberg's theory *as if* it were a decently elaborated Marxism of an ultraleftist kind, one which issues in certain mistaken views (which I criticize) but which need not so issue and which might still provide, cleansed of those errors, a good vantage for a history of our culture.

lished began with an embattled article by Dwight MacDonald entitled "National Defense: The Case for Socialism," whose two parts were headed "Death of a World" and "What Must We Do to Be Saved?" The article was a preliminary to the "Ten Propositions on the War" which MacDonald and Greenberg were to sign jointly a year later, in which they argued—still in the bleak days of 1941—for revolutionary abstention from a war between capitalist nation-states. It was a bleak time, then, in which Marxist convictions were often found hard to sustain, but still a time characterized by a certain energy and openness of Marxist thought, even in its moment of doubt. MacDonald had just finished a series of articles—an excellent series, written from an anti-Stalinist point of view—on Soviet cinema and its public. (It is one main point of reference in the closing sections of "Avant-Garde and Kitsch.") Edmund Wilson in Fall 1938 could be seen pouring scorn on "The Marxist Dialectic," in the same issue as André Breton and Diego Rivera's "Manifesto: Towards a Free Revolutionary Art." Philip Rahv pieced out "The Twilight of the Thirties" or "What Is Living and What Is Dead" in Marxism. Victor Serge's *Ville Conquise* was published, partly, in translation. Meyer Schapiro took issue with *To the Finland Station*, and Bertram Wolfe reviewed Boris Souvarine's great book on Stalin.

And so on. The point is simply that this *was* a Marxist culture—a hectic and shallow-rooted one, in many ways, but one which deserved the name. Its appetite for European culture—for French art and poetry in particular—is striking and discriminate, especially compared with later New York French enthusiasms. This was the time when Lionel Abel was translating Lautréamont and Delmore Schwartz, *A Season in Hell*. The pages of *Partisan Review* had Wallace Stevens alongside Trotsky, Paul Eluard next to Allen Tate, "East Coker"—I am scrupulous here—following "Marx and Lenin as Scapegoats." No doubt the glamour of all this is misleading; but at least we can say, all reservations made, that a comparable roster of names and titles from any later period would look desultory by contrast, and rightly so.

Greenberg's first contribution to the magazine, in early 1939, was a review of Bertolt Brecht's *Penny for the Poor*, the novel taken from *The Threepenny Opera*. In it he discussed, sternly but with sympathy, the "nerve-wracking" formal monotony which derived, so he thought, from Brecht's effort to write a parable—a *consistent* fiction—of life under capitalism. In the same issue as "Avant-Garde and Kitsch" there appeared an account of an interview which Greenberg had had, the previous year, with Ignazio Silone. The interviewer's questions told the tale of his commitments without possibility of mistake: "What, in the light of their relations to political parties," he asked, "do you think should be the role of revolutionary writers in the present situation?"; and then, "When you speak of liberty, do you mean *socialist* liberty?"; and then,

"Have you read Trotsky's pamphlet, *Their Morals and Ours?* What do you think of it?"[3]

I am aware of the absurdity of paying more heed to Greenberg's questions than to Silone's grand replies; but you see the point of all this for anyone trying in the end to read between the lines of the "Newer Laocoon." And I hope that when, in a little while, I use the phrase "Eliotic Trotskyism" to describe Greenberg's stance, it will seem less forced a coinage. Perhaps one should even add Brecht to Eliot and Trotsky here, since it seems that the example of Brecht was especially vivid for Greenberg in the years around 1940, representing as he did a difficult, powerful counterexample to all the critic wished to see as the main line of avant-garde activity: standing for active engagement in ideological struggle, not detachment from it, and suggesting that such struggle was not necessarily incompatible with work on the *medium* of theatre, making that medium explicit and opaque in the best avant-garde manner. (It is a pity that Greenberg, as far as I know, wrote only about Brecht's novels and poetry.[4] Doubtless he would have had critical things to say also about Brecht's epic theatre, but the nature of his criticism—and especially his discussion of the tension between formal concentration and political purpose—might well have told us a great deal about the grounds of his ultimate settling for "purity" as the only feasible artistic ideal.)

All this has been by way of historical preliminary: if we are to read Greenberg's essays of 1939 and 1940, it is necessary, I think, to bear this history in mind.

Let me begin my reading proper, then, by stating in summary form what I take to be the arguments of "Avant-Garde and Kitsch" and the "Newer Laocoon." They are, as I have said, historical explanations of the course of avant-garde art since the mid–nineteenth century. They are seized with the strangeness of the avant-garde moment—that moment in which "a part of Western bourgeois society . . . produced something unheard of heretofore"; seized with its strangeness and not especially optimistic as to its chances of survival in the face of an ongoing breakdown of bourgeois civilization. For that *is* the context in which an avant-garde culture comes to be: it is a peculiar, indeed unique, reaction to a far from unprecedented cultural situation—to put it bluntly, the decadence of a society, the familiar weariness and confusion of a culture in its death throes. "Avant-Garde and Kitsch" is explicit on this: Western society in the nineteenth century reached that fatal phase in which, like Alexandrian Greece or late Mandarin China, it became "less and less able . . . to justify the inevitability of its particular forms" and thus to

3. Greenberg, "An Interview with Ignazio Silone," *Partisan Review* 6 (Fall 1939): 23, 25, 27
4. See Greenberg, "Bertolt Brecht's Poetry" (1941), *Art and Culture* (Boston, 1961).

keep alive "the accepted notions upon which artists and writers must depend in large part for communication with their audiences" ("AK," p. 34). Such a situation is usually fatal to seriousness in art. At the end of a culture, when all the verities of religion, authority, tradition, and style—all the ideological cement of society, in other words—are either disputed or doubted or believed in for convenience' sake and not held to *entail* anything much—at such a moment "the writer or artist is no longer able to estimate the response of his audience to the symbols and references with which he works." In the past that had meant an art which therefore left the really important issues to one side and contented itself with "virtuosity in the small details of form, all larger questions being [mechanically, listlessly] decided by the precedent of the old masters" ("AK," pp. 34–35).

Clearly, says Greenberg, there has been a "decay of our present society"—the words are his—which corresponds in many ways to all these gloomy precedents. What is new is the course of art in this situation. No doubt bourgeois culture is in crisis, more and more unable since Marx "to justify the inevitability of its particular forms"; but it has spawned, half in opposition to itself, half at its service, a peculiar and durable artistic tradition—the one we call modernist and what Greenberg then called, using its own label, avant-garde. "It was to be the task of the avant-garde to perform in opposition to bourgeois society the function of finding new and adequate cultural forms for the expression of that same society, without at the same time succumbing to its ideological divisions and its refusal to permit the arts to be their own justification" ("NL," p. 301).

There are several stresses here worth distinguishing. First, the avant-garde is "part of Western bourgeois society" and yet in some important way estranged from it: needing, as Greenberg phrases it, the revolutionary gloss put on the very "concept of the 'bourgeois' in order to define what they were *not*" ("AK," p. 35) but at the same time performing the function of finding forms "for the expression" of bourgeois society and tied to it "by an umbilical cord of gold." Here is the crucial passage: "it is to the [ruling class] that the avant-garde belongs. No culture can develop without a social basis, without a source of stable income. [We might immediately protest at this point at what seems to be the text's outlandish economism: "social basis" is one thing, "source of income" another; the sentence seems to elide them. But let it pass for the moment.] In the case of the avant-garde this [social basis] was provided by an elite among the ruling class of that society from which it assumed itself to be cut off, but to which it has always remained attached by an umbilical cord of gold" ("AK," p. 38).

That is the first stress: the contradictory belonging-together-in-opposition of the avant-garde and its bourgeoisie; and the sense—the pressing and anxious sense—of that connection-in-difference being attenuated, being on the point of severance. For "culture is being abandoned by those to whom it actually belongs—our ruling class" ("AK," p. 38): the avant-garde, in its specialization and estrangement, *had always been* a sign of that abandonment, and now it seemed as if the breach was close to final.

Second, the avant-garde is a way to protect art from "ideological divisions." "Ideological confusion and violence" are the enemies of artistic force and concentration: art seeks a space of its own apart from them, apart from the endless uncertainty of meanings in capitalist society ("AK," p. 36). It is plain how this connects with my previous wondering about Greenberg on Brecht, and I shall not press the point here, except to say that there is a special and refutable move being made in the argument: to compare the conditions in which, in late capitalism, the meanings of the ruling class are actively disputed with those in which, in Hellenistic Egypt, say, established meanings stultified and became subject to skepticism—this is to compare the utterly unlike. It is to put side by side a time of economic and cultural dissolution—an epoch of weariness and unconcern—and one of articulated and fierce class struggle. Capital may be uncertain of its values, but it is not weary; the bourgeoisie may have no beliefs worth the name, but they will not admit as much: they are hypocrites, not skeptics. And the avant-garde, I shall argue, has regularly and rightly seen an *advantage* for art in the particular conditions of "ideological confusion and violence" under capital; it has wished to take part in the general, untidy work of negation and has seen no necessary contradiction (rather the contrary) between doing so and coming to terms once again with its "medium."

But I shall return to this later. It is enough for now to point to this second stress, and to the third: the idea that one chief purpose of the avant-garde was to oppose bourgeois society's "refusal to permit the arts to be their own justification." This is the stress which leads on to the more familiar—and trenchant—arguments of the essays in question, which I shall indicate even more briefly: the description of the ersatz art produced for mass consumption by the ruling classes of late capitalism as part of their vile stage management of democracy, their pretending—it becomes perfunctory of late—"that the masses actually rule"; and the subtle account of the main strands in the avant-garde's history and the way they have all conspired to narrow and raise art "to the expression of an absolute" ("AK," p. 36). The pursuit has been purity, whatever the detours and self-deceptions. "The arts lie safe now, each within its 'legitimate' boundaries, and free trade has been replaced by autarchy. Purity in art consists in the acceptance . . . of the limitations of the medium. . . . The arts, then, have been hunted back [the wording is odd and pondered] to their mediums, and there they have been isolated, concentrated and defined" ("NL," p. 305). The logic is ineluctable, it "holds the artist in a vise," and time and again it overrides the most impure and ill-advised intentions:

> A good many of the artists—if not the majority—who contributed importantly to the development of modern painting came to it with the desire to exploit the break with imitative realism for a more powerful expressiveness, but so inexorable was the logic of the development that in the end their work constituted but another step towards abstract art, and a further sterilization of the expressive factors. This has been true, whether the artist was Van Gogh, Picasso or Klee. All roads lead to the same place. ["NL," pp. 309–10]

This is enough of summary. I do not want now, whatever the temptation, to pitch in with questions about specific cases (Is that *true* of van Gogh? What is the balance in collage between medium and illusion? etc.) Greenberg's argument of course provokes such questions, as arguments should do, but I want to restrict myself, if I can, to describing its general logic, inexorable or not, choosing my examples for their bearing on the author's overall gist.

Let me go back to the start of "Avant-Garde and Kitsch." It seems to be an unstated assumption of that article—and an entirely reasonable one, I believe—that there once was a time, before the avant-garde, when the bourgeoisie, like any normal ruling class, possessed a culture and an art which were directly and recognizably its own. And indeed we know what is meant by the claim: we know what it means, whatever the provisos and equivocations, to call Chardin and Hogarth bourgeois painters or Samuel Richardson and Daniel Defoe novelists of the middle class. We can move forward a century and still be confident in calling Balzac and Stendhal likewise, or Constable and Géricault. Of course there are degrees of difference and dissociation always—Balzac's politics, Géricault's alienation, Chardin's royal clientele—but the bourgeoisie, we can say, in some strong sense *possessed* this art: the art enacted, clarified, and criticized the class' experiences, its appearance and values; it responded to its demands and assumptions. There was a distinctive bourgeois culture; this art is part of our evidence for just such an assertion.

But it is clear also that from the later nineteenth century on, the distinctiveness and coherence of that bourgeois identity began to fade. "Fade" is too weak and passive a word, I think. I should say that the bourgeoisie was obliged to dismantle its focused identity, as part of the price it paid for maintaining social control. As part of its struggle for power over other classes, subordinate and voiceless in the social order but not placated, it was forced to dissolve its claim to culture—and in particular forced to revoke the claim, which is palpable in Géricault or

Stendhal, say, to take up and dominate and preserve the absolutes of aristocracy, the values of the class it displaced. "It's Athene whom we want," Greenberg blurts out in a footnote once, "formal culture with its infinity of aspects, its luxuriance, its large comprehension" ("AK," p. 49 n.5). Add to those qualities intransigence, intensity and risk in the life of the emotions, fierce regard for honour and desire for accurate self-consciousness, disdain for the commonplace, rage for order, insistence that the world cohere: these are, are they not, the qualities we tend to associate with art itself, at its highest moments in the Western tradition. But they are specifically feudal ruling-class superlatives: they are the ones the bourgeoisie believed they had inherited and the ones they chose to abandon because they became, in the class struggles after 1870, a cultural liability.

Hence what Greenberg calls kitsch. Kitsch is the sign of a bourgeoisie contriving to lose its identity, forfeiting the inconvenient absolutes of *Le Rouge et le noir* or *The Oath of the Horatii*. It is an art and a culture of instant assimilation, of abject reconciliation to the everyday, of avoidance of difficulty, pretence to indifference, equality before the image of capital.

Modernism is born in reaction to this state of affairs. And you will see, I hope, the peculiar difficulty here. There had once been, let me say again, a bourgeois identity and a classic nineteenth-century bourgeois culture. But as the bourgeoisie built itself the forms of mass society and thereby entrenched its power, it devised a massified pseudoart and pseudoculture and destroyed its *own* cultural forms—they had been, remember, a long time maturing, in the centuries of patient accommodation to and difference from aristocratic or absolutist rule. Now, Greenberg says, I think rightly, that some kind of connection exists between this bourgeoisie and the art of the avant-garde. The avant-garde is engaged in finding forms for the expression of bourgeois society: that is the phrase again from the "Newer Laocoon." But what could this mean, exactly, in the age of bourgeois decomposition so eloquently described in "Avant-Garde and Kitsch"? It seems that modernism is being proposed as bourgeois art in the absence of a bourgeoisie or, more accurately, as aristocratic art in the age when the bourgeoisie abandons its claims to aristocracy. And how will art keep aristocracy alive? By keeping *itself* alive, as the remaining vessel of the aristocratic account of experience and its modes; by preserving its own means, its media; by proclaiming those means and media *as* its values, as meanings in themselves.

This is, I think, the crux of the argument. It seems to me that Greenberg is aware of the paradox involved in his avant-garde preserving *bourgeoisie*, in its highest and severest forms, for a bourgeoisie which, in the sense so proposed, no longer existed. He points to the paradox, but he believes the solution to it has proved to be, in practice, the density and resistance of artistic values per se. They are the repository, as it were, of affect and intelligence that once inhered in a complex form of life but do so no longer; they are the concrete form of intensity and self-consciousness, the only one left, and therefore the form to be preserved at all costs and somehow kept apart from the surrounding desolation.

It is a serious and grim picture of culture under capitalism, and the measure of its bitterness and perplexity seems to me still justified. Eliotic Trotskyism, I called it previously; the cadencies shifting line by line from "Socialism or Barbarism" to "Shakespeare and the Stoicism of Seneca." (And was Greenberg a reader of *Scrutiny*, I wonder? It was widely read in New York at this time, I believe.)[5] From his Eliotic stronghold he perceives, and surely with reason, that much of the great art of the previous century, including some which had declared itself avant-garde and anti-bourgeois, had depended on the patronage and mental appetites of a certain fraction of the middle class. It had in some sense *belonged* to a bourgeois intelligentsia—to a fraction of the class which was self-consciously "progressive" in its tastes and attitudes and often allied to the cause not just of artistic experiment but of social and political reform. And it is surely also true that in late capitalism this independent, critical, and progressive intelligentsia was put to death by its own class. For late capitalism—by which I mean the order emerging from the Great Depression—is a period of cultural uniformity: a leveling-down, a squeezing-out of previous bourgeois élites, a narrowing of distance between class and class *and* between fractions of the same class. In this case, the distance largely disappears between bourgeois intelligentsia and unintelligentsia: by our own time one might say it is normally impossible to distinguish one from the other.

(And lest this be taken as merely flippant, let me add that the kind of distance I have in mind—and distance here does not mean detachment but precisely an active, uncomfortable difference from the class one belongs to—is that between Walter Lippmann's salon, say, and the American middle class of its day; or that between the circle around Léon Gambetta and the general ambience of Ordre Moral. This last is especially to the purpose, since its consequences for culture were so vivid: one has only to remember the achievement of Antonin Proust in his brief tenure of the Direction des Beaux-Arts or Georges Clemenceau's patronage of and friendship with Claude Monet.)[6]

5. Mr. Greenberg informs me the answer here is yes and points out that he even once had an exchange with F. R. Leavis, in *Commentary*, on Kafka—one which, he says, "I did not come out of too well!" ("How Good Is Kafka?," *Commentary* 19 (June 1955).

6. I think this state of affairs lies at the root of those ills of present-day Marxist criticism to which Edward Said refers in "Opponents, Audiences, Constituencies, and Community." In the years around 1910, for example, it was possible for Marxist intellectuals to identify a worthwhile enemy within the ranks of the academy—there was a

This description of culture is suitably grim, as I say, and finds its proper echoes in Eliot, Trotsky, F. R. Leavis, and Brecht. And yet—and here at last I modulate into criticism—there seem to me things badly wrong with its final view of art and artistic value. I shall offer three, or perhaps four, kinds of criticism of the view: first, I shall point to the difficulties involved in the very notion of art itself becoming an independent source of value; second, I shall disagree with one of the central elements in Greenberg's account of that value, his reading of "medium" in avant-garde art; and third, I shall try to recast his sketch of modernism's formal logic in order to include aspects of avant-garde practice which he overlooks or belittles but which I believe are bound up with those he sees as paramount. What I shall point to here—not to make a mystery of it—are *practices of negation* in modernist art which seem to me the very form of the practices of purity (the recognitions and enactments of medium) which Greenberg extols. Finally, I shall suggest some ways in which the previous three criticisms are connected, in particular, the relation between those practices of negation and the business of bourgeois artists making do without a bourgeoisie. I shall be brief, and the criticisms may seem schematic. But my hope is that because they are anyway simple objections to points in an argument where it appears palpably weak, they will, schematic or not, seem quite reasonable.

The first disagreement could be introduced by asking the following

---

group of progressive bourgeois intellectuals whose thought and action had some real effect in the polity. That state of things was fortunate in two regards. It enabled middle-class Marxist intellectuals to attain to some kind of lucidity about the limits of their own enterprise—to see themselves as bourgeois, lacking roots in the main earth of class struggle. It meant they did not spend much of their time indulging in what I regard as the mainly futile breast-beating represented so characteristically by Terry Eagleton's bathetic question, which Said quotes: "'How is a Marxist-structuralist analysis of a minor novel of Balzac to help shake the foundations of capitalism?'" (p. 21). Those earlier Marxists did not need this rhetoric, this gasping after class positions which they did not occupy, because there was an actual job for them to do, one with a measure of importance, after all—the business of opposing the ideologies of a bourgeois élite and of pointing to the falsity of the seeming contest between that élite and the ordinary, power-wielding mass of the class. (I am thinking here, e.g., of the simple, historical *ground* to Georg Lukács' battle with positivism in science, Kantianism in ethics, and Weberianism in politics. It was the evident link between that circuit of ideas and an actual, cunning practice of social reform that gave Lukács' essays their intensity and also their sense of not having to apologize for intellectual work.) I believe it is the absence of any such bourgeois intelligentsia, goading and supplying the class it belongs to—the absence, in other words, of a bourgeoisie worth attacking in the realm of cultural production—that lies behind the quandary of Eagleton et al. And let me be clear: the quandary seems to me at least worth being in, which is more than I can say for most other academic dilemmas. I just now applied the adjective "bathetic" to Eagleton's question, and perhaps it will have seemed a dismissive choice of word. But bathos implies an attempt at elevation and a descent from it, and of the general run of contemporary criticism—the warring solipsisms and scientisms, the exercises in spot-the-discourse or discard-the-referent—I think one can fairly say that it runs no such risk. Its tone is ludicrously secure.

(Wittgensteinian) question: What would it be *like*, exactly, for art to possess its own values? Not just to have, in other words, a set of distinctive effects and procedures but to have them somehow be, or provide, the standards by which the effects and procedures are held to be of worth? I may as well say at once that there seem, on the face of it, some insuperable logical difficulties here, and they may well stand in the way of ever providing a coherent reply to the Wittgensteinian question. But I much prefer to give—or to sketch—a kind of *historical* answer to the question, in which the point of asking it in the first place might be made more clear.

Let us concede that Greenberg may be roughly right when he says in "Avant-Garde and Kitsch" that "a fairly constant distinction" has been made by "the cultivated of mankind over the ages" "between those values only to be found in art and the values which can be found elsewhere" ("AK," p. 42). But let us ask how that distinction was actually made— made and maintained, as an active opposition—in practice, in the first heyday of the art called avant-garde. For the sake of vividness, we might choose the case of the young speculator Dupuy, whom Camille Pissarro described in 1890 as "mon meilleur amateur" and who killed himself the same year, to Pissarro's chagrin, because he believed he was faced with bankruptcy. One's picture of such a patron is necessarily speculative in its turn, but what I want to suggest is nothing very debatable. It seems clear from the evidence that Dupuy was someone capable of savouring the *separateness* of art, its irreducible difficulties and appeal. That was what presumably won him Pissarro's respect and led him to buy the most problematic art of his day. (This at a time, remember, when Pissarro's regular patrons, and dealers, had quietly sloped off in search of something less odd.) But I would suggest that he also saw—and in some sense insisted on—a kind of consonance between the experience and value that art had to offer and those that belonged to his everyday life. The consonance did not need to be direct and, indeed, could not be. Dupuy was not in the market for animated pictures of the Stock Exchange—the kind he could have got from Jean Béraud—or even for scenes à la Degas in which he might have been offered back, dramatically, the shifts and upsets of life in the big city. He purchased landscapes instead and seems to have had a taste for those painted in the neo-impressionist manner— painted, that is, in a way which tried to be tight, discreet, and uniform, done with a disabused orderliness, seemingly scientific, certainly analytic. And all of these qualities, we might guess, he savoured and required as the signs of art's detachment.

Yet surely we must also say that his openness to such qualities, his ability to understand them, was founded in a sense he had of some play between those qualities occurring in art and the same occurring in life—occurring in his life, not on the face of it a happy one but one at the cutting edge of capitalism still. And when we remember what capitalism *was* in 1890, we are surely better able to understand why Dupuy invested in Georges Seurat. For this was a capital still confident in its powers, if shaken; and not merely confident, but scrupulous: still in active dialogue with science; still producing distinctive rhetorics and modes of appraising experience; still conscious of its own values—the tests of rationality, the power born of observation and control; still, if you wish, believing in the commodity as a (perplexing) form of freedom.

You see my point, I hope. I believe it was the interplay of these values and the values of art which made the distinction between them an active and possible one—made it a distinction at all, as opposed to a rigid and absolute disjunction. In the case of Dupuy, there was difference-yet-consonance between the values which made for the bourgeois' sense of himself in practical life and those he required from avant-garde painting. The facts of art and the facts of capital were in active tension. They were still negotiating with each other; they could still, at moments, in particular cases like Dupuy's, contrive to put each other's categories in doubt.

This, it seems to me, is what is meant by "a fairly constant distinction [being] made between those values only to be found in art and the values which can be found elsewhere." It is a negotiated distinction, with the critic of Diderot's or Baudelaire's or Félix Fénéon's type the active agent of the settlement. For critics like these, and in the art they typically address, it is true that the values a painting offers are discovered, time and again and with vehemence, as different and irreducible. And we understand the point of Fénéon's insistence; but we are the more impressed by it precisely because the values are found to be different as part of a real cultural dialectic, by which I mean that they are visibly under pressure, in the text, from the demands and valuations made by the ruling class in the business of ruling—the meanings it makes and disseminates, the kinds of order it proposes as its own. It is this pressure—and the way it is enacted in the patronage relation or in the artist's imagining of his or her public—which keeps the values of art from becoming a merely academic canon.

I hope it is clear how this account of artistic standards—and particularly of the ways in which art's separateness as a social practice is secured—would call into question Greenberg's hope that art could become a provider of value in its own right. Yet I think I can call that belief in question more effectively simply by looking at one or another of the facts of art which Greenberg takes to have become a value, in some sense: let me look, for simplicity's sake, at the notorious fact of "flatness." Now it is certainly true that the literal flatness of the picture surface was recovered at regular intervals as a striking fact by painters after Courbet. But I think that the question we should ask in this case is *why* that simple, empirical presence went on being interesting for art. How could a fact of effect or procedure stand in for value in this way? What was it that made it vivid?

The answer is not far to seek. I think we can say that the fact of flatness was vivid and tractable—as it was in the art of Cézanne, for example, or that of Matisse—because it was made to stand for something: some particular and resistant set of qualities, taking its place in an articulated account of experience. The richness of the avant-garde, as a set of contexts for art in the years between 1860 and 1918, say, might thus be redescribed in terms of its ability to give flatness such complex and compatible values—values which necessarily derived from elsewhere than art. It could stand, that flatness, as an analogue of the "popular"— something therefore conceived as plain, workmanlike, and emphatic. Or it could signify "modernity," with flatness meant to conjure up the mere two dimensions of posters, labels, fashion prints, and photographs. Equally, unbrokenness of surface could be seen—by Cézanne, for example—as standing for the truth of *seeing*, the actual form of our knowledge of things. And that very claim was repeatedly felt, by artist and audience, to be some kind of aggression on the latter: flatness appeared as a barrier to the ordinary bourgeois' wish to enter a picture and dream, to have it be a space apart from life in which the mind would be free to make its own connections.

My point is simply that flatness in its heyday *was* these various meanings and valuations; they were its substance, so to speak; they were what it was seen *as*. Their particularity was what made it vivid—made it a matter to be painted over again. Flatness was therefore in play—as an irreducible, technical "fact" of painting—with all of these totalizations, all of these attempts to make it a metaphor. Of course in a sense it resisted the metaphors, and the painters we most admire insisted also on it as an awkward, empirical quiddity; but the "also" is the key word here: there was no fact without the metaphor, no medium without its being the vehicle of a complex act of meaning.

This leads me directly to my third criticism of Greenberg's account. It could be broached most forcefully, I think, by asking the question, How does the medium most often *appear* in modernist art? If we accept (as we ought to, I feel) that avant-garde painting, poetry, and music are characterized by an insistence on medium, then what kind of insistence has it been, usually? My answer would be—it is hardly an original one—that the medium has appeared most characteristically as the site of negation and estrangement.

The very way that modernist art has insisted on its medium has been by negating that medium's ordinary consistency—by pulling it apart, emptying it, producing gaps and silences, making it stand as the opposite of sense or continuity, having matter be the synonym for resistance. (And why, after all, should matter be "resistant"? It is a modernist piety with a fairly dim ontology appended.) Modernism would have its medium be *absence* of some sort—absence of finish or coherence, indeterminacy, a ground which is called on to swallow up distinctions.

These are familiar avant-garde strategies; and I am not for a moment suggesting that Greenberg does not recognize their part in the art he admires. Yet he is notoriously uneasy with them and prepared to declare them extrinsic to the real business of art in our time—the business of each art "determin[ing], through the operations peculiar to itself, the effects peculiar and exclusive to itself."[7] It is Greenberg's disdain for the rhetoric of negation which underlies, one supposes, the ruefulness of his description of Jackson Pollock as, after all, a "Gothic" whose art harked back to Faulkner and Melville in its "violence, exasperation and stridency."[8] It is certainly the same disdain which determines his verdict on Dada, which is only important, he feels, as a complaisant topic for journalism about the modern crisis (or the shock of the new). And one does know what he means by the charge; one does feel the fire of his sarcasm, in 1947, when, in the middle of dealing well with Pollock's unlikely achievement, he writes: "In the face of current events, painting feels, apparently, that it must be more than itself, that it must be epic poetry, it must be theatre, it must be an atomic bomb, it must be the rights of Man. But the greatest painter of our time, Matisse, preeminently demonstrated the sincerity and penetration that go with the kind of greatness particular to twentieth century painting by saying that he wanted his art to be an armchair for the tired business man."[9]

It is splendid, it is salutary, it is congenial. Yet surely in the end it will not quite do as description. Surely it is part of modernism's problem—even Matisse's—that the tired businessman be so weary and vacant and so little interested in art as his armchair. It is this situation—this lack of an adequate ruling class to address—which goes largely to explain modernism's negative cast.

I think that finally my differences with Greenberg centre on this one. I do not believe that the practices of negation which Greenberg seeks to declare mere *noise* on the modernist message can be thus demoted. They are simply inseparable from the work of self-definition which he takes to be central: inseparable in the case of Pollock, for certain, or Miro or Picasso or, for that matter, Matisse. Modernism is certainly that art which insists on its medium and says that meaning can henceforth only be found in *practice*. But the practice in question is extraordinary and desperate: it presents itself as a work of interminable and absolute decomposition, a work which is always pushing "medium" to its limits—to its ending—to the point where it breaks or evaporates or

7. Greenberg, "Modernist Painting," *Art and Literature* 4 (Spring 1965): 194.
8. Greenberg, "The Present Prospects of American Painting and Sculpture," *Horizon* 16 (October 1947): 26.
9. Greenberg, "Art," *Nation* 8 (March 1947): 284.

turns back into mere unworked material. That is the form in which medium is retrieved or reinvented: the fact of Art, in modernism, *is* the fact of negation.

I believe that this description imposes itself: that it is the only one which can include Mallarmé alongside Rimbaud, Schoenberg alongside Webern, or (dare I say it?) Duchamp beside the Monet of the *Nymphéas*. And surely that dance of negation has to do with the social facts I have spent most of my time rehearsing—the decline of ruling-class élites, the absence of a "social base" for artistic production, the paradox involved in making bourgeois art in the absence of a bourgeoisie. Negation is the sign inside art of this wider decomposition: it is an attempt to *capture* the lack of consistent and repeatable meanings in the culture—to capture the lack and make it over into form.

I should make the extent of this, my last disagreement with Greenberg, clear. The extent is small but definite. It is not, of course, that Greenberg fails to recognize the rootlessness and isolation of the avant-garde; his writing is full of the recognition, and he knows as well as anyone the miseries inherent in such a loss of place. But he does believe—the vehemence of the belief is what is most impressive in his writing—that art can substitute *itself* for the values capitalism has made valueless. A refusal to share that belief—and that is finally what I am urging—would have its basis in the following three observations. First, to repeat, negation is inscribed in the very practice of modernism, as the form in which art appears to itself as a value. Second, that negativity does not appear as a practice which guarantees meaning or opens out a space for free play and fantasy—in the manner of the joke, for example, or even of irony—but, rather, negation appears as an absolute and all-encompassing fact, something which once begun is cumulative and un-controllable; a fact which swallows meaning altogether. The road leads back and back to the black square, the hardly differentiated field of sound, the infinitely flimsy skein of spectral colour, speech stuttering and petering out into etceteras or excuses. ("I am obliged to believe that these are statements having to do with a world, . . . but you, the reader, need not. . . . And I and You, oh well. . . . The poem offers a way out of itself, hereabouts. . . . But do not take it, wholly. . . ." And so on.) On the other side of negation is always emptiness: that is a message which mod-ernism never tires of repeating and a territory into which it regularly strays. We have an art in which ambiguity becomes infinite, which is on the verge of proposing—and does propose—an Other which is comfort-ably ineffable, a vacuity, a vagueness, a mere mysticism of sight.[10]

10. The editor of *Critical Inquiry* suggested that I say a little more about the negative cast I ascribe to modernism and give an example or two. Too many examples crowd to mind, and I ought to avoid the more glamorous, since what I am referring to is an *aspect* or *moment* of modernist art, most often mixed up with other purposes or techniques, though often, I would argue, dominating them. Nevertheless a phrase from Leavis' *New Bearings*

There is a way—and this again is something which happens *within* modernism or at its limits—in which that empty negation is in turn negated. And that brings me back finally to the most basic of Greenberg's assumptions; it brings me back to the essays on Brecht. For there is an art—a modernist art—which has challenged the notion that art stands only to suffer from the fact that now all meanings are disputable. There is an art—Brecht's is only the most doctrinaire example—which says that we live not simply in a period of cultural decline, when meanings have become muddy and stale, but rather in a period when one set of meanings—those of the cultivated classes—is fitfully contested by those who stand to gain from their collapse. There is a difference, in other words, between Alexandrianism and class struggle. The twentieth century has elements of both situations about it, and that is why Greenberg's description, based on the Alexandrian analogy, applies as well as it does. But the end of the bourgeoisie is not, or will not be, like the end of Ptolemy's patriciate. And the end of its art will be likewise unprecedented. It will involve, and has involved, the kinds of inward turning that Greenberg has described so compellingly. But it will also involve—and has involved, as part of the practice of modernism—a search for another place in the social order. Art wants to address someone, it wants something precise and extended to do; it wants *resistance*, it needs criteria; it will take risks in order to find them, including the risk of its own dissolution.[11] Greenberg is surely entitled to judge that risk

---

occurs, in which the critic describes T. S. Eliot's "effort to express formlessness itself as form," and the lines (among others) which that phrase applies to: "Shape without form, shade without colour, / Paralysed force, gesture without motion." Yet we would do best to descend from these obvious heights and, if glamour is what is wanted, contemplate Ad Reinhardt's description of his own black painting in 1962:

> A square (neutral, shapeless) canvas, five feet wide, five feet high, as high as a man, as wide as a man's outstretched arms (not large, not small, sizeless), trisected (no composition), one horizontal form negating one vertical form (formless, no top, no bottom, directionless), three (more or less) dark (lightless) non-contrasting (color-less) colors, brushwork brushed out to remove brushwork, a matt, flat, free-hand painted surface (glossless, textureless, non-linear, no hard-edge, no soft-edge) which does not reflect its surroundings—a pure, abstract, non-objective, timeless, spaceless, changeless, relationless, disinterested painting—an object that is self-conscious (no unconsciousness), ideal transcendent, aware of no thing but art (absolutely no anti-art). [*Art, USA, Now* (New York, 1963), p. 269]

This pretends to be ironical, of course, and the art it gives rise to is negligible now, I dare say, even by received modernist standards; but the passage only puts into words a kind of attitude and practice which is by no means eccentric since Baudelaire and which has often issued in art of peculiar forcefulness and gravity.

11. This is not to smuggle in a demand for realism again by the back door; or at least, not one posed in the traditional manner. The weakness or absence I have pointed to in modern art does not derive, I think, from a lack of grounding in "seeing" (for example) or a set of realist protocols to go with that; rather, it derives from its lack of grounding in some (any) specific practice of representation, which would be linked in turn to other social

too great and, even more, to be impatient with the pretense of risk so dear to one fringe of modernist art and its patrons—all that stuff about blurring the boundaries between art and life and the patter about art being "revolutionary." Entitled he is; but not in my opinion right. The risk is large and the patter odious; but the alternative, I believe, is on the whole worse. It is what we have, as the present form of modernism: an art whose object is nothing but itself, which never tires of discovering that that self is pure as only pure negativity can be, and which offers its audience that nothing, tirelessly and, I concede, adequately made over into form. A verdict on such an art is not a matter of taste—for who could fail to admire, very often, its refinement and ingenuity—but involves a judgment, still, of cultural possibility. Thus while it seems to me right to expect little from the life and art of late capitalism, I still draw back from believing that the best one can hope for from art, even *in extremis,* is its own singular and perfect disembodiment.

---

practices—embedded in them, constrained by them. The question is not, therefore, whether modern art should be figurative or abstract, rooted in empirical commitments or not so rooted, but whether art is now provided with sufficient constraints of any kind—notions of appropriateness, tests of vividness, demands which bring with them measures of importance or priority. Without constraints, representation of any articulateness and salience cannot take place. (One might ask if the constraints which modernism declares to be its own and sufficient—those of the medium or of an individual's emotions and sense of inner truth—are binding or indeed coherent; or, to be harsh, if the areas of practice which it points to as the *sites* of such constraint—medium, emotion, even "language" [sacred cow]—are existents at all, in the way that is claimed for them.)

How Modernism Works: A Response to T. J. Clark

Michael Fried

In the remarks that follow, I challenge the interpretation of modernism
put forward in T. J. Clark's provocative essay, "Clement Greenberg's
Theory of Art." As will become clear, my aim in doing so is not to defend
Greenberg against Clark's strictures. On the contrary, although my own
writings on recent abstract art are deeply indebted to the example of
Greenberg's practical criticism (I consider him the foremost critic of new
painting and sculpture of our time), I shall suggest that Clark's reading
of modernism shares certain erroneous assumptions with Greenberg's,
on which indeed it depends. I shall then go on to rehearse an alternative
conception of the modernist enterprise that I believe makes better sense
of the phenomena in question than does either of theirs, and, in an
attempt to clinch my case, I shall conclude by looking briefly at an interesting phase in the work of the contemporary English sculptor Anthony
Caro, whose achievement since 1960 I take to be canonical for modernism generally.

1

At the center of Clark's essay is the claim that the practices of modernism in the arts are fundamentally practices of negation. This claim is
false.

Not that there is nothing at all to the view he espouses. In the first
place, there is a (Gramscian?) sense in which a given cultural expression

may be thought of as occupying a social space that might otherwise be occupied by another and, therefore, as bearing a relation to that other that might loosely be characterized as one of negation. Furthermore, particular modernist developments in the arts have often involved a negative "moment" in which certain formal and expressive possibilities were implicitly or indeed explicitly repudiated in favor of certain others, as when, for example, Edouard Manet in the early 1860s rejected both dramatic mise-en-scène and traditional sculptural modelling as vehicles of pictorial coherence, or as when Caro almost a century later came to feel the inadequacy to a dawning vision of sculptural possibility of the techniques of modelling and casting in which he had been trained.[1]

It is also true that entire episodes in the history of modern art— Dada, for example, or the career of Marcel Duchamp—can be construed as largely negative in motivation, and it is part of Clark's critique that Greenberg gives those episodes short shrift, treating them, Clark says, as mere noise on the surface of the modernist message. But Clark goes far beyond these observations to insist that "negation is inscribed in the very practice of modernism, as the form in which art appears to itself as a value," or, as he more baldly puts it, "the fact of Art, in modernism, *is* the fact of negation" (p. 218). And these claims, to the extent that I find them intelligible, seem to me mistaken.

Now it is a curious feature of Clark's essay that he provides no specific examples for his central argument. Instead, he merely cites the names Mallarmé, Rimbaud, Schoenberg, Webern, Duchamp, and Monet (of the *Nymphéas*), and in footnote 10, added, we are told, at the request of the editor, he quotes (irrelevantly in my view) a phrase of F. R. Leavis' on two lines by T. S. Eliot, along with a description by Ad Reinhardt—a distinctly minor figure who cannot be taken as representative of

1. Clark writes in his n. 10 (p. 218) that "what I am referring to is an *aspect* or *moment* of modernist art, most often mixed up with other purposes or techniques, though often, I would argue, dominating them." This introduces a hint of qualification, almost of moderation, that can be found nowhere else in his essay. The present response addresses the hard, unqualified position taken by his essay as a whole, which stands virtually as it was read aloud at the "Politics of Interpretation" conference in Chicago. Perhaps I ought to add, inasmuch as my assessment of his views on modernism will be severe, that I think highly of his studies of French art during the Second Republic, *Image of the People* (Princeton, N.J., 1973) and *The Absolute Bourgeois* (Princeton, N.J., 1973).

Michael Fried, professor of humanities and the history of art and director of the Humanities Center at the Johns Hopkins University, is the author of *Morris Louis* and *Absorption and Theatricality: Painting and Beholder in the Age of Diderot* and is currently at work on a book on Courbet.

modernism—of his own black paintings. (The latter are evidently the "black square" to which, Clark asserts, "the road leads back and back"— except it doesn't [p. 218].)

How are we to understand this refusal to discuss specific cases? In an obvious sense, it makes Clark's position difficult to rebut: one is continually tempted to imagine what he would say about particular works of art—Manet's *Déjeuner sur l'herbe* (fig. 1), or Cézanne's *Gulf of Marseilles Seen from L'Estaque,* or Matisse's *Blue Nude,* or Picasso's *Ma Jolie,* or Jackson Pollock's *Lavender Mist,* or David Smith's *Zig IV,* or Caro's *Prairie*—and then to argue against those invented descriptions. I found myself doing this again and again in preliminary drafts of this response until I realized that it was pointless. For the burden of proof is Clark's, the obligation is his, to establish by analyzing one or more indisputably major works of modernist art (I offer him the short list I have just assembled) that negation functions in those works as the radical and all-devouring principle he claims it is. And here it is worth stipulating that it will not be enough to say of Manet's *Déjeuner* (I'm anticipating Clark again) that it represents a situation or an action that is psychologically and narratively unintelligible; not enough because it would still be

FIG. 1.—Edouard Manet, *Le Déjeuner sur l'herbe,* 1862–63. Louvre, Paris. Phot. Réunion des musées nationaux.

possible to argue, as I would wish to argue, that unintelligibility in Manet, far from being a value in its own right as mere negation of meaning, is in the service of aims and aspirations that have in view a new and profound and, for want of a better word, positive conception of the enterprise of painting.[2] I would make the same sort of argument about the violation of ordinary spatial logic in Cézanne, or the distorted drawing and bizarre color in Matisse, or the near dissolution of sculptural form in Picasso, or the embracing of abstraction and the exploration of new means of picture-making in Pollock, or the use of industrial materials and techniques in Smith and Caro. In all these instances of "mainstream" modernism—a notion Clark is bound to reject as reinstituting the very distinction he wishes to collapse—there is at most a negative "moment," the significance of which can only be understood (and the form of that understanding can only be historical, which is to say, provisional or at any rate not final) in terms of a relation to a more encompassing and fundamental set of positive values, conventions, sources of conviction.[3] If Clark disagrees with this, and I'm sure he does, let him accept the challenge and offer examples that prove his point. Otherwise his sweeping generalizations lack all force.

2

Clark's essay stages itself as a critique of Greenberg's theory of modernism; yet the gist of Clark's argument, his equation of modernism with negation, involves a largely uncritical acceptance of Greenberg's account of how modernism works.

The story Greenberg tells is this.[4] Starting around the middle of the nineteenth century, the major arts, threatened for the first time with

2. I associate those aims and aspirations with the search for a new and more perspicuous mode of pictorial unity as well as with the desire to achieve a specific relation between painting and beholder (two aspects of the same undertaking). This is not the place for a detailed discussion of these matters, but I will simply note that the unintelligibility of the action or situation promotes an effect of *instantaneousness*, not of the action itself so much as of one's perception of the scene, the painting, as a whole. For more on Manet's aims in the first half of the 1860s, see my "Manet's Sources: Aspects of His Art, 1859–1865," *Artforum* 7 (March 1969): 28–82. In that essay I suggest that the *Déjeuner* combines elements of several genres of painting (e.g., landscape, portraiture, still life) and that this too is to be understood in terms of Manet's pursuit of a more radical and comprehensive mode of unification than was provided by the pictorial culture of his day.

3. On the distinction between "mainstream" modernism and its shadow, the phenomenon Greenberg calls avant-gard*ism,* see n. 17 below.

4. My presentation of Greenberg's theory of modernism is based chiefly on two of his later essays, "Modernist Painting" (1961), in *The New Art: A Critical Anthology,* ed. Gregory Battcock (New York, 1966), pp. 100–110, and "After Abstract Expressionism" (1962), in *New York Painting and Sculpture: 1940–1970,* ed. Henry Geldzahler (New York, 1969), pp. 360–71.

being assimilated to mere entertainment, discovered that they could save themselves from that depressing fate "only by demonstrating that the kind of experience they provided was valuable in its own right and not to be obtained from any other kind of activity." (The crucial figure in painting is Manet, whose decisive canvases belong to the early 1860s.)

> Each art, it turned out, had to effect this demonstration on its own account. What had to be exhibited and made explicit was that which was unique and irreducible not only in art in general but also in each particular art. Each art had to determine, through the operations peculiar to itself, the effects peculiar and exclusive to itself. By doing this, each art would, to be sure, narrow its area of competence, but at the same time it would make its possession of this area all the more secure.
>
> It quickly emerged that the unique and proper area of competence of each art coincided with all that was unique to the nature of its medium. The task of self-criticism became to eliminate from the effects of each art any and every effect that might conceivably be borrowed from or by the medium of every other art. Thereby each art would be rendered "pure," and in its "purity" find the guarantee of its standards of quality as well as of its independence. "Purity" meant self-definition, and the enterprise of self-criticism in the arts became one of self-definition with a vengeance.[5]

As described by Greenberg, the enterprise in question involved testing a wide range of norms and conventions in order to determine which were inessential, and therefore to be discarded, and which on the contrary constituted the timeless and unchanging essence of the art of painting. (Greenberg doesn't use either of the last two adjectives, but both are implicit in his argument.) By the early 1960s, the results of this century-long project, Greenberg's famous modernist "reduction," appeared to be in:

> It has been established by now, it would seem, that the irreducibility of pictorial art consists in but two constitutive conventions or norms: flatness and the delimitation of flatness. In other words, the observance of merely these two norms is enough to create an object which can be experienced as a picture: thus a stretched or tacked-up canvas already exists as a picture—though not necessarily as a *successful* one.[6]

Greenberg may have been somewhat uneasy with this conclusion; at any rate, he goes on to state that Barnett Newman, Mark Rothko, and Clyfford Still, three of the most advanced painters of the postwar period,

5. Greenberg, "Modernist Painting," p. 102.
6. Greenberg, "After Abstract Expressionism," p. 369.

"have swung the self-criticism of Modernist painting in a new direction by dint simply of continuing it in its old one. The question now asked in their art is no longer what constitutes art, or the art of painting, as such, but what constitutes *good* art as such. What is the ultimate source of value or quality in art?" (The answer he gives, or finds their art to give, is "conception.")[7] But here, too, the governing notion is one of reduction to an essence, to an absolute and unchanging core that in effect has been there all along and which the evolution of modernist painting has progressively laid bare.

I don't say that Clark swallows Greenberg whole. In particular he refuses to accept the proposition that with the advent of modernism art becomes or is revealed to be "a provider of value in its own right" (p. 215), arguing instead that modernist art has always reflected the values of modern society (more on this presently). But I do suggest that Clark's insistence that modernism proceeds by ever more extreme and dire acts of negation is simply another version of the idea that it has evolved by a process of radical reduction—by casting off, negating, one norm or convention after another in search of the bare minimum that can suffice. Indeed I believe that it is because Clark accepts Greenberg's reductionist and essentialist conception of the modernist enterprise that he is led to characterize the medium in modernism as "the site of negation and estrangement"—as pushed continually "to the point where it breaks or evaporates or turns back into mere unworked material"—and to assert that in modernism "negation appears as an absolute and all-encompassing fact, something which once begun is cumulative and uncontrollable" (pp. 216, 217–18, 218). From this perspective, Clark's attitude toward the developments to which he alludes is less important than the assumptions underlying his interpretation of those developments. His attitude, of course, is the reverse of Greenberg's, but his assumptions derive directly from Greenberg's schema.

3

As long ago as 1966–67 I took issue with what I called a reductionist conception of modernism. In an essay on a group of paintings by Frank Stella, I wrote:

> I take a reductionist conception of modernist painting to mean this: that painting roughly since Manet is seen as a kind of cognitive enterprise in which a certain quality (e.g., literalness), set of norms (e.g., flatness and the delimiting of flatness), or core of problems (e.g., how to acknowledge the literal character of the support) is

7. Ibid. Greenberg spells out what he means by "conception" when he says of Newman's paintings: "The onlooker who says his child could paint a Newman may be right, but Newman would have to be there to tell the child *exactly* what to do" (p. 370).

progressively revealed as constituting the *essence* of painting—and, by implication, as having done so all along. This seems to me gravely mistaken, not on the grounds that modernist painting is *not* a cognitive enterprise, but because it radically misconstrues the *kind* of cognitive enterprise modernist painting is. What the modernist painter can be said to discover in his work—what can be said to be revealed to him in it—is not the irreducible essence of *all* painting, but rather that which, at the present moment in painting's history, is capable of convincing him that it can stand comparison with the painting of both the modernist and the pre-modernist past whose quality seems to him beyond question.[8]

And in another essay written later that year I quoted Greenberg's remarks about a tacked-up canvas already existing as a picture though not necessarily as a successful one and commented:

> It is not quite enough to say that a bare canvas tacked to a wall is not "necessarily" a successful picture; it would, I think, be more accurate to say that it is not *conceivably* one. It may be countered that future circumstances might be such as to *make* it a successful painting; but I would argue that, for that to happen, the enterprise of painting would have to change so drastically that nothing more than the name would remain. . . . Moreover, seeing something as a painting in the sense that one sees the tacked-up canvas as a painting, and being convinced that a particular work can stand comparison with the painting of the past whose quality is not in doubt, are altogether different experiences: it is, I want to say, as though unless something compels conviction as to its quality it is no more than trivially or nominally a painting. . . . This is not to say that painting *has no essence*; it *is* to claim that essence—i.e., that which compels conviction—is largely determined by, and therefore changes continually in response to, the vital work of the recent past. *The essence of painting is not something irreducible.* Rather, the task of the modernist painter is to discover those conventions which, at a given moment, alone are capable of establishing his work's identity as painting.[9]

8. Fried, "Shape as Form: Frank Stella's New Paintings" (1966), in *New York Painting and Sculpture*, p. 422.

9. Fried, "Art and Objecthood" (1967), in *Minimal Art: A Critical Anthology*, ed. Battcock (New York, 1968), pp. 123–24 n.4 (with a few minor changes). The Wittgensteinian view of essence and convention propounded in these passages and indeed the basic conception of the modernist enterprise outlined in them were worked out during a period of close intellectual comradeship with Stanley Cavell; see, e.g., Cavell, "The Availability of Wittgenstein's Later Philosophy," "Music Discomposed," and "A Matter of Meaning It," *Must We Mean What We Say?* (New York, 1969), as well as his *The Claim of Reason: Wittgenstein, Skepticism, Morality, and Tragedy* (New York, 1979), esp. pp. 86–125. For a highly intelligent, at once sympathetic and deconstructive, reading of my account of modernism, see Stephen Melville, "Notes on the Reemergence of Allegory, the Forgetting of Modernism, the Necessity of Rhetoric, and the Conditions of Publicity in Art and Criticism," *October* 19 (Winter 1981): 55–92.

My aim in quoting these passages is not to spare myself the trouble of formulating afresh the thoughts they express but rather to show that a sharply critical but emphatically pro-modernist reading of Greenberg's reductionism and essentialism has been available for some considerable time. And my aim in showing *this* is not to suggest that Clark ought to have felt obliged to come to grips with or at least to acknowledge that reading (though I tend to think he should have) so much as to under-score his dependence on Greenberg's theory of modernism, even perhaps his solidarity with Greenberg in the face of certain criticisms of the latter's ideas. In any case, I hope it is evident that the conception of modernism adumbrated in the passages just quoted is consistent with the arguments I have already mounted against Clark's essay. The following observations will help spell this out.

1. The less inclined we are to accept the view that modernism pro-ceeds by discarding inessential conventions in pursuit of a timeless con-stitutive core, the more improbable we are bound to find the claim that negation in modernism is "cumulative and uncontrollable," that (to quote Clark in full) "the road leads back and back to the black square, the hardly differentiated field of sound, the infinitely flimsy skein of spectral colour, speech stuttering and petering out into etceteras and excuses" (p. 218). There is no road, if by that one means a track laid down in advance and ending in a predetermined destination, which is to say that there are no theoretical grounds for believing (or inclining to believe) that the evolution of modernist painting or sculpture or any other art will be from greater to lesser complexity, from differentiation to nondifferenti-ation, from articulateness to inarticulateness, and so on. (Nor are there theoretical grounds for believing the reverse.) Of course, it may simply be the case that some such evolution has occurred, but that is precisely what I dispute. Try understanding the history of Impressionism in those terms, or the art of Picasso and Braque between 1906 and 1914, or the emergence in the past seventy years of a tradition of constructed sculpture culminating in Smith and Caro, or the sequence of recent modernist painters Pollock-Helen Frankenthaler-Morris Louis-Kenneth Noland-Jules Olitski-Larry Poons (more challenges to Clark). My point here, however, is not that Clark's account of modernism belies the facts so much as that it is captive to an idea of how modernism works that all but screens the facts from view.

2. To the extent that we acknowledge the need for a putative work of modernist art to sustain comparison with previous work whose quality or level, for the moment anyway, is not in doubt, we repudiate the notion that what at bottom is at stake in modernism is a project of negation. For it is plainly not the case that the art of the old masters—the ultimate term of comparison—can usefully be seen as negative in essence: and implicit in my account is the claim that the deepest impulse or master convention of what I earlier called "mainstream" modernism has never been to

overthrow or supersede or otherwise break with the pre-modernist past but rather to attempt to equal its highest achievements, under new and difficult conditions that from the first were recognized by a few writers and artists as stacking the deck against the likelihood of success.[10] (For Baudelaire in 1846, those conditions included the disappearance of the great schools of painting that in the past had sustained relatively minor talents and, more broadly, the advent of an extreme form of individualism that in effect threw the modern artist solely on his personal resources and thereby ensured that only the most gifted and impassioned natures could hope to create lasting art.)[11] Here too, of course, someone might wish to argue that the various measures and strategies by which the modernist arts have sought to measure up to the great works of the past have been cumulatively and overwhelmingly negative in import. But this would require serious discussion of specific works, careers, movements, and so on, and once again I would bet heavily against the persuasiveness of the result.

3. The interpretation of modernism that I have been propounding implies a view of the relation of the artistic enterprise to the wider culture in which it is situated that differs from both Greenberg's and Clark's. According to Greenberg, modernism gets started at least partly in response to sociopolitical developments, but once under way its evolution is autonomous and in the long run even predetermined.[12] According to Clark, on the other hand, artistic modernism must be understood as something like a reflection of the incoherence and contradictoriness of modern capitalist society. In his words, "Negation is the sign inside art of this wider decomposition: it is an attempt to *capture* the lack of consistent and repeatable meanings in the culture—to capture the lack and make it over into form" (p. 218).

10. That the historical mission of modernism has been to preserve the standards of the high art of the past is one of Greenberg's major themes. The closing words of "Modernist Painting" are these: "Nothing could be further from the authentic art of our time than the idea of a rupture of continuity. Art is, among many other things, continuity. Without the past of art, and without the need and compulsion to maintain past standards of excellence, such a thing as Modernist art would be impossible" (p. 110).

11. See Charles Baudelaire, "The Salon of 1846," *Art in Paris 1845–1862: Salons and Other Exhibitions,* trans. and ed. Jonathan Mayne (Ithaca, N.Y., 1981), pp. 115–16. What the great schools chiefly provided to artists belonging to them was "faith" or, as Baudelaire shrewdly goes on to say, "the impossibility of doubt" (p. 115). In the same vein, Baudelaire writes of Delacroix more than a decade later: "He is as great as the old masters, in a country and a century in which the old masters would not have been able to survive" ("The Salon of 1859," p. 168).

12. Let me emphasize that I am speaking here of the implications of his theoretical essays (or of primarily theoretical passages in essays like "After Abstract Expressionism"); as a practical critic, Greenberg is at pains to eliminate all suggestion of predetermination and in fact would surely claim that he wished to do so in his theoretical writings as well. As we have seen, however, the terms of his analysis—reduction to an essence—make such a suggestion unavoidable.

Now it may seem that my own views on this topic are closer to Greenberg's than to Clark's, and in a sense they are. I find Clark's thumbnail analysis of the sociopolitical content of modernism both crude and demeaning, quite apart from the absurdity of the idea that this culture or any culture can be said to lack "consistent and repeatable meanings." What on earth can he be thinking of? Furthermore, the modernist artist—say, the modernist painter—is represented in my account as primarily responsible to an exalted conception or at any rate to an exacting practice of the enterprise of painting. And this, in addition to perhaps striking some readers as elitist and inhumane (their problem, not mine),[13] may appear to commit me to a view of art and society as mutually exclusive, forever sealed off from one another without possibility of interpenetration or even communication. But this would be wrong: in the first place because my argument expressly denies the existence of a distinct *realm* of the pictorial—of a body of suprahistorical, non–context-specific, in that sense "formalist," concerns that define the proper aims and limits of the art of painting—maintaining on the contrary that modernist painting, in its constantly renewed effort to discover what it must be, is forever driven "outside" itself, compelled to place in jeopardy its very identity by engaging with what it is not. (The task of understanding modernism politically is itself misunderstood if it is thought of as constructing a bridge over an abyss.)[14] And in the second

13. I say that it is their problem because it is based on unexamined assumptions or simply wishful thinking about what art (and life) should be like. This is perhaps the place to mention that in a lecture at a conference on art criticism and social theory held at Blacksburg, Virginia (9–11 October 1981), Donald Kuspit of the State University of New York at Stony Brook (author of a study of Greenberg) characterized my views on modernism as "authoritarian" and even as "fascistic." These are hard words. Presumably what justifies them is my insistence that some art is better than other art and my claim to know, to be able to tell, which is which. (Sometimes, of course, what I am able to tell is that previously I was wrong.) But what would be the use of a critic who regarded all art as equally indifferent, or who claimed not to be able to distinguish good from bad, or who considered all such questions beside the point? Moreover, my emphasis on the primacy of conviction means precisely that the reader of my criticism is barred from being persuaded, simply by reading me, of the rightness (or wrongness) of the judgments I make; rather, he *must* test those judgments against his firsthand experience of the works in question if he is to arrive at a view of the matter that is truly his. Is this authoritarianism? Fascism? Only, it seems to me, if we are prepared to characterize in those terms the assertion that while "the doors of the temple stand open, night and day, before every man, and the oracles of this truth cease never, it is guarded by one stern condition; this namely; It is an intuition. It cannot be received at second hand" (Ralph Waldo Emerson, "The Divinity School Address," *Nature, Addresses, and Lectures,* ed. Robert E. Spiller and Alfred R. Ferguson [Cambridge, Mass., 1979], p. 80).

14. Early in his essay, Clark cites Bertolt Brecht as a modern artist for whom "active engagement in ideological struggle . . . was not necessarily incompatible with work on the *medium* of theatre, making that medium explicit and opaque in the best avant-garde manner" (p. 207), and again toward the end he mentions Brecht with approval. This is true as far as it goes, but it fails to consider the possibility that it was precisely Brecht's prior concern with problems and issues relating to what might be called the inescapable theatri-

place because my emphasis on the utterly crucial role played in modern-ism by conviction or its' absence invites inquiry into what might be called the politics of conviction, that is to say, the countless ways in which a person's deepest beliefs about art and even about the quality of specific works of art have been influenced, sometimes to the point of having been decisively shaped, by institutional factors that, traced to their limits, merge imperceptibly with the culture at large. In a particular instance this may result in the undermining of certain beliefs and their replace-ment by others (a state of no belief is impossible). But it doesn't follow merely from the recognition of influence, even powerful influence, that the original beliefs are not to be trusted. A host of institutional factors must have collaborated long ago to incline me to take Manet seriously; but I can no more imagine giving up my conviction about the greatness of his art than I can imagine losing interest in painting altogether. (Both events could happen and perhaps will, but if they do I will scarcely be the same person. Some convictions are part of one's identity.)

4. To repeat: my insistence that the modernist painter seeks to discover not the irreducible essence of all painting but rather those con-ventions which, at a particular moment in the history of the art, are capable of establishing his work's nontrivial identity as painting leaves wide open (in principle though not in actuality) the question of what, should he prove successful, those conventions will turn out to be. The most that follows from my account, and I agree that it is by no means negligible, is that those conventions will bear a perspicuous relation to conventions operative in the most significant work of the recent past, though here it is necessary to add (the relation of perspicuousness con-sists precisely in this) that significant new work will inevitably transform our understanding of those prior conventions and moreover will invest the prior works themselves with a generative importance (and isn't that to say with a measure of value or quality?) that until that moment they may not have had. Thus the evolution since the early 1950s of what is often called color-field painting has entailed a continual reinterpretation of Pollock's allover drip paintings of 1947–50 as well as an ever more authoritative identification of those pictures as the fountainhead of an entire tradition of modernist painting.[15]

---

cality of the theatrical arts that enabled him to make an engagement in ideological struggle *count* artistically. Brecht himself describes his discovery of Marx as that of an ideal audi-ence: "When I read Marx's *Capital* I understood my plays. . . . It wasn't of course that I found I had unconsciously written a whole pile of Marxist plays; but this man Marx was the only spectator for my plays I'd ever come across" (*Brecht on Theater*, trans. and ed. John Willett [New York, 1964], pp. 23–24). (A similar line of argument might be pursued in connection with Godard.) The question as regards modernist painting and sculpture is therefore whether the present state of those arts is such as to facilitate an analogous development. I think the answer is no, but not because of any fact of *closure*.

15. See, e.g., my *Morris Louis* (New York, 1970), pp. 13–22 and passim.

So intensely perspectival and indeed so circular a view of the modernist enterprise—both the meaning and the value of the present are conceived as underwritten by a relation to a past that is continually being revised and reevaluated by the present—has close affinities with modern antifoundationalist thought both in philosophy proper and in theory of interpretation. (Recent discussions of Wittgenstein's treatment in the *Philosophical Investigations* of "following a rule," with its problematizing of how we "go on in the same way"—e.g., making objects capable of eliciting conviction as paintings—are pertinent here.) But what I want to emphasize at this juncture is that insofar as the practice I have just described involves something like radical self-criticism, the nature of that self-criticism is altogether different from what Greenberg means by the term; and insofar as the process in question may be figured as a version of the dialectic, it throws into relief just how *un*dialectical Clark's reading of modernism is.[16]

4

Toward the close of his essay, Clark writes that the end (in the sense of death) of the art of the bourgeoisie will involve, in fact has already involved (he is thinking of Brecht), "a search for another place in the social order." He continues: "Art wants to address someone, it wants something precise and extended to do; it wants *resistance*, it needs criteria; it will take risks in order to find them, including the risk of its own dissolution" (p. 217). And in a footnote to this he adds:

16. Two further ramifications of my account of modernism should at least be mentioned. First, it implies that the conviction of quality or value is always elicited by putative paintings and sculptures and not by putative works of art as such. The way I put this in "Art and Objecthood" was to claim that "the concepts of quality and value—and to the extent that these are central to art, the concept of art itself—are meaningful . . . only *within* the individual arts. What lies *between* the arts is theatre" (p. 142). (See n. 18 below, and cf. Greenberg, "Intermedia," *Arts* 56 [October 1981]: 92–93.) Second, the situation of the critic is analogous to that of the modernist artist in that criticism has no neutral, context-free, in that sense suprahistorical, descriptive categories at its disposal (not even, or especially not, "painting" and "sculpture") but rather must seek to elicit the conviction that the concepts it finds itself motivated to deploy actually illuminate the works under discussion. Moreover, as the context changes, largely as the result of subsequent artistic developments, even the concepts in widest use will require modification. For example, during the past fifteen or twenty years the concept "flatness" that at least since the late nineteenth century had been indispensable to the construal of modernist painting has lost much of its urgency; which is not to say that ambitious painting in our time has been freed from the demand that it come to terms with issues of *surface*—if anything the pressure there is more intense than before. Larry Poons' recent "pour" paintings incorporating bits and pieces of styrofoam, shown at the Emmerich Gallery in New York in April 1982, are a case in point.

This is not to smuggle in a demand for realism again by the back door; or at least, not one posed in the traditional manner. The weakness or absence I have pointed to in modern art does not derive, I think, from a lack of grounding in "seeing" (for example) or a set of realist protocols to go with that; rather, it derives from its lack of grounding in some (any) specific practice of representation, which would be linked in turn to other social practices—embedded in them, constrained by them. The question is not, therefore, whether modern art should be figurative or abstract, rooted in empirical commitments or not so rooted, *but whether art is now provided with sufficient constraints of any kind*—notions of appropriateness, tests of vividness, demands which bring with them measures of importance or priority. Without constraints, representation of any articulateness and salience cannot take place. [Pp. 219–20 n. 11; my emphasis]

Here as elsewhere Clark's argument is unpersuasive. For one thing, to personify art itself as "wanting" to do certain things that are now not being done is palpably absurd. (Need I add that it is also alien to a materialist view of the subject?) For another, Clark's use of notions like resistance and criteria is obscure. Is it his considered view that in modernist art literally anything goes? Does he simply dismiss the insistence by Greenberg and others on the need to distinguish between the large mass of ostensibly difficult and advanced but in fact routine and meretricious work—the product, according to those critics, of an ingratiating and empty avant-gardism—and the far smaller and often less obviously extreme body of work that really matters, that can survive comparison with what at that juncture they take to be the significant art of the past?[17] True, the distinction is not enforced by appeal to objective

17. In a lecture delivered at the University of Sydney in 1968, Greenberg distinguishes between the authentic avant-garde, which he sees as dedicated to preserving the values of the high art of the past, and the "popular" avant-garde—the invention of Duchamp and Dada—which he characterizes as seeking to evade the issue of quality altogether (see Greenberg, "Avant-Garde Attitudes: New Art in the Sixties," The John Power Lecture in Contemporary Art, 17 May 1968 [Sydney, 1969], pp. 10–11). (One recurrent tactic of evasion has been to raise the pseudoquestion of art as such.) In that lecture too Greenberg notes the emergence in the 1960s of what he calls "novelty" art, in which the "easiness" of the work—its failure to offer a significant challenge to advanced taste—"is . . . knowingly, aggressively, extravagantly masked by the guises of the difficult" (p. 12). And in a subsequent essay, Greenberg substitutes the pejorative term "avant-gardism" for that of the "popular" avant-garde ("Counter Avant-Garde," *Art International* 15 [May 1971]: 16–19).

In my "Art and Objecthood" I argue that the best contemporary painting and sculpture seek an ideal of self-sufficiency and what I call "presentness" whereas much seemingly advanced recent work is essentially *theatrical*, depending for its effects of "presence" on the staging, the conspicuous manipulation, of its relation to an audience. (In the years since "Art and Objecthood" was written, the theatrical has assumed a host of new

criteria—but are those what Clark is asking for? Does he think, against Kant and Wittgenstein, that such criteria have a role to play in the arts? In any case, despite his disclaimers, the whole passage bears witness to an uneasiness with abstract art that makes Clark a dubious guide to the events of the past century or more.

My strongest objection to his remarks, however, is that they fail to recognize not just the magnitude of the achievement of modernist painters and sculptors I admire but also, more to the point, the formative importance in their art of what can only be called constraints. I shall conclude with a brief example.

In 1966 Caro, who had been making abstract sculptures in welded steel since 1960, became interested in making *small* sculptures—pieces that would extend no more than a foot or two in any dimension and thus would tend to be placed on a table or other convenient locus for small portable objects rather than directly on the ground, the compulsory (i.e., the only right) siting for his abstract pieces until that moment.[18] Now it may seem that this ought not to have presented a problem: Why not

---

guises and has acquired a new name: post-modernism.) Recently Melville has challenged the hardness of this distinction, arguing, for example, that the desire to defeat the theatrical can find satisfaction only in a theatrical space, or at any rate in circumstances that cannot wholly escape the conditions of theater (I make this point in my writings on pre-modernist art), and going on to claim that today "the field we call 'painting' includes, and cannot now be defined without reference to, its violations and excesses—performance work in particular" ("Notes," p. 80). In this connection he cites figures such as Rauschenberg and Acconci, whose endeavors I continue to see as trivial. But the fact that I am unimpressed by his exemplary artists by no means deflects the force of his general argument, which compels an awareness that, as he puts it, neatly paraphrasing me on Diderot, the art of painting is inescapably addressed to an audience that must be gathered (see p. 87). On the other hand, as Melville is aware, the impossibility of a pure or absolute mode of antitheatricality by no means implies that I am mistaken in my assessment of the best work of our time or even, by and large, in the terms in which I have described it. (Effects of presentness can still amount to grace.)

On theatricality as an issue for pre-modernist art, see my *Absorption and Theatricality: Painting and Beholder in the Age of Diderot* (Berkeley, 1980); "Thomas Couture and the Theatricalization of Action in Nineteenth-Century French Painting," *Artforum* 8 (June 1970): 36–46; "The Beholder in Courbet: His Early Self-Portraits and Their Place in His Art," *Glyph* 4 (1978): 85–129; "Representing Representation: On the Central Group in Courbet's *Studio*," in *Allegory and Representation: Selected Papers from the English Institute, 1979–80*, ed. Stephen J. Greenblatt (Baltimore, 1981), pp. 94–127, rpt. in *Art in America* 69 (September 1981): 127–33, 168–73; and "Painter into Painting: On Courbet's *After Dinner at Ornans* and *Stonebreakers*," *Critical Inquiry* 8 (Summer 1982): 619–49. Theatricality in Manet is discussed in my "Manet's Sources," pp. 69–74.

18. On Caro, see, e.g., my introduction to the exhibition catalog, *Anthony Caro*, Hayward Gallery, London, 1969; Richard Whelan et al., *Anthony Caro* (Baltimore, 1974); and William Rubin, *Anthony Caro* (New York, 1975). The Whelan book contains additional texts by Greenberg, John Russell, Phyllis Tuchman, and myself. The following discussion of Caro's table sculptures is based on my essay in the catalog to the travelling exhibition, *Anthony Caro: Table Sculptures, 1966–77*, British Council, 1977–78 (rpt. in *Arts* 51 [March 1977]: 94–97).

simply make small (i.e., tabletop) versions of the larger sculptures that normally would have been placed on the bare ground, and let it go at that? But the fact of the matter is that such a solution was unacceptable to Caro, by which I mean that even without giving it a try he knew with perfect certainty that it would not do, that it was incapable of providing the basis for proceeding that he sought. But why?

Here I want to say, because it failed to respond to the *depth of Caro's need* for something, call it a convention,[19] that would articulate smallness in a manner consistent with the prior logic of his art, that would be faithful to his commitment to a particular mode of thinking, feeling, and willing sculpture, in short that would not run counter to his acceptance (but that is too contractual a term: his internalization, his appropriation) of a particular set of constraints, the initial and at first only partial un-earthing of which roughly six years before had been instrumental in his sudden emergence as a major artist (itself a characteristically modernist phenomenon).[20] I associate those constraints with a radical notion of *abstractness,* which I contrast not with *figurativeness,* an uninteresting op-position, but rather with *literalness,* in the present context a compelling one.[21] Reformulated in these terms, the problem of smallness that Caro found so challenging may be phrased quite simply. How was he to go about making pieces whose modest dimensions would strike the viewer not as a contingent, quantitative, in that sense merely literal fact about them but rather as a crucial aspect of their identity as abstract works of art—as internal to their "form," as part of their very essence as works of sculpture? To put this another way, by what means was he to make small sculptures that could not be seen, that would effectively defeat being perceived, either as models for or as reduced versions of larger ones? In obvious respects, the task he faced involved departing from norms that had been operative in his art up to that time. More importantly, how-ever, his task was one of remaining responsible to a particular vision of his art (may we not lift a phrase from Clark and say to a particular vision of "cultural possibility"?) according to which a sculpture's scale—indeed

19. "It is as if this expressed the essence of form.—I say, however: if you talk about *essence*—, you are merely noting a convention. But here one would like to retort: there is no greater difference than that between a proposition about the depth of the essence and one about—a mere convention. But what if I reply: to the *depth* that we see in the essence there corresponds the *deep* need for the convention" (Ludwig Wittgenstein, *Remarks on the Foundations of Mathematics,* ed. G. H. Von Wright, R. Rhees, and G. E. M. Anscombe, trans. Anscombe [Oxford, 1956], p. 23e).

20. See my discussion of Louis' "breakthrough" to major achievement in *Morris Louis,* pp. 10–13.

21. The opposition between abstractness and literalness is developed in my essays "Shape as Form" and "Art and Objecthood," as well as in two short reviews, "Two Sculptures by Anthony Caro" and "Caro's Abstractness," both available in Whelan et al., *Anthony Caro,* pp. 95–101 and 103–10; see also in this collection Greenberg's remarks on Caro's abstractness or "radical unlikeness to nature" ("Anthony Caro," pp. 87–93, esp. p. 88).

all its features that matter, including its mode of self-presentation—must be secured abstractly, made part of its essence, in order to convince the viewer (in the first instance the sculptor) of their necessity or at any rate their lack of arbitrariness.

Caro's solution to this problem involved two distinct steps, the first of which soon proved dispensable. First, he incorporated handles of various sorts in a number of pieces in an attempt to key the "feel" of each work to that of graspable and manipulable objects. The chief precedent for this was Picasso's *Glass of Absinthe* (1914), a small painted bronze sculpture that incorporates a real silver sugar strainer. (Recognizable handles disappear from Caro's art around 1968.) Second, as in *Table Piece XXII* of 1967 (fig. 2), Caro ran at least one element in every piece *below* the level of the tabletop or other elevated plane surface on which it was to be placed. This had the effect of precluding the transposition of the sculpture, in fact or in imagination, to the ground—of making the placement of the sculpture on (i.e., partly off) the tabletop a matter not of arbitrary choice but of structural necessity. And it at once turned out that tabling or precluding grounding the sculptures in this way was tantamount to establishing their smallness in terms that are not a function of actual size. More precisely, the distinction between tabling and

FIG. 2.—Anthony Caro, *Table Piece XXII,* 1967. Private Collection, London. Phot. John Goldblatt.

grounding, determined as it is by the sculptures themselves, makes itself felt as equivalent to a qualitative as opposed to quantitative, essential as opposed to contingent, or abstract as opposed to literal difference in scale. (Not only did the abstract smallness of the table sculptures later prove compatible with surprising largeness of actual size; it soon became apparent that a certain minimum size, on the order of feet rather than inches, was required for their tabling to be experienced in these terms.)[22]

Caro's table sculptures thus embody a sense of scale for which there is no obvious precedent in earlier sculpture. And although it seems clear that our conviction on this score relates intimately to the fact that in everyday life smallish objects of the sort we grasp, manipulate, and shift casually from place to place tend to be found on tables, within easy reach, rather than on the ground, it is also true that we encounter nothing quite like the abstract smallness of Caro's table sculptures in our ordinary dealings with the world. From this point of view, an ontological one, the table sculptures are endlessly fascinating. And the source of that fascination could not have less to do with everything Clark means by negation, decomposition, absence, emptiness— the entire battery of concepts by means of which he tries to evoke the futility of modernism as he sees it.

A further glance at *Table Piece XXII* and I am done. The sculpture consists of three primary elements—a section of curved, broad-diameter pipe, a longer section of straight, narrow-diameter pipe, and a handle—welded together in a configuration, a structure of relations, that subtly, abstractly, asserts not only the disparateness but also the separateness of the two sections of pipe. (The pipe sections strike us as above all *disjoined* from one another by the handle that runs between them.) And one consequence of this is that, far from being tempted to reach out and grasp the handle, we sense as if subliminally that we are being invited to take hold of a gap, a spacing, and we draw back. In short, the everyday, literal function of a handle is here eclipsed by *this* handle's abstract function of enforcing a separation and thereby attuning us all the more finely to apprehending *Table Piece XXII* abstractly rather than literally, as a work of art and not, or not merely, a physical object. A Marxist critic might wish to say that this last distinction and indeed my larger advocacy of abstractness versus literalness are epitomes of bourgeois ideology. But he would have to grant that my analysis of Caro's table sculptures could hardly be further from Clark's fantasy of

---

22. Between 1966 and 1974, Caro made roughly two hundred table sculptures of this type. Around 1974–75, however, he began making table sculptures that no longer dipped below the level of the tabletop, without loss of quality. It is as though by then Caro had acquired a mastery of what might be called table scale that enabled him to give up anchoring the pieces to the tabletop and nevertheless to establish abstractly the specificity of their dimensions and mode of presentation. (On the other hand, many of these pieces also "work" on the ground and in that sense are presentationally looser than the earlier pieces.)

the medium in modernism reverting to the state of "mere unworked material."

Finally, beyond and embracing the considerations I have so far invoked, the convincingness of *Table Piece XXII* as art depends on something that defies exhaustive analysis, namely, the sheer rightness of *all* the relevant relations at work in it, including the appropriateness of its color, a metallic gray-green, to everything else. Intuition of that rightness is the critic's first responsibility as well as his immediate reward, and if Clark shared more than a fraction of that intuition, about this Caro or any Caro, or any Smith, Pollock, Frankenthaler, Louis, Noland, Olitski, or Poons, not to mention the antecedent masters whose painting and sculptures, continually reinterpreted, stand behind theirs, his understanding of the politics of modernism would be altogether different from what it is.

Arguments about Modernism:
A Reply to Michael Fried

T. J. Clark

1. *The argument about negation.* I think that the thesis of my paper Michael Fried chooses mainly to attack—namely, that there is a strong negative cast to modernism, one that characterizes it as an episode in art—is, if banal, pretty well supported by the evidence. Attempts to contradict it always end up seeming strained and over-ingenious (which is not always the case with refutations of the commonplace). Fried's attempts seem to me no exception and not much better in their present form than in the previous ones he wonders I did not mention.

But obviously I should have been clearer about what I took the argument to *be;* that I was not allows Fried to run rings round various imaginary opponents. First of all, it is hardly likely that I should agree with the later Clement Greenberg on some version of essentialism, for example, "that modernism proceeds by discarding inessential conventions in pursuit of a timeless constitutive core" (p. 228). To the extent that Fried's self-quotations are disputes with some such notion—and I cannot see that they are much more—I can cordially agree with them and pass on. My argument is about historical cases and how best to interpret them, or how best to interpret the overall sequence they make.

Of course it was a large part of my case in the paper that the same was true of Greenberg's argument in its original form. Both the articles of 1939–40 in *Partisan Review,* "Avant-Garde and Kitsch" and "Towards a Newer Laocoon," depended on a picture—quite a powerful picture, I still think—of the social circumstances of late capitalism, and the discussion of medium in "Towards a Newer Laocoon" was largely free of the a priori reasoning characteristic of Greenberg later in his career. Fried is evidently very little interested in the Trotskyite writer of 1939–40. I can see why. But if he wants to pass judgement on how much or how little of Greenberg I have swallowed, it might help to get clear which Greenberg we are talking.about.

Hereabouts another misunderstanding seems to creep in. For to say of a series of artworks that they show modernist art proceeding by leaps and bounds of negation is not to say that these negations result continually in *nothing*, or next to nothing, or even that modernism is habitually nay-saying or nihilistic. It is not to make the claim—which I would find as absurd as Fried does—that modernism has left behind it no complex account of experience and its modes, or no viable work on the means and materials of representation. Of course it has. The argument is rather (1) that it should strike us as important that these accounts depended on such a "casting off of norms and conventions," one which in the end included most of the kinds of descriptive work which had previously given art its *raison d'être*, and (2) that this process progressively tended to overwhelm modernist practice and become a peculiar end in itself, or at least to obscure all others. So that the "new conception of the enterprise of painting" became, in my view, more and more etiolated and self-obsessed.[1]

Thus to describe Pollock's *Lavender Mist*—it would take, of course, quite a long discussion of its peculiar place in the sequence of Pollock's drip canvases—as representing a delectable *impasse* of painting, from which its author sought to escape, months later, by means of a desperate backtrack to figuration—this would not be to call the picture empty or insubstantial but to point to the unrepeatable, incorrigible nature of its wholeness. (The account could be supported by reference to the artist's own doubts and hesitations about abstraction, for which there is a re-

---

1. The core of this argument is commonplace, as I say; in no sense is it Greenberg's special property, still less mine. For a more elegant and emphatic phrasing of it, apropos the nineteenth-century invention of "literature," see Michel Foucault's *Les Mots et les choses* (Paris, 1966), p. 313:

> De la révolte romantique contre un discours immobilisé dans sa cérémonie, jusqu'à la découverte mallarméenne du mot en son pouvoir impuissant, on voit bien quelle fut, au XIXe siècle, la fonction de la littérature par rapport au mode d'être moderne du langage. Sur le fond de ce jeu essentiel, le reste est effet: la littérature se distingue de plus en plus du discours d'idées, et s'enferme dans une intransitivité radicale; elle se détache de toutes les valeurs qui pouvaient à l'âge classique le faire circuler (le goût, le plaisir, le naturel, le vrai), et elle fait naître dans son propre espace tout ce qui peut en assurer la dénégation ludique (le scandaleux, le laid, l'impossible); elle rompt avec toute définition de "genres" comme formes ajustées à un ordre de représentations, et devient pure et simple manifestation d'un langage qui n'a pour loi que d'affirmer—contre tous les autres discours—son existence escarpée; elle n'a plus alors qu'à se recourber dans un perpétuel retour sur soi.

I am not suggesting, by the way, that Foucault sees no advantages in this round of negation and intransitivity—any more than I do.

markable and poignant body of evidence; for this kind of reason and others, Fried's remarks about my "uneasiness with abstract art" making me "a dubious guide to the events of the past century" [p. 234] have an anachronistic ring.) Or to place Picasso's *Ma Jolie* (fig. 1) in a series of pictures from 1909 onward in which the female body seems pulled out of shape or dispersed by the very act of representing it, to say that painting itself is seen here as a form of doleful violence against the nude, to point to the grim and obvious irony of the picture's title, inscribed as it is on the scaffold of monochrome shards—none of this would be to say that there *is* no body in *Ma Jolie* but rather that painting here seems obliged to push toward an area in which every vestige of integrity or sensual presence is done to death—every vestige but that of "paint itself," put on with such delicate, sober virtuosity—in the belief, apparently, that only there would some genuine grasp of the body be possible.[2] Fried and I may disagree in either case about whether the grasp or the wholeness is achieved; but I simply want us to be struck again by the violence with which the normal repertoire of likeness is annihilated and to wonder if any other ground for representation had been secured, or could possibly be secured, in the process.

Why is it, I wonder, that modernist critics (Fried is typical here), when they encounter a history of modernism in which its masterpieces are not all pictured as triumphant openings on to fullness and positivity, are so ready to characterize that history as merely hostile, telling a story of "futility" and waste? Part of the problem may simply be this: for me a strategy of negation and refusal is not an unreasonable response to bourgeois civilization since 1871, and indeed it is the ruthlessness of negation which lies at the root of what I admire—certainly what I feel is still usable—in modern art. The line of wit is replaced by the line of dissolution: there is no modernism to speak of, as far as I am concerned, apart from *Mauvais Sang* and *Ecce Homo,* from *The Cloud in Trousers* and the *Dictionnaire des idées reçues,* from the black square (Malevich's not Ad Reinhardt's) and the *Wooden Horse* (fig. 2). "I consider *The Cloud in Trousers* a catechism for modern art," said its author, V. Mayakovsky. "It is in four parts, with four rallying cries: 'Down with your Love!'; 'Down with your Art!'; 'Down with your Social Order!'; 'Down with your Reli-

2. Interested readers might like to compare *Ma Jolie* with the further extremes of reduction and schematization of the female body in several canvases done some months before, in spring 1911, e.g., *La Mandoliniste* (P. Daix, *Le Cubisme de Picasso,* no. 390), *La Violiniste* (393), *Tête* (395), *Soldat et fille* (394), and the ultimate *Tête de jeune fille* (376; the title is firmly accredited). In comparison *Ma Jolie* does represent a return to a less desolate and rebarbative mode, but only in comparison.

In other paintings by Picasso from this time the presence of a guitar or mandolin gives rise to a play of analogy—it may anyway strike us as perfunctory—between the shape of the instrument and that of the woman. *Ma Jolie* is apparently playing a zither, and its rectilinear form does not allow even this much of metaphor.

Fig. 1.—Pablo Picasso, *Ma Jolie,* 1911–12, winter. Lillie P. Bliss Bequest, Collection, The Museum of Modern Art, New York. Phot. Museum.

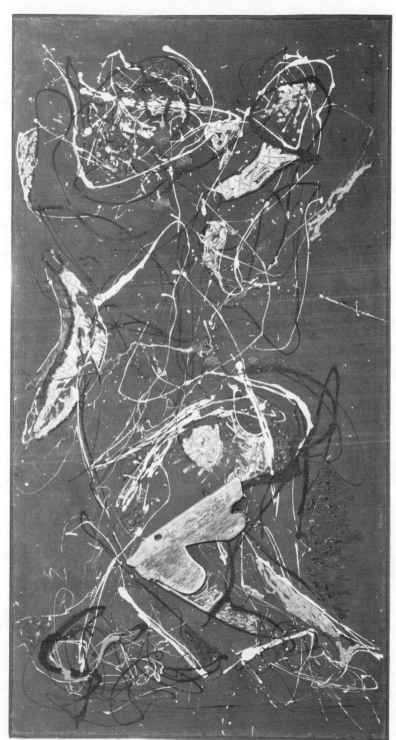

FIG. 2.—Jackson Pollock, *The Wooden Horse: 1*, 1948. Collection, Moderna Museet, Stockholm. Phot. Museum.

gion!' "[3] "Voilà les forces qui se sont déployées," as an old book has it, "pour introduire dans les consciences des hommes un peu de la moississure des valeurs pourissantes."[4] The problem remains, however, whether art on its own has anything to offer *but* the spectacle of decomposition.

I find myself swapping lists of favourite works. This is a pity. For let it be said that no decent historical account of modern art can be framed solely round a selected set of its "masterpieces." (Though if a contrary account can only be managed by excluding those masterpieces or admitting them all as exceptions, that account is equally in trouble.)[5] I think that my reading of modernism could make various sense of the works Fried cites and put them in contact with a host of others that are now declared, by modernist fiat not by any process of historical enquiry, to be irrelevant to them. To take the example Fried mentions: I still find it striking that modernist writers so confidently outlaw the real impulse of Dada and early Surrealism from their account of twentieth-century art, while giving such weight to artists—like Arp or Miro or Pollock—who were profoundly affected by it. Nor is the problem solved, I think, by claiming that what Pollock and Miro took from the Surrealists, by some miracle of probity, was a set of techniques which they quickly cleansed and turned to higher purpose rather than a whole strategy of release, exacerbation, emptying, and self-splitting. Some such description might just apply to Arp's way with his masters, but that it does is the key to his limitations as an artist. It is what puts him outside the "modern tradition," if such a contradiction in terms is conceivable.

These points could be pursued further. It is particularly in its treatment of the period between 1910 and 1930 that modernist art history is inadequate, because it is faced most dramatically there with the break-up of its received tradition, the end of Parisian hegemony over the arts, and the emergence of a set of competing art practices in which the limits and autonomy of art are at stake. The question is not whether one approves of or dislikes Marcel Duchamp, who in any case is largely the entrepreneur of "anti-art" attitudes in the period, giving them commodity form. The question is how one should deal with the whole decenter-

3. V. Mayakovsky, foreword to the second edition of his *Cloud in Trousers* as cited in his *Bedbug and Selected Poetry* (New York, 1960), p. 306.

4. R. Vaneigem, *Traité de savoir-vivre à l'usage des jeunes générations* (Paris, 1967), p. 182.

5. Since so much of Michael Fried's argument turns on my reluctance to address particular works of modern art and discuss their negations in detail, I suppose I have to state the obvious here: I do not admit to any such reluctance, and of course I agree that detailed study of particular instances—pictures and their circumstances—is part of the business of understanding modernism. Readers can judge for themselves whether two articles of mine on Manet—"Preliminaries to a Possible Treatment of 'Olympia' in 1865," *Screen* 21 (Spring 1980), and "The Bar at the Folies-Bergère," in *Popular Culture in France: The Wolf and the Lamb: From the Old Regime to the Twentieth Century,* ed. Jacques Beauroy, Marc Bertrand, and Edward T. Gargan (Saratoga, Calif., 1977)—do that job or not.

ing of art after 1917. A history which has nothing to say about the November Group and the Russian Productivists, about VKhUTEMAS and *Der Ventilator,* while lavishing attention on the dispirited efforts of Matisse and Kandinsky in the same decade, should flinch, I would have thought, from too confident a trading of examples.

2. *The argument about consistent meanings.* This can be dealt with briefly. I am surprised that Fried finds the idea that modern culture lacks "consistent and repeatable meanings" absurd. I used the phrase as a shorthand for *patterns* of meaning, systems of belief and instantiation, by which a culture fixes—and opens to refutation— some complex account of its central experiences and purposes. The word "consistent" was meant to suggest both coherence and substance—a power to convince, a seeming depth. The word "repeatable" has that pattern of belief surviving through time, dealing with new evidence without coming apart, becoming something like a tradition or a mythology.

The idea that modern culture is characterized by the absence of such forms of knowledge goes back at least as far as the Jena school or the English writers of the same period and does not seem to me absurd then or later. It has certainly been an important idea for modernist art. To adopt Fried's own tactic for a moment, I should be interested to hear a plausible account of *Bouvard et Pécuchet,* say, or *The Trial* or *The Waste Land* (no minor figures now), which did not take such doubts and un certainties to be somewhere near the heart of things.

As for Fried's further claim that it makes no sense to picture *any* culture as lacking "consistent and repeatable meanings," I recommend a good read of social anthropology—say, the literature on cargo cults.

3. *The argument about cases.* My answer to Fried is bound to be as inconclusive as responses-to-replies-to-rejoinders normally are, because really there is so little common ground between us on which to argue. This comes out most clearly in Fried's exultant pointing to cases and his certainty that in doing so he poses a serious challenge to my main account.

The reader is entitled to feel a bit baffled. So Fried finds my analyses crude and demeaning, and I find his fulsome and aggrandizing. Apart from the usual academic *corrida,* what does this exchange of courtesies amount to? I do not think it turns on contrary intuitions of Anthony Caro; intuitions about Caro (and so forth) do not seem to me tests of anything very important. Of course their not seeming so derives in a sense from judgements of Caro's work, but these derive from other (primary) interests and commitments. The point at issue is this, I think: Fried is interested in preserving a certain set of practices and sensibilities (let's call them those of "art" or "sculpture"); the set is specific; at the heart of it I detect a form of pristine experience had by an individual in front of an object, an "intuition of rightness" if you like. The relation of this experience to the normal identities and relations of history is obscure, but the language of Fried's actual descriptions, here and elsewhere, suggests that it somehow abrogates them and opens on to a ground or plenitude of knowledge which is normally closed to us. Caro's sculpture provides such experiences (Fried says); the experience seems valuable (to him). And no doubt it does and is; or rather, since there is no rational ground *for* doubt, let's talk about something else—for instance, about why one person should be interested in preserving this kind of experience and the talk that goes with it and another be interested in its destruction.

Let me put the point another way. I take it that many of Fried's disagreements with me centre or depend on a version of the priority-of-perception thesis. Differences on this subject seem to me largely unresolvable, because behind them lie commitments and interests which are not susceptible to proof or disproof; but nonetheless I shall have my brief say. The priority-of-perception thesis in criticism owes its appeal, surely, to its uncontroversial insistence on the special nature of artistic statements, its reminding us that we are very often dealing with complex and self-conscious cases of description or enunication, ones which admit the odd materiality of the means they employ. Art is a practice—or at least can be a practice, in certain historical circumstances—in which the mismatching of beliefs and instances can be recognised and played with. Thus artistic statements are likely to be specially demanding on the viewer or reader's attention.

The priority-of-perception thesis therefore insists on close reading, quite properly I think. The mistake it makes is in its notion of what close reading *is:* the question being whether it is an exclusive and intensive focusing, a bracketing of knowledge, a giving-over of consciousness to its object, or whether successful reading is a mobilization of complex assumptions, commitments, and skills, in which the object is always being seen against (as *part* of) a ground of interest and argument. I certainly think the latter is the case. In the critics whose close reading I most admire (and my preferences are not eccentric; I have in mind T. S. Eliot or F. R. Leavis, or for that matter Diderot and Coleridge), objects are attended to as instances of a certain history. They are construed from a political point of view. And these perspectives and commitments are present in the reading, shaping and informing it; they are what gives it precision and substance; the writing of the reading admits as much. The same is true of Greenberg's criticism, or was true in its active and fruitful first period from 1939 to 1948. Again, this was one of the things I tried to suggest in my paper; but perhaps I should state more clearly here that it seems to me Greenberg's best years as a critic were these, when his readings were still openly worked by wider historical concerns and partisanship. Why these were eventually abandoned, and why he retreated to a notoriously intransigent version of the primacy-of-perception thesis, is another story. The Cold War and McCarthyism are not our subject at present.

4. One of the reasons I cannot see Caro's or Jules Olitski's work very well any longer is that I have become more aware over time of the ground of interests and arguments it serves, and that, woodenly. I find them so uncongenial and boring that I cannot now perceive anything much. (I don't intuit the work's rightness: Is that it? I think I'm still capable of noticing that a Caro is small, but I fail to see why I should take facts of this kind very seriously. And as to accepting them as *constraints,* in the sense I gave the word! . . .) This will seem critical gain to some and loss to others; doubtless the real hardliners will want to say that I never could have genuinely *seen* in the first place if I am thrown off track thus easily by ideology. My hard line in return would be that "seeing" in such statements seems to me nothing—I mean that more or less literally—but the instrumentation of a different ideology.

There is a danger that all this talk of interests and arguments will seem obscure, and rather than have it remain so I shall spell out what I mean quite crudely (no doubt demeaningly too). The bourgeoisie has a small but considerable interest, I believe, in preserving a certain myth of the aesthetic consciousness, one where a transcendental ego is given something appropriate to contemplate in a situation essentially detached from the pressures and deformities of history. The interest is considerable because the class in question has few other areas (since the decline of the sacred) in which its account of consciousness and freedom can be at all compellingly phrased.

It is not enough, in this connection, for Fried to deny that he posits "a distinct *realm* of the pictorial," since his critical practice so insistently reinstates one; in the same sentence we find him saying that painting's engagement "with what it is not," though inevitable, "place[s] in jeopardy its very identity" (p. 230). But why on earth should it? And isn't an account of painting which sees it as *gaining* its various identities through engagement with what it is not automatically foreclosed by Fried's formulations? Won't he rule out my account of Picasso, say, on the ground that it does not grasp how separate and sustaining the "enterprise of painting" was for the artist in question? In critical practice, isn't *any* account of modern art's engagement with what it is not dismissed as being beside the great ontological point? And when it comes to ontology, all the nods to Merleau-Ponty cannot save Fried's prose from sounding like old-time religion.

One is reminded, if I too can quote from a founding text, of the climax of "Art and Objecthood" (1967), where Fried draws a distinction between the theatrical, literalist modes of the sculpture he dislikes—preeminently Morris' and Judd's—and the "presentness" of a Caro, its being at every moment "wholly manifest." "It is this continuous and entire presentness, amounting, as it were, to the perpetual creation of itself, that one experiences as a kind of *instantaneousness:* as though if only one were infinitely more acute, a single infinitely brief instant would be long enough to see everything, to experience the work in all its depth and fullness, to be forever convinced by it." The essay concludes famously: "More generally, however, I have wanted to call attention to the utter pervasiveness—the virtual universality—of the sensibility or mode of being which I have characterized as corrupted or perverted by theater. We are all literalists most or all of our lives. Presentness is grace."[6]

I do not mean to insinuate, finally, that a religious point of view is indefensible in criticism; how could I, with Eliot as reminder? It may even be that a religious perspective is the only possible one from which a cogent defence of modernism in its recent guise can be mounted. But the view is not defended here, it seems to me, just noised abroad in an odd manner; and that is its usual status in such writing.[7] If on the contrary a defence *were* offered, arguments about modernism, other than the name-calling kind, would be made much easier.

---

6. Fried, "Art and Objecthood," *Artforum* 5 (Summer 1967): 22, 23.

7. There is a curious twofold structure to Fried's writing at this point and others like it, which again seems to me typical of a certain discourse on the arts. The metaphysical buzzwords—"presentness," "perpetual creation of itself," "infinitely," "depth and fullness," "forever convinced," "grace," etc.—seem to provide the ground on which the more persistent, not to say strident, appeals to "intuition" rest. But what is it in the text that gives the metaphysics substance apart from the category, "intuition," which it appears to validate? The intuition *is* the religion—not a very satisfactory one, I should imagine, and certainly unlike Eliot's or Coleridge's. For in their kind of criticism, religious commitments are articulated in the form of full-fledged histories. It is clear that these writers possess a test of truth which to their minds exceeds the historical and puts the mere sequence of human events in question; but nonetheless that perspective *constructs* a history—not just a sequence of "great works"—in which art takes a special, subordinate place. (Consider the duties performed by descriptions of Shakespeare in *Biographia Literaria*, or the nature of the close reading of *Rameau's Nephew* offered by Hegel in the *Phenomenology*.) There is an essay to be written on when and how the religious attitude in criticism declines from this complex building and questioning of the past into a set of merely metaphysical episodes in an earth-bound, present-bound discussion of cases.

Critical Exchange II:

The Politics of Legal Interpretation

Law as Interpretation

Ronald Dworkin

I shall argue that legal practice is an exercise in interpretation not only when lawyers interpret particular documents or statutes but generally. Law so conceived is deeply and thoroughly political. Lawyers and judges cannot avoid politics in the broad sense of political theory. But law is not a matter of personal or partisan politics, and a critique of law that does not understand this difference will provide poor understanding and even poorer guidance. I propose that we can improve our understanding of law by comparing legal interpretation with interpretation in other fields of knowledge, particularly literature. I also expect that law, when better understood, will provide a better grasp of what interpretation is in general.

I. Law

The central problem of analytical jurisprudence is this: What sense should be given to propositions of law? I mean the various statements lawyers make reporting what the law is on some question or other. Propositions of law can be very abstract and general, like the proposition that states of the United States may not discriminate on racial grounds in supplying basic services to citizens, or they can be relatively concrete, like the proposition that someone who accepts a check in the normal course of business without notice of any infirmities in its title is entitled to collect against the maker, or very concrete, like the proposition that Mrs. X is liable in damages to Mr. Y in the amount of $1,150 because he slipped on her icy sidewalk and broke his hip. In each case a puzzle arises. What are propositions of law really about? What in the world could make them true or false?

The puzzle arises because propositions of law seem to be descriptive—they are about how things are in the law, not about how they should be—and yet it has proved extremely difficult to say exactly what it is that they describe. Legal positivists believe that propositions of law are indeed wholly descriptive: they are in fact pieces of history. A proposition of law, in their view, is true just in case some event of a designated law-making kind has taken place, and otherwise not. This seems to work reasonably well in very simple cases. If the Illinois legislature enacts the words "No will shall be valid without three witnesses," then the proposition of law, that an Illinois will needs three witnesses, seems to be true only in virtue of that historical event.

But in more difficult cases the analysis fails. Consider the proposition that a particular affirmative action scheme (not yet tested in the courts) is constitutionally valid. If that is true, it cannot be so just in virtue of the text of the Constitution and the fact of prior court decisions, because reasonable lawyers who know exactly what the Constitution says and what the courts have done may yet disagree whether it is true. (I am doubtful that the positivists' analysis holds even in the simple case of the will; but that is a different matter I shall not argue here.)

What are the other possibilities? One is to suppose that controversial propositions of law, like the affirmative action statement, are not descriptive at all but are rather expressions of what the speaker wants the law to be. Another is more ambitious: controversial statements are attempts to describe some pure objective or natural law, which exists in virtue of objective moral truth rather than historical decision. Both these projects take some legal statements, at least, to be purely evaluative as distinct from descriptive: they express either what the speaker prefers—his personal politics—or what he believes is objectively required by the principles of an ideal political morality. Neither of these projects is plausible, because someone who says that a particular untested affirmative action plan is constitutional does mean to describe the law as it is rather than as he wants it to be or thinks that, by the best moral theory, it should be. He might, indeed, say that he regrets that the plan is constitutional and thinks that, according to the best moral theory, it ought not to be.

There is a better alternative: propositions of law are not simply

Ronald Dworkin, professor of jurisprudence at Oxford University, is the author of *Taking Rights Seriously* and editor of *The Philosophy of Law.*

descriptive of legal history, in a straightforward way, nor are they simply evaluative in some way divorced from legal history. They are interpretive of legal history, which combines elements of both description and evaluation but is different from both. This suggestion will be congenial, at least at first blush, to many lawyers and legal philosophers. They are used to saying that law is a matter of interpretation; but only, perhaps, because they understand interpretation in a certain way. When a statute (or the Constitution) is unclear on some point, because some crucial term is vague or because a sentence is ambiguous, lawyers say that the statute must be interpreted, and they apply what they call "techniques of statutory construction." Most of the literature assumes that interpretation of a particular document is a matter of discovering what its authors (the legislators, or the delegates to the constitutional convention) meant to say in using the words they did. But lawyers recognize that on many issues the author had no intention either way and that on others his intention cannot be discovered. Some lawyers take a more skeptical position. They say that whenever judges pretend they are discovering the intention behind some piece of legislation, this is simply a smoke screen behind which the judges impose their own view of what the statute should have been.

Interpretation as a technique of legal analysis is less familiar in the case of the common law, but not unfamiliar. Suppose the Supreme Court of Illinois decided, several years ago, that a negligent driver who ran down a child was liable for the emotional damage suffered by the child's mother, who was standing next to the child on the road. Now an aunt sues another careless driver for emotional damage suffered when she heard, on the telephone many miles from the accident, that her niece had been hit. Does the aunt have a right to recover for that damage? Lawyers often say that this is a matter of interpreting the earlier decision correctly. Does the legal theory on which the earlier judge actually relied, in making his decision about the mother on the road, cover the aunt on the telephone? Once again skeptics point out that it is unlikely that the earlier judge had in mind any theory sufficiently developed so as to decide the aunt's case either way, so that a judge "interpreting" the earlier decision is actually making new law in the way he or she thinks best.

The idea of interpretation cannot serve as a general account of the nature or truth value of propositions of law, however, unless it is cut loose from these associations with speaker's meaning or intention. Otherwise it becomes simply one version of the positivist's thesis that propositions of law describe decisions taken by people or institutions in the past. If interpretation is to form the basis of a different and more plausible theory about propositions of law, then we must develop a more inclusive account of what interpretation is. But that means that lawyers must not treat legal interpretation as an activity *sui generis*. We must study interpretation as a general activity, as a mode of knowledge, by attending to other contexts of that activity.

Lawyers would do well to study literary and other forms of artistic interpretation. That might seem bad advice (choosing the fire over the frying pan) because critics themselves are thoroughly divided about what literary interpretation is, and the situation is hardly better in the other arts. But that is exactly why lawyers should study these debates. Not all of the battles within literary criticism are edifying or even comprehensible, but many more theories of interpretation have been defended in literature than in law, and these include theories which challenge the flat distinction between description and evaluation that has enfeebled legal theory.

II. Literature

1. The Aesthetic Hypothesis

If lawyers are to benefit from a comparison between legal and literary interpretation, however, they must see the latter in a certain light, and in this section I shall try to say what that is. (I would prefer the following remarks about literature to be uncontroversial among literary scholars, of course, but I am afraid they will not be.) Students of literature do many things under the titles of "interpretation" and "hermeneutics," and most of them are also called "discovering the meaning of a text." I shall not be interested, except incidentally, in one thing these students do, which is trying to discover the sense in which some author used a particular word or phrase. I am interested instead in arguments which offer some sort of interpretation of the meaning of a work as a whole. These sometimes take the form of assertions about characters: that Hamlet really loved his mother, for example, or that he really hated her, or that there really was no ghost but only Hamlet himself in a schizophrenic manifestation. Or about events in the story behind the story: that Hamlet and Ophelia were lovers before the play begins (or were not). More usually they offer hypotheses directly about the "point" or "theme" or "meaning" or "sense" or "tone" of the play as a whole: that *Hamlet* is a play about death, for example, or about generations, or about politics. These interpretive claims may have a practical point. They may guide a director staging a new performance of the play, for example. But they may also be of more general importance, helping us to an improved understanding of important parts of our cultural environment. Of course, difficulties about the speaker's meaning of a particular word in the text (a "crux" of interpretation) may bear upon these larger matters. But the latter are about the point or meaning of the work as a whole, rather than the sense of a particular phrase.

Critics much disagree about how to answer such questions. I want, so far as is possible, not to take sides but to try to capture the disagreements in some sufficiently general description of what they are disagreeing about. My apparently banal suggestion (which I shall call the "aesthetic hypothesis") is this: an interpretation of a piece of literature attempts to show which way of reading (or speaking or directing or acting) the text reveals it as the best work of art. Different theories or schools or traditions of interpretation disagree, on this hypothesis, because they assume significantly different normative theories about what literature is and what it is for and about what makes one work of literature better than another.

I expect that this suggestion, in spite of its apparent weakness, will be rejected by many scholars as confusing interpretation with criticism or, in any case, as hopelessly relativistic, and therefore as a piece of skepticism that really denies the possibility of interpretation altogether. Indeed the aesthetic hypothesis might seem simply another formulation of a theory now popular, which is that since interpretation creates a work of art and represents only the fiat of a particular critical community, there are only interpretations and no best interpretation of any particular poem or novel or play. But the aesthetic hypothesis is neither so wild nor so weak nor so inevitably relativistic as might first appear.

Interpretation of a text attempts to show *it* as the best work of art *it* can be, and the pronoun insists on the difference between explaining a work of art and changing it into a different one. Perhaps Shakespeare could have written a better play based on the sources he used for *Hamlet* than he did, and in that better play the hero would have been a more forceful man of action. It does not follow that *Hamlet,* the play he wrote, really is like that after all. Of course, a theory of interpretation must contain a subtheory about identity of a work of art in order to be able to tell the difference between interpreting and changing a work. (Any useful theory of identity will be controversial, so that this is one obvious way in which disagreements in interpretation will depend on more general disagreements in aesthetic theory.)

Contemporary theories of interpretation all seem to use, as part of their response to that requirement, the idea of a canonical text (or score, in the case of music, or unique physical object, in the case of most art). The text provides one severe constraint in the name of identity: all the words must be taken account of and none may be changed to make "it" a putatively better work of art. (This constraint, however familiar, is not inevitable. A joke, for example, may be the same joke though told in a variety of forms, none of them canonical; an interpretation of a joke will choose a particular way in which to put it, and this may be wholly original, in order to bring out its "real" point or why it is "really" funny.) So any literary critic's style of interpretation will be sensitive to his theoretical beliefs about the nature of and evidence for a canonical text.

An interpretive style will also be sensitive to the interpreter's opinions about coherence or integrity in art. An interpretation cannot make a work of art more distinguished if it makes a large part of the text irrelevant, or much of the incident accidental, or a great part of the trope or style unintegrated and answering only to independent standards of fine writing. So it does not follow, from the aesthetic hypothesis, that because a philosophical novel is aesthetically more valuable than a mystery story, an Agatha Christie novel is really a treatise on the meaning of death. This interpretation fails not only because an Agatha Christie, taken to be a tract on death, is a poor tract less valuable than a good mystery but because the interpretation makes the novel a shambles. All but one or two sentences would be irrelevant to the supposed theme; and the organization, style, and figures would be appropriate not to a philosophical novel but to an entirely different genre. Of course some books originally offered to the public as mysteries or thrillers (and perhaps thought of by their authors that way) have indeed been "re-interpreted" as something more ambitious. The present critical interest in Raymond Chandler is an example. But the fact that this re-interpretation can be successful in the case of Chandler, but not Christie, illustrates the constraint of integrity.

There is nevertheless room for much disagreement among critics about what counts as integration, about which sort of unity is desirable and which irrelevant or undesirable. Is it really an advantage that the tongue of the reader, in reading a poem aloud, must "mime" motions or directions that figure in the tropes or narrative of the poem? Does this improve integrity by adding yet another dimension of coordination? Is it an advantage when conjunctions and line endings are arranged so that the reader "negotiating" a poem develops contradictory assumptions and readings as he goes on, so that his understanding at the end is very different from what it was at discrete points along the way? Does this add another dimension of complexity to unity, or does it rather compromise unity because a work of literature should be capable of having the same meaning or import when read a second time? Schools of interpretation will rise or fall in response to these questions of aesthetic theory, which is what the aesthetic hypothesis suggests.

The major differences among schools of interpretation are less subtle, however, because they touch not these quasi-formal aspects of art but the function or point of art more broadly conceived. Does literature have (primarily or substantially) a cognitive point? Is art better when it is in some way instructive, when we learn something from it about how people are or what the world is like? If so and if psychoanalysis is true (please forgive that crude way of putting it), then a psychoanalytic interpretation of a piece of literature will show why it is successful art. Is art good insofar as it is successful communication in the ordinary sense? If so, then a good interpretation will focus on what the author intended, because communication is not successful unless it expresses what a speaker wants it to express. Or is art good when it is expressive in a different sense, insofar as it has the capacity to stimulate or inform the lives of those who experience it? If so, then interpretation will place the reader (or listener or viewer) in the foreground. It will point out the reading of the work that makes it most valuable—best as a work of art—in that way.

Of course theories of art do not exist in isolation from philosophy, psychology, sociology, and cosmology. Someone who accepts a religious point of view will probably have a different theory of art from someone who does not, and recent critical theories have made us see how far interpretive style is sensitive to beliefs about meaning, reference, and other technical issues in the philosophy of language. But the aesthetic hypothesis does not assume that anyone who interprets literature will have a fully developed and self-conscious aesthetic theory. Nor that everyone who interprets must subscribe entirely to one or another of the schools I crudely described. The best critics, I think, deny that there is one unique function or point of literature. A novel or a play may be valuable in any number of ways, some of which we learn by reading or looking or listening, rather than by abstract reflection about what good art must be like or for.

Nevertheless anyone who interprets a work of art relies on beliefs of a theoretical character about identity and other formal properties of art, as well as on more explicitly normative beliefs about what is good in art. *Both* sorts of beliefs figure in the judgment that one way of reading a text makes it a better text than another way. These beliefs may be inarticulate (or "tacit"). They are still genuine beliefs (and not merely "reactions") because their force for any critic or reader can be seen at work not just on one isolated occasion of interpretation but in any number of other occasions, and because they figure in and are amenable to argument.[1] (These weak claims do not, of course, take sides in the running debate whether there are any necessary or sufficient "principles of value" in art or whether a theory of art could ever justify an interpretation in the absence of direct experience of the work being interpreted.)[2]

None of this touches the major complaint I anticipated against the aesthetic hypothesis: that it is trivial. Obviously (you might say) different

1. See Gareth Evans, "Semantic Theory and Tacit Knowledge," in *Wittgenstein: To Follow a Rule,* ed. Steven H. Holtzman and Christopher M. Leich (London, 1981).

2. It may be one of the many important differences between interpretation in art and law, which I do not examine in this essay, that nothing in law corresponds to the direct experience of a work of art, though some lawyers of the romantic tradition do speak of a good judge's "sixth sense" which enables him to grasp which aspects of a chain of legal decisions reveal the "immanent" principle of law even though he cannot fully explain why.

interpretive styles are grounded in different theories of what art is and what it is for and what makes art good art. The point is so banal that it might as well be put the other way around: different theories of art are generated by different theories of interpretation. If someone thinks stylistics are important to interpretation, he will think a work of art better because it integrates pronunciation and trope; if someone is attracted by deconstruction, he will dismiss reference in its familiar sense from any prominent place in an account of language. Nor does my elaboration of the hypothesis in any way help to adjudicate amongst theories of interpretation or to rebut the charge of nihilism or relativism. On the contrary, since people's views about what makes art good art are inherently subjective, the aesthetic hypothesis abandons hope of rescuing objectivity in interpretation except, perhaps, among those who hold very much the same theory of art, which is hardly very helpful.

No doubt the aesthetic hypothesis is in important ways banal—it must be abstract if it is to provide an account of what a wide variety of theories disagree about—but it is perhaps not so weak as all that. The hypothesis has the consequence that academic theories of interpretation are no longer seen as what they often claim to be—analyses of the very idea of interpretation—but rather as candidates for the best answer to the substantive question posed by interpretation. Interpretation becomes a concept of which different theories are competing conceptions. (It follows that there is no radical difference but only a difference in the level of abstraction between offering a theory of interpretation and offering an interpretation of a particular work of art.) The hypothesis denies, moreover, the sharp distinctions some scholars have cultivated. There is no longer a flat distinction between interpretation, conceived as discovering the real meaning of a work of art, and criticism, conceived as evaluating its success or importance. Of course some distinction remains because there is always a difference between saying how good a particular work can be made to be and saying how good that is. But evaluative beliefs about art figure in both these judgments.

Objectivity is another matter. It is an open question, I think, whether the main judgments we make about art can properly be said to be true or false, valid or invalid. This question is part of the more general philosophical issue of objectivity, presently much discussed in both ethics and the philosophy of language, and no one is entitled to a position who studies the case of aesthetic judgment alone. Of course no important aesthetic claim can be "demonstrated" to be true or false; no argument can be produced for any interpretation which we can be sure will commend itself to everyone, or even everyone with experience and training in the appropriate form of art. If this is what it means to say that aesthetic judgments are subjective—that they are not demonstrable— then of course they are subjective. But it does not follow that no normative theory about art is better than any other, nor that one theory cannot be the best that has so far been produced.

The aesthetic hypothesis reverses (I think to its credit) a familiar strategy. E. D. Hirsch, for example, argues that only a theory like his can make interpretation objective and particular interpretations valid.[3] This seems to me a mistake on two connected grounds. Interpretation is an enterprise, a public institution, and it is wrong to assume, a priori, that the propositions central to any public enterprise must be capable of validity. It is also wrong to assume much about what validity in such enterprises must be like—whether validity requires the possibility of demonstrability, for example. It seems better to proceed more empirically here. We should first study a variety of activities in which people assume that they have good reasons for what they say, which they assume hold generally and not just from one or another individual point of view. We can then judge what standards people accept in practice for thinking that they have reasons of that kind.

Nor is the point about reversibility—that a theory of art may depend upon a theory of interpretation as much as vice versa—an argument against the aesthetic hypothesis. I am not defending any particular explanation of how people come to have either theories of interpretation or theories of art but only a claim about the argumentative connections that hold between these theories however come by. Of course even at the level of argument these two kinds of theories are mutually reinforcing. It is plainly a reason for doubting any theory of what an object of art is, for example, that that theory generates an obviously silly theory of interpretation. My point is exactly that the connection is reciprocal, so that anyone called upon to defend a particular approach to interpretation would be forced to rely on more general aspects of a theory of art, whether he realizes it or not. And this may be true even though the opposite is, to some extent, true as well. It would be a mistake, I should add, to count this fact of mutual dependence as offering, in itself, any reason for skepticism or relativism about interpretation. This seems to be the burden of slogans like "interpretation creates the text," but there is no more immediate skeptical consequence in the idea that what we take to be a work of art must comport with what we take interpreting a work of art to be than in the analogous idea that what we take a physical object to be must sit well with our theories of knowledge; so long as we add, in both cases, that the connection holds the other way around as well.

2. Author's Intention

The chief test of the aesthetic hypothesis lies, however, not in its resistance to these various charges but in its explanatory and particularly its critical power. If we accept that theories of interpretation are not independent analyses of what it means to interpret something but are

3. See E. D. Hirsch, Jr., *Validity in Interpretation* (New Haven, Conn., 1967).

rather based in and dependent upon normative theories of art, then we must accept that they are vulnerable to complaints against the normative theory in which they are based. It does seem to me, for example, that the more doctrinaire authors' intention theories are vulnerable in this way. These theories must suppose, on the present hypothesis, that what is valuable in a work of art, what should lead us to value one work of art more than another, is limited to what the author in some narrow and constrained sense intended to put there. This claim presupposes, as I suggested earlier, a more general thesis that art must be understood as a form of speaker-audience communication; but even that doubtful thesis turns out, on further inspection, not to support it.

Of course the intentionalists would object to these remarks. They would insist that their theory of interpretation is not an account of what is valuable in a book or poem or play but only an account of what any particular book or poem or play means and that we must understand what something means before we can decide whether it is valuable and where its value lies. And they would object that they do not say that only intentions of the author "in some narrow and constrained sense" count in fixing the meaning of his work.

In the first of these objections, the author's intention theory presents itself not as the upshot of the aesthetic hypothesis—not as the best theory of interpretation within the design stipulated by that hypothesis—but rather as a rival to it, a better theory about what kind of thing an interpretation is. But it is very difficult to understand the author's intention theory as any sort of rival to the present hypothesis. What question does it propose to answer better? Not, certainly, some question about the ordinary language or even technical meaning of the words "meaning" or "interpretation." An intentionalist cannot suppose that all his critics and those he criticizes mean, when they say "interpretation," the discovery of the author's intention. Nor can he think that his claims accurately describe what every member of the critical fraternity in fact does under the title "interpretation." If that were so, then his strictures and polemics would be unnecessary. But if his theory is not semantic or empirical in these ways, what sort of a theory is it?

Suppose an intentionalist replies: "It points out an important issue about works of literature, namely, What did the author of the work intend it to be? This is plainly an important question, even if its importance is preliminary to other equally or more important questions about significance or value. It is, in fact, what most people for a long time have called 'interpretation'. But the name does not matter, so long as the activity is recognized as important and so long as it is understood that scholars are in principle capable of supplying objectively correct answers to the question it poses."

This reply comes to this: we can discover what an author intended (or at least come to probabilistic conclusions about this), and it is important to do so for other literary purposes. But why is it important? What other purposes? Any answer will assume that value or significance in art attaches primarily to what the author intended, just because it is what the author intended. Otherwise, why should we evaluate what this style of interpretation declares to be the work of art? But then the claim that interpretation in this style is important depends on a highly controversial, normative theory of art, not a neutral observation preliminary to any coherent evaluation. Of course no plausible theory of interpretation holds that the intention of the author is always irrelevant. Sometimes it is plainly the heart of the matter, as when some issue turns on what Shakespeare meant by "hawk" as distinguished from "handsaw." But it is nevertheless controversial that we must know whether Shakespeare thought Hamlet was sane or a madman pretending to be mad in order to decide how good a play he wrote. The intentionalist thinks that we do, and that is exactly why his theory of interpretation is not a rival to the aesthetic hypothesis but rather a suitor for the crown that hypothesis holds out.

The second objection to my charge against author's intention theories may prove to be more interesting. Intentionalists make the author's state of mind central to interpretation. But they misunderstand, so far as I can tell, certain complexities in that state of mind; in particular they fail to appreciate how intentions *for* a work and beliefs *about* it interact. I have in mind an experience familiar to anyone who creates anything, of suddenly seeing something "in" it that he did not previously know was there. This is sometimes (though I think not very well) expressed in the author's cliché, that his characters seem to have minds of their own. John Fowles provides an example from popular fiction.

> When Charles left Sarah on her cliff edge, I ordered him to walk straight back to Lyme Regis. But he did not; he gratuitously turned and went down to the Dairy. Oh, but you say, come on—what I really mean is that the idea crossed my mind as I wrote that it might be more clever to have him stop and drink milk . . . and meet Sarah again. That is certainly one explanation of what happened; but I can only report—and I am the most reliable witness—that the idea seemed to me to come clearly from Charles, not myself. It is not only that he has begun to gain an autonomy; I must respect it, and disrespect all my quasi-divine plans for him, if I wish him to be real.

Fowles changed his mind about how the story in *The French Lieutenant's Woman* "really" goes in the midst of writing it, if we are to credit this description. But he might also have changed his mind about some aspect of the novel's "point" years later, as he is rumored to have done after seeing the film made from his book. He might have come to see Sarah's motives very differently after reading Harold Pinter's screenplay or watching Meryl Streep play her; Pinter and Streep were interpreting the novel, and one or both of their interpretations might have led Fowles to change *his* interpretation once again. Perhaps I am wrong in supposing that this sort of thing happens often. But it happens often enough, and it is important to be clear about what it is that happens.

The intentionalist wants us to choose between two possibilities. Either the author suddenly realizes that he had a "subconscious intention" earlier, which he only now discovers, or he has simply changed his intention later. Neither of these explanations is at all satisfactory. The subconscious is in danger of becoming phlogiston here, unless we suppose some independent evidence, apart from the author's new view of his work, to suggest that he had an earlier subconscious intention. I do not mean that features of a work of art of which an author is unaware must be random accidents. On the contrary. If a novel is both more interesting and more coherent if we assume the characters have motives different from those the novelist thought of when he wrote (or if a poet's tropes and style tend to reinforce his theme in ways he did not appreciate at the time), the cause of this must in some way lie in the artist's talent. Of course there are unsolved mysteries in the psychology of creation, but the supposition of subconscious *intentions,* unsupported by other evidence of the sort a psychoanalyst would insist on, solves no mysteries and provides no explanation. This is not crucial to the point, however, because whether or not Fowles had a subconscious intention to make Charles or Sarah different characters from the "quasi-divine plan" he thought he had, his later decisions and beliefs neither consist in nor are based on any discovery of that earlier intention. They are produced by confronting not his earlier self but the work he has produced.

Nor is any new belief Fowles forms about his characters properly called (as in the intentionalist's second suggestion) a new and discrete intention. It is not an intention about what sort of characters to create because it is a belief about what sort of characters he has created; and it is not an intention about how others should understand the book, though it may or may not include an expectation of that sort. Fowles changed his view in the course of writing his book, but he changed it, as he insists, by confronting the text he had already written, by treating its characters as real in the sense of detachable from his own antecedent designs, in short by interpreting it, and not by exploring the subconscious depths of some previous plan or finding that he had a new plan. If it is true that he changed his mind again, after seeing the film, then this was, once again, not a retrospective new intention or a rediscovered old one. It was another interpretation.

An author is capable of detaching what he has written from his earlier intentions and beliefs, of treating it as an object in itself. He is capable of reaching fresh conclusions about his work grounded in aesthetic judgments: that his book is both more coherent and a better analysis of more important themes read in a somewhat different way from what he thought when he was writing it. This is, I think, a very important fact for a number of reasons; but I want, for my present purpose, only to emphasize one. Any full description of what Fowles "intended" when he set out to write *The French Lieutenant's Woman* must include the intention to produce something capable of being treated that way, by himself and therefore by others, and so must include the intention to create something independent of his intentions. I quote Fowles once again, and again as a witness rather than for his metaphysics: "Only one reason is shared by all of us [novelists]: *we wish to create worlds as real as, but other than, the world that is.* Or was. That is why we cannot plan. . . . We also know that a genuinely created world must be independent of its creator."

I suspect that regarding something one has produced as a novel or poem or painting, rather than a set of propositions or marks, *depends* on regarding it as something that can be detached and interpreted in the sense I described. In any case this is characteristically how authors themselves regard what they have done. The intentions of authors are not simply conjunctive, like the intentions of someone who goes to market with a shopping list, but structured, so that the more concrete of these intentions, like intentions about the motives of a particular character in a novel, are contingent on interpretive beliefs whose soundness varies with what is produced and which might be radically altered from time to time.

We can, perhaps, isolate the full set of interpretive beliefs an author has at a particular moment (say at the moment he sends final galleys to the printer) and solemnly declare that these beliefs, in their full concreteness, fix what the novel is or means. (Of course, these beliefs would inevitably be incomplete, but that is another matter.) But even if we (wrongly) call this particular set of beliefs "intentions," we are, in choosing them, ignoring another kind or level of intention, which is the intention to create a work whose nature or meaning is not fixed in this way, because it is a work of art. That is why the author's intention school, as I understand it, makes the value of a work of art turn on a narrow and constrained view of the intentions of the author.

III. Law and Literature

1. The Chain of Law

These sketchy remarks about literary interpretation may have suggested too sharp a split between the role of the artist in creating a work of art and that of the critic in interpreting it later. The artist can create nothing without interpreting as he creates; since he intends to produce art, he must have at least a tacit theory of why what he produces is art and why it is a better work of art through this stroke of the pen or the brush or the chisel rather than that. The critic, for his part, creates as he interprets; for though he is bound by the fact of the work, defined in the more formal and academic parts of his theory of art, his more practical artistic sense is engaged by his responsibility to decide which way of seeing or reading or understanding that work shows it as better art. Nevertheless there is a difference between interpreting while creating and creating while interpreting, and therefore a recognizable difference between the artist and the critic.

I want to use literary interpretation as a model for the central method of legal analysis, and I therefore need to show how even this distinction between artist and critic might be eroded in certain circumstances. Suppose that a group of novelists is engaged for a particular project and that they draw lots to determine the order of play. The lowest number writes the opening chapter of a novel, which he or she then sends to the next number who adds a chapter, with the understanding that he is adding a chapter to that novel rather than beginning a new one, and then sends the two chapters to the next number, and so on. Now every novelist but the first has the dual responsibilities of interpreting and creating because each must read all that has gone before in order to establish, in the interpretivist sense, what the novel so far created is.[4] He or she must decide what the characters are "really" like;

4. Even the first novelist has the responsibility of interpreting to the extent any writer must, which includes not only interpreting as he writes but interpreting the genre in which he sets out to write. Will novelists with higher numbers have less creative "freedom" than those with lower? In one sense, no novelist has any freedom at all, because each is constrained to choose that interpretation which (he believes) makes the continuing work of art the best it can be. But we have already seen (and the discussion of law below will elaborate) two different dimensions along which any interpretation can be tested: the "formal" dimension, which asks how far the interpretation fits and integrates the text so far completed, and the "substantive" dimension, which considers the soundness of the view about what makes a novel good on which the interpretation relies. It seems reasonable to suppose that later novelists will normally—but certainly not inevitably—believe that fewer interpretations can survive the first of these tests than would have survived had they received fewer chapters. Most interpreters would think that a certain interpretation of *A Christmas Carol*—that Scrooge was inherently evil, for example—would pass the test of integrity just after the opening pages, but not toward the end of that novel. Our sense that later novelists are less free may reflect just that fact. This does not mean, of course, that there is more likely to be consensus about the correct interpretation later rather than earlier in the chain or that a later novelist is more likely to find an argument that "proves" his interpretation right beyond rational challenge. Reasonable disagreement is available on the formal as well as the substantive side, and even when most novelists would think only a particular interpretation could fit the novel to a certain point, some novelist of imagination might find some dramatic change in plot that (in his opinion) unexpectedly unifies what had seemed unnecessary and redeems what had seemed wrong or trivial. Once again, we should be careful not to confuse the fact that consensus would rarely be reached, at any point in the process, with the claim that any particular novelist's interpretation must be "merely subjective." No novelist, at any point, will be able simply to read the correct interpretation of the text he receives in a mechanical way, but it does not follow from that fact alone that one interpretation is not superior to others overall. In any case it will nevertheless be true, for all novelists beyond the first, that the assignment to find (what they believe to be) the correct interpretation of the text so far is a different assignment from the assignment to begin a new novel of their own. See, for a fuller discussion, my forthcoming "Natural Law Revisited," *University of Florida Law Review*.

what motives in fact guide them; what the point or theme of the developing novel is; how far some literary device or figure, consciously or unconsciously used, contributes to these, and whether it should be extended or refined or trimmed or dropped in order to send the novel further in one direction rather than another. This must be interpretation in a non–intention-bound style because, at least for all novelists after the second, there is no single author whose intentions any interpreter can, by the rules of the project, regard as decisive.

Some novels have in fact been written in this way (including the softcore pornographic novel *Naked Came the Stranger*), though for a debunking purpose; and certain parlor games, for rainy weekends in English country houses, have something of the same structure. But in my imaginary exercise the novelists are expected to take their responsibilities seriously and to recognize the duty to create, so far as they can, a single, unified novel rather than, for example, a series of independent short stories with characters bearing the same names. Perhaps this is an impossible assignment; perhaps the project is doomed to produce not simply a bad novel but no novel at all, because the best theory of art requires a single creator or, if more than one, that each have some control over the whole. But what about legends and jokes? I need not push that question further because I am interested only in the fact that the assignment makes sense, that each of the novelists in the chain can have some idea of what he or she is asked to do, whatever misgivings each might have about the value or character of what will then be produced.

Deciding hard cases at law is rather like this strange literary exercise. The similarity is most evident when judges consider and decide common-law cases; that is, when no statute figures centrally in the legal issue, and the argument turns on which rules or principles of law "underlie" the related decisions of other judges in the past. Each judge is then like a novelist in the chain. He or she must read through what other judges in the past have written not simply to discover what these judges have said, or their state of mind when they said it, but to reach an opinion about what these judges have collectively *done*, in the way that each of our novelists formed an opinion about the collective novel so far written. Any judge forced to decide a lawsuit will find, if he looks in the appropriate books, records of many arguably similar cases decided over decades or even centuries past by many other judges of different styles and judicial and political philosophies, in periods of different orthodoxies of procedure and judicial convention. Each judge must regard himself, in deciding the new case before him, as a partner in a complex chain enterprise of which these innumerable decisions, structures, conventions, and practices are the history; it is his job to continue that history into the future through what he does on the day. He *must* interpret what has gone before because he has a responsibility to advance the enterprise in hand rather than strike out in some new direction of his own. So he must determine, according to his own judgment, what the earlier decisions come to, what the point or theme of the practice so far, taken as a whole, really is.

The judge in the hypothetical case I mentioned earlier, about an aunt's emotional shock, must decide what the theme is not only of the particular precedent of the mother in the road but of accident cases, including that precedent, as a whole. He might be forced to choose, for example, between these two theories about the "meaning" of that chain of decisions. According to the first, negligent drivers are responsible to those whom their behavior is likely to cause physical harm, but they are responsible to these people for whatever injury—physical or emotional—they in fact cause. If this is the correct principle, then the decisive difference between that case and the aunt's case is just that the aunt was not within the physical risk, and therefore she cannot recover. On the second theory, however, negligent drivers are responsible for any damage they can reasonably be expected to foresee if they think about their behavior in advance. If that is the right principle, then the aunt may yet recover. Everything turns on whether it is sufficiently foreseeable that a child will have relatives, beyond his or her immediate parents, who may suffer emotional shock when they learn of the child's injury. The judge trying the aunt's case must decide which of these two principles represents the better "reading" of the chain of decisions he must continue.

Can we say, in some general way, what those who disagree about the best interpretation of legal precedent are disagreeing about? I said that a literary interpretation aims to show how the work in question can be seen as the most valuable work of art, and so must attend to formal features of identity, coherence, and integrity as well as more substantive considerations of artistic value. A plausible interpretation of legal practice must also, in a parallel way, satisfy a test of two dimensions: it must both fit that practice and show its point or value. But point or value here cannot mean artistic value because law, unlike literature, is not an artistic enterprise. Law is a political enterprise, whose general point, if it has one, lies in coordinating social and individual effort, or resolving social and individual disputes, or securing justice between citizens and between them and their government, or some combination of these. (This characterization is itself an interpretation, of course, but allowable now because relatively neutral.) So an interpretation of any body or division of law, like the law of accidents, must show the value of that body of law in political terms by demonstrating the best principle or policy it can be taken to serve.

We know from the parallel argument in literature that this general description of interpretation in law is not license for each judge to find in doctrinal history whatever he thinks should have been there. The same distinction holds between interpretation and ideal. A judge's duty is to interpret the legal history he finds, not to invent a better history. The dimensions of fit will provide some boundaries. There is, of course, no algorithm for deciding whether a particular interpretation sufficiently fits that history not to be ruled out. When a statute or constitution or other legal document is part of the doctrinal history, speaker's meaning will play a role. But the choice of which of several crucially different senses of speaker's or legislator's intention is the appropriate one cannot itself be referred to anyone's intention but must be decided, by whoever must make the decision, as a question of political theory.[5] In the common-law cases the question of fit is more complex. Any particular hypothesis about the point of a string of decisions ("these decisions establish the principle that no one can recover for emotional damage who did not lie within the area of physical danger himself") is likely to encounter if not flat counterexamples in some earlier case at least language or argument that seems to suggest the contrary. So any useful conception of interpretation must contain a doctrine of mistake—as must any novelist's theory of interpretation for the chain novel. Sometimes a legal argument will explicitly recognize such mistakes: "Insofar as the cases of *A* v. *B* and *C* v. *D* may have held to the contrary, they were, we believe, wrongly decided and need not be followed here." Sometimes the doctrine of precedent forbids this crude approach and requires something like: "We held, in *E* v. *F*, that such-and-such, but that case raised special issues and must, we think, be confined to its own facts" (which is not quite so disingenuous as it might seem).

This flexibility may seem to erode the difference on which I insist, between interpretation and a fresh, clean-slate decision about what the law ought to be. But there is nevertheless this overriding constraint. Any judge's sense of the point or function of law, on which every aspect of his approach to interpretation will depend, will include or imply some conception of the integrity and coherence of law as an institution, and this conception will both tutor and constrain his working theory of fit—that is, his convictions about how much of the prior law an interpretation must fit, and which of it, and how. (The parallel with literary interpretation holds here as well.)

It should be apparent, however, that any particular judge's theory of fit will often fail to produce a unique interpretation. (The distinction between hard and easy cases at law is perhaps just the distinction between cases in which they do and do not.) Just as two readings of a poem may each find sufficient support in the text to show its unity and coherence, two principles may each find enough support in the various decisions of the past to satisfy any plausible theory of fit. In that case substantive political theory (like substantive considerations of artistic merit) will play a decisive role. Put bluntly, the interpretation of accident

5. See my "The Forum of Principle," *New York University Law Review* 56 (1981).

law, that a careless driver is liable to those whose damage is both sub-stantial and foreseeable, is probably a better interpretation, if it is, only because it states a sounder principle of justice than any principle that distinguishes between physical and emotional damage or that makes recovery for emotional damage depend on whether the plaintiff was in danger of physical damage. (I should add that this issue, as an issue of political morality, is in fact very complex, and many distinguished judges and lawyers have taken each side.)

We might summarize these points this way. Judges develop a par-ticular approach to legal interpretation by forming and refining a politi-cal theory sensitive to those issues on which interpretation in particular cases will depend; and they call this their legal philosophy. It will include both structural features, elaborating the general requirement that an interpretation must fit doctrinal history, and substantive claims about social goals and principles of justice. Any judge's opinion about the best interpretation will therefore be the consequence of beliefs other judges need not share. If a judge believes that the dominant purpose of a legal system, the main goal it ought to serve, is economic, then he will see in past accident decisions some strategy for reducing the economic costs of accidents overall. Other judges, who find any such picture of the law's function distasteful, will discover no such strategy in history but only, perhaps, an attempt to reinforce conventional morality of fault and re-sponsibility. If we insist on a high order of neutrality in our description of legal interpretation, therefore, we cannot make our description of the nature of legal interpretation much more concrete than I have.

2. Author's Intention in Law

I want instead to consider various objections that might be made not to the detail of my argument but to the main thesis, that interpretation in law is essentially political. I shall not spend further time on the general objection already noticed: that this view of law makes it irreducibly and irredeemably subjective, just a matter of what particular judges think best or what they had for breakfast. Of course, for some lawyers and legal scholars this is not an objection at all, but only the beginnings of skeptical wisdom about law. But it is the nerve of my argument that the flat distinction between description and evaluation on which this skepti-cism relies—the distinction between finding the law just "there" in his-tory and making it up wholesale—is misplaced here, because interpreta-tion is something different from both.

I shall want, therefore, to repeat the various observations I made about subjectivity and objectivity in literary interpretation. There is no obvious reason in the account I gave of legal interpretation to doubt that one interpretation of law can be better than another and that one can be best of all. Whether this is so depends on general issues of philosophy not peculiar to law any more than to literature; and we would do well, in considering these general issues, not to begin with any fixed ideas about the necessary and sufficient conditions of objectivity (for example that no theory of law can be sound unless it is demonstrably sound, unless it would wring assent from a stone). In the meantime we can sensibly aim to develop various levels of a conception of law for ourselves, to find the interpretation of a complex and dramatically important practice which seems to us at once the right kind of interpretation for law and right as that kind of interpretation.

I shall consider one further, and rather different, objection in more detail: that my political hypothesis about legal interpretation, like the aesthetic hypothesis about artistic interpretation, fails to give an adequate place to author's intention. It fails to see that interpretation in law is simply a matter of discovering what various actors in the legal process—constitutional delegates, members of Congress and state legislatures, judges and executive officials—intended. Once again it is important to see what is at stake here. The political hypothesis makes room for the author's intention argument as a conception of interpretation, a conception which claims that the best political theory gives the intentions of legislators and past judges a decisive role in interpretation. Seen this way, the author's intention theory does not challenge the political hypothesis but contests for its authority. If the present objection is really an objection to the argument so far, therefore, its claim must be understood differently, as proposing, for example, that very "meaning" of interpretation in law requires that only these officials' intentions should count or that at least there is a firm consensus among lawyers to that effect. Both of these claims are as silly as the parallel claims about the idea or the practice of interpretation in art.

Suppose, therefore, that we do take the author's intention theory, more sensibly, as a conception rather than an explication of the concept of legal interpretation. The theory seems on firmest ground, as I suggested earlier, when interpretation is interpretation of a canonical legal text, like a clause of the Constitution, or a section of a statute, or a provision of a contract or will. But just as we noticed that a novelist's intention is complex and structured in ways that embarrass any simple author's intention theory in literature, we must now notice that a legislator's intention is complex in similar ways. Suppose a delegate to a constitutional convention votes for a clause guaranteeing equality of treatment, without regard to race, in matters touching people's fundamental interests; but he thinks that education is not a matter of fundamental interest and so does not believe that the clause makes racially segregated schools unconstitutional. We may sensibly distinguish an abstract and a concrete intention here: the delegate intends to prohibit discrimination in whatever in fact is of fundamental interest and also intends not to prohibit segregated schools. These are not isolated, dis-

crete intentions; our descriptions, we might say, describe the same intention in different ways. But it matters very much which description a
theory of legislative intention accepts as canonical. If we accept the first
description, then a judge who wishes to follow the delegate's intentions,
but who believes that education is a matter of fundamental interest, will
hold segregation unconstitutional. If we accept the second, he will not.
The choice between the two descriptions cannot be made by any further
reflection about what an intention really is. It must be made by deciding
that one rather than the other description is more appropriate in virtue
of the best theory of representative democracy or on some other openly
political grounds. (I might add that no compelling argument has yet
been produced, so far as I am aware, in favor of deferring to a delegate's
more concrete intentions, and that this is of major importance in arguments about whether the "original intention" of the framers requires
abolishing, for example, racial discrimination or capital punishment.)

When we consider the common-law problems of interpretation, the
author's intention theory shows in an even poorer light. The problems
are not simply evidentiary. Perhaps we can discover what was "in the
mind" of all the judges who decided cases about accidents at one time or
another in our legal history. We might also discover (or speculate) about
the psychodynamic or economic or social explanations of why each judge
thought what he or she did. No doubt the result of all this research (or
speculation) would be a mass of psychological data essentially different
for each of the past judges included in the study, and order could be
brought into the mass, if at all, only through statistical summaries about
which proportion of judges in which historical period probably held
which opinion and was more or less subject to which influence. But this
mass, even tamed by statistical summary, would be of no more help to
the judge trying to answer the question of what the prior decisions, taken
as a whole, really come to than the parallel information would be to one
of our chain novelists trying to decide what novel the novelists earlier in
the chain had collectively written. That judgment, in each case, requires
a fresh exercise of interpretation which is neither brute historical research nor a clean-slate expression of how things ideally ought to be.

A judge who believed in the importance of discerning an author's
intention might try to escape these problems by selecting one particular
judge or a small group of judges in the past (say, the judges who decided
the most recent case something like his or the case he thinks closest to
his) and asking what rule that judge or group intended to lay down for
the future. This would treat the particular earlier judges as legislators
and so invite all the problems of statutory interpretation including the
very serious problem we just noticed. Even so it would not even escape
the special problems of common-law adjudication after all, because the
judge who applied this theory of interpretation would have to suppose
himself entitled to look only to the intentions of the particular earlier

judge or judges he had selected, and he could not suppose this unless he thought that it was the upshot of judicial practice as a whole (and not just the intentions of some *other* selected earlier judge) that this is what judges in his position should do.

IV. Politics in Interpretation

If my claims about the role of politics in legal interpretation are sound, then we should expect to find distinctly liberal or radical or conservative opinions not only about what the Constitution and laws of our nation should be but also about what they are. And this is exactly what we do find. Interpretation of the Equal Protection Clause of the United States Constitution provides especially vivid examples. There can be no useful interpretation of what that clause means which is independent of some theory about what political equality is and how far equality is required by justice, and the history of the last half-century of constitutional law is largely an exploration of exactly these issues of political morality. Conservative lawyers argued steadily (though not consistently) in favor of an author's intentions style of interpreting this clause, and they accused others, who used a different style with more egalitarian results, of inventing rather than interpreting law. But this was bluster meant to hide the role their own political convictions played in their choice of interpretive style, and the great legal debates over the Equal Protection Clause would have been more illuminating if it had been more widely recognized that reliance on political theory is not a corruption of interpretation but part of what interpretation means.

Should politics play any comparable role in literary and other artistic interpretation? We have become used to the idea of the politics of interpretation. Stanley Fish, particularly, has promoted a theory of interpretation which supposes that contests between rival schools of literary interpretation are more political than argumentative: rival professoriates in search of dominion. And of course it is a truism of the sociology of literature, and not merely of the Marxist contribution to that discipline, that fashion in interpretation is sensitive to and expresses more general political and economic structures. These important claims are external: they touch the causes of the rise of this or that approach to literature and interpretation.

Several of the essays for this conference discuss these issues. But we are now concerned with the internal question, about politics in rather than the politics of interpretation. How far can principles of political morality actually count as arguments for a particular interpretation of a particular work or for a general approach to artistic interpretation? There are many possibilities and many of them are parasitic on claims developed or mentioned in these essays. It was said that our commitment to feminism, or our fidelity to nation, or our dissatisfaction with the rise of the New Right ought to influence our evaluation and appreciation of literature. Indeed it was the general (though not unanimous) sense of the conference that professional criticism must be faulted for its inattention to such political issues. But if our convictions about these particular political issues count in deciding how good some novel or play or poem is, then they must also count in deciding, among particular interpretations of these works, which is the best interpretation. Or so they must if my argument is sound.

We might also explore a more indirect connection between aesthetic and political theory. Any comprehensive theory of art is likely to have, at its center, some epistemological thesis, some set of views about the relations that hold among experience, self-consciousness, and the perception or formation of values. If it assigns self-discovery any role in art, it will need a theory of personal identity adequate to mark off the boundaries of a person from his or her circumstances, and from other persons, or at least to deny the reality of any such boundaries. It seems likely that any comprehensive theory of social justice will also have roots in convictions about these or very closely related issues. Liberalism, for example, which assigns great importance to autonomy, may depend upon a particular picture of the role that judgments of value play in people's lives; it may depend on the thesis that people's convictions about value are beliefs, open to argument and review, rather than simply the givens of personality, fixed by genetic and social causes. And any political theory which gives an important place to equality also requires assumptions about the boundaries of persons, because it must distinguish between treating people as equals and changing them into different people.

It may be a sensible project, at least, to inquire whether there are not particular philosophical bases shared by particular aesthetic and particular political theories so that we can properly speak of a liberal or Marxist or perfectionist or totalitarian aesthetics, for example, in that sense. Common questions and problems hardly guarantee this, of course. It would be necessary to see, for example, whether liberalism can indeed be traced, as many philosophers have supposed, back into a discrete epistemological base, different from that of other political theories, and then ask whether that discrete base could be carried forward into aesthetic theory and there yield a distinctive interpretive style. I have no good idea that this project could be successful, and I end simply by acknowledging my sense that politics, art, and law are united, somehow, in philosophy.

Working on the Chain Gang: Interpretation in the Law and in Literary Criticism

Stanley Fish

In his essay "Law as Interpretation," Ronald Dworkin is concerned to characterize legal practice in such a way as to avoid claiming either that in deciding a case judges find the plain meaning of the law "just 'there' " or, alternatively, that they make up the meaning "wholesale" in accordance with personal preference or whim. It is Dworkin's thesis that neither of these accounts is adequate because "interpretation is something different from both" (p. 266). Dworkin is right, I think, to link his argument about legal practice to an argument about the practice of literary criticism, not only because in both disciplines the central question is, What is the source of interpretive authority? but because in both disciplines answers to that question typically take the form of the two positions Dworkin rejects. Just as there are those in the legal community who have insisted on construing statutes and decisions "strictly" (that is, by attending only to the words themselves), so are there those in the literary community who have insisted that interpretation is, or should be, constrained by what is "in the text"; and just as the opposing doctrine of "legal realism" holds that judges' "readings" are always rationalizations of their political or personal desires, so do proponents of critical subjectivity hold that what a reader sees is merely a reflection of his predispositions and biases. The field is divided, in short, between those who believe that interpretation is grounded in objectivity and those who believe that interpreters are, for all intents and purposes, free. Dworkin moves to outflank both of these positions by characterizing legal and critical practice as "chain enterprises," as enterprises in which interpretation is always an extension of an institutional history made up of "innumerable decisions, structures, conventions, and practices" (p. 263). Interpretation so conceived is not purely objective since its results will not "wring assent from a stone" (there is still "room for disagreement"), but neither is it wholly subjective since the interpreter does not proceed independently of what others in the institution have done or said.

In general I find this account of interpretation and its constraints attractive, in part because I find it similar in important ways to the account I have recently offered under the rubric of "interpretive communities" in *Is There a Text in This Class?* (Cambridge, Mass., 1980). There are, however, crucial differences between the two accounts, and in the course of explicating those differences, I will argue that Dworkin repeatedly falls´ away from his own best insight into a version of the fallacies (of pure objectivity and pure subjectivity) he so forcefully challenges.

We can begin by focusing on the most extended example in his essay of a chain enterprise, the imagined literary example of a novel written not by a single author but by a group of coauthors each of whom is responsible for a separate chapter. The members of the group draw lots and the

> lowest number writes the opening chapter of a novel, which he or she then sends to the next number who adds a chapter, with the understanding that he is adding a chapter to that novel rather than beginning a new one, and then sends the two chapters to the next number, and so on. Now every novelist but the first has the dual responsibilities of interpreting and creating because each must read all that has gone before in order to establish, in the interpretivist sense, what the novel so far created is. He or she must decide what the characters are "really" like; what motives in fact guide them; what the point or theme of the developing novel is; how far some literary device or figure, consciously or unconsciously used, contributes to these, and whether it should be extended or refined or trimmed or dropped in order to send the novel further in one direction rather than another. [Pp. 262–63]

In its deliberate exaggeration, this formulation of a chain enterprise is helpful and illuminating, but it is also, I think, mistaken in several

---

Stanley Fish is the William Kenan, Jr. Professor of English and the Humanities at the Johns Hopkins University. His most recent publication is *Is There a Text in This Class? The Authority of Interpretive Communities,* and he is currently completing a book entitled *Milton's Aesthetic of Testimony.*

important respects. First, it assumes that the first person in the chain is in a position different in kind from those who follow him because he is only creating while his fellow authors must both create and interpret. In an earlier draft of the essay, Dworkin had suggested that as the chain extends itself the freedom enjoyed by the initiator of the sequence is more and more constrained until at some point the history against which "late novelists" must work may become so dense "as to admit only one good-faith interpretation"; and indeed that interpretation will not be an interpretation in the usual sense because it will have been *demanded* by what has already been written. Dworkin has now withdrawn this suggestion (which he had qualified with words like "probably"), but the claim underlying it—the claim that constraints thicken as the chain lengthens—remains so long as the distinction between the first author and all the others is maintained. The idea is that the first author is free because he is not obliged "to read all that has gone before" and therefore doesn't have to decide what the characters are "really" like, what motives guide them, and so on. But in fact the first author has surrendered his freedom (although, as we shall see, surrender is exactly the wrong word) as soon as he commits himself to writing a novel, for he makes his decision under the same constraints that rule the decisions of his collaborators. He must decide, for example, how to begin the novel, but the decision is not "free" because the very notion "beginning a novel" exists only in the context of a set of practices that at once enables and limits the act of beginning. One cannot think of beginning a novel without thinking within, as opposed to thinking "of," these established practices, and even if one "decides" to "ignore" them or "violate" them or "set them aside," the actions of ignoring and violating and setting aside will themselves have a shape that is constrained by the preexisting shape of those practices. This does not mean that the decisions of the first author are wholly determined but that the choices available to him are "novel writing choices," choices that depend on a prior understanding of what it means to write a novel, even when he "chooses" to alter that understanding.[1] In short he is neither free nor constrained (if those words are understood as referring to absolute states) but free *and* constrained. He is free to begin whatever kind of novel he decides to write, but he is constrained by the finite (although not unchanging) possibilities that are subsumed in the notions "kind of novel" and "beginning a novel."

Moreover, those who follow him are free and constrained in exactly the same way. When a later novelist decides to "send the novel further in one direction rather than in another," that decision must follow upon a decision as to what direction has already been taken; and *that* decision

1. Dworkin makes a similar but not exactly parallel point when he acknowledges in his note 4 that the first novelist will have the responsibility of "interpreting the genre in which he sets out to write."

will be an interpretive one in the sense that it will not be determined by the independent and perspicuous shape of the words but will be the means by which the words are given a shape. That is, later novelists do not read directly from the words to a decision about the point or theme of the novel but from a prior understanding (which may take a number of forms) of the points or themes novels can possibly have to a novelistic construction of the words. Just as the first novelist "creates" within the constraints of "novel-practice" in general, so do his successors on the chain interpret him (and each other) within those same constraints. Not only are those constraints controlling but they are uniformly so; that is, they do not relax or tighten in relation to the position an author happens to occupy on the chain. The last author is as free, within those constraints, to determine what the characters are really like as is the first. It is of course tempting to think that the more information one has (the more history) the more directed will be one's interpretation; but information only comes in an interpreted form (it does not announce itself), and no matter how much or how little you have, it cannot be a check against interpretation because even when you first "see" it, interpretation has already done its work. So that rather than altering the conditions of interpretation, the accumulation of chapters merely extends the scope of its operation.

If this seems counterintuitive, imagine the very real possibility of two (or more) later novelists who have different views of the direction the novel has taken and are therefore in disagreement as to what would constitute a continuation of "that" novel as opposed to "beginning a new one." To make the example more specific, let us further imagine that one says to another, "Don't you see that it's ironic, a social satire?" and the second replies, "Not at all, at most it's a comedy of manners," while a third chimes in, "You're both wrong; it's obviously a perfectly straightforward piece of realism." If Dworkin's argument is to hold, that is, if the decisions he talks about are to be constrained, in a strong sense, by an already-in-place text, it must be possible to settle this disagreement by appealing to that text. But it is precisely because the text appears differently in the light of different assumptions as to what is its mode that there is a disagreement in the first place. Or, to put it another way, "social satire," "comedy of manners," and "piece of realism" are not labels applied mechanically to perspicuous instances; rather, they are names for ways of reading, ways which when put into operation make available for picking out the "facts" which those who are proceeding within them can then cite. It is entirely possible that the parties to our imagined dispute might find themselves pointing to the same "stretch of language" (no longer the same, since each would be characterizing it differently) and claiming it as a fact in support of opposing interpretations. (This history of literary criticism abounds in such scenarios.) Each would then believe, and be able to provide reasons for his belief, that only he is continuing the novel in the direction it has taken so far and that the others are striking out in a new and unauthorized direction.

Again, this does not mean that a later novelist is free to decide anything he likes (or that there is no possibility of adjudicating a disagreement) but that, within the general boundaries of novel-reading practice, he is as free as anyone else, which means that he is as constrained as anyone else. He is constrained in that he can only continue in ways that are recognizable novel ways (and the same must be said of the first novelist's act of "beginning"), and he is free in that no amount of textual accumulation can make his choice of one of those ways inescapable. Although the boundaries of novel practice mark the limits of what anyone who is thinking within them can think to do, within those limits they do not *direct* anyone to do this rather than that. (They are not a "higher" text.) Every decision a later novelist makes will rest on his assessment of the situation as it has developed; but that assessment will itself be an act of interpretation which will in turn rest on an interpreted understanding of the enterprise in general.

This, then, is my first criticism of Dworkin's example: the distinction it is supposed to illustrate—the distinction between the first and later novelists—will not hold up because everyone in the enterprise is equally constrained. (By "equally" I mean equally with respect to the condition of freedom; I am making no claim about the number or identity of the constraints.) My second criticism is that, in his effort to elaborate the distinction, Dworkin embraces both of the positions he criticizes. He posits for the first novelists a freedom that is equivalent to the freedom assumed by those who believe that judges (and other interpreters) are bound only by their personal preferences and desires; and he thinks of later novelists as bound by a previous history in a way that would be possible only if the shape and significance of that history were self-evident. Rather than avoiding the Scylla of legal realism ("making it up wholesale") and the Charybdis of strict constructionism ("finding the law just 'there'"), he commits himself to both. His reason for doing so becomes clear when he extends the example to an analysis of the law:

> Deciding hard cases at law is rather like this strange literary exercise. The similarity is most evident when judges consider and decide common-law cases; that is, when no statute figures centrally in the legal issue, and the argument turns on which rules or principles of law "underlie" the related decisions of other judges in the past. Each judge is then like a novelist in the chain. He or she must read through what other judges in the past have written not simply to discover what these judges have said, or their state of mind when they said it, but to reach an opinion about what these judges have collectively *done*, in the way that each of our novelists formed an opinion about the collective novel so far written. Any judge forced

to decide a lawsuit will find, if he looks in the appropriate books, records of many arguably similar cases decided over decades or even centuries past by many other judges of different styles and judicial and political philosophies, in periods of different orthodoxies of procedure and judicial convention. Each judge must regard himself, in deciding the new case before him, as a partner in a complex chain enterprise of which these innumerable decisions, structures, conventions, and practices are the history; it is his job to continue that history into the future through what he does on the day. He *must* interpret what has gone before because he has a responsibility to advance the enterprise in hand rather than strike out in some new direction of his own. [Pp. 263–64]

The emphasis on the word "must" alerts us to what is at stake for Dworkin in the notion of a chain enterprise. It is a way of explaining how judges are kept from striking out in a new direction, much as later novelists are kept by the terms of their original agreement from beginning a new novel. Just as it is the duty of a later novelist to continue the work of his predecessors, so is it the duty of a judge "to advance the enterprise in hand." Presumably, the judge who is tempted to "strike out in some new direction of his own" will be checked by his awareness of his responsibility to the corporate enterprise; he will then comport himself as a partner in the chain rather than as a free and independent agent. The force of the account, in other words, depends on the possibility of judges comporting themselves in ways other than the chain-enterprise way. But is there in fact any such possibility? What would it mean for a judge to strike out in a new direction? Dworkin doesn't tell us, but presumably it would mean deciding a case in such a way as to have no relationship to the history of previous decisions; but it is hard to imagine what such a decision would be like since any decision, to be recognized as a decision by a judge, would have to be made in recognizably judicial terms. A judge who decided a case on the basis of whether or not the defendant had red hair would not be striking out in a new direction; he would simply not be acting as a judge because he could give no reasons for his decision that would be seen *as* reasons by competent members of the legal community. (Even in so extreme a case it would not be accurate to describe the judge as striking out in a new direction; rather he would be continuing the direction of an enterprise—perhaps a bizarre one— *other* than the judicial.) And conversely, if in deciding a case a judge *is* able to give such reasons, then the direction he strikes out in will not be new because it will have been implicit in the enterprise as a direction one could conceive of and argue for. This does not mean that his decision will be above criticism but that it will be criticized, if it is criticized, for having gone in one judicial direction rather than another, neither direction being new in the sense that would give substance to Dworkin's fears. Those fears are equally groundless with respect to the other alternative Dworkin imagines, that is, the judge who looks at the chain of previous decisions and decides to see in it "whatever he thinks should have been there." Here the danger is not so much arbitrary action (striking out in a new direction) as it is the willful imposition of a personal perspective on materials that have their own proper shape. "A judge's duty," Dworkin asserts, "is to interpret the legal history he finds, not to invent a better history" (pp. 264–65). Interpretation that is constrained by the history one finds will be responsible, whereas interpretation informed by the private preferences of the judge will be wayward and subjective. The opposition is one to which Dworkin repeatedly returns in a variety of forms, but in whatever form it is always vulnerable to the same objection: neither the self-declaring or found entity nor the dangerously free or inventing agent is a possible feature of the enterprise.

First, one doesn't just find a history; rather one views a body of materials within the assumption that it is organized by judicial concerns; and it is that assumption which gives a shape to the materials, a shape that can *then* be described as having been "found." Moreover, not everyone will find the same shape because not everyone will be proceeding within the same notion of what constitutes a proper judicial concern, either in general or in particular cases. One sees this clearly in Dworkin's own account of what is involved in legal decision making. A judge, he explains, will look in the "appropriate books" for cases "arguably similar" to the one before him. Notice that the similarity is "arguable" which means that it must be argued *for;* similarity is not something one finds but something one must establish, and when one establishes it, one establishes the configurations of the cited cases as well as of the case that is to be decided. Similarity, in short, is not a property of texts (similarities do not announce themselves) but a property conferred by a relational argument in which the statement *A* is like *B* is a characterization (one open to challenge) of *both A* and *B.* To see a present-day case as similar to a chain of earlier ones is to resee that chain by finding in it an applicability that had not always been apparent. Paradoxically one can be faithful to legal history only by revising it, by redescribing it in such a way as to accommodate and render manageable the issues raised by the present.[2]

2. I am not saying that the present-day case comes first and the history then follows but that they emerge together in the context of an effort to see them as related embodiments of some legal principle. Indeed a case could not even be seen as a case if it were not from the very first regarded as an item in a judicial field and therefore as the embodiment of some or other principle. This does not mean, however, that it is to judicial principles that we must look for the anchoring ground of interpretation, for they cannot be separated out from the history to which they give form; one can no more think of a judicial principle apart from a chain of cases than one can think of a chain of cases apart from a judicial principle. No one of the entities that make up judicial reasoning exists independently— neither the present-day case, nor the chain of which it is to be the continuation, nor the principle of which they are both to be the realizations.

This is a function of the law's conservatism which will not allow a case to remain unrelated to the past and so assures that the past, in the form of the history of decisions, will be continually rewritten. In fact, it is the *duty* of a judge to rewrite it (which is to say no more than that it is the duty of a judge to decide), and therefore there can be no simply found history in relation to which some other history could be said to be invented. All histories are invented in the weak sense that they are not simply "discovered" but assembled under the pressure of some present urgency; but no history is invented in the strong sense that the urgency which led to its assembly was unrelated to any generally acknowledged legal concern.

To put it another way, there could be no such strongly invented history because there could be no such strong inventor, no judge whose characterization of legal history displayed none of the terms, distinctions, and arguments that would identify it (for competent members) as a *legal* history. Of course someone who stood apart from the enterprise, someone who was not performing as a judge, might offer such a history (a history, for example, in which the observed patterns were ethnic or geographical). But to accuse such a historian of striking out in a new direction or inventing a better history would be beside the point since whatever he did or didn't do would have no legal (as opposed to sociological or political) significance. And, conversely, someone who was in fact standing within the enterprise, in the sense that his ways of thinking were enterprise ways, could only put forward a history that was enterprise specific, and that history could not be an invented one. It is true of course that jurists can and do accuse each other of inventing a history, but that is a charge you level at someone who has found a history different from yours, and it should not be confused with the possibility (or the danger) of really inventing one. The distinction between a found history and an invented one is finally nothing more than a distinction between a persuasive interpretation and one that has failed to convince. One man's found history will be another man's invented history, but neither will ever be, because it could not be, either purely found or purely invented.

As one reads Dworkin's essay, the basic pattern of his mistakes becomes more obvious. Repeatedly he makes two related and mutually reinforcing assumptions: he assumes that history in the form of a chain of decisions has, at some level, the status of a brute fact; and he assumes that wayward or arbitrary behavior in relation to that fact is an institutional possibility. Together these two assumptions give him his project, the project of explaining how a free and potentially irresponsible agent is held in check by the self-executing constraints of an independent text. Of course by conceiving of his project in this way—that is, by reifying the mind in its freedom and the text in its independence—he commits himself to the very alternatives he sets out to avoid, the alternatives of legal realism on the one hand and positivism on the other. As a result these alternatives rule his argument, at once determining its form and emerging, again and again, as its content.

An example, early in the essay, involves the possibility of reading an Agatha Christie mystery as a philosophical novel. Such a reading, Dworkin asserts, would be an instance of "changing" the text rather than "explaining" it because the text *as it is* will not yield to it without obvious strain or distortion. "All but one or two sentences would be irrelevant to the supposed theme; and the organization, style, and figures would be appropriate not to a philosophical novel but to an entirely different genre" (p. 254). The assumption is that sentences, figures, and styles announce their own generic affiliation and that a reader who would claim them for an inappropriate genre would be imposing his will on nature. It is exactly the same argument by which judges are supposedly constrained by the obvious properties of the history they are to continue, and it fails by the same analysis. First of all, generic identification, like continuity between cases, is not something one finds but something one establishes, and one establishes it for a reason. That is, readers don't just "decide" to recharacterize a text; there has to be some reason why it would occur to someone to treat a work identified as a member of one genre as a possible member of another; there must already be in place ways of thinking that will enable the recharacterization to become a project, and there must be conditions in the institution such that the prosecution of that project seems attractive and potentially rewarding. With respect to the project Dworkin deems impossible, those ways and conditions already exist. It has long been recognized that authors of the first rank—Poe, Dickens, Dostoyevsky—have written novels of detection, and the fact that these novels have been treated seriously means that the work of less obviously canonical authors—Wilkie Collins, Conan Doyle, among others—are possible candidates for the same kind of attention. Once this happens, and it has already happened, any novel of detection can, at least provisionally, be considered as a serious work without a critic or his audience thinking that he is doing something bizarre or irresponsible by treating it as such; and in recent years just such consideration has been given to the work of Dashiell Hammett, Raymond Chandler (whom Dworkin mentions), Patricia Highsmith, Dorothy Sayers, Georges Simenon, Nicolas Freeling, and MacDonald (both Ross and John D.). In addition, the emergence of semiotic and structural analysis has meant that it is no longer necessarily a criticism to say of something that it is "formulaic"; a term of description, which under a previous understanding of literary value would have been invoked in a gesture of dismissal, can now be invoked as a preliminary to a study of "signifying systems." The result has been the proliferation of serious (not to say somber) formalist readings of works like Ian Fleming's *Goldfinger;* and whatever one might think of this phenomenon, it is now a recognized and respectable part of the academic literary scene. At the same time the advocates of popular culture have been pressing their claim with a new insistence and a new rigor (prompted in part by the developments I have already cited), and a measure of their success is the number of courses in detective fiction now offered at all levels in colleges and universities.

Given these circumstances (and others that could be enumerated), it would be strange if a sociological or anthropological or philosophical interpretation of Agatha Christie had *not* been put forward (in fact, here we have an embarrassment of riches),[3] and as a longtime reader of her novels it has occurred to me to put one forward myself. I have noticed that Christie's villains are often presented as persons so quintessentially evil that they have no moral sense whatsoever and can only simulate moral behavior by miming, without understanding, the actions and attitudes of others. It is also typical of these villains to be chameleons, capable almost at will of changing their appearance, and one can see why: since they have no human attachments or concerns, they can clothe themselves in whatever attachment or concern suits their nefarious and often unmotivated ends. (The parallel with Shakespeare's Iago and Milton's Satan is obvious.) It would seem then that Christie has a theory of evil in relation to personal identity that accounts for (in the sense of generating a description of) many of the characteristics of her novels—their plots, the emphasis on disguise, the tolerance for human weakness even as it is being exposed, and so forth.

Were I to extend this general hypothesis about Christie into a reading of one or more of her works, I would not be proceeding as Dworkin's

---

3. One hardly knows where to begin, perhaps simply with the title of David Grossvogel's study, *Mystery and Its Fictions: From Oedipus to Agatha Christie* (Baltimore, 1979). The title of Dennis Porter's *The Pursuit of Crime: Art and Ideology in Detective Fiction* (New Haven, Conn., 1981) suggests a scope and a thesis somewhat less grand, but Porter does find Christie "working in the tradition of Poe, Collins, and Doyle" (p. 137), and he devotes some very serious pages to a stylistic analysis of the first paragraph of her first novel in the context of V. N. Voloshinov's *Marxism and the Philosophy of Language.* Christie is taken no less seriously by Stephen Knight in *Form and Ideology in Crime Fiction* (Bloomington, Ind., 1980). Knight speaks without any self-consciousness of Christie as a "major writer" and analyzes her "art" in terms that might well be applied to, say, Henry James: "The rigidity of the time and place structure emphasizes the obscurity of the thematic shape, challenges us all the more urgently to decide it. The dual structure enacts the central drama of the novel, a threat to order that only careful observation can resolve" (p. 126). Knight's book, like Porter's, is replete with references to Lacan, Jameson, Machery, Marx, Freud, and Barthes and bears all the marks of sophisticated academic criticism. See also in a similarly academic mode, Robert Champigny, *What Will Have Happened: A Philosophical and Technical Essay on Mystery Stories* (Bloomington, Ind., 1977), and Jerry Palmer, *Thrillers: Genesis and Structure of a Popular Genre* (New York, 1979). As this essay goes to press, I have just received in the mail the most recent issue of *Poetics Today* (3 [Winter 1982]) and find Joseph Agassi, a professor of philosophy, discussing the relationship of the novels of Christie, Chandler, Doyle, and others to the scientific theories of Francis Bacon and Thomas Kuhn ("The Detective Novel and Scientific Method," pp. 99–108). Dworkin, it would seem, could not have chosen a worse example to support his case.

pronouncement suggests. I would not, that is, be changing the novel by riding roughshod over sentences bearing obvious and inescapable meanings; rather I would be reading those sentences within the assumption that they were related to what I assumed to be Christie's intention (if not this one, then some other), and as a result they would appear to me in an already related form. Sentences describing the weaknesses of characters other than the villain would be seen as pointing to the paradoxical strength of human frailty; sentences detailing the topography and geography of crucial scenes would be read as symbolic renderings of deeper issues, and so on. This interpretive action, or any other that could be imagined, would not be performed in violation of the facts of the text but would be an effort to establish those facts; and if in the course of that effort I were to dislodge another set of facts, they would be facts that had emerged within the assumption of another intention and would therefore be no less interpretive than the facts I was putting in their place. Of course my efforts might very well fail in that no one else would be persuaded to my reading. But neither success nor failure would prove anything about what the text does or does not allow; rather it would attest to the degree to which I had mastered or failed to master the rules of argument and evidence as they are understood (tacitly, to be sure) by members of the professional community.

The point is one that I have made before: it is neither the case that interpretation is constrained by what is obviously and unproblematically "there," nor the case that interpreters, in the absence of such constraints, are free to read into a text whatever they like (once again Dworkin has put himself in a corner with these unhappy alternatives). Interpreters are constrained by their tacit awareness of what is possible and not possible to do, what is and is not a reasonable thing to say, and what will and will not be heard as evidence in a given enterprise; and it is within those same constraints that they see and bring others to see the shape of the documents to whose interpretation they are committed.

Dworkin's failure to see this is an instance of a general failure to understand the nature of interpretation. The distinction between explaining a text and changing it can no more be maintained than the others of which it is a version (finding versus inventing, continuing versus striking out in a new direction, interpreting versus creating). To explain a work is to point out something about it that had not been attributed to it before and therefore to change it by challenging other explanations that were once changes in their turn. Explaining and changing cannot be opposed activities (although they can be the names of claims and counterclaims) because they are the same activities. Dworkin opposes them because he thinks that interpretation is itself an activity in need of constraints, but what I have been trying to show is that interpretation is a *structure* of constraints, a structure which, because it is always and already in place, renders unavailable the independent or uninterpreted text and renders unimaginable the independent and freely interpreting reader. In searching for a way to protect against arbitrary readings (judicial and literary), Dworkin is searching for something he already has and could not possibly be without, and he conducts his search by projecting as dangers and fears possibilities that could never be realized and by imagining as discrete, entities that are already filled with the concerns of the enterprise they supposedly threaten.

One of those entities is intention. Dworkin spends a great deal of time refuting the view that interpretation in law and in literature must concern itself with the intentions of the author. He argues first that the intention of a novelist or legislator is "complex" and therefore difficult to know and, second, that, even if it were known, it would be only a piece of "psychological data" and therefore irrelevant to the determination of a meaning that was not psychological but institutional (pp. 267–68). In short, to make intention the key to interpretation is to bypass the proper interpretive context—the history of practices and conventions—and substitute for it an interior motion of the mind. This argument would make perfect sense if intentions were, as Dworkin seems to believe, private property and more or less equivalent with individual purpose or even whim. But it is hard to think of intentions formed in the course of judicial or literary activity as one's own, since any intention one could have will have been stipulated in advance by the understanding of what activities are possible to someone working in the enterprise. One could no more come up with a unique intention with respect to the presentation of a character or the marshaling of legal evidence than one could come up with a new way of beginning a novel or continuing a chain of decisions. Simply to do something in the context of a chain enterprise is *ipso facto* to "have" an enterprise-specific intention, and to read something identified as a part of a chain enterprise is *ipso facto* to be in the act of specifying that same intention. That is to say, the act of reading itself is at once the asking and answering of the question, What is it that is meant by these words?, a question asked not in a vacuum but in the context of an already-in-place understanding of the various things someone writing a novel or a decision (or anything else) might mean (that is, intend).

In Dworkin's analysis, on the other hand, reading is simply the construing of sense and neither depends nor should depend on the identification of intention. He cites as evidence the fact that authors themselves have been known to reinterpret their own works. This, Dworkin asserts, shows that "an author is capable of detaching what he has written from his earlier intentions . . . , of treating it as an object in itself" (p. 260). But in fact it only shows that an author is capable of becoming his own reader and deciding that he meant something other by his words than he had previously thought. Such an author-reader is not ignoring intention but recharacterizing it; he is not interpreting in a "non–intention-bound style" but interpreting in a way that leads to a new understanding of his intention (p. 263). Nor is there anything mysterious about this; it is no more than what we all do when sometime after having produced an utterance (it could be in less than a second) we ask ourselves, What did I mean by that? This will seem curious if intentions are thought of as unique psychological events; but if intentions are thought of as forms of possible conventional behavior that are to be conventionally "read," then one can just as well reread his own intentions as he can reread the intentions of another.

The crucial point is that one cannot read *or* reread independently of intention, independently, that is, of the assumption that one is dealing with marks or sounds produced by an intentional being, a being situated in some enterprise in relation to which he has a purpose or a point of view. This is not an assumption that one adds to an already construed sense in order to stabilize it but an assumption without which the construing of sense could not occur. One cannot understand an utterance without *at the same time* hearing or reading it as the utterance of someone with more or less specific concerns, interests, and desires, someone with an intention. So that when Dworkin talks, as he does, of the attempt to "discover" what a judge or a novelist intended, he treats as discrete, operations that are inseparable. He thinks that interpretation is one thing and the assigning of intention is another, and he thinks that, because he thinks that to discover intention is to plumb some psychological depth that is unrelated to the meaning of chain-enterprise texts; whereas, in fact, to specify the meaning of a chain-enterprise text is exactly equivalent to specifying the intention of its author, an intention which is not private but a form of conventional behavior made possible by the general structure of the enterprise. This of course does not mean that intention anchors interpretation in the sense that it stands outside and guides the process. Intention like anything else is an interpretive fact; that is, it must be construed. It is just that it is impossible *not* to construc it and therefore impossible to oppose it either to the production or the determination of meaning.

The fact that Dworkin does so oppose it is of a piece with everything else in the essay and is one more instance of its basic pattern. Once again he has imagined a free-floating and individualistic threat to interpretation—in this case it is called "intention"—and once again he has moved to protect interpretation by locating its constraints in a free-standing and self-declaring object—in this case "the work itself" detached from the antecedent designs of its author. And of course this means that once again he has committed himself in a single stroke to the extremes he set out to avoid, the objectivity of meanings that are just there and the subjectivity of meanings that have been made up by an unconstrained agent.

I cannot conclude without calling attention to what is perhaps the most curious feature of Dworkin's essay, the extent to which it contains its own critique. Indeed, a reader sympathetic to Dworkin might well argue that he anticipates everything I have said in the preceding pages. He himself says that "the artist can create nothing without interpreting . . . since . . . he must have at least a tacit theory of why what he produces is art" (p. 261); and he also points out that the facts of legal history do not announce themselves but will vary with the beliefs of particular judges concerning the general function of the law (see p. 266). In another place he admits that the constraint imposed by the words of a text "is not inevitable," in part because any theory of identity (that is, any theory of what is the same and what is different, of what constitutes a departure from the same) "will be controversial" (p. 253). And after arguing that the "constraint of integrity" (the constraint imposed by a work's coherence with itself) sets limits to interpretation, he acknowledges that there is much disagreement "about what counts as integration"; he acknowledges, in other words, that the constraint is itself interpretive.

Even more curious than the fact of these reservations and qualifications is Dworkin's failure to see how much they undercut his argument. Early in the essay he distinguishes between simple cases in which the words of a statute bear a transparent relationship to the actions they authorize or exclude (his sample statute is "No will shall be valid without three witnesses") and more difficult cases in which reasonable and knowledgeable men disagree as to whether some action or proposed action is lawful. But immediately after making the distinction he undermines it by saying (in a parenthesis), "I am doubtful that the positivists' analysis holds even in the simple case of the will; but that is a different matter I shall not argue here" (p. 250). It is hard to see how this is a different matter, especially since so much in the essay hangs on the distinction. One doesn't know what form the argument Dworkin decides *not* to make would take, but possibly it might take the form of pointing out that even in a simple case the ease and immediacy with which one can apply the statute to the facts is the result of the same kind of interpretive work that is more obviously required in the difficult cases. That is, in order for a case to appear readable independently of some interpretive strategy consciously employed, one must already be reading within the assumption of that strategy and employing, without being aware of them, its stipulated (and potentially controversial) definitions, terms, modes of inference, and so on. This, at any rate, would be the argument I would make, and in making it I would be denying the distinction between hard and easy cases not, of course, as an empirical fact (as something one might experience) but as a fact that reflected a basic difference between cases that are self-settling and cases that can be settled only by referring them to the history of procedures, practices, and conventions; all cases are so referred (not after reading but in the act of reading) and could not be anything but so referred and still be seen as cases.[4] The point is an important one because Dworkin later says that his account of chain enterprises is offered as an explanation of how we "[decide] hard cases at law"; that is, his entire essay depends on a distinction that he himself suggests may not hold, and therefore, as we have seen, his entire essay depends on the positivist analysis he rejects in the parenthesis.[5]

    4. One must question too, and for the same reason, Dworkin's distinction between common-law cases and cases where there is a statute, at least insofar as it is a distinction between cases whose interpretation is straightforward and cases that must be referred to the background of an institutional history. In cases where there is a statute for a judge to look at, he must still look at it, and his look will be as interpretive—as informed by the practices and conventions that define the enterprise—as it would be in a common-law case. That is, a statute no more announces its own meaning than does the case to which it is to be applied, and therefore cases where statutes figure are no more or less grounded than cases where no statute exists. In either circumstance one must interpret from the beginning, and in either circumstance one's interpretation will be at once constrained and enabled by a general and assumed understanding of the goals, purposes, concerns, and procedures of the enterprise. See on these and related points Kenneth S. Abraham, "Statutory Interpretation and Literary Theory: Some Common Concerns of an Unlikely Pair," *Rutgers Law Review* 32, no. 4 (1979): 676–94, and "Three Fallacies of Interpretation: A Comment on Precedent and Judicial Decision," *Arizona Law Review* 23, no. 2 (1981): 771–83.
    5. In its strengths and weaknesses "Law as Interpretation" is at once like and unlike Dworkin's other writings. I find that in *Taking Rights Seriously* (Cambridge, Mass., 1977), Dworkin more than occasionally falls into a way of talking that reinstitutes the positions against which he is arguing. As an example I will consider briefly some moments in the key essay "Hard Cases" (chap. 4). At one point in that essay Dworkin begins a paragraph by asserting that "institutional history acts not as a constraint on the political judgment of judges but as an ingredient of that judgment" (p. 87). The point is that what a judge decides is inseparable from his understanding of the history of past decisions, and it is a point well taken. It is, however, a point that is already being compromised in the second half of this same sentence: "because institutional history is part of the background that any plausible judgment about the rights of an individual must accommodate." With the word "accommodate" what had been inseparable suddenly falls apart, for it suggests that, rather than having his judgment informed by the history (in the sense that his ways of thinking are constrained by it), the judge takes an independent look at an independent history and decides (in a movement of perfect freedom) to accommodate it; it suggests, in short, that he could have chosen otherwise. The notion of choice, here only implied, is explicitly invoked later in the paragraph when Dworkin discusses the situation in which "a judge chooses between the rule established in precedent and some new rule thought to be fairer." But in accordance with what principle is the choice to be made? Dworkin doesn't tell us, but clearly it is a principle that stands apart from either the body of precedent or the new rule (both of which have been reified) and apart too from the judge himself who freely chooses to employ it as a way of reconciling two independent entities.
    The movement in this paragraph is from an understanding of judgment in which the judge, the context of judgment, and the principles of judgment are mutually constitutive to an understanding in which each has its own identity and can only be integrated by invoking some neutral mechanism or calculus. Later Dworkin slides into the same (mis)understanding when he says of Hercules (his name for an imaginary, all-knowing judge) that in deciding between competing theories he "must turn to the remaining constitutional rules and settled practices under these rules to see which of these two theories provides a

One can only speculate as to what Dworkin intends by these qualifications, but whether they appear in a parenthesis or in an aside or in the form of quotation marks around a key word, their effect is the same: to place him on both sides of the question at issue and to blur the supposedly hard lines of his argument. As a result we are left with two ways of reading the essay, neither of which is comforting. If we take the subtext of reservation and disclaimer seriously, it so much weakens what he has to say that he seems finally not to have a position at all; and if we disregard the subtext and grant his thesis its strongest form, he will certainly have a position, but it will be, in every possible way, wrong.

---

smoother fit with the constitutional scheme as a whole" (p. 106). Here the difficulty (and the sleight of hand) resides in the phrase "smoother fit." On what basis is the smoothness of fit determined? Again Dworkin doesn't tell us, but an answer to the question could take only one of two forms. Either the rules and practices have their own self-evident shape and therefore themselves constrain what does or does not fit with them, or there is some abstract principle by which one can calculate the degree to which a given theory fits smoothly with "the constitutional scheme as a whole." But these alternatives are simply flip sides of the same positivism. If the shape of the constituent parts is self-evident, then no independent principle is required to decide whether or not they fit together; and by the same reasoning an independent principle of fit will be able to do its job only if the shape of the constituent parts is self-evident. For as soon as the shape of the parts becomes a matter of dispute (as it would for judges who conceived the constitutional rules or the settled practices differently), the judgment of what fits with what will be in dispute as well. In short, the criterion of fitness is no less theoretical than the theories Dworkin would have it decide between, and by claiming an independence for it, he once again compromises the coherence of his position.

In general Dworkin's confusions have the same form: he argues against positivism, but then he has recourse to positivist notions. At one point he observes that Hercules' decision about a "community morality" will sometimes be controversial, especially when the issue concerns "some contested political concept, like fairness or liberality or equality," and the institutional history "is not sufficiently detailed so that it can be justified by only one among different conceptions of that concept" (p. 127). The language is somewhat vague here, but it would seem that Dworkin is assuming the possibility of a history that *was* "sufficiently detailed": that is, a history so dense (a favorite word of his) that it was open to only one reading of the morality informing it. In relation to such a history Hercules would be in the position of the later novelists in Dworkin's imagined chain, obliged to "admit only one good-faith interpretation"; but at that point Hercules would be doing what Dworkin himself says no judge can possibly do, mechanically reading off the meaning of a text that constrained its own interpretation.

I trust that I have said enough to support my contention that the errors I find in the present essay can also be found in Dworkin's earlier work. But I must also say that, at least in the case of "Hard Cases," those errors are less damaging. "Hard Cases" is primarily an argument against "classical theories of adjudication . . . which suppose that a judge follows statutes or precedent until the clear direction of these runs out, after which he is free to strike out on his own" (p. 118). Dworkin's critique of these theories seems to me powerful and entirely persuasive, and, moreover, in its main lines it does not depend on the general account of interpretation that occasionally and (to my mind) disconcertingly surfaces. In "Law as Interpretation," on the other hand, Dworkin is concerned to elaborate that general account, and in that essay, as I have tried to show, the incidental weaknesses of the earlier work become crucial and even fatal.

My Reply to Stanley Fish (and Walter Benn Michaels): Please Don't Talk about Objectivity Any More

Ronald Dworkin

I

Stanley Fish's critical essay is more instructive than it looks. His "reading" of my own essay, "Law as Interpretation," is incompetent. But we can find, just beneath the surface of his essay, an intriguing set of dogmas about truth and reference which helps to explain not only his misinterpretation of what I said but also the fashionable quasi skepticism of much modern literary theory. Walter Benn Michaels shares some of these dogmas, and these help to explain both his comments on my text and his own views about the ubiquity of intention in interpretation (see p.335).

My principal aim here is to identify these hidden and malign assumptions and to comment on the unfortunate interest literary scholars now take in what they call the problem of objectivity and relativism. It is, however, important that I support my charge that Fish has brutally misread my own essay, because his misreading is part of my case that critics have misunderstood that problem. I offer a point-by-point analysis of Fish's major arguments (and also Michaels' single argument) against me. But I defer this analysis to the last part of the present essay so that readers who are uninterested in these details can ignore it.

I must, however, state my main complaint at once. Fish devotes the bulk of his essay to identifying my many "mistakes," but when he has almost finished, he announces the "curious" fact that I seem to have anticipated all his objections (p. 284). My basic claim, he says, is that in law and literature texts compel their own correct interpretation through some self-enforcing set of constraints, and he notices that I *also* say, on almost every page, that this is not so, that competent and reasonable students of any text or department of the law will in fact disagree over any serious issue of interpretation, that nothing forces a reader to a particular interpretation except his own judgment. Fish offers an explanation of these inconvenient remarks. The many passages in which I deny that the text alone forces an interpretation must be read as a "subtext of reservation and disclaimer" which effectively undermines my main arguments. So the reader must make a choice: if he attends to this "subtext," then I have no position at all; if he ignores it, then what I say is "in every possible way, wrong" (p. 286).

Fish disregards another (much less exciting) possibility which will nevertheless occur to many readers. Perhaps I never do say that the text forces a particular interpretation on its students. Perhaps I never say anything which the "subtext" can possibly "undermine." That is, in fact, the surprising truth. Fish has simply invented my major thesis for me and complained that I am churlish enough to try to wriggle out of it.

Here is his summary of the position I am meant to hold.

> As one reads Dworkin's essay, the basic pattern of his mistakes becomes more and more obvious. Repeatedly he makes two related and mutually reinforcing assumptions: he assumes that history in the form of a chain of decisions has, at some level, the status of a brute fact; and he assumes that wayward or arbitrary behavior in relation to that fact is an institutional possibility. Together these two assumptions give him his project, the project of explaining how a free and potentially irresponsible agent is held in check by the self-executing constraints of an independent text. [P. 278]

It would no doubt be possible to construct a more treacherous report of my assumptions, but it would not be easy.

Nowhere do I announce, or even whisper, the "project" of showing how "self-executing constraints" hold readers in check. I said, at the beginning, that my project was to explain what people who disagree in matters of interpretation are disagreeing about (see p. 249). I suggested, as my main hypothesis about literature, that "an interpretation of a piece of literature attempts to show which way of reading (or speaking or directing or acting) the text reveals it as the best work of art" (p. 253). I emphasized what would in any case have been obvious, that this hypothesis links interpretation with controversial arguments of aesthetic theory about the value of art and about what makes one work of art better, as art, than another. I said that two competent scholars with different aesthetic convictions will just for that reason even disagree about how to identify the text to be interpreted. I said that interpreters are constrained by their own complex aesthetic judgments and by nothing more interpersonal, and I developed an argument why such constraints are nevertheless genuine. There is no trace in my essay of any claim that the identity or characterization or interpretation of a work of art is a "brute fact" (whatever that might be), or that the nature of a work of art is "independent" of the interpreter, or that the constraints of interpretation are "self-executing." The force of the aesthetic hypothesis (and of the parallel political hypothesis in the case of law) is exactly to deny each one of these claims. So we have an interesting puzzle. Fish has read my essay through lenses of quite amazing power. They enable him to see, in what I said, claims I never embrace and firmly reject. How has he managed this?

II

1. Two Questions about Interpretation

People interpret texts and statutes and cases and pictures. The most striking fact about this practice is a certain shared conviction. Interpreters for the most part assume that interpreting a text is different from changing it into a new text, that one interpretation may be better than another even when this is controversial, that arguments exist for and against interpretations, that some of these arguments are stronger, more probative than others, that someone who now accepts a particular interpretation of some text may be persuaded rather than simply pushed out of it, and so forth. Together these second-order beliefs compose what we might call a "right-wrong" picture of interpretation, a picture which supposes that interpretations may be sound or unsound, better or worse, more or less accurate. This is not a picture philosophers impose on interpretation from the outside. The second-order beliefs I describe are part of the practices that constitute the institution of interpretation; they are, in fact, at the center of that practice. If most people who interpret did not accept them, the practice would be very different from what it is, if it continued to exist at all.

This striking fact poses two connected problems for any theory of interpretation. First, it must explain how it is possible for interpreters even to hold this view of what they are doing. For of course no interpreter can accept a right-wrong picture unless he can distinguish (or in any case think he can distinguish) between his own interpretive beliefs and his own inventions, unless the activities of interpreting and inventing seem different to him. And his way of making these distinctions, for himself, must correspond with the way others make the same distinctions for themselves. They must have some grasp of what he means even to disagree with him and enough grasp of what he will count as an argument to argue against him. So we must ask: How *do* we distinguish between interpreting and inventing? How *do* we decide that one interpretation or one argument for an interpretation is better than another?

Interpretive judgments are not isolated elements of our intellectual life. They are dependent upon and yet distinguished from other kinds of beliefs, attitudes, and convictions we have, and these will vary even within a single professional community however narrowly described. We must try to identify these connections and distinctions, try to discover the place interpretive judgments occupy in our mental topology. If we decide—as we will—that there are different kinds or levels of interpretation, then we must try to identify the structure these form, to see how one level of interpretation draws upon and yet is distinct from another.

The second kind of question posed by the right-wrong picture of interpretation might be called, in contrast, the question of objectivity. Is the right-wrong picture right? Is interpretation really different from invention, as ordinary interpreters think, or is this just an illusion they share? Can judgments of interpretation be sound or unsound, true or false, or is this just another illusion? I have great reservations about the sense of this second question, which I shall describe later. But if we do wish to take it up, then we must at least attack the first question first. It would be silly to construct theories about whether interpretive judgments can be "objectively" true or false before we understand what these judgments mean to those who make them, because until then we have no good idea of what the claim, that one interpretation of a text is better than another, really means.

2. Block That Metaphor

I can now offer my diagnosis of Fish's inability to read my essay. He has reversed this sensible order of attacking the two questions I just distinguished. He has his own theory, drawn from what philosophers call a "copy" theory of truth, about what the world would have to be like in order to make the right-wrong picture accurate.[1] Or rather he thinks he has such a theory, because he can only state it using metaphors and scare-quotes. The right-wrong picture supposes, he says, that meanings are "just there" or "self-executing" or "independent" or "already in place" in the text. Since he believes that meanings can be none of these things, the right-wrong picture must be false. There can be no genuine distinction between interpretation and invention, and if two interpretations are each recognizable as interpretations—if they are both "institutional possibilities"—one cannot be said to be any better than the other.

Fish's a priori model is the distorting lens that made him misread my essay. I tried to answer the first question. I tried to show how our interpretive beliefs and convictions are connected to other kinds of beliefs so as to permit us to make the distinctions and discriminations the right-

---

1. See, e.g., Hilary Putnam, *Reason, Truth, and History* (Cambridge, 1981), p. ix.

wrong picture requires. My purpose was pragmatic. Once we understand how people can and do make these discriminations, then we can grasp the special character of enterprises, like law, in which people aim to interpret rather than invent. I was careful to say, three times, that it was not necessary for this purpose to consider the second question I set aside, the question whether interpretive judgments can be said to be objectively true or false (see pp. 184, 192 n. 4, and 266–67).

But since Fish has reversed the proper order of these two questions, he has missed my warnings about confusing them (see p. 257). He simply assumed his own answer to the question I was trying to answer, about how people make the discriminations and judgments that are licensed by the right-wrong picture. He assumed that these discriminations depend on the impossible idea that meanings are "already in place" or "just there." He thought, when he began my essay, that I was joining him and his skeptical colleagues in rejecting the idea that interpretive judgments could be "purely objective." But then he discovered, to his disgust, that I was actually relying on rather than making fun of the right-wrong picture. I suggested that if I were a novelist in the game I described I might think myself constrained by a text to a certain interpretation of that text, even though, were I beginning the novel, I would have written a different kind of novel. I suggested that if I were a judge I might feel myself constrained by past judicial decisions in the same way. Fish's "copy" theory reflexes were triggered. He declares that I mean that meanings are self-executing or already in place, that texts announce their own generic affiliations and so forth. He offers, as proof that I am wrong, exactly the fact I myself insisted on, which is that two interpreters will have a very different idea of what a text is—that one may think it ironic while another insists that it is a piece of realism. He acknowledges that I deny that everyone agrees about issues of interpretation. But since I rely on a right-wrong vocabulary, which itself assumes that interpretations are "just there," he thinks I cannot deny this consistently. So he dismisses my denials as a self-contradictory subtext and concludes this extraordinary career of error by announcing that I have embraced both the positions I was trying to escape.

Fish is not the only literary scholar who makes the mistake of bringing an a priori theory of objectivity to the enterprise of interpretation instead of taking it from the enterprise. Others share his view that one interpretation could be better than another only if meanings were "just there." So they take up varying kinds and degrees of skepticism about interpretation. The most radical say that interpretation is just a matter of one person's emotional reactions to a text confronting another's, and that it is nonsense to suppose that one interpretation could be "really" better than another. The less radical, like Fish, try to build alternative descriptions of interpretation which, while not falling back into the supposed mistakes of the right-wrong picture, nevertheless preserve something of the idea that interpretation is not just emotional reaction, that interpretation is not wholly subjective. They turn, for this purpose, to the currently fashionable idea of a practice and find, in the traditions and conventions of the "professional community," some pale form of the constraints the right-wrong picture would provide if it were not absurd.

I do not know what it means to say that meanings are "already in place" or "just there" or "self-executing."[2] Does it mean that if we take a very sharp scalpel to a book and carve away the paper and ink we will find something else left on the table? Or that everyone who reads the book in a good light will agree about its genre or theme or point? Or that people who reach the wrong conclusions about texts will be punished, perhaps by being denied tenure? If so, then we can be confident that ordinary interpreters, who hold the right-wrong picture, do *not* think that meanings are "just there," and so on.

So Fish and his skeptical colleagues have not answered the first question any theory of interpretation must face. They have not explained how people who think one interpretation can be better than another make the discriminations necessary to hold on to that second-order belief. (Indeed, even if people did think that meanings are "just there" in one of these ways, this would not explain that ability either but only deepen the mystery.) Fish and the others have been tricked into thinking they have an explanation of the ordinary second-order beliefs of interpretation, an explanation that justifies their skeptical conclusions. They have been tricked by their own metaphors, which seem to provide an explanation until we ask what these metaphors really mean to attribute to those whom they accuse.

3. Theory Dependence

Fish's explicit arguments for his claim that interpretation cannot be different from inventing, whatever ordinary interpreters think, rest on the further hidden assumption that interpretation must be homogenous (see pp. 274–86). He says that texts cannot constrain interpretation because interpretation creates texts. His argument for this paradox begins in an important and sensible point, which I myself stressed, and which no one who is himself engaged in any interpretive activity would deny. Any interpreter's beliefs about the genre and characterizations of a novel, for example, will reflect his more general aesthetic beliefs and attitudes, including, as I suggested in the most controversial part of my

---

2. I myself used the different phrase, "just 'there' in history," only to refer to the specific theory I had described earlier, that propositions of law are true in virtue of "straightforward" historical claims about official behavior (pp. 266, 250). That theory does have a clear sense, of course, but this is not what Fish means to rule out in denying that meanings can be "just 'there' " in the world.

essay, his convictions about what is valuable in art. These other beliefs will furnish, for him, whatever grounds he has for thinking his interpretation better than others. No feature of an interpretation is exempt from this description—not even the threshold question of what counts as the physical text—the canonical set of marks on paper—that identifies the work to be interpreted.

But this fact, that interpretations are in this way theory-dependent all the way down, provides no argument that interpreting is really no different from inventing. On the contrary, it is the beginning of an explanation of what I said any decent theory of interpretation must explain, which is how interpreters can make that distinction for themselves. It is now a familiar thesis among philosophers of science and epistemology, after all, that people's beliefs even about the facts that make up the physical world are the consequence of their more general scientific theories. According to one prominent version of this argument, the entire body of our beliefs about logic, mathematics, physics, and the rest confronts experience together, as an interdependent system, and there is no part of this system which could not, in principle, be revised and abandoned if we were willing and able to revise and adjust the rest. If we held very different beliefs about the theoretical parts of physics and the other sciences, we would, in consequence, divide the world into very different entities, and the facts we "encountered" about these different entities would be very different from the facts we now take to be unassailable.

Now suppose we accepted this general view of knowledge and drew from it the startling conclusion that discrete scientific hypotheses cannot be tested against facts at all, because once a theory has been adopted there are no wholly independent facts against which to test that theory. We would have misunderstood the philosophical thesis we meant to apply. For the point of that thesis is not to deny that facts constrain theories but to explain how they do. There is no paradox in the proposition that facts both depend on and constrain the theories that explain them. On the contrary, that proposition is an essential part of the picture of knowledge as a complex and interrelated set of beliefs confronting experience as a coherent whole.

On this view the constraints of scientific investigation are imposed not by the self-announcing reality philosophers invent only to mock but by the internal tensions, checks, and balances of the complex structure of what we recognize as scientific knowledge. Of course the constraint would be illusory if that system were not sufficiently complex and structured, if there were no functional distinctions, within that system, among the various kinds and levels of belief. But there are, and that is why scientists can abandon theories on the ground that they are inconsistent with the facts deployed by the remaining structure of the body of knowledge. It is perhaps true that we could in principle replace the entire

system of our scientific beliefs with an entirely new system, equally coherent. But it is not clear whether this is in any sense a genuine possibility for human beings. Even if it is, the fact that something like this would
be necessary to rid ourselves of certain facts shows how powerful the
constraint of fact on theory really is. Much has been made, in recent
philosophy of science, about scientific "revolutions" in which the
paradigms and deep methodological structures of science, along with
more ordinary propositions, are called into question. But even the most
dramatic changes in scientific paradigm are not instances of anything
like replacing one entire structure of ideas with another. These are
rather instances (to adapt Otto Neurath's happy figure) of rebuilding the
boat one plank at a time at sea.

Fish's claim, that texts cannot constrain interpretation, would be an
important claim if he meant to argue the following thesis. Interpretive
convictions are different from scientific beliefs because the system of
interpretive beliefs any particular interpreter has at any particular time
is either too simple or too unstructured to allow a genuine distinction
between those beliefs he proposes to test, in some particular argument,
and the other departments of that structure he holds fixed for the purpose of testing these. It does, after all, seem silly to say that our preferences for vanilla over chocolate are constrained by facts about the ice
cream itself. This seems silly, I think, exactly because the relevant beliefs
are not interdependent and structured in a way that could give sense to
this claim. Indeed, Fish does sometimes suggest that our interpretive
convictions are simple and unstructured in the same way as our preferences in ice cream, particularly when he falls back on the metaphor of
sight to explain what interpretation is like.[3] But he does not offer anything like an argument to that effect because he does not realize that this
is the only way his paradoxical claims could make genuine sense within
the institution of interpretation.

In any case, this issue—about the internal structure and complexity
of judgments of interpretation—is exactly what any debate over whether
texts can constrain interpretation should be about. That is why I wrote
the essay I did. I tried to bring something of the great complexity of
these judgments to the surface, by stressing the difference between what
I called convictions about integrity, pertinent to the dimension of fit, and
convictions about artistic merit, pertinent to the dimension of value. I
tried to show how each interpreter finds, in the interaction between

3. He says about the chain novel: "No matter how much or how little [prior text] you
have, it cannot be a check against interpretation because even when you first 'see' it,
interpretation has already done its work" (p. 262). This suggests that a reader's initial
interpretive impressions form one simple "gestalt" of projection, which cannot be checked
because it already expresses every interpretive and aesthetic conviction of the interpreter.
The preposterous simplification of a complex process is at the root of Fish's iterated
mistake, that everything involving some interpretation is alike.

these two sets of attitudes and beliefs, not only constraints and standards for interpretation but the essential circumstance of that activity, the grounds of his capacity to give discrete sense to interpretive judgments.

I will return to this idea later, in considering Michaels' objection to my essay. But I realize that some readers will want to say, just here, that I have already said enough to establish the very skepticism I resist. If the only constraints on interpretation are those supplied by a particular interpreter's other convictions, then there can be no independent test of interpretation that everyone, no matter what his other beliefs, can accept. It follows, according to this argument, that no interpretive judgment can be objectively right or wrong.

Even if this objection were sound, the point of my own essay, which was to describe interpretation rather than to establish the objectivity of interpretive judgments, would be untouched. We would simply add, to our description of the kind of argument the enterprise of interpretation requires, that in the last analysis there is no genuine or real truth to interpretive judgments. I do not think this argument is sound, however, and I think its flaw is connected to this last observation—accepting the argument could not change what interpreters do about interpretation. The premise is sound. there can be no argument for any interpretation that must persuade everyone no matter what his other aesthetic beliefs and values. But it does not follow, simply from this, that no interpretation can be "objectively" right.

I shall turn to that issue in a moment; but first I want to say something about Fish's own solution to the skeptical position he has created for himself. He thinks that the right-wrong picture is impossible because meanings are not "already in place." But he insists that interpretation is not "wholly subjective" either because an interpreter must respect the practices of the professional community on pain of not producing an interpretation at all. I cannot imagine a weaker constraint; anything that others could even recognize as an interpretation, no matter how juvenile or silly, by hypothesis passes this test. If Fish has not made interpretation wholly subjective, the difference is not noticeable to the naked eye. In any event, however, this account does not show what I said any theory of interpretation must. It does not show what an interpreter must believe in order to believe that his interpretation is better than other interpretations of the same material, because these may also respect the weak constraints imposed by the practice of his professional peers.

Fish comes closest to facing this question when he discusses his *own* interpretation of Agatha Christie novels. He says:

> This interpretive action, or any other that could be imagined, would not be performed in violation of the facts of the text but would be an effort to establish those facts; and if in the course of that effort I were to dislodge another set of facts, they would be facts that had emerged within the assumption of another intention

and would therefore be no less interpretive than the facts I was putting in their place. Of course my efforts might very well fail in that no one else would be persuaded to my reading. But neither success nor failure would prove anything about what the text does or does not allow; rather it would attest to the degree to which I had mastered or failed to master the rules of argument and evidence as they are understood (tacitly, to be sure) by members of the professional community. [P. 281]

Now the first part of this passage is simply the message as before, though its skeptical tone is now more in the foreground. It appears that the only claim Fish can make about his own interpretation against rivals is that his has "emerged within the assumption of another intention," and this does not seem much of a claim. We want to know why Fish thinks his interpretation superior to rival interpretations. (If he does not think it superior, then why has he offered it?) His efforts might fail, Fish says, in that no one would be persuaded by his arguments. Of course he may mean by this only that if his interpretation fails to persuade then it has failed to persuade. But it is, as I said, the closest he comes to explaining what an interpreter must believe in order to believe in his own interpretation. This seems to be his attempt to preserve, from the skeptical wreck he has made of interpretation, something of the idea that interpretation can be done well or badly, that some interpretations are better than others.

This ambition is confirmed in the next sentence when he explains that his failure would "attest to the degree" to which he had failed to master the "rules" of interpretation as they are understood by the "professional community." Fish cannot mean by this that an interpreter will believe his interpretation better than rival interpretations only if he thinks that it is uniquely dictated by rules of interpretation accepted by all professionals. No one could think that any particular interpretation of anything was uniquely dictated by such rules, least of all Fish himself who denies that there are any rules sufficiently narrow as to make one interpretation of a Christie novel "inescapable." But what else could this dark reference to the "rules" mean? Does it mean that an interpreter will think his interpretation better if he thinks it is dictated by his own interpretation (which others might not accept) of such rules as the community does share? But this merely pushes the problem back one step. What must an interpreter believe to believe that his interpretation of these rules is better than alternate interpretations of them? And if an interpretation of the second-order rules can be controversial, then the failure of a first-order interpretation to persuade others would not "attest" to the inadequacy of anything.

If we are to make any sense of the quoted passage we must ignore the reference to rules accepted by the professional community. For all the fuss Fish makes about the idea of such rules, and about the critical practices of the professional community, these ideas in fact play no real part in his account of interpretation, which is therefore much more skeptical than he seems to realize. If Fish has any explanation of how an interpreter can come to think that his interpretation is superior to others, it can only be this: he will think his interpretation superior if he thinks that it will in fact persuade others.

But this plainly will not do. No one who has a new interpretation to offer believes his interpretation better because it will convince others, though he may believe that it will convince others because it is better. Many critics, in fact, think their interpretations better in spite of their suspicion, confirmed by experience, that they will win no converts at all. Even if this were not so, even if people thought their own interpretations better only because they thought they would convince others, it would still be necessary to explain what those others must think in order to be convinced. On Fish's account they could be persuaded to a particular interpretation only if they thought that still others would be persuaded by it. The boundaries of intelligibility are indistinct. But we have passed them now.

III. Objectivity

My interest in the second question I distinguished—the question of objectivity—is largely negative. I see no point in trying to find some *general* argument that moral or political or legal or aesthetic or interpretive judgments are objective. Those who ask for an argument of that sort want something different from the kind of arguments I and they would make for particular examples or instances of such judgments. But I do not see how there could be any such different arguments. I have no arguments for the objectivity of moral judgments except moral arguments, no arguments for the objectivity of interpretive judgments except interpretive arguments, and so forth.

I believe, for example, that slavery is unjust in the circumstances of the modern world. I think I have arguments for this view, though I know that if these arguments were challenged I would in the end have to rest on convictions for which I had no further direct argument. I say "I think" I have arguments not because I am worried about the philosophical standing of the arguments I have but because I know that others have taken a contrary view, that I might not be able to convince them, and that they might, in fact, be able to convince me if I gave them a decent opportunity to do so. But now suppose someone, having heard my arguments, asks me whether I have any different arguments for the further view that slavery is objectively or really unjust. I know that I do not because, so far as I can tell, it is not a further claim at all but just the same claim put in a slightly more emphatic form.

Of course someone might stipulate a sense for the word "objectively" that would make the "further" proposition really different. He might say that the further question, about whether slavery is objectively unjust, asks whether everyone agrees that it is, for example, or would agree under favorable conditions for reflection. In that case I would say that I do not believe slavery is objectively unjust. But this would in no way affect or qualify my original judgment, that slavery is unjust. I never thought everyone did or would agree.

So I have no interest in trying to compose a general defense of the objectivity of my interpretive or legal or moral opinions. In fact, I think that the whole issue of objectivity, which so dominates contemporary theory in these areas, is a kind of fake. We should stick to our knitting. We should account to ourselves for our own convictions as best we can, standing ready to abandon those that do not survive reflective inspection. We should make such arguments to others, who do not share our opinions, as we can make in good faith and break off arguing when no further argument is appropriate. I do not mean that this is all we can do because we are creatures with limited access to true reality or with necessarily parochial viewpoints. I mean that we can give no sense to the idea that there is anything else we could do in deciding whether our judgments are "really" true. If some argument should persuade me that my views about slavery are not really true, then it should also persuade me to abandon my views about slavery. And if no argument could persuade me that slavery is not unjust, no argument could persuade me that it is not "really" unjust.

But I am not allowed to turn my back on the problem of objectivity in the way I would like, and Fish's essay shows why not. People like Fish say there is something radically wrong with what I and others think about law and morality and literature. Our arguments assume, they say, that judgments in these enterprises can be objectively right and wrong, but in fact they cannot be. Since I take the view I do about what the claim of objectivity in these disciplines can mean, I am tempted to reply by arguing in favor of the judgments they say cannot be objective. I want to meet the claim that moral judgments cannot be objective by repeating my arguments why slavery is unjust, for example. But they do not mean their arguments to be taken in this spirit. A moral philosopher who denies that slavery can be really or objectively unjust does not wish to be understood as holding the same position as a fascist who argues that there is nothing wrong with slavery. He insists that his arguments are not moral arguments at all but philosophical arguments of a very different character to which I must respond in a very different way.

I cannot do this, however, until I understand the difference between the proposition that slavery is unjust, which the fascist denies, and the proposition that slavery is really or objectively unjust, which the skeptical philosopher denies. The philosopher says: the latter proposition is different because it claims that the injustice of slavery is part of the furniture of the universe, that it is really "out there" in some way. We are back in the land of the incomprehensible metaphors. I do think that slavery is unjust, that this is not "just my opinion," that everyone ought to think so, that everyone has a reason to oppose slavery, and so forth. Is this what it means to think that the injustice of slavery is part of the furniture of the universe? If so, then I do think this, but then I cannot see the difference between the proposition that slavery is unjust and the proposition that the injustice of slavery is part of the furniture of the universe. The proposition about furniture, interpreted in this way, has become a moral proposition about what I and others should believe and do, and I do not see how there can be any argument against that moral proposition which is not a moral argument. What other kind of argument could possibly persuade me to abandon these claims about what others should think and do?

But the philosopher will insist that I am missing the point. When it comes to moral opinions, he will say, he has the same ones I do. He also thinks that slavery is unjust. He disagrees with me not *within* morality but *about* morality. How is this possible? How can he believe that slavery is unjust and also believe that no propositions of political morality can be really or objectively true? For some decades one explanation was very popular. Skeptical philosophers said that what seem to be moral beliefs are not really beliefs at all but only emotional reactions. So when a philosopher says, off duty, that slavery is unjust, he is only reporting or expressing his own subjective reaction to slavery, and there is no inconsistency when he confirms, back on duty, that no moral propositions can be true. But this explanation will not work because the convictions philosophers try to explain away in this fashion do not function, on their own mental stage, as emotional reactions. They entertain arguments, take up or abandon different positions in response to arguments, see and respect logical and other connections among these positions, and otherwise behave in a style appropriate to belief rather than mere subjective reaction. So the redescription of their moral beliefs as emotional reactions is just bad reporting. The fact is: they think that slavery is unjust.

Now consider a more contemporary explanation of how it is possible to think this and yet be a skeptic. Suppose we distinguish between truth within a special game or enterprise and real or objective truth outside it. Taking fiction as a model, we might say that within the enterprise of a certain story someone killed Roger Ackroyd. But in the real world, outside that enterprise, Roger Ackroyd never existed, so that it cannot be true that anyone killed him. We might want to conceive the social practices of morality, art, law, and interpretation in some such way. Within the enterprise we make arguments and have beliefs of a certain sort— that slavery is unjust, for example, or that Christie novels display a certain view of evil. But when we stand outside the enterprise we know that no such proposition can be really or objectively true.

This strategy is appealing because, as I just said, skeptics not only have moral or interpretive opinions but also treat these as beliefs, and this new picture explains how and why. When people make interpretive or moral or legal judgments, it says, they are playing a certain game of make-believe, asking themselves which interpretation would be better if any really could be better, or what would be morally right if anything really could be morally right, and so forth. There is no reason why skeptical philosophers themselves should not "play the game," even though they know it is really, objectively speaking, all nonsense.

But now we are back at the beginning, and my initial problem, that I do not see what difference could be made by the word "objectively," remains. For this explanation supposes that we can distinguish between the game and the real world, that we can distinguish between the claim that slavery is unjust, offered as a move in some collective enterprise in which such judgments are made and debated, and the claim that slavery is really or objectively unjust in the actual world; or that we can distinguish between the claim that Christie novels are about evil, offered as a move in a different kind of enterprise, and the claim that they are really about evil, offered as a claim about how things really are. It supposes that we can distinguish these as two different kinds of claims the way we distinguish claims about Roger Ackroyd as a character in a novel from claims about Roger Ackroyd as a historical character. And this is exactly what we cannot do, because the words "objectively" and "really" cannot change the sense of moral or interpretive judgments. If moral or aesthetic or interpretive judgments have the sense and force they do just because they figure in a collective human enterprise, then such judgments cannot have a "real" sense and a "real" truth value which transcend that enterprise and somehow take hold of the "real" world.

I have yet been given no reason to think that any skeptical argument about morality can be other than a moral argument, or skeptical argument about law other than a legal argument, or skeptical argument about interpretation other than an interpretive argument. I think that the problem of objectivity, as it is usually posed, is a fake because the distinction that might give it meaning, the distinction between substantive arguments within and skeptical arguments about social practices, is itself a fake. I must now take some care, however, to guard against misunderstandings of what I have said. Someone might say that my position is the deepest possible form of skepticism about morality, art, and interpretation because I am actually saying that moral or aesthetic or interpretive judgments cannot possibly describe an independent objective reality. But that is not what I said. I said that the question of what "independence" and "reality" are, for any practice, is a question within that practice, so that whether moral judgments can be objective is itself a moral question, and whether there is objectivity in interpretation is itself a question of interpretation. This threatens to make skepticism not inevitable but impossible.

It threatens to make skepticism impossible because it seems to deny that someone can criticize morality, for example, without himself taking up the moral point of view. Skepticism, on this account, would be self-defeating, for if the skeptic must make moral arguments in order to challenge morality, he must concede the sense and validity of arguments whose sense and validity he wants to deny. But this, too, is an overstatement because it ignores what I tried to stress throughout my original essay, which is the complexity of the moral and interpretive practices skeptics want to challenge. My arguments about objectivity leave even very general skepticism possible as a position *within* the enterprise it challenges.

I have already pointed out one kind of skeptical argument about interpretive judgments. Someone might try to show that interpretive judgments are too unstructured and disconnected to be checked by other judgments in the way the enterprise of interpretation supposes such judgments to be checked—too unstructured to count as beliefs even within that enterprise. This form of skepticism does require taking up some minimal position, which might nevertheless be controversial among interpreters, about the point and value of interpretation. It seems to rest, in fact, on exactly the view I urged in my essay—that plausible interpretations must be connected to normative aesthetic or political theories that are themselves plausible. It uses that very general assumption about the point of interpretation to argue for the impossibility of successful interpretations, and that should be sufficiently skeptical for anyone. (Of course it also assumes a false psychology of interpretation, and that is why it fails.) This kind of skepticism, however, while very general, is nevertheless internal in the sense I am now assuming. No one who accepts this argument could then add that, in his personal opinion, a Christie novel is really an exploration of the nature of evil.

There are many other, and more plausible, possibilities for skepticism within interpretation. An interpreter might accept some theory about the point or value of art according to which certain interpretive questions (or even all of them) simply have no answer, because no answer to these questions could make any difference to the value of a work of art. Someone might well think, for example, that the old question whether Hamlet and Ophelia were lovers has no answer because neither answer would intersect any criterion of value in drama. The play could not be read better one way rather than the other. Almost any theory of art would have that consequence for some issues—whether Hamlet slept on his side, for example. But some would have it for most of the questions that exercise critics, and these theories would furnish very skeptical accounts of interpretation.

We can even imagine a skeptical argument rising from the issues that seem important to Fish and his skeptical colleagues. They dwell on the fact that two interpreters will often disagree about the correct characterization of a work of fiction because characterizations are so theory-dependent. That is, apparently, what they mean to argue in those unfortunate metaphors about meanings not being "just there." If someone thinks that the point of interpretation is to secure a large measure of interpersonal agreement, he will notice that interpretation as presently practiced offers no such prospect, and he will draw the appropriate global and skeptical conclusions. But his arguments will then depend on the plausibility of that view of the point of the enterprise.

These different forms of skepticism about interpretation are all internal to that enterprise. They adopt some controversial view about the point or nature of interpretation, as do positive theories, but they adopt a view that has skeptical consequences. We can easily construct parallel examples of internal skepticism about the value of art and about political morality. No problem of consistency arises for this sort of skepticism because we are no longer dealing with the myth of two standpoints, an internal standpoint from which an interpreter has his own answer to interpretive questions, and an external standpoint from which he acknowledges that such questions can have no answers. No one who says there is no answer to the question about Hamlet and Ophelia, because neither answer makes the play better or worse than the other, will go on to say that in his personal opinion they were lovers.

If we abandon that myth we threaten not the impossibility of skepticism but the impossibility of what we might call, in contrast to the kinds of skepticism we have recognized, external skepticism. The external skeptic supposes he can check all interpretive judgments against some external reality whose content is not to be determined by arguments of the sort made familiar by the practice but which is to be apprehended in some other way. He supposes that he can step wholly outside the enterprise, give some different sense to interpretive judgments from the sense they have within it, test these judgments so conceived in some way different from confronting the arguments deployed for and against them in the ordinary practice of interpretation, and find them all false or senseless when measured against this supposedly more objective standard. If we reject external skepticism of this sort, then we shall say, to Fish and other would-be skeptics, that the only way they can make good their extravagant claim—that any text allows any interpretation whatsoever—is to make a genuine argument to that effect, by setting out some appealing normative theory of artistic integrity that has that consequence. If Fish wishes us to entertain such an argument, then he must begin by assuring us of his own good faith. If he really does hold such a theory himself, then he must abandon, as inconsistent, his own favorite interpretations of texts, including, for example, his interpretation of *Paradise Lost,* not to mention *Peril at End House.*

Of course if he did make such an argument he might end by convincing us. We cannot say for certain, in advance, that he would not. The only kind of skepticism that is ruled out by my earlier observations is skepticism brought to an enterprise from the outside, skepticism which engages no arguments of the sort the enterprise requires, skepticism which is simply tacked on at the end of our various interpretive and political convictions, leaving them all somehow unruffled and in place. This kind of skepticism can make no difference to our own efforts to understand and improve interpretation, art, and law. What do we lose in giving it up?

IV. Reply to Fish (and Michaels)

1. Naked Came the Critic

Fish begins his essay with an extended discussion of my chain-novel construction, which he says is "helpful and illuminating" but also "mistaken in several important respects" (pp. 272–73). I suggested that the first novelist, who has the job of beginning the novel, is in a different position from the rest, who have the "dual responsibilities of interpreting and creating" (p. 262). But I added, in a footnote, that "even the first novelist has the responsibility of interpreting to the extent any writer must, which includes not only interpreting as he writes but interpreting the genre in which he sets out to write," and I had already pointed out that any writer must interpret as he writes (p. 262 n. 4). Unfortunately all Fish has to say, by way of criticism, is that I have neglected this latter point. And he knows I have not, because when he has finished stating it he acknowledges that I made a "similar but not exactly parallel point" myself (p. 273 n. 1). (I am unclear, however, why my point is not exactly parallel.) Why should Fish think I have made any mistake at all in distinguishing between the first and later novelists? We must be alert to this possibility. Perhaps he thinks, as I suggested earlier he might, that interpretation is a unique and unstructured act, so that any judgment that involves interpretation is essentially like any other such judgment. In that case he would read my statement, that even the first novelist must interpret something, as contradicting my general claim, that later novelists have a different assignment from the first. It seems unlikely that anyone familiar with interpretation would make this mistake, but please bear the possibility in mind.

This is not Fish's only objection to my chain-novel story. I raise the question whether later novelists in the chain will have less creative "freedom" than earlier novelists and try to explain why it seems natural to say that normally (but not inevitably) they will. I offer this example: most chain novelists would think that certain interpretations of Scrooge's character would be incompatible with the final sections of *A Christmas Carol,* but not with the opening pages alone. "In any case," I add, "it will nevertheless be true, for all novelists beyond the first, that the assignment to find (what they believe to be) the correct interpretation of the text so far is a different assignment from the assignment to begin a new novel of their own" (p. 262 n. 4). Fish finds all this unsatisfactory. He says: "This, then, is my first criticism of Dworkin's example: the distinction it is supposed to illustrate—the distinction between the first and later novelists—will not hold up because everyone in the enterprise is equally constrained" (p. 275).[4]

Fish ignores the long section preceding the chain-novel construction, in which I describe the kind of constraint that I believe can change as the prior text increases. Even so, something very odd happens to his argument. He adds, directly after the remark I just quoted: "By 'equally' I mean equally with respect to the condition of freedom; I am making no claim about the number or identity of the constraints" (p. 275). This does contradict much of what has gone before. He has said, for example, that both the first novelist and "those who follow him are free and constrained in exactly the same way" and that "not only are those constraints [of interpretation] controlling but they are uniformly so; that is, they do not relax or tighten in relation to the position an author happens to occupy on the chain. The last author is as free, within those constraints, to determine what the characters are really like as is the first" (pp. 273, 274). This sounds like the assumption I asked you to bear in mind, that interpretation is always and everywhere essentially the same. But the parenthetical qualification seems to say exactly the opposite. If the later novelists are subject to more and different constraints, how can they all be equally constrained? If a novelist at the end of the *Christmas Carol* chain will have more difficulty seeing Scrooge as inherently evil than a novelist second in line would have, how can they both be equally free to determine "what the characters are really like?"

If we take the qualification at face value, we must conclude that Fish only means, by his more paradoxical claims, that neither the first nor the early nor the late novelists are *totally* "free," that all are subject to some constraints, though later novelists may be subject to more and different ones. But then why does he object to my crucial claim that the program of continuing a novel is different from that of beginning a new novel and

---

4. Fish thought he had to reach back to the unpublished draft of my essay in order to convict me of this mistake. But this surprising maneuver was unnecessary; I had not "withdrawn" the offending observation but only removed it to a footnote and expanded upon it (see p. 262 n. 4).

that this is so precisely because the "number and identity" of the constraints are different? I try to show how these are different in the two cases, and if Fish is really "making no claims" about this issue, then he actually has nothing to say that is relevant to my essay, for all the heavy weather he makes.

Unfortunately this is also true of the discussion of judicial interpretation which immediately follows. I distinguished, using the chain novel as a model, between two assignments a judge might take up: he might try to find the best justification of the statutes and past judicial decisions that are part of the prior law and carry the principles of that justification forward in deciding new cases, or he might ignore the past record of statutes and decisions to decide cases "on a clean slate" instead. How could a judge, Fish asks, possibly decide a case by striking out in a new direction of his own (see p. 276)? We need not strain for an answer. A judge might say, or at least think, that though the correct interpretation of past decisions, or the correct interpretation of a statute, requires a decision for the defendant, he is deciding for the plaintiff because that would make the community better off on the whole. Some judges do think about their decisions that way, and some very few actually say so, if not in their judicial decisions then in their memoirs.

Presumably Fish would say that a judge who decides in this way does not think himself totally free from judicial practice and convention, because he offers, in his claim that the community would be better off were he to ignore precedent or the statute, the kind of reason that is at least conventionally associated with political decisions. He is not like the judge who, in Fish's well-worn example, decides on the ground of the defendant's hair coloring (see p. 276).[5] But once again this is beside the point. It argues only that no one who wishes to be understood as judging, rather than playing some bizarre kind of game, is totally free from all the abstract and contestable conventions pertinent to that role. He must do something that could be construed by others as taking up a view about what judges should do, just as the first novelist in the chain must do something that could be construed as beginning a kind of novel. There is nevertheless a critical difference between two assignments a judge might accept: to reach the best interpretation of the past judicial decisions of his jurisdiction or to produce the best forward-looking decision without regard to whether that decision represents the best interpretation of what has gone before. Each represents a way of continuing the "practice" of judging, but they are radically different ways.

If Fish denies this then he must, after all, think that any judgment which involves some kind of interpretation is essentially like any other

---

5. Suppose the judge believed that redheads were the victims of pervasive discrimination in our society and therefore decided cases in their favor whenever possible. Or, to make the example a bit more realistic, he decided in favor of poor people when the other party was rich. Would either of these count as not judging?

judgment that also involves interpretation. He gives ample evidence of this assumption elsewhere. He says that the only way for a judge to behave other than "the chain-enterprise way" would be to decide "a case in such a way as to have no relationship to the history of previous decisions," and he says that is not possible (p. 276). But this is a false contrast. A judge who accepts the responsibility of the chain tries to decide in a way that has a *particular* relationship to the past, described in the chain-enterprise construction, and it is certainly possible to aim to decide in a way that has a *different* relationship to the past. Fish describes how a judge constructs a particular judicial history by interpreting past decisions in the light of his own political convictions (see pp. 278–79). His discussion could be simply a summary of my own description of that process. But then Fish adds, gratuitously, that "all histories are invented in the weak sense that they are not simply 'discovered' but assembled under the pressure of some present urgency; but no history is invented in the strong sense that the urgency which led to its assembly was unrelated to any generally acknowledged legal concern" (p. 278). Once again this is a false contrast. Fish uses "discovered" and "invented in the strong sense" to describe processes that are, even on his account, impossible. He says that "neither the self-declaring or found entity nor the dangerously free or inventing agent is a possible feature of the enterprise" and concludes that, because nothing judges do about the past could be either pure finding or pure inventing, everything they do about it must be the same (p. 277). So he misses the crucial distinction between the two assignments a judge might take up. The judge who ignores statutes and precedent to establish the rule he believes will serve society best is certainly not acting in a way "unrelated to any generally acknowledged legal concern." But if he reports his conclusions as the best interpretation of past decisions, in spite of the fact that he has made no effort to interpret them, then he will be inventing a judicial history in the only sense in which that epithet is or can be used within professional practice.[6]

This is a strategy Fish uses again and again. He imposes meanings on phrases used within critical or judicial practice, like "finding," "discovering," "inventing," "free," "constrained," and the like which are, in fact, wholly alien to the way in which these phrases function in that practice. He then announces, as important conclusions, that the crucial distinctions made through these phrases are bogus. They would be

---

6. Fish's ear has betrayed him here. He thinks that when lawyers accuse a judge of inventing judicial history they only mean that he has reached a different interpretation than they have (see p. 279). Normally they mean that he has only pretended to interpret past judicial decisions, that he has actually taken up the different assignment I described, and that he is therefore acting deceitfully, rather than simply making a mistake. Fish misses this because his categories do not allow him the distinction on which this specialized critical judgment depends.

bogus if they were used in the sense he supposes; but, as I tried to show, that sense is drawn from Fish's a priori philosophical assumptions and not from the practice he wants to discredit.

2. The Mysterious Affair of Styles

Now consider Fish's next excursion into my essay: his comments about Christie. I imagined that someone might say, as a kind of *reductio ad absurdum* of my "aesthetic" hypothesis, that, if we accept the hypothesis and suppose that a philosophical novel about the meaning of death is a more substantial literary achievement than an ordinary thriller, it would follow that the best interpretation of a Christie novel, in which deaths almost always occur, is that its theme is the meaning of death (see p. 254). I said that this does not follow. Any attempt to read a Christie mystery as an essay about the meaning of death would produce not a more distinguished work of art but a shambles, because our view of a novel's worth depends not only on what we take to be its theme but also on our assessment of its execution of that theme. I assumed that we would judge the execution of a Christie novel, interpreted as an essay on the meaning of death, to be a miserable failure. Fish gathers together the resources of his library to prove—what? That important novelists have written thrillers, that well-known critics have analyzed the mystery as a genre, that some of them think Christie was a distinguished writer, that different interpretations of her work have been offered, and that Fish himself has developed an analysis of Christie's villains with "obvious" parallels to Iago and Milton's Satan (see pp. 279–80). Depressing, all of this, but stunningly irrelevant.

I have not checked Fish's citations, but I doubt any of the scholars he cites tried to read Christie's novels as essays on the meaning of death, and Fish offers no reason to think that they would have succeeded if they had. (He says I could not have chosen a worse example of my point; but his own failure to engage my point, though he turns out to be a Christie scholar, suggests that I perhaps chose rather well.) He must have persuaded himself that I meant to make a very different point. He apparently thinks I said that nothing interesting at all could be made of Christie, that mysteries could not be considered important as art, or something of that sort. Once again he attributes an "assumption" to my discussion which is not only unjustified but disavowed. "The assumption is that sentences, figures, and styles announce their own generic affiliation and that a reader who would claim them for an inappropriate genre would be imposing his will on nature" (p. 279). The idea of sentences announcing their generic affiliation is another metaphor, like self-enforcement, designed to make the theory they describe seem ridiculous. Fish means, I suppose, that I believe that everyone who sets out to interpret any particular work of literature will reach the same conclusion about its genre; or, perhaps, that only one such conclusion can ever succeed on what I called an interpretation's dimension of fit. So when I suggest that a certain way of reading Christie would be wrong, he assumes I mean that everyone who reads her novels reaches the same conclusions about their genre or character or value.

But I said exactly the opposite in the course of my discussion of Christie, and I gave, as Fish himself acknowledges, Raymond Chandler as an example of a writer who has been interpreted in very different ways (see p. 254). It does not however follow, from the fact that texts do not "announce their genre," that any attribution of any genre to any text will be plausible. I said that calling a Christie mystery a novel about the meaning of death would be a mistake because it would make the novel a shambles, and that is not because all novels announce their own genre but because her novels become wrecks if we try to read them in that particular way. Of course I rely, in saying this, on my own judgment and my expectation that almost all readers will agree. That is not to say that no one will disagree. Fish's bizarre reading of my article is proof of its own claim, that the most implausible interpretations of texts can be put forward as serious efforts. I would nevertheless want to say, of both the hypothetical claim that Christie writes about the meaning of death and Fish's actual claims about my essay, that these interpretations are wrong and plainly wrong.

3. The New Intentional Fallacy

Fish's final argument fixes on my remarks about the author's intention school of interpretation. Critics who belong to that school use "intention" in the way people normally do, to refer to a certain conscious or unconscious psychological state. Fish, for the most part, uses it in a very different way. He thinks a statement of an author's intention is just another way of reporting an interpretation of that author's work. The author's intention critics could not use the idea of intention in that way because that would make their claims empty. They could no longer argue that a particular interpretation is correct because it matches the intention of the author; for the claim, that the author intended something, would be simply the claim that the parallel interpretation is correct for some *other* reason. Fish reveals the emptiness of his concept of intention in his discussion of Christie. He says that his own interpretation attributes a particular intention to Christie which is different from the intentions assumed by competing interpretations. But he does not suggest that his assumptions about intention are in any way more accurate as a matter of psychological history than those other assumptions, and he offers no evidence for the intention he assumes beyond the evidence he says he has for the interpretation he favors. The idea of intention, so construed, can play no useful role in interpretation because it is simply a phrase used to report interpretations already established in some other way.

Fish does not recognize that he is simply assigning a different—and less useful—sense to the word "intention." He thinks there is something wrong with the way I and others use that word to describe a kind of psychological state. His reasons for thinking this, however, are mistaken in just the way his reasons for thinking that there can be no difference between interpreting and inventing are mistaken. He begins his argument with a familiar and important point, which is that an author cannot frame literary intentions except by employing his own conception—his own interpretation—of the practices and conventions of literature. No one could intend to write a novel without some conception of what counts as a novel within the practices that provide his culture with that form of art. Nor could we attribute that intention to him unless we ourselves had some conception of that practice. But Fish loses this point, characteristically, in overstatement. He loses it through a failure I have already noted: he thinks that any judgment which involves any kind of interpretation must be essentially like any other judgment which involves any interpretation. So he thinks we cannot discriminate between assigning someone a literary intention and asking whether the text he has created succeeds in expressing that intention, or whether the best interpretation of that text matches that intention. But we must make that distinction in order to have even the dimmest understanding of what the practice of interpreting texts is like.

Of course we can, if we wish, express the latter of these two questions as a question about the psychological state of some imaginary author other than the actual author. We can ask whether the text in question is best interpreted by supposing that it was written by someone who had a very different intention. This might be, heuristically, a useful way to put the question of interpretation. But it would be a terrible confusion to say that, if the text is best understood that way, then the actual author's "real" intention was this different intention, not the one we first assigned him. That would be to confuse two different issues, both of which engage our interpretive convictions and our understandings of the literary and other traditions of our own culture, but in very different ways.

Fish apparently thinks that we must assign the real author the intentions that comport with our own interpretation of what he wrote because "one cannot understand an utterance without *at the same time* hearing or reading it as the utterance of someone with more or less specific concerns, interests, and desires, someone with an intention" (p. 283). This is an ambiguous claim, however. Does he mean that we cannot understand a text in a certain way without supposing ourselves to have captured the intentions of the particular historical person whom we identify as its actual author? Or only that we cannot understand a text in a certain way without seeing how someone might have written that text intending it to be understood that way? Only if Fish means to make the first of these claims are his observations even relevant to my remarks about intention. And the first claim is wrong.

I drew a distinction, in my essay, between questions which it might be plausible to think we can only answer by attending to the intentions of a particular "author," like questions about the sense in which an ambiguous word should be read and more general interpretive questions (pp. 252, 259). It is plain, I think, that we can form beliefs about these larger interpretive questions without attributing the pertinent intentions to anyone who meets our quite different tests for counting as the historical author of the text in question. We can understand the equal protection clause as forbidding racial segregation without supposing that any particular historical statesman or draftsman intended that it should do this. We can read *Hamlet* in a psychodynamic way without supposing that Shakespeare either did or could have intended that we do so. The fact that we *can* read texts in this way allows the author's intention theory to be a significant theory because it allows that theory to claim that this is the wrong way to read texts.

4. A Feeble Dilemma

Michaels believes that I confront a dilemma (see p. 338). I say that interpretation aims to show a work of art as the best work of art it can be and that this is different from changing it into something else. So we cannot show a Christie novel in its best light by taking it to be an essay on the meaning of death because this makes it a shambles. Michaels does not make Fish's general argument, that the distinction between interpreting and inventing is always illusory. But he follows Fish in supposing that interpretation is necessary to identify a particular text, and this is the source of the supposed dilemma. If we cannot define a text without relying on a particular theory of aesthetic value, then it is nonsense to say that the text constrains interpretation because the text will have been created by the theory it supposedly tests. If, on the other hand, the text is given independently of the aesthetic theory it is supposed to constrain, through some other kind of interpretation which does not draw on a theory of aesthetic value, then my account of interpretation is self-defeating, because it supposes that some other kind of interpretation is logically prior to the kind I describe.

If this really were a dilemma, of course, then it would defeat any theory of interpretation except a wholly skeptical one. It would certainly defeat the theory Michaels says he holds himself, which is that "interpretation is just a matter of trying to figure out [the author's] intention" (p. 344). For we must have *some* idea of what constitutes a particular text in order to decide who its author is, and we cannot decide what a single text is, even physically, without some act of interpretation of literary conventions. So there must be some kind of interpretation which is logically prior to an author's intention interpretation. This argument does not, of course, actually defeat the author's intention school. For they may simply make the point I made several times earlier in this essay, that there are different kinds or levels of interpretation. Perhaps we do need to interpret our common practice of reading and writing books to know that the marks to be found within the pages of a bound volume are to count as a single and entire text provided they bear a certain causal relation to words which were written or spoken earlier by someone who intended them so to count, and the volume in question is the causal consequence of his having written or spoken those words with that intention. (Even this is too crude a statement of our criteria for this judgment, and even this would be, in some circumstances, controversial.) But once we have decided on this test for identifying a single text we can then interpret texts in a rather different way, by asking the different kinds of questions about them I discussed in my essay. Interpretation at this further and more interesting level may then be said to be only a matter of discovering the author's intention.

Can the aesthetic hypothesis rely on a parallel argument to escape the supposed dilemma? Someone might say no, because the claim that a Christie novel is a mess when read as an essay about death must not only identify the text physically, as a particular collection of marks on paper, but must also assign particular meanings to those marks. It must define the text so that when the marks read "Samantha administered a dose of Veronal," the text, read literally, says that Samantha administered a dose of Veronal and not that she refuted Lucretius. Otherwise it would be easy to define a Christie text in such a way that it becomes an excellent treatise on the meaning of death: we would simply assign meanings to the marks it contains so that it has exactly the same content as a work of Kierkegaard. So now we are back, Michaels might claim, in the grip of the dilemma. If we define the meanings of words without reference to the aesthetic test, by asking what assignment of meanings makes the work best as a work of art, we can convert Christie into Kierkegaard. But if we define these meanings through some other test, we are conceding that some other kind of interpretation lies behind the kind of interpretation we are trying to defend.

My reply to all this is obvious enough. Once we notice that any theory of interpretation requires, for its application, some prior act of interpretation, the aesthetic hypothesis is in no different position from the author's intention theory. It is only necessary to specify the kind or level of interpretation that is under discussion. Of course we must decide what the words on a page mean, at least if they are to be taken literally, before we can ask the questions the aesthetic hypothesis contemplates, including the question of whether they should be taken literally. We might well decide that this prior question, about the literal meaning of the words on the page, is best answered by some theory of "speaker's meaning" which makes certain complex intentions of the author decisive. This is, in fact, exactly what I said in my essay, because I anticipated that someone might make the objection Michaels has made. Deciding what series of marks constitutes a physical text is one question. Deciding upon the speaker's meaning of those words is another. Deciding what the theme or tone or genre is, or what the characters are really like, or how the novel behind the play goes is plainly different from both, and these last questions are the ones I said I had in mind. Only someone who really thought interpretation was homogenous, so that there was only one kind of interpretive question, could think these were all the same question.

In this way I can easily defeat the dilemma by repeating what I said about the scope of the aesthetic hypothesis. It can be only a theory about the third set of issues I just distinguished. In fact I want to make a larger claim for it and in this way to expand my original essay. The speaker's meaning hypothesis is, after all, only one way of identifying what the literal meaning of the marks on the page should be taken to be. Someone might suggest, for example, that we should fix the literal meaning of the text by asking what they mean to a contemporary audience, which might be different from the meaning of the historical speaker. So a hawk is a bird after all, and Hamlet must be understood as the kind of person who would think it appropriate to claim he could tell a bird from a tool. How should we think about this contest between rival theories about how to decide what the marks literally mean?

Suppose we say: we need to interpret the practice of interpretation in the fashion of the aesthetic hypothesis and therefore to propose some theory about the point of the practice to see which method of assigning meaning to the marks makes the practice go better. Of course any particular interpreter's answer will, in the end, be a matter of his most general convictions about the point of literature and its study. Does *this* lead us back into Michaels' dilemma? No, only back to the general observations about theory complexity I made earlier. For our beliefs about how to assign meanings to the individual words that make up the text (and also—why not?—about how to identify the actual physical text) will form elements in a global normative theory of interpretation which will nevertheless be sufficiently structured and disjointed so that one part of this theory can supervise and constrain another. We will not be able to read Christie's words as meaning what Kierkegaard meant when he used very different words because we cannot accept any theory about the point of reading and writing that would permit this. I do not mean that no rational being could possibly accept such a theory. Just that *we* could not, because it would be, in the only sense we can give this judgment, plainly wrong.

I shall end by reporting a suspicion I have about Michaels' own views about the connection between interpretation and intention. I suspect he is using "intention" in the unusual way Fish does. Otherwise Michaels' suggestion would be incredible, that everyone who interprets is actually seeking the author's intention no matter what he says he is seeking, including those who propose interpretations the author could not possibly have intended in the ordinary sense, even subconsciously.

Law as Hermeneutics:
A Response to Ronald Dworkin

Gerald L. Bruns

I want to respond briefly, and only in a very general way, to Ronald Dworkin's fine essay, "Law as Interpretation." I agree that in order to speak adequately about interpretation it is necessary to study what goes on in the theory and practice of the law, since the law is not only a *sort* of hermeneutical discipline; rather, it can be taken as exemplary of what it means to understand and interpret anything at all.

I think, however, that Dworkin obscures the exemplary character of the law by trying to describe legal interpretation from the standpoint of literary criticism. Thus he characterizes legal interpretation variously in terms of our experience of a work of art, in terms of the relation of text and reader, and in terms of a literary tradition figured as the unending re-inscription of a form (for example, the novel). I want to discuss how difficult it is to get from this literary and aesthetic way of thinking to the question of the politics of interpretation. My main point, however, is that recourse to literary and aesthetic models upholds a view of interpretation that the hermeneutical character of the law appears to call into question.

Dworkin's concern is to speak of interpretation in terms of a relation between work and critic or text and reader, or according to a subject-object relationship that necessarily reduces the study of interpretation to a branch of epistemology where sooner or later you will be required to ask, "How do you know that you have interpreted the text correctly?" The scramble to explain how norms of correctness are to be determined follows hard upon this question, and (as Stanley Fish can testify) working yourself out of the ensuing tangle is hard work. Thus you will have to decide whether norms of correct interpretation are logical and necessary or whether they are social and contingent—or whether, among other alternatives, they are a little bit of both. Most of us want it both ways, and so we take regular advantage of notions like convention, paradigm, ideology, theory (conceived as a shared point of view whose practical equivalent is called a method) in order to explain how interpretations are always under control yet capable of individual variation. Some, of course, want to repudiate the notion of norms altogether.

If you want to understand interpretation explicitly on an epistemological model, that is, as a sort of knowing, then you will want norms of correctness to be analytical and productive of objective results, or of judgments or constructions of meaning that are above suspicion because they are rooted in the rigorous analysis of propositions. An inescapable companion of this view, however, is that interpretation, in order to be logically correct (or what is called valid), must be what interpretation never quite manages to be, namely, the objectification of a hidden or authorial intention. The strict construction of an original meaning is always going to fall a little short of strictness, whence interpretation in practice will always seem abnormal—a little less like knowing than like having opinions, or analytically weak in the manner of rhetorical constructions rooted in probability. Strict construction tends to breed deconstruction as a matter of course. Thus Dworkin's thinking is clearly shaped by the modern analytical tradition, but he is also obviously suspicious of where such thinking, strictly pursued, leads (it leads, inescapably, to positivism). Dworkin's recourse to literary and aesthetic models as a way of reflecting differently upon "analytical jurisprudence" is thus perfectly understandable; it follows a precedent set by John Stuart Mill over a century ago.

The attempt to describe norms that are conventional or paradigmatic, that is, authoritative under certain conditions but not possessing logical or universal validity, does help to loosen things up a bit. But how loose things get depends on whether we think of conventions grammatically in terms of mental constraints or socially in terms of prevailing customs (as when one says that what counts as a normal interpretation of anything will always be determined by practices current among those who interpret things in one another's company). On this point most of us divide (loosely) into grammarians and pragmatists, and here is where most arguments in current literary criticism go on. Thus grammarians will be inclined to worry about interpretations going too far and needing to be restrained—or, much to the same point, going on

---

Gerald L. Bruns, professor of English at the University of Iowa, is the author of *Modern Poetry and the Idea of Language* and *Inventions: Writing, Textuality, and Understanding in Literary History.* He is currently working on the early history of interpretation.

according to "tacit" rules or unconscious forces that require to be made theoretically explicit or to be polemically exposed—whereas pragmatists will speak of "conditions" of a worldly rather than mental nature that enable a particular interpretation to be intelligible (perhaps even authoritative) among those who hear it. Having (at last) arrived at this point, one might be in a position to reflect in earnest about the politics of interpretation.

I would have thought that the study of what goes on in legal interpretation would have taken us to this point more directly, but it appears that legal scholars do not think about interpretation much differently from the way most literary grammarians think about it. (There's not much room for disagreement between Dworkin and Fish.)

What would happen, however, if you were to think of legal interpretation not just in terms of the epistemological relationship between the reader of the law and the writer of it, or between the analyst of jurisprudence and the legal proposition, but also in terms of the hermeneutical relationship between tradition and application?[1] On this hermeneutical model it would not be enough to say that the law is a product of an intention or the work of writing; it would not be enough to say that the law exists in the form of propositions or as a text. On the contrary, on this model the law is simply a superior example of what is meant by tradition. Tradition is the mode of being of the law. The law comes down to us from the past, that is, from a world of situations different from our own, and our hermeneutical task is to determine the applicability of the law to the situation in which we now find ourselves, where we are called upon to address issues and resolve dilemmas that are particular to the moment at hand, or where we are required to provide for what the law, up until now, had never foreseen. Interpretation in this event will be an adjudication of past and present, or between a written text, the history of the understanding of it (that is, the history of its application), and the question currently to be decided. The law will be that by which we understand our present situation, even as our situation will throw its light upon the law or help us to understand the law more fully, or in a way that will enable the law to remain forceful instead of lapsing into a merely documentary existence.

The virtue of this model is that it raises straightforwardly the question of whether anything can be meant by strict construction except the recovery of what the law means in relation to the situation in which it was originally handed down. (Notice that this is different from speaking of the law simply in relation to an original intention.) A strict constructionist might well read the law in the same attitude as that of the legal historian—one who reads, however, not only with an eye on the

---

1. See Hans-Georg Gadamer, *Truth and Method*, ed. Garrett Barden and John Cumming (New York, 1975), esp. pp. 274–304.

proposition of the law and the legal and political views of its author but also in explicit consideration of the legal, social, and political situation in which the law made its first appearance in the world. A loose construction, on this view, would be simply the attempt to determine the sense of the law in relation to subsequent and perforce different states of affairs, or where the law is required to be applied in a new way and not as if the present had to be judged strictly in light of the past. Hence the appropriateness for the law of the hermeneutical formula that to understand at all is to understand differently. How loose an interpretation would become would presumably depend upon how far a subsequent state of affairs differed from the situation that originally caused the law to be handed down. The point here is that the law is always answerable to a situation for its meaning. On this model, there could be no interpretation, whether strict or loose, that was not also, and at the same time, an application of the law to a concrete, historical situation.

In other words, this model allows us to speak of the historicality of the law or of the historicity of legal meaning. Much more explicitly than art or literature, the law is worldly rather than mental. This is why the study of what goes on in the law is so important for an understanding of interpretation and particularly for an understanding of the politics of interpretation. I assume one does not have to argue for the worldliness of politics.

Whether recourse to the hermeneutical model of tradition and application will prove fruitful for an understanding of interpretation will depend, of course, on what sort of *nature* we want interpretation to have. Dworkin writes as if he had decided already (or perhaps necessarily) in favor of a romantic theory of interpretation, where interpretation means recovering or construing an intention in behalf of a text. It does not matter whether this construction is said to correspond to an author's original intention, or whether it is a construction produced by a reader on his own (or on someone else's) authority. The point is that the relationship between text and mind takes precedence over (and frequently excludes without a second thought) the relationship between text and situation. I take it that Dworkin would not count application to a situation as part of the *nature* of interpretation, since application clearly goes on outside of the relationship between mind and text. Thus one would have to speak of the *use* of a legal text the way one speaks of the *use* of the Bible as something secondary to the understanding of it. To my ear, however, it sounds odd to speak of the *use* of the law.

This helps to explain why Dworkin does not find it strange to speak of the rewriting of the law, even though it would be excessive, or at least highly metaphorical, to say that the application of a law is a rewriting of it. To apply the law is not to change it but to take it in a certain way—now this way, now that—depending on the situation that calls for the law to be applied. The traditional division of letter and spirit reflects the belief that the law must always be open, not to new versions of itself but to the special claims of unforeseen human situations. A good law possesses, as Dworkin himself suggests, foresight. The question of how the law is in fact altered by its subsequent interpretations is interesting, but it does not seem to me that Dworkin really addresses this question. My opinion is that the romantic model of interpretation makes it difficult to address this question in a way commensurable with its interest. The romantic model discourages the idea of law as a tradition of understanding in favor of the idea that the law is a text or "chain" of texts, a tradition of authorship rather than of interpretation.

For this same reason I think that the romantic model, with its preference for minds as against situations, discourages attempts to understand the political nature of interpretation. It is this preference for minds that has inspired us to think of political reality chiefly in terms of ideology, or in terms of what goes on in our minds, rather than in terms of action, or what goes on in the world. Thus Dworkin thinks of politics in terms of a philosophy or a theory held by a judge as he sits down to write a legal text. On this view, in order to be political it is enough to have convictions of one sort or another; politics in this sense reduces to belief.

My own position would be that the hermeneutical model of tradition and application is much more open to political reflection than the romantic model with its relentless epistemological bias in favor of authors, texts, and readers. Here I can only refer to the Habermas-Gadamer debates, which have raised the question of how to understand the essentially political nature of tradition, with its power of binding us to it, and also the question of appropriation, which is the activity that defines our relationship to tradition, and which, incidentally, cannot be adequately described as a mental act, since it is, like application, an action that draws its meaning and purpose from the situation in which it takes place. It seems to me that in the context of these hermeneutical themes, the law, with its extraordinary power of binding us to itself, becomes philosophically interesting in a way that novels and poems figured as aesthetic or textual objects can never be.

This metaphor of binding deserves a final word. From a phenomenological point of view, it is in the question of how a text becomes binding upon a community that the subject of politics and interpretation begins to emerge with proper clarity and as a substantive issue. One needs to speak here of the conditions that enable a text to become forceful and to hold a community in its power. This community does not need to be a community of readers or interpreters—one does not have to be a reader of the law in order to be bound by it, in fact one need not even be aware of the law in order to stand under its jurisdiction. Our relationship to the law is not epistemological; it is not a relationship of reader and text, not even when the interpretation of the law—how it applies specifically to us in the way it constrains our action—is what is in question. However, it would be the case that to understand the law means to understand how it is binding upon us; or, alternatively, to understand the law would be to be able to say what would happen if it were applied in this or that way. One can see here an analogy between Law and Scripture as binding texts, and one can also speak of the power of the literary text to bind us aesthetically—to hold us in thrall or in captivity, spellbound or in a trance, which has always been the prerogative of beauty, magic, and monumental achievement. In each case, however, one needs to understand that these legal, sacred, and enchanting texts do not come down to us on their own but belong to traditions of understanding that underwrite these texts in ways that we have not examined. The politics of interpretation has yet to be discussed.

Critical Exchange III:

The Politics of Interpretation

The Politics of Theories of Interpretation

E. D. Hirsch, Jr.

All interpretations originate in politics, which is to say, in values. As in other human affairs, we choose one activity over another because we have values or habits which could be termed, in the broadest sense, "political." Scientific interpretations are no exception. Scientists prosecute many more interpretations in medicine than in astrophysics for reasons that are not themselves scientific. But even if our interpretations do originate in politics, must it follow that their final character is also politically predetermined? Not necessarily. Although we may ask an interpretive question for political reasons, its answer may not necessarily be dictated by those same reasons. If we ask whether laetrile cures cancer, our question is political in origin and could have a politically predetermined answer. But we might be more interested in getting at the truth of the case. Some scientific interpreters might be much more interested in the truth about laetrile than in having the answer come out on one side or the other. Their main political interest might be in getting the answer right, getting the interpretation right.

No doubt an interpretation can be politically predetermined. That would happen if the interpreter cared more about fostering a particular result than about being right. A proponent of political predetermination could object that the aim of being right is also a political aim which usually masks a conservative, status-quo ideology. That could be so, for who would deny that the aim of being right is itself an ideology and therefore political? On the other hand, isn't it also the case that the ideology of truth is structurally different from any other political ideology? Under other political ideologies, we desire and sometimes pre-determine a particular result. Under the ideology of truth, our desire for a particular result is subordinated to our desire to be right. Our orienta-tion is a posteriori, not a priori. We decide after the fact, not before the fact. And even if an interpreter is told that there are no disinterested, theory-free facts, the ideologue of truth still *tries* to operate under the control of some "other," of some reality beyond predisposition and pref-erence.

This choice between predetermined and revisable, postdetermined interpretations has an importance beyond textual exegesis. Interpreta-tion is the central activity of cognition. Our perceived meanings or, metaphorically, our objects-in-the-world are always interpreted con-structs, that is, they are always other than the "language" of vibrations (light, sound, heat, and so on) through which we perceive them. We always perceive (construct) something other than the language through which we know that thing. This constructive process is interpretation. Since our interpretations are always other than the language by which they are construed, a space of uncertainty exists between the vehicle (our language of cognition) and the meanings (or objects) interpreted from it. This gap, which cannot be overcome, is a space in which different inter-pretations can be played out. Hence there is always an element of un-certainty in every possible sphere of interpretation. This gap of un-certainty is the defining feature of interpretation—the gap between the vibrations and the object, between the vehicle and the meaning, between the sign and the signified.

One of the most influential ideas of our time, which is drawn from Kant, is that the form of our interpretive constructs is predetermined from within, rather than imposed from without. This is the doctrine of the synthetic a priori. Since Kant, the most significant development of the a priori has been its application to the changing realm of culture rather than just to the permanent structures of our minds.[1] This cultural

1. The term "a priori" is of course familiar to readers in philosophy. Taken loosely and in a broad sense it sometimes means the totality of prior givens which enable us to interpret experience: such prior cognitive frameworks as space, time, object, person, and so on. These givens "ground" our experience; we never confront experience with an innocent eye—on that point all parties agree, including empirical psychologists of various schools. The more specific doctrine that I call the "a priori" here is a Kantian form of idealism which holds that we cannot change our formative givens in a fundamental way. Thus, I use the term a priori to specify the doctrine of the *unrevisability* of our cognitive givens. This unrevisability doctrine, central to Kant, is held, *mutatis mutandis,* by the cultural Kantians of our time. The a posteriorist, by contrast, while not contesting the idea of

E. D. Hirsch, Jr., professor of English at the University of Virginia, is the author of numerous works, including *Validity in Interpretation* and *The Aims of Interpretation.*

Kantianism has had an immense influence on the popular mind as well as on recent theories of interpretation. Language, for instance, is said to predetermine the forms and limits of our ideas. Culture, in a still larger sense, is said to predetermine the forms and limits of all realities in our world. Ideology is said to predetermine the results of our inquiries, and politics (the extension of ideology) is said unconsciously to predetermine our interpretations.[2]

The staying power of the synthetic a priori comes partly from the impossibility of refuting it. Any empirical counterclaim advanced against the a priori can always be seen as occurring within its predetermined forms. Thus, even Kant's original claims about the a priori character of causality and Euclidian space, though long since called into doubt by physics, still leads a vigorous life in science and philosophy—on the grounds that such "refutations" already take place within an a priori structure. But the impossibility of refuting the a priori also means the impossibility of confirming it. Therefore, the a posteriori is also alive and well in the sciences, if not in the humanities. Philosophically speaking, the *revisability* of interpretations is an idea just as impregnable as the predetermination of interpretations. The a priori claim that a revision "always already" occurs within a predetermining scheme can be met by the counterclaim that the scheme itself is revisable. Revisability is as reasonable an ultimate as predetermination. Thus, neither the a priori nor the a posteriori could ever be definitively proved or falsified. Both are "metaphysical" concepts. The political a priori is a metaphysical doctrine that, like all forms of cultural Kantianism, has no compelling logical application to practice. Psychologically, of course, it strongly influences practice, as do all metaphysical beliefs. But, logically, the doctrine of the synthetic a priori is neutral with regard to politics. Any and all interpretive choices are equally governed by its imperial force. If a political a priorist tried to distinguish between authentic and inauthentic interpretations, his theory would lose its epistemological generality and would then be seen to be what it really is: rhetorical exhortation. Exhortations imply choices; metaphysical a priori theories imply universal necessity. A priorism is, in Hegel's phrase, "the night in which all cows are black."

cognitive frameworks, does contest the idea of their unrevisability. There is no limit in principle to the revisability and corrigibility of our interpreted constructs. The a posteriorist regards our prior givens as provisional rather than as ultimate. For extended discussion, see Arthur Pap, *The A Priori in Physical Theory* (New York, 1946), and the recent translation of Hans Reichenbach's pathbreaking book of 1919, *The Theory of Relativity and A Priori Knowledge,* ed. and trans. Maria Reichenbach (Berkeley, 1965).

2. See, e.g., Fredric Jameson, *The Political Unconscious* (Ithaca, N.Y., 1981), p. 17: "This book will argue the priority of the literary interpretation of literary texts. It conceives of the political perspective not as some supplementary method, not as an optional auxiliary to other interpretive methods current today . . . but rather as the absolute horizon of all reading and all interpretation."

The only philosophical theory that could describe the politics of interpretation would be one that described interpretive choice as a theoretical ultimate. This, cultural Kantianism fails to do. Its political efficacy lies in its secondary rhetorical effect—in its suggesting that we do not *really* have ultimate interpretive choices, in its showing that we cannot *really* prosecute "objective" interpretations, and so on. My contrary thesis here is that interpretive choice can be described in ultimate theoretical terms and that interpreters can and should resist the rhetorical force of the a priori if they want to make those genuine political choices. I wish to expose the sheer rhetoricity of a priori theories and at the same time explore the most basic political choices governing interpretation.

Let me start with a simple example. Suppose that we are interpreting Blake's well-known poem "The Lamb." According to most a priori theories, we are not fully able to recover the original meaning of that poem. My efforts at historical reconstruction would necessarily be filtered through my own prior cultural or political categories. Since that secondary filtering cannot be overcome, the attempt to do so is an illusioned charade. To this, the ideologue of truth replies: "Maybe; but in light of multiple vectors of evidence, and continual revision, we might sometimes achieve an accurate reconstruction, despite our cultural predispositions." One of the interpretive questions that has been asked of "The Lamb" is whether its original meaning was sentimental or ironic.[3] Many readers take the poem to be straightforward, while Harold Bloom and others take it to be ironic. So far, that is an argument about how *Blake* meant the poem to be taken. It is, therefore, the typical, old-fashioned kind of question to which historical interpretation has always dedicated its energies. Can we, should we, try to resolve that historical question?

In providing this example, I do not intend to discuss the merits of ironic versus nonironic historical interpretations of "The Lamb." I use it to focus instead on another kind of choice. A mere disagreement between ironic and nonironic readings is a disagreement about the nature of an historical event, namely, Blake's original purpose. But there is another and more fundamental kind of disagreement which underlies the real politics of interpretation. It is a disagreement about the norm of interpretation itself. Whatever may be said for choosing an ironic versus nonironic reading of "The Lamb," the choice would usually be governed by the attempt to reconstruct an historical event. But a very different kind of norm would be invoked if the interpreter decided to choose whatever meaning seemed preferable quite apart from its historicality. I

3. The a priorist would quickly observe that these questions themselves fall within a predetermined scheme. Yes, they do. The more fundamental issue is whether these pregiven questions (or frameworks) are themselves revisable. If so, they are predetermining only in a "Pickwickian" sense, that is, not absolutely predetermining at all.

shall argue that *this,* rather than disagreements about an historical event, is the ultimate political choice in interpretation.

To explain this basic choice, it will be convenient to steer a detour around all the irrelevant questions that have been raised concerning authorial intent. I confess to feeling personally responsible for some of the irrelevancies surrounding this issue, and I am at work on a book that tries to untangle those interesting problems. But that is another topic. In order to perceive the political essence of interpretive norms, we can circumvent the whole question of author psychology by adopting a semiotic account of interpretation.[4] Instead of referring an interpretation back to an original author, we could just for the moment refer it back to an original code or convention system. Let us say that the historical interpretation is the one that applies an earlier code system to the text. For instance, one historical problem in interpreting "The Lamb" would then be whether the original code system made the poem ironic or not. This semiotic account can be simplified still further if, instead of talking about particular conventions, we talk about the choice between different convention systems and we pretend that the choice is controlled by the selection of a particular "cypher key." Under this semiotic account, then, the political choices of interpretation have to do with the choice of a cypher key.

This model for dealing with the matter has another advantage besides simplicity. It not only avoids digressive issues connected with author psychology, it avoids confusions about the social and conventional character of linguistic meaning. Those who attack the author norm, or some other individualistic version of interpretation, rightly observe that no one could ever impose an arbitrary linguistic mode of interpretation. Nobody can act quite as Humpty-Dumpty did when he told Alice that he could make a word mean whatever he wanted it to mean. But the real political question does not concern the conventionality versus the individuality of interpretation; it concerns, rather, the locus of authority. *Who* chooses the cypher key?

It would be wrong to see this as anything but a political question. When Alice asked Humpty-Dumpty whether he really could apply any arbitrary meaning to a text, Humpty replied, "The question is, which is to be master—that's all." Although the choice of cypher keys is not unlimited, as Humpty-Dumpty claimed, that fact does not have the theoretical importance which some theorists have attached to it. Much more important is the fact that several conventional codes can be applied to any text. That being so, Humpty-Dumpty's question, *Who* shall be master? *Who* shall choose the cypher key? is the ultimate political question in interpretation.

4. By no means do I consider semiotics to be an adequate account by itself, nor have I abandoned the principle of authorial intent. I have simply set aside that issue for the moment in order to focus on the nature of basic political choices in interpretation.

In the a priori view, the real chooser of norms is, of course, willy-nilly the reader. So, the short answer to the question, Who chooses the cypher key? is the reader chooses. But this short answer hides an important detail, namely, that the reader can decide to let somebody other than the reader choose the cypher key. Under that kind of arrangement, the reader, like the ideologue of truth, would take an a posteriori approach. The reader would accept whatever cypher key seemed, on the evidence, to be one that governed a past event. That kind of interpretation is inherently and necessarily historical, since it always refers back to a decision made in the past. Therefore, the structure of the historical norm, which is always open to revision, is different from the structure of a norm based on ad hoc reader preferences, which are open only to change by whim.

This distinction between a reader's present, ad hoc choice of a cypher key and the reader's decision to accept somebody's past choice of a cypher key is applicable to every act of interpretation whether of speech or of writing. Let us call the reader's choice of his or her own preferred cypher key a "self-governing" or "autocratic" norm. In contrast, let us call the reader's decision to defer to a past choice of a cypher key an "other-governing" or "allocratic" norm.

This distinction is more general and useful than "author-norm" and "reader-norm," since "author" usually refers to an original author and to one single historical event, and that is not the only important kind of historical interpretation in the humanities. Take this example of nonauthorial yet historical interpretation. Suppose I say that my goal is to interpret "The Lamb" not as Blake understood it but as Bloom did. It is true that I would then conceive of Bloom as a kind of secondary author, and so I would still be conducting an interpretation under a kind of authorial norm. Structurally speaking, to conduct an accurate historical interpretation of Bloom's "Lamb," I would follow the same sort of allocratic procedure as I would in conducting an historic interpretation of Blake's.[5] Both would be historical a posteriori investigations, and evidence relevant to either historical event would help provisionally in choosing the cypher key to be applied. The historical, allocratic norm would govern both, thus giving that term a greater generality than authorial norm.

This autocratic/allocratic distinction holds also for those interpretive communities celebrated by Stanley Fish. In the example just mentioned, I might choose to belong either to the Blakean community or the Bloomian community, but in both cases I would have to look back to an historical act of choice by which the community adopted some cypher key which defines it as an interpretive community. On the other hand, if

5. I have noted before that a priorist, autocratic critics invite us to pursue an allocratic interpretation of their own writings—thus recognizing implicitly the reality of the autocratic/allocratic choice—by their actions if not by their theories.

I decided to disregard *anybody's* choice of a cypher key and chose the one that I preferred, or that seemed right to me, or that was always already given to me, I then would be following the autocratic norm. It's true that such a norm is not merely an individualistic one, since the cypher key I have chosen consists of social conventions. Moreover it's true that other people might independently choose as I do, thus making me a member of a transindividual interpretive community. But the only way anyone could deliberately join me in that community would be to practice an historical, allocratic interpretation in order to find out what the cypher key of my community was. To do that they would have to engage in straightforward allocratic, historical interpretation.

From the standpoint of logical coherence and even legitimacy, I do not think there is anything to choose between an autocratic or allocratic norm of interpretation. I must not object that the autocratic norm is linguistically implausible, since any choice of any cypher key would actualize some existing conventional, legitimate system. But this very plurality of legitimate code systems requires an interpreter to choose one cypher key rather than another, without having any *logical* reason for choosing one over another. So, the decision between the autocratic and the allocratic norm is at bottom an ethical and political choice, and only that. Against Fish's insistence that interpretation is always already autocratic (whether we know it or not) must be set P. D. Juhl's insistence that interpretation is always already allocratic (whether we know it or not).[6] Both of these monolithic descriptions are rhetorical exhortations masked as theory (whether they know it or not). For the claim that we have no choice between the autocratic and allocratic norms is in practice an exhortation to make one choice rather than another; the political choice itself is very real. Ironically, the a priori theory that interpretations are always already politically predetermined is an evasion of the very real political choice between the autocratic and allocratic norms.

Let me briefly summarize the analysis to this point. First, the politics of interpretation resides in the choice between the autocratic and allocratic norm. Under the autocratic norm, authority resides in the reader, while under the allocratic norm, the reader delegates authority to the reconstructed historical act of another person or community. Second, autocratic interpretation is not in principle revisable except by accidental change of preference, whereas allocratic interpretation is revis-

---

6. Stanley Fish: "No longer is the critic the humble [allocratic] servant of texts whose glories exist independently of anything he might do; it is what he [autocratically] does, within the constraints embedded in the literary institution, that brings texts into being and makes them available for analysis and appreciation" (*Is There a Text in This Class?* [Cambridge, Mass., 1980] p. 368). P. D. Juhl: "There is a logical connection between statements about the meaning of a literary work and [allocratic] statements about the author's intention such that a statement about the meaning of a work *is* a statement about the author's intention" (*Interpretation* [Princeton, N.J., 1980], p. 12).

able ex post facto on the basis of changing theories and evidence about a determinative historical event. Hence the autocratic norm is a priori and incorrigible; the allocratic norm is a posteriori and revisable. The authority to choose one of these norms lies with the reader, and this choice, being free, is ethical or political in nature; it is entirely unconstrained by epistemological considerations. I will now amplify this last point.

Broadly speaking, those who claim that all interpretations are prestructured by cultural schemas may be called "idealists": Nihil in interpretatione nisi prius in schema. In the deepest sense, in this view, interpretation is always already autocratic, that is, always constituted by the reader's predetermining schemas, whether cultural, political, or what have you. The contrasting view, that interpretation can be either autocratic or allocratic, assumes that the truth about an historical event (say, another person's choice of a cypher key) is something that might be objectively known despite the influence of cultural schemas. Those who hold this latter view may be called "realists." (In recent polemics, they are called "naive realists" with "naive" being a nonseparable prefix.) This contrast between realism and idealism seems to be the epistemological bottom line between the autocratic–a priori and the allocratic–a posteriori principles in interpretation. As Richard Rorty has pointed out, the rise of a prioristic, post-modern literary theory is a resurgence of nineteenth-century cognitive idealism—in a new guise.[7]

In calling the views of Foucault, Fish, Derrida, and de Man "idealistic," I do not suppose that I score a telling point. Quite the contrary. Idealism is one of the durable positions in epistemology. Furthermore, when I assume the philosophical respectability of cognitive realism, I do not suppose that philosophical problems are circumvented merely by appealing to the universal realism of common sense. The realist position, like the idealist, is beset by embarrassments (though they happen to embarrass me less than the idealist ones). My observation that postmodern theorists are idealists has a practical, not a philosophical, motivation. I want to claim that *neither* epistemological idealism nor epistemological realism has any direct practical bearing on the politics of interpretation. Ultimately, nothing argued at the grandiose level of epistemology, such as the turn from "logocentrism" (Derrida), "the historical a priori" (Foucault), "the political unconscious" (Jameson)—none of these high-level generalizations can decide the issue between autocratic and allocratic norms of interpretation.

This truth is acknowledged by both idealist and realist arguments in their more thoughtful forms. A sophisticated idealist would never deny that we can act like realists—that is, act *as though* our beliefs were indefinitely revisable and *as though* they sometimes corresponded to reality.

7. See Richard Rorty, "Nineteenth-Century Idealism and Twentieth Century Textualism," *The Monist* 64 (1981): 155–74.

The idealist simply proposes that these beliefs are either wrong or un-justifiable. A sophisticated realist, on the other side, would not deny that our beliefs might, at some unknown, ultimate, not-yet-defined level be unrevisable, nor that we couldn't sometimes *act* like idealists if we wanted to. People do act like realists even if the idealist position should (in some undemonstrable way) be right; they can go on acting like idealists, at least in the sphere of intellectual affairs, even if the realist position should (in some undemonstrable way) be right. This influence on action constitutes what I would call the "rhetoricity" of interpretive theories. In short, even a sophisticated idealist would grant that we can *act* as though we have a choice between autocratic and allocratic interpretation, and action is the medium of politics and ethical choice.

Thus, to be a realist or idealist in an ultimate epistemological sense is rather like being a theist or an atheist. Such metaphysical belief is a psychological sanction for action rather than a position that can be proved or demolished. Neither position is certainly decidable. As Pascal once observed with regard to religious belief: "We are incapable of knowing either what He is or whether He exists. This being so, who will be so rash as to decide?"[8] Yet, in practical terms, as Pascal also observed, we are put into the position of having to choose, that is, having to act. Pascal proposed, therefore, the further question: How shall we act in the absence of any decisive grounding for theism or atheism? He argued that in the end such a decision had to be a gamble: "Let us weigh the gain and loss in calling heads—that God exists. Let us estimate the two chances. If you win, you win everything. If you lose, you lose nothing. Do not hesitate then, gamble on His existence."

The analogy between Pascal's famous wager and the situation of the interpreter is this: no philosopher, including whichever current sage one chances to revere—Foucault, Heidegger, Rorty, Derrida—has put forward a decisive argument for preferring an idealist over a realist view. As with theism versus atheism, no decisive ground could be put forward. This fact has led Rorty, for example, to adopt what he calls a "prag-matist" (in my view, an idealist) position. But the same facts and argu-ments which lead Rorty to repudiate traditional epistemology can, fol-lowing Pascal's argument, lead to a different imperative, namely: choose that position among the two undecidable ones which sanctions the most desired or desirable practice. The modern version of Pascal's wager would be: Let us weigh the practical gain and loss in calling heads—that is, that objective historical truth exists. Let us estimate the two chances. If you win, you win something. If you lose, you lose nothing. Do not hesi-tate then, gamble on the existence of objective truth.

How does that wager play itself out in the sphere of interpretive practice? I have suggested that the realist (a posteriori) viewpoint sanc-

8. Pascal, *The "Pensées,"* trans. J. M. Cohen (Harmondsworth, 1961), no. 451.

tions the possibility that we might sometimes know the objective truth about the following historical question: What was the code of conventions that somebody chose at some historical moment to apply to this text? To the extent that this historical question might be answered correctly, historical, allocratic interpretation might be carried out correctly. Allocratic interpretation, moreover, is the only sort that can in principle be revised, and thus make practical use of scholarship, evidence, logical argument, and could even look to the possibility of empirical progress. Allocratic interpretation, then, offers the possibility of being wrong. Autocratic interpretation, by contrast, is always right or, more exactly, could be neither right nor wrong; it offers itself no external standard with respect to which it could be one or the other. That doesn't nullify autocratic interpretation, which in a particular circumstance could serve the more valuable purpose.[9] But such a value judgment would be a practical, not a theoretical, decision. It would be a genuine political decision.

What have I tried to achieve with this Pascalian argument? First, a negative goal—I want to remove the delusion that philosophers, theorists, and cultural sages could ever definitively show that objective truth is impossible or that accurate historical interpretation is a delusion. They have not shown this, and they cannot do so. This means that the field of interpretation is, in its large theoretical structure (and despite some genuine technical advances), more or less where it was 100 years ago. That is where big theoretical issues are likely to remain, along with the big epistemological questions to which they are allied—forever in the realm of the never-surely-decidable. I have argued that the practical consequence of this theoretical aporia is not to subordinate the politics of interpretation to big theory but rather to subordinate big theory to politics. In the end, the debate between autocratic and allocratic interpretation is a political, not an epistemological, issue. And the political issue is: What sort of culture do we want to foster?

When I was first starting on a career in scholarship, I was thrilled to read Max Weber's lecture to young scholars called "Wissenschaft als Beruf," "Science as a Vocation." No one will venture to contend that Weber neglected or underestimated the cultural, personal, social, and

9. For instance, we might prefer to interpret Benjamin Franklin's proverb "A rolling stone gathers no moss" *autocratically* as an admonishment to keep out of a rut, rather than allocratically as his admonishment to stay put. In this case my own preference is for the autocratic interpretation, and I would be willing to argue that in certain contexts it is the more valuable one. But in making that political choice, I haven't the slightest need of epistemological theories.

political influences that impinge upon the seeking of objective truth. He was the master of that subject. Yet no one has spoken of the goal of objective truth—*Wissenschaft*—with more impressive and infectious fervor than Weber did in that 1919 lecture. His message to young scholars was: In the academy beware of politics as an adjunct to science and, equally, beware of science as an adjunct to politics. Fourteen years later, in 1933, Ernst Krieck, the first Nazi rector of the University of Frankfort, pronounced in his inaugural address a different view: "Nowadays the task of the universities is not to cultivate objective science, but soldier-like, militant science"—a succinct statement of the politics of interpretation.[10]

The word "science" *(Wissenschaft)* of course meant to Weber more than the word "science" can convey in English, since *Wissenschaft* embraces the humane as well as the natural sciences. Indeed the interpretation of texts was one of the memorable examples Weber used in his lecture to illustrate what he meant by science:

> Whoever lacks the capacity . . . to come up to the idea that the fate of his soul depends upon whether or not he makes the correct conjecture at this passage of this manuscript may as well stay away from science. He will never have what one may call the "personal experience" of science. If you lack this strange intoxication, ridiculed by every outsider, if you lack this passion . . . you have no calling for science and should do something else. For nothing is worthy of man as man unless he can pursue it with passionate devotion.[11]

In the 1980s, we who find ourselves in the profession of textual interpretation cannot respond wholeheartedly to Weber's example. Too many children of science have already pored over too few canonical texts

10. Gerald Graff has quoted Mussolini in a similar vein in *Literature against Itself* ([Chicago, 1979], p. 188), and the two examples together show pretty well that the politics of interpretation, though now espoused by the intellectual Left, is not the exclusive property of any political group. Nor is it only a characteristic of the Right to take on the cloak of realism and "spurious objectivity." A political leftist can be an ideologue of truth and a realist-objectivist—such was Lenin. See the account of Lenin's realism and objectivism in Roger Trigg, *Reality at Risk: A Defense of Realism in Philosophy and the Sciences* (New York, 1980), pp. 27–39. See also the spirited defense of realism by a thinker whom nobody would call conservative, Paul Feyerabend, especially in his "Realism and Instrumentalism," *Realism, Rationalism, and Scientific Method: Philosophical Papers* (Cambridge, 1981), pp. 176–202. Another example would be the cohabitation of realism with Maoism in Hilary Putnam a few years back (see Putnam, *Philosophical Papers,* 2 vols. [London, 1975]). All of this further documents a primary thesis of this essay: that politics and epistemology are independent variables and that the attempt to sanction either of them by the other is basically a rhetorical (political) maneuver.

11. Max Weber, "Science as a Vocation," *From Max Weber: Essays in Sociology,* ed. and trans. H. H. Gerth and C. W. Mills (New York, 1946), p. 131.

with just the intensity that Weber so inspiringly described. The allocratic exegesis of our major canonical texts has pretty much reached a dead end because our texts are few and our interpreters, over the years, have been many. The allocratic exegesis of Chaucer, Shakespeare, Spenser, and Milton on narrow literary principles cannot provide us with an endless frontier, and it is the closing down of that New Critical frontier rather than "advances" in epistemology which now draws our profession toward autocratic interpretation (for which the frontier no doubt seems endless, even if intellectually uninteresting). But it is doubtful that autocratic interpretation will long continue to satisfy either its practitioners or its readers.

Unfortunately, the forty-year-old doctrine that textual exegesis (interpretation in the New Critical sense) is our only legitimate critical activity still holds sway in the academy. It is the hidden assumption that joins allocrats and autocrats together; it is the common bond of Derridians and Robertsonians. But without this assumption that only interpretation of the "literary work" is legitimate, would we still feel an institutional pressure to continue to produce new readings whether autocratic or allocratic? Does not this restriction of our activity to interpretation in a narrow sense betray a certain habit-bound lack of imagination? What is needed for the future is a genuinely new frontier for allocratic, historical interpretation—interpretation with an object, but with a new kind of object.

This can be found only in history. And it will have to be found beyond the narrow boundaries of the aesthetic and the text-in-itself. Interpretation, as the general term for cognition, is hardly limited to the boundaries of texts or to the arbitrary confines of fiction and poetry. Historical interpretation is the humanistic pursuit par excellence and embraces not just texts but contexts. On this score, the contextual urgings of Foucault (minus his a priori obfuscations) are all in the right direction.

Whether professors of literature shall find new objects of historical inquiry is a political, not a theoretical, question, even though in a large perspective it is perhaps an insignificant political question. Sometimes, however, academic humanists do enter the sphere of significant politics in addition to their considerable influence in the classroom. Once in a while some professor in the humanities is named to an important panel or called on to testify before a legislative committee. When that happens, the humanist is never asked to put forward an autocratic interpretation of texts or of the world. The humanist is called on to tell, as far as possible, the objective historical truth about some facet of reality that he or she has closely studied. Nobody outside the academy is interested in autocratic interpretations, even when they follow the conventions of some established interpretive community. Interpretation is intellectually interesting inside the academy mainly when it is trying to determine some objective historical truth. It is politically significant outside the academy *only* when it is trying to determine some objective historical truth. Whether or not an interpretation *is* telling the historical truth is a question that nobody can answer. Nonetheless, the interpreter's decision to try to tell this truth is a genuine political decision, too important to be yielded by default to the rhetoricity of interpretive theories.

Is There a Politics of Interpretation?

Walter Benn Michaels

The answer I want to give to the question posed by my title is no, but for that answer to be at all plausible it must also be severely qualified. In some sense, there surely is a politics of interpretation; acts of interpretation are often influenced by political interests, and even more often they have political consequences. The fact that the interests may be unconscious and the consequences unintended does not make them any less political. But, in asserting the importance of politics in interpretation, several of the contributors to this volume—E. D. Hirsch, Hayden White, to some extent Wayne Booth, and several others—have meant something more than the relatively uncontroversial points made above. They have meant that interpretation is a political act in the sense that interpretations or ways of interpreting are the results of "free" (Hirsch) political choices for which we should be held "responsible" (White), as we are for other political acts.

These claims seem to me wrong, not so much in their emphasis on politics as in their account of interpretations as freely chosen and their consequent invocation of the ethical categories we think appropriate for describing choices. I want to begin by suggesting that interpretations are not chosen and that the only sense in which interpretation is an act is when it is taken as the understanding of meaning in general, not of the meaning of any particular text. Next, I want to give some account of the epistemological scenario that leads so many theorists to think that interpretations are chosen. My example here will be Ronald Dworkin's "Law as Interpretation" which, never explicitly concerned with choice,

nevertheless relies heavily on the epistemology that makes choice seem
so central. Last, I want to show how the attempt to imagine a situation in
which interpretations *could* be chosen is fundamentally incoherent since
it involves constructing a scenario in which the possibility of choice depends on the impossibility of having any criteria by which to choose. My
examples here will be White's "Politics of Historical Interpretation" and
Hirsch's description of "the ideology of truth" in his "Politics of Theories
of Interpretation."

Obviously there is some relation between interpretation and choice.
You can, for example, choose to interpret a text as opposed to putting it
aside or throwing it away. Going one step further, you can choose to do a
Marxist (or deconstructive or psychoanalytic or whatever) interpretation
of the text you have decided to interpret. This sort of thing is the staple
of introductory graduate courses in method. But can you choose to
believe your Marxist interpretation? Here is where it seems your choices
run out. For while it makes sense to say that you can choose to interpret a
text and that you can choose to interpret it in a particular way, it does not
make sense to say that you can choose to believe that the interpretation
you come up with is true (or false, or good or bad). Indeed, it does not
make sense to say that you choose to believe anything at all. If, in Booth's
example, you believe that Rabelais is sexist, can you choose to believe
that he isn't? Did you ever choose to believe that he was? You might, of
course, become convinced that he was, but are being convinced and
freely choosing the same? The whole point of being convinced is that we
cannot help believing whatever it is we are convinced of, whereas the
whole point of freely choosing is that we might freely choose otherwise.

One might conclude from this that the point is to separate the activity of interpretation into its two constituent parts: acting and believing.
But these two parts are not really parts at all, they are just two descriptions of the same thing. Under one description, interpretation is an act
you can control; under another description, interpretation is an account
of a meaning over which you have no control. To separate these would
be to imagine that you could choose to do interpretation in general
without thereby committing yourself to some particular interpretation
that you will not have chosen. But this is just what you cannot do. To
interpret is to interpret something, and while you can choose to interpret, you cannot choose the meaning of the thing you are interpreting.

Walter Benn Michaels, an associate professor of English at the University of California, Berkeley, is working on the relation between literary and economic forms of representation in nineteenth-century
America.

Hence the question of *whether* to interpret may be considered, in these terms, a political one, but the question of what interpretation to produce may not—the first question involves a choice, the second does not.

Nevertheless, many, if not most, of the authors in this volume forcefully assert that interpretation is, as Dworkin puts it, "essentially political." For Dworkin, interpretation in law depends on the choice between competing political theories; for White, what is wrong with traditional history is that, pretending to be "above politics," it prevents people from creating the "openly political" history they need, a history endowed by them "with a meaning for which they alone are fully responsible" (p. 134); and for Hirsch, the ultimate choice in interpretation is "entirely unconstrained by epistemological considerations," and "being free, is ethical or political in nature" (p. 328). Clearly the account of interpretation underlying these views is radically different from mine. It must involve a very different notion of the kinds of constraints at work in interpretation, by which I mean not necessarily a sense that there are fewer or different constraints but that, however many there may be and whatever they are, they come into play independent of and outside of the actual interpretive process; they are obtained before interpretation takes place or applied after it takes place. This vague-sounding concept can be made more concrete by looking for a moment at Dworkin's explanation of how his own theory of interpretation avoids the pitfalls of relativism.

In Dworkin's view, "interpretation of a piece of literature attempts to show which way of reading . . . the text reveals it as the best work of art" (p. 253). Put this way, the "aesthetic hypothesis" immediately looks vulnerable, since an interpreter of (say) *Hamlet* might have a conception of what the best tragedy would be which had nothing in common with *Hamlet*. Why would we want to call this a reading of *Hamlet*? Wouldn't the aesthetic hypothesis simply license interpreters to produce the works of art they liked best and call their creations interpretation? To forestall this objection, Dworkin asserts the necessity of a distinction between "interpreting and changing a work": "Interpretation of a text attempts to show *it* as the best work of art *it* can be, and the pronoun insists on the difference between explaining a work of art and changing it into a different one" (p. 253). Dworkin thus answers the charge of relativism by reminding us that interpretation is not absolutely free; it is always interpretation *of* something. And this something ("it") will permit a number of interpretations but not just any interpretation. Hence the text itself serves as a "constraint," admitting without prejudice all interpretations that attempt to explain it but prohibiting all those that attempt to change it.

The problem with this defense is that it depends heavily on an aspect of the interpretive process that Dworkin leaves mysterious—our relation to the text before or independent of our decision as to what its best interpretation is. That for Dworkin we must have some such relation is clear since he thinks that in choosing an interpretation we distinguish between readings that explain the text and readings that alter it by comparing them to the text itself. But what is our relation to the point of comparison? Have we already got an account of its meaning? Have we already interpreted it? Since Dworkin's central argument is for the aesthetic hypothesis as an account of interpretation, the answer to these questions would seem to be no—interpreting a text is attempting to show "which way of reading . . . the text reveals it as the best work of art." But the problem with this negative answer is obvious: If we don't know what "it" means, how can "it" possibly serve as a constraint on our choice of its best interpretation? How can we use something meaningless to adjudicate between two different accounts of its meaning?

Hence, for the "it" to do what Dworkin wants it to do, we must apparently have some sense of what it means. But the problems posed by this positive answer are as great as those posed by the negative one. For if we do already know what "it" means, we have clearly not relied on the aesthetic hypothesis to discover this meaning, and so the aesthetic hypothesis turns out to be dependent on some other unstated account of interpretation. Is it formalist or, despite Dworkin's polemic, intentionalist? And, whatever it is, once we've got it, why do we need the aesthetic hypothesis? If the best meaning turns out to be identical to the meaning we've already got, then it is superfluous; and if it turns out to be different, then it has changed the meaning we've got and, by Dworkin's own stipulation, is inadmissible.

Of course, in defense of the aesthetic hypothesis it could be argued that the alternatives as I have depicted them are far too extreme. When we find ourselves in the position of selecting the best meaning, we are neither completely uninformed about the text nor in full possession of an interpretation. Rather, we are confronted with a range of equally plausible possible meanings, and so we can, indeed must, choose among them on the basis of our own (nonsubjective) political or aesthetic theoretical preferences. (As we shall see, some version of this scenario lies at the heart of all the arguments for a politics of interpretation.) But this more moderate description of what we need to know before the aesthetic hypothesis can come into play is vulnerable to the same objections made against the more extreme versions. How did we get our range of choices? What model of interpretation gives us a limited number of meanings and offers no clue (reliable or not) as to which among them is the most plausible? And, assuming such a model can be produced, what warrant do we have for choosing among the meanings it gives us? If a text really is ambiguous with respect to any one of a number of possible meanings, how does preferring one of those meanings to all the others count as explaining rather than altering? Don't we change an ambiguous text when we choose to interpret it as if it were not ambiguous?

These difficulties all derive from Dworkin's conception of interpretation as a two-stage process: first an encounter with the text, then a decision about what the text means. In an argument for the politics of interpretation, the virtue of this conception is that it makes room at the second stage for choice—within the constraints first provided by the "fact of the work," you are free to choose a meaning according to political (or ethical or aesthetic) criteria. The defect of this conception, at least for someone with Dworkin's interests, is that it fails to establish any coherent relation between its constraints and its choices. The constraints turn out to be available only by a prior act of interpretation, and that interpretation makes the choices either supererogatory or illegitimate— supererogatory if you are choosing a meaning you have already got, illegitimate if you are choosing a meaning different from the one you have already got. But of course one might not share Dworkin's sense of the need for constraints, and so one might accept an epistemological scenario much like his and be utterly unscandalized by its inability to fend off relativism. This, in fact, is the position occupied by White, who welcomes relativism as "the moral equivalent of . . . skepticism" which he sees in turn as "the basis of social tolerance" (p. 125 n.12).

In contrast to the conservative view of historical events as "understandable" and the radical view of them as "explainable," White thinks that the "truth" of history is its meaninglessness. This meaninglessness represents to him not a catastrophe but an opportunity, since it is "meaninglessness which alone can goad the moral sense of living human beings to make their lives different for themselves and their children, which is to say, to endow their lives with a meaning for which they alone are fully responsible" (p. 134). Crudely (but not, I think, inaccurately) put, White thinks that recognizing history's meaninglessness makes it necessary, or at least possible, for people to choose a history for themselves: since "there are no grounds to be found in the record itself for preferring one way of construing its meaning rather than another," people should see themselves as free to "impose . . . a meaning where none is to be found" (p. 136). Interpretations of history are thus political acts in the fullest sense—the products of political choices for which people should be held responsible.

For Dworkin, the fact of the text itself is constraining but only partially so; hence, it makes choice possible while at the same time limits the number of possible choices. For White, the fact of the text is replaced by the meaninglessness of "history . . . 'in itself,' " and so, he thinks, "any historical object can sustain a number of equally plausible descriptions" (pp. 143, 137). In its political application, this epistemological pluralism enables him to applaud both the Zionist and Palestinian interpretations of their relations with the world and one another as "morally responsible" responses "to the meaninglessness of a certain history" (p. 141). The meaninglessness at the first stage guarantees the possibility of moral choice at the second stage.

White thus thinks of the Israelis and the Palestinians as having chosen their interpretations of history from any number of equally plausible descriptions, as if the question of whether these interpretations were true had been superseded by the question of whether they were morally responsible. But do the Israelis and the Palestinians understand their interpretations in this light? Surely they think of their own descriptions as not merely morally responsible but true, and they think of other descriptions as not merely morally reprehensible but false. Indeed, White himself finds it impossible to sustain a description of their views as simply moral. He calls the Zionist interpretation of the Holocaust "a product . . . of a conception of Jewish history that is conceived to be meaningless to Jews insofar as this history was dominated by agencies, processes, and groups who encouraged or permitted policies that led to the 'final solution' of the 'Jewish Question' " (p. 141). But what can it mean to call a history described in this way "meaningless"? The Jews in White's example may regard their history with horror and anger but not because they cannot understand it—they understand it perfectly well and, understanding it, hate it. There is precisely no point in their understanding of their history (or in the Palestinians' understanding of theirs) at which that history seems meaningless and in need of an interpretation. White is nevertheless forced to imagine such a moment because without it historical interpretation ceases to be a political act and becomes only an account of what seems true.

At the heart of his argument is thus the sense that really nothing seems true: "It is often overlooked," he writes, "that the conviction that one *can* make sense of history stands on the same level of epistemic plausibility as the conviction that it makes no sense whatsoever" (p. 135). In one respect, at least, this is right—there are no epistemological reasons for thinking either that we can or cannot understand historical events. In other words, nothing about the conditions of our knowing things guarantees that we really do know them correctly. But, of course, the conviction that we can and do understand at least some historical events does not stem from an original claim that we are epistemologically well equipped to do history: it stems from the fact that we often give explanations of historical events that seem convincing, to ourselves and to others. White's doubt as to whether such explanations can be true imagines, like its Cartesian ancestor, a moment in which one simply has no beliefs whatsoever, no sense at all of what is true. But where Descartes thought he could argue himself out of this position (grounding all belief in the *cogito*), White thinks the appropriate behavior is not to argue but to choose. Believing nothing, he chooses to believe whatever he wants to believe, or rather whatever seems morally responsible to believe.

In arguing against this position I have claimed that no one ever is in the position of believing nothing and so no one ever is required (or enabled) to choose beliefs irrespective of how true they seem. But one might also argue that if you *could* inhabit the space of epistemological innocence imagined by White, you would not be free to choose your beliefs but would instead be unable to make any choices at all. And, surprisingly enough, the clearest example of this interpretive predicament occurs not in White's unabashedly utopian manifesto but in Hirsch's defense of the ideology of truth. The surprise, of course, is that Hirsch and White, who are usually thought to hold opposing theoretical views, turn out to hold almost identical views: where White thinks the idea that we can know the truth about history "stands on exactly the same level of epistemic plausibility" as the idea that we cannot, Hirsch argues that no "decisive argument" has been put forward for thinking that we can know the truth about anything and indeed that "no decisive ground *could* be put forward" (p. 329; italics mine).

Hirsch's remarks, coming from a longtime defender of objectivity and determinate meanings, may strike some readers as a little odd or at least unusually concessive. But one of the merits of our topic, the politics of interpretation, is that it brings out commitments which, not in themselves political, are nevertheless required if interpretation is to be political. Another way of putting this is to say that White and Hirsch can achieve their political differences only by sharing a prepolitical commitment to the primacy of choice, and so Hirsch, like White, is willing to do whatever seems epistemologically necessary to maintain this primacy. Hence, instead of urging the merits of what he calls realism over those of what he calls idealism, he maintains here that the two positions are equally plausible—the difference between them is "undecidable." By which, of course, he does not mean that one should make no decision. The point is rather that since one can make no decision on the basis of what seems true (they both seem true), one must choose instead on political or ethical grounds. Hirsch is implicitly acknowledging the point made earlier—you can't choose what will seem right to you. And since he is interested above all in arguing that the choice of a theory of interpretation is a real political and ethical choice, he must imagine a situation in which neither realism nor idealism seems more right. Realists who become realists because they think that realism is closer to the truth than idealism are no good for his purposes since they can't be said to have chosen realism, they have just been convinced by the arguments. Hence, to become an "ideologue of truth," Hirsch must suppress his sense that the arguments for realism are better than the arguments for idealism. He wants to choose truth, not simply say what seems true to him. Indeed, he cannot be in a position to choose truth until nothing seems true to him. The ideologue of truth cannot become an ideologue of truth until he gets himself into a position where he hasn't the faintest idea what the truth is. Only then, unconstrained by any idea of what might really be true, can he assert the moral superiority of his principled attachment to the truth.

As a description of what it means to be a realist or idealist, this seems fairly implausible. In their writings, at least, Richard Rorty, Stanley Fish, and others argue for their views and against the views of others just as if they believed that their views were right and others wrong. And Hirsch himself cannot quite shake the sense that realism's superiority to idealism may not be merely moral; admitting (or perhaps boasting) that realism is just as "beset by embarrassments" as idealism, he nonetheless confesses to being "less" embarrassed by realist failings than by idealist ones. But the fact that realists and idealists characteristically believe that they hold whatever views they hold because those views are more accurate than other views need not constitute a fatal objection to Hirsch's account of the situation. Perhaps they are just invariably mistaken about their own motives; and perhaps once their mistake is pointed out to them they will agree that the question as to whether idealism or realism is more true is just a "rhetorical" question and should be replaced by the real political question: "What sort of culture do we want to foster?" (p. 330).

This is Hirsch's question, and he has an answer to it, although not a very direct one. His answer takes the form of an anecdotal contrast between Max Weber's "passion" for objective science and the Nazi Ernst Krieck's preference for "soldier-like, militant science," in which Weber apparently stands in for allocratic realists and Krieck for autocratic idealists. I say "apparently" for Hirsch nowhere makes this allegory explicit, but, of course, the introduction of Weber and Krieck makes no sense except as an example of the political and ethical issues at stake in the choice between realism and idealism. The moral here seems to be that we should choose realism because idealism leads to fascism. Which is not to say that the humanist has no responsibility to the state; occasionally, Hirsch notes, a professor in the humanities will be "named to an important panel or called on to testify before a legislative committee," and on such occasions the government is interested in "the objective historical truth," not in the "conventions of some established interpretive community" (p. 332). Realism thus has two political advantages over idealism: it keeps us from becoming intellectual servants to fascism, and it equips us to become intellectual servants to liberal democracy American-style.

Many (although not all) would agree with Hirsch that these advantages really would be advantages if the assertions supporting them were true; that is, if idealism really did lead to fascism and realism really did support American democracy. But quoting one Nazi who sounds (to Hirsch) like an idealist does not exactly prove that all, most, or any idealists besides Krieck are fascists. And the notion that we should choose truth because some day a Senate subcommittee might want the real story on Wordsworth does not sound too convincing either. But, of course, the real problem with Hirsch's account of why we should choose truth is not that his political arguments in support of the choice are so weak. No doubt he could think of some better arguments. The real problem is that to have any arguments for or, for that matter, against choosing truth, you have to already know the truth about a great many things. And if you already know many truths (that idealism leads to fascism, for instance), in what sense can you be in the position Hirsch imagines the ideologue of truth starting out from—utterly agnostic as to whether we can ever know the truth?

To see the problem here, we have only to remember the delicacy of Hirsch's original position. He understands that for truth to be a matter of choice, it must not in the usual sense be a matter of conviction. As ideologues of truth, we must have no convictions whatsoever about whether we can or do know the truth; hence, if we choose to act as though we can, our choice is a "free" one, not a response to what already seems to us true. Anyone, however, who actually occupied the position prescribed for Hirsch's ideologue could have no criteria by which to make a choice. How could you argue for any historical relation between idealism and fascism if you were not already committed to the idea that you could and did know things about the past? And if you did not think you knew something about the past, how could any arguments about the relation between idealism and fascism possibly lead you to choose realism?

Hirsch, then, encounters in more spectacular fashion the same difficulty faced by White in his account of how and why people should choose their interpretations of history. The difficulty for White is that to make a choice you have to have some criteria, and if you argue that these criteria too are freely chosen, you just push the problem one step further back. The difficulty for Hirsch is more spectacular because he thinks not simply that the truth of history is up for grabs but that truth itself is at issue. In both cases, however, the difficulty is a function of an epistemological scenario in which the interpreter is understood first as believing nothing and second as responding to this "meaningless" or "undecidable" situation by choosing beliefs for political reasons. I have tried to indicate two lines of argument against this scenario. One is that the first stage—having no interpretation, believing nothing—does not ever take place and hence that the conditions required for the second stage—the moment of ethical choice—never exist. The other is that even if the first stage were possible—if we could for a moment believe nothing—the second stage would still be impossible since, believing nothing, we would have no criteria for making the choices we would have imagined ourselves as free to make. Of these two arguments, the second is, at least potentially, more damaging since it suggests that the whole project of conceiving interpretations as chosen is incoherent and thus wrong from the start. But the first argument, not that we cannot make choices but that we never need to, seems to me a good deal more relevant to a description of the way interpretation actually works.

I have attempted no such description here, but regular readers of *Critical Inquiry* will know that Steven Knapp and I have tried to give something like a positive account of interpretation in "Against Theory" (vol. 8 [Summer 1982]). There we argue that our understanding of what a text means and what its author intends it to mean are the same thing and that interpretation is just a matter of trying to figure out this intention. This is a position that, Dworkin says, no intentionalist can hold. "An intentionalist cannot," he writes, "suppose that all his critics and those he criticizes mean, when they say 'interpretation,' the discovery of the author's intention. Nor can he think that his claims accurately describe what every member of the critical fraternity in fact does under the title 'interpretation.' If that were so, then his strictures and polemics would be unnecessary" (p. 258). Dworkin is certainly right about what critics *say*, but he is wrong about what critics *do*. In "Against Theory," we argue that every interpreter is always an intentionalist, that language can be rightly understood only as a set of intentional acts, and hence that to use language at all (as speaker or hearer, writer or reader) is to acknowledge the centrality of intention. The whole point of this polemic is that, practically speaking, it is unnecessary. Dworkin wonders what "sort of a theory" it could be that would insist on the superfluousness of its own claims, and the answer, of course, implicit in our title, is no sort of theory at all.

What are the consequences of such a view for the politics of interpretation? Obviously negative. If interpretation is just a matter of finding out what some author meant, then it can hardly be understood as a political act like voting or campaigning or kneecapping. But even if we set aside the intentionalist account of interpretation, we have no good reason for thinking of interpretation as a political activity in the sense that voting and kneecapping are. This does not mean, of course, that interpretations may not be put to political uses, or that they may not be a consequence of political beliefs, or even that the decision to do interpretation in the first place may not be a political one. But it does mean that we are not morally responsible for our interpretations and that our commitment to the idea of truth is no cause for ethical or political satisfaction. The notion that interpretation is a moral and political issue depends, as I have tried to show, on an implausible and ultimately incoherent epistemology. That writers whose views and purposes are in many respects utterly opposed should share this epistemology testifies to the strength of the desire to install free choice at the heart of interpreta-tion. This seems to me a mistake, but it should be clear that, in arguing against what Booth calls "freedom of interpretation," I am not in any way attempting to undermine the notion of free choice. Indeed, my fundamental strategy involves contrasting acts which seem to us free (like voting) with acts which do not (like believing). That this contrast may itself be open to question is notoriously the case; perhaps nothing is freely chosen. But, assuming that some things are, I have tried only to show that interpretations are not and hence that there is no politics of interpretation.

The Politics of Interpretations

Gayatri Chakravorty Spivak

It is difficult to speak of a politics of interpretation without a working notion of ideology as larger than the concepts of individual conscious-ness and will. At its broadest implications this notion of ideology would undo the oppositions between determinism and free will and between conscious choice and unconscious reflex. Ideology in action is what a group takes to be natural and self-evident, that of which the group, as a group, must deny any historical sedimentation. It is both the condition and the effect of the constitution of the subject (of ideology) as freely willing and consciously choosing in a world that is seen as background. In turn, the subject(s) of ideology are the conditions and effects of the self-identity of the group as a group. It is impossible, of course, to mark off a group as an entity without sharing complicity with its ideological definition. A persistent critique of ideology is thus forever incomplete. In the shifting spectrum between subject-constitution and group-constitution are the ideological apparatuses that share the condition/effect oscillation.

I am always obliged to quote Stuart Hall's excellent historical study of ideology whenever I refer to the notion in the U.S. context: "two radically different styles of thought—the European (where the concept [of ideology] has played a significant role) and the American (where it had up to [1949] been largely absent). . . . An interesting essay could be written on what concepts did duty, in American social theory, for the absent concept of 'ideology': for example, the notion of norms in struc-tural functionalism, and of 'values' and the 'central value system' in

[Talcott] Parsons."¹ I would add to this list a concept of the "unconscious" as a continuous and homogeneous part of the mind that is simply "not conscious."

I will here suggest the usefulness of a broader concept of ideology and note some marks of ideology at work: conserving the sovereign subject; excluding a monolithic Marx(ism); and excluding or appropriating a homogeneous woman. The text of the symposium does not contain a hidden ideological truth but is operated by as it operates an imperfectly hidden ideological agenda; that is one of its structural alterities.

It is in Stephen Toulmin's "The Construal of Reality" that the absence of a theory of ideology is felt the most; for Toulmin's project is to undo the disciplinary-ideological opposition between the human sciences and the natural sciences, between logic and rhetoric.² Toulmin writes: "What P. F. Strawson calls a 'conceptual framework,' and Bakhtin—*a little misleadingly*—an 'ideology,' the theoretical physicist thus calls a 'treatment' " (p. 113; italics mine). A broader notion of ideology would of course situate the merely conceptual framework within a more extended and heterogeneous field. The physicist's treatment, a decision where "the interpretive element is quite explicit," would occupy a different place within a field similarly heterogeneous and extended.

In the absence of a heterogeneous concept of ideology, Toulmin's text produces definitions that keep the ideology-constitutive distinctions between center and periphery, explanation and interpretation, cause and effect intact:

1. Stuart Hall, "The Hinterland of Science: Ideology and the 'Sociology of Knowledge,' " *On Ideology*, Working Papers in Cultural Studies, no. 10 (Birmingham, 1977), p. 9. See also Douglas Kellner, "A Bibliographical Note on Ideology and Cultural Studies," *Praxis* 5 (1981): 84–88.

2. See Newton Garver, intro. to Jacques Derrida, *"Speech and Phenomena" and Other Essays on Husserl's Theory of Signs*, trans. David B. Allison (Evanston, Ill., 1973), for a summary of the opposition between logic and rhetoric in the disciplinary ideology of philosophy. Not only does Garver parallel Toulmin but he also describes Derrida's work as seeking to undo that opposition. Whatever the validity of Garver's broader analysis, it is interesting to speculate what Toulmin would make of such a suggestion of propinquity. I should perhaps add here that Derrida is suspicious of the concept of ideology because, in his view, it honors too obstinate a binary opposition between mind and matter.

Gayatri Chakravorty Spivak is professor of English at the University of Texas at Austin. She is the translator of Jacques Derrida's *De la grammatologie* and is presently finishing a book in the areas of Marxist feminism and deconstructive practice.

In dealing with [peripheral factors that may influence the work of professionals], we are centrally concerned with a larger and more turbulent world of *causes*, for example, the interactions between the professionals and their human contexts, as well as with any consequential influences that contextual factors may exert on the professional argument itself. [Pp. 110–11]

Accordingly, in both today's postmodern natural and human sciences and the critical disciplines of the humanities, we are concerned with a mix, or blend, of explanation and interpretation. [P. 115]

A critical view of the subject of ideology would call the clarity of these distinctions into question and thus ask the critic to address a less simplified view of the world. It would deconstitute and situate (*not* reject) the "we" who experiences the productivity of alternative investigative postures, the "legitima[cy]" and "power" of the "acceptable standpoints." Such a view does not allow for a personal-subjective category to be set up over against an intellectual-interpretive category either, since it would see complicity between the constitution of subjectivity and the desire for objective identity.

These problematic distinctions are necessary for Toulmin's argument because it cannot accommodate the concept of ideology. The never fortuitous choice of normative metaphors sometimes seems to suggest this necessity: "There is more *temptation* to present *all* [author's italics] interpretations in the human sciences as being essentially political in character than there is in the physical sciences. Still, it is a *temptation* that we *ought to resist*" (p. 108; italics mine). This resistance wins a space for us where it is possible to overlook the tremendous ideological over-determination of the relationship between the "pure" and "applied" sciences, as well as their relationship with private- and public-sector technology and the inscription of the whole into the social and material relations of production. All is reduced to the classical split between subject and object—"two-way interactions between the observer and the system being observed" (p. 112). If the clarity of the theory is dependent upon so stringent a reduction, it loses persuasive value when applied to the sociopolitical scene. A statement like the following, concluded from the subject-object premises I quote above, remains *merely* theoretical, *normed* into ethical decoration: "That being so, there is, a fortiori, no longer any reason to assume that studying human beings from a scientific point of view necessarily involves dehumanizing them" (p. 112).

Ronald Dworkin attempts to cut loose from the task of recovering the legislator's intention in the interpretation of the law. He takes literary interpretation as a model, however self-divided, and offers us two interesting and related versions of the subject of lawmaking: a pluralized subject that is one link in a chain of supplementations and a double subject who is at once writer and reader. I shall give a brief example of how a general theory of ideology would enhance his argument.

Following through the notion of the pluralized subject in the interpretation of the law, Dworkin is obliged to call a halt at a point which is worth remarking:

> Perhaps [putting together a collective novel sequentially] is an impossible assignment . . . because the best theory of art requires a single creator or, if more than one, that each have some control over the whole. But what about legends and jokes? I need not push that question further because I am interested only in the fact that the assignment makes sense, that each of the novelists in the chain can have some idea of what he or she is asked to do, whatever misgivings each might have about the value or character of what will then be produced. [P. 263]

That Dworkin has made fiction and the law each other's tenor and vehicle is in itself significant. In this passage yet another possibility is implicit. Legends and jokes are phenomena where the condition-effect relationship with ideology (in the U.S. the preferred word in this case is "culture") is readily granted. The point might be to see that the difference between these phenomena and the novel is, in the ideological view, one of degree rather than of kind. The single author also has only "*some* idea" of what he is asked to do, for the *entire* idea is spread like a map across the text of ideology. The nonexhaustive constitution of the subject *in* ideology (which is in turn constitutive *of* ideology) would include, in this revised version of Dworkin's argument, the so-called ideology-free language of Western European and U.S. law. It is only a homogeneous, isomorphic, and adequate cause-and-effect view of social production that would advance the doubtful claim that "liberalism can . . . be traced [to] . . . a discrete epistemological base . . . [which] could be carried forward into aesthetic theory and there yield a distinctive interpretive style" (p. 270). The view I am describing would suggest that such items are related as the interanimating complicity of the shifting components of an ideological system. The productive undecidability of the borderlines of politics, art, law, and philosophy, as they sustain and are sustained by the identity of a composite entity such as the state, is operated by the heterogeneous and discontinuous concept of ideology. Lacking such a concept, Dworkin is obliged to indicate it in the name of a unifying philosophy. It is the strength of his essay that the unification is not seen as a necessarily sublating synthesis: "I end simply by acknowledging my sense that politics, art, and law are united, somehow, in philosophy" (p. 270).

If Dworkin, without pronouncing the word, seems to make room for a broader concept of ideology, Donald Davie would choose to "bypass" its workings: "Doubtless such interrelations exist, and doubtless they can be exploited to sinister purposes. Rather than inveighing against this, or (with [Stanley] Fish) more or less blithely acquiescing in it, we can best spend our time bypassing the network altogether, as the truly independent and illuminating interpreters always have" (p. 49).

One cannot of course "choose" to step out of ideology. The most responsible "choice" seems to be to know it as best one can, recognize it as best one can, and, through one's necessarily inadequate interpretation, to work to change it, to acknowledge the challenge of: "*Men* make their own history, but they do not choose the script" (italics mine).[3] In fact, I would agree with Edward Said that the ideological system that one might loosely name as contemporary USA expects its poets to *seem* to choose to ignore it and thus allows its businessmen to declare: "Solid business practices transcend ideology if you are willing to work for it."[4]

Both Hayden White and Said concentrate upon ideological formations—the former with respect to a group identity called "a discipline," the latter with respect to the discipline in the service of the group identity called "the state." I shall not linger on their arguments here. It is my feeling, however, that in the absence of an articulated notion of ideology as larger than and yet dependent upon the individual subject, their essays sometimes seem a tirade against the folly or knavery of the practitioners of the discipline. The relationship between art and ideology—in this case, bourgeois ideology in the *broader* sense—is T. J. Clark's explicit subject matter. In his comments on Terry Eagleton, Clark suggests that, "in the years around 1910, . . . it was possible for Marxist intellectuals . . . to see themselves as bourgeois . . . [and oppose] the ideologies of a bourgeois élite" (pp. 212–13 n. 6). The critical practice Clark describes is close to what I suggest as an alternative to Davie's conviction of "bypassing" the ideological network or Said and White's ideology-free accusations.

It is Wayne Booth who pronounces the word "ideology" most often; and in his essay, it is the word "language" that performs the curious function of covering over the absence of a broader concept of ideology. In Mikhail Bakhtin's text, language is not immediately understood as verbal discourse. Ideology as language is an effect that assumes a subject for its cause, defining it within a certain convention of signification. For Booth, language as ideology is the expression of a (group) subject who must constantly assure us, and himself, that he is not merely of the group but also unique. There is a moment in the essay when Booth is almost within reach of Bakhtin's position, a position that today would call itself the politics of textuality, seeing that the network of politics-history-

3. Karl Marx, "The Eighteenth Brumaire of Louis Bonaparte," *Karl Marx, Frederick Engels: Collected Works,* trans. Richard Dixon et al., 15 vols. (New York, 1975–), 2:103; all translated material has been modified when necessary.

4. Armand Hammer, "A Primer for Doing Business in China," *New York Times,* 11 Apr. 1982.

society-sexuality, and the like, defines itself in ideology by acknowledging a textual or weblike structure. Booth's language, however, like Toulmin's, articulates Bakhtin's position within a vocabulary of free choice: "Each language we take in is a *language,* something already blessed or cursed with symbolic richness, with built-in effects of past choices, invitations to new choices, and a knowledge that some choices are in fact better than the others" (I quote from an earlier version of the essay). Bakhtin's implicit dialectical hinging of subject and language in/of ideology seems to elude Booth here.

When Booth thinks of ideology as beliefs and practices rather than, strictly speaking, language or voice, it is possible for him to hint at this dialectical structure: "Ideology springs from and in turn influences systems of belief and human practice" (p. 56).* Yet he constantly reduces the situation of art and ideology to the conscious-unconscious opposition that I invoked at the outset as one of the substitutes for ideology upon the Anglograph scene. Bakhtin is laudable because he "plac[es] as high a value as he does on the deliberate introduction of counter-ideologies," whereas "conventional Marxists [hold that] . . . selves and societies are radically dependent on the ideologies of art" (earlier version). Here consciousness and the unconscious are understood with reference to a pre-psychoanalytic model, as if they belonged to a continuous system where the mark of good practice was to raise the unconscious into consciousness. The strongest diagnosis of ideological victimization in this view is: "I confess, with considerable diffidence, that I think the revelation [of Rabelais' double standard] quite unconscious" (p. 71). The sense of ideology as free choice is the goal: "The question we now face, then, as believers in feminist (or any other) ideology, is this: Am I free, in interpreting and criticizing a work of art, to employ that ideology as one element in my appraisal of the artistic value of that work?" (p. 62).

It is not too far from the truth to suggest that this freedom of choice by a freely choosing subject, which operates the essays of Toulmin, Davie, Dworkin, and Booth, is the ideology of free enterprise at work—recognizably a politics of interpretation. That is why we accepted as common sense that the best theory of art required a single author. Within a broad concept of ideology, the subject does not lose its power to act or resist but is seen as *irretrievably* plural. In that perspective, all novels are seen to be composed as serials by various hands. Dworkin's analogy between literature and the law can, in that perspective, be read differently as a *case* of this politics of interpretation, just as the novelist and his reader, requiring a single creator and therefore overlooking the novel's being an effect within a larger text, are another case. In a serial novel by various hands of the kind Dworkin presupposes, the narrative is supposed to advance while preserving some presumed *unity,* whereas in

*Booth has since changed the word "ideology" to "art" in this sentence.—*Editor's note*

a series of interpretations of the *same* law, we have not progress but repetition—each repetition presumably claiming to be most adequate to the ipseity of the law in question. Lawyers, even when they, like Dworkin, grant the actual plurality of interpretations, are bent on the search for the "real" law, the "proper" law, the "best" interpretation, its single true intention. As cases of ideology formation, Dworkin's analogy and its attendant definition of authorship seem to betray their "politics"—free enterprise and the rule of law.

"Betray their 'politics.'" A better formulation of this is to be found in Pierre Macherey: "We always eventually find, *at the edge of the text,* the language of ideology, momentarily hidden, but eloquent by its very absence."[5] Let us consider moments on the edges or borders of some of these essays, the ideological traces that allow them to define their interiors. Such a gesture will yield a hint of their politics as well, a politics of the freely choosing subject who, divining his own plurality, breaks his theory as he takes a stand.

Such a definitive moment comes at the end of Stanley Cavell's piece: "If deconstruction, as in de Man's recommendation of it, is to disillusion us, it is a noble promise and to be given welcome. Disillusion is what fits us for reality, whether in Plato's terms or in D. W. Winnicott's. But then we must be assured that this promise is based on a true knowledge of what our illusions are" (p. 202). I am not altogether convinced by Cavell's reading of deconstruction in this essay, especially when he associates de Man and Derrida without much differentiation.[6] I will merely remark that the assurance to the subject of true knowledge, a self-evident ideological requirement for self-evidence, is the one thing deconstruction cannot promise. A number of arguments that Cavell undoubtedly can anticipate might be advanced here: there is no disillusion without illusion; a true knowledge of illusions can lead to a knowledge of reality only as that which is not illusion; to predicate reality as the death of illusion is to ignore the syntax or practice that passes from illusion to reality via dis-illusion; not to acknowledge that deconstruction distinguishes itself from dialectics precisely by this attention to the syntax that is otherwise ignored in the interest of the semantics of reality is not to speak of deconstruction at all.[7] I shall not dwell upon these arguments here but suggest that Cavell's interpretation of voice and writing is also in the interest of this ideological requirement.

5. Pierre Macherey, *A Theory of Literary Production,* trans. Geoffrey Wall (London, 1978), p. 60; italics mine.

6. See Cavell, "Politics as Opposed to What?" (p. 197). For a discussion of this difference, see my review of *Allegories of Reading: Figural Language in Rousseau, Nietzsche, Rilke, and Proust* by Paul de Man, *Studies in the Novel* (forthcoming). See also my "Revolutions That as Yet Have No Model: Derrida's *Limited Inc,*" *Diacritics* 10 (Winter 1980): 17–40.

7. For an articulation of deconstruction as syntactic or micrological resistance against the hegemony of semantics or macrology, see Derrida, "White Mythology: Metaphor in the Text of Philosophy," trans. F. C. T. Moore, *New Literary History* 6 (Autumn 1974): 73–74.

Cavell writes: "For me it is evident that the reign of repressive philosophical systematizing—sometimes called metaphysics, sometimes called logical analysis—has depended upon the suppression of the human voice. It is as the recovery of this voice (as from an illness) that ordinary language philosophy is . . . to be understood" (p. 197). Derrida admires this project and relates it to Nietzsche's attention to the force of language rather than its signification alone. What Derrida critiques is what Cavell seems to be showing here: the tendency common to most radical philosophies, including speech-act theory, to perceive their task as the restoration of voice. The systematic philosophies, on the other hand, although their aura seems to be altogether mediated and therefore akin to the common understanding (here Cavell's) of writing, develop systems which depend upon *phono*centrism as their final reference. Thus the commonsense perception—that systematic philosophies suppress and radical philosophies restore voice—depends upon varieties of phonocentric assumptions. "Writing" in this view becomes the name for that which must be excluded so that the interiority of a system can be defined and guarded. "The essential predicate of [the] *specific difference*" between writing and the field of voice is seen in such a reading as "the absence of the sender [and] of the receiver *(destinateur),* from the mark that he abandons."[8] The place of such an understanding of writing within a self-professed project of the restoration of speech should be clear.

Writing as the name of that which must be excluded as the other in order to conserve the identity of the same can be related to Macherey's other formulation: "What is important in the work is what it does not say. This is not the same as the careless notation 'what it refuses to say,' although that would in itself be interesting. . . . But rather than this, what the work cannot say is important because there the elaboration of the journey is acted out, in a sort of journey to silence."[9] It is not surprising that, within a definition of writing as a *deliberate* withholding of voice, the one sense of "turn"— in Thoreau's "You only need sit still long enough in some attractive spot in the woods that all its inhabitants may exhibit themselves to you by turns"—that Cavell does not (cannot?) mention is "trope," the irreducible turn of figuration that is the condition of (im)-possibility of any redemption of voice.

It is in terms of saving the freely choosing subject whose concept insinuates itself into the most radical commun(al)ist politics of collectivity that Said uses *écriture* as a code word suggesting (I cannot be sure, since the word hangs unexplained on the borders of his essay) linguistic reductionism at a second remove. The thumbnail explanation of *écriture* as the excluded other that I have given above would have helped his gen-

8. Derrida, "Signature Event Context," trans. Jeffrey Mehlman and Samuel Weber, *Glyph* 1 (1977): 179, 177.

9. Macherey, *Theory of Literary Production,* p. 86.

eral argument: "A principle of silent exclusion operates within and at the boundaries of discourse; this has now become so internalized that fields, disciplines, and their discourses have taken on the status of immutable durability" (p. 22).

Since I find myself more than usually sympathetic with Said's position, I must point out another mark of ideology at work in his essay. The essay is written by a subject who is not only freely choosing but is also a star within a star system. There is no recognition or support here for the thousands of teachers and students across the country who are attempting to keep alive a critical cultural practice. Their track is to be picked up not only in journals such as *Radical Teacher* or *Radical America* but in course syllabi, in newsletters, and increasingly on the rolls of young teachers denied tenure. In order to recognize these workers, pedagogy as political interpretation must be seriously considered. A phenomenon cannot be nonexistent when a political spectrum extending from Michael Harrington to *U.S. News and World Report* accounts for its workings.[10] Said's statement that "the Left [is] in a state of intellectual disarray" is indeed true with respect to political sectarianism (p. 9). But if our own field of work is seen as outside of generalizations such as "high culture here is assumed to be above politics as a matter of unanimous convention" and also outside of the perspective of self-described Marxist "celebrities" (the third item in the title of Regis Debray's *Teachers, Writers, Celebrities,* which Said cites) who seem obliged to hear themselves as lonely personalities proselytizing in the wilderness, then the extent of our predicament, that *all this effort* goes awry, is seen as a much more menacing problem.

An awareness of solidarity with the ongoing pedagogic effort would have allowed Said to step out of the chalk circle of the three thousand critics and recognize that the task—"to use the visual faculty (which also happens to be dominated by visual media such as television, news photography, and commercial film, all of them fundamentally immediate, 'objective,' and ahistorical) to restore the nonsequential energy of lived historical memory and subjectivity as fundamental components of meaning in representation"—is attempted every day by popular-culture teachers on the Left (p. 31). I quote *Tabloid* as a metonym: "Many of our articles over the past months have given examples of this daily subversion—women in the home mutating the 'planned' effect of TV soap operas, political activists creating pirate radio stations, the customization of cars, clothing, etc."[11]

One of the most productive moments at the "Politics of Interpreta-

10. See Michael Harrington, "Getting Restless Again," *New Republic,* 1 and 8 Sept. 1979, and David B. Richardson, "Marxism in U.S. Classrooms," *U.S. News and World Report,* 25 Jan. 1982.

11. "On / Against Mass Culture III: Opening Up the Debate," *Tabloid* 5 (Winter 1982): 1.

tion" symposium was an exchange between Davie and Said. Davie singled out Said's work for Palestine (Lebanon in Davie's script) as an example of patriotism. Said appropriately amended that praise by suggesting that he was working for the Palestinian state to establish itself so that he could then become its critic. Consciousness of national identity is marked by the use to which it is put. The thin line between national liberation and maintenance of the ideology of the state must be kept clean by the critic's vigilance. Otherwise, Davie's endorsement of patriotism becomes the condition and effect of a political ideology that denies the workings of an economic multinationalism. The production of archaic politico-nationalist explanations, irreducibly asymmetrical with the economico-multinationalist network, shows itself most brutally as war and most divisively as the indoctrination of the labor force. The mechanics of that denial are implicit in Davie's lament:

> By thus loftily declaring ourselves "citizens of the world" [which is of course not what I suggest above] we cut ourselves off not just from the majority of our fellow-citizens at the present day but from the far more numerous multitude of the dead. For there can be no doubt that to Virgil and Dante and Machiavelli, to Milton and Wordsworth, to Washington and Jefferson and Walt Whitman, the patria was meaningful, and its claims upon us were real and must be honoured, in just the ways that this sort of modern enlightenment refuses to countenance. [P. 35]

The march of capital has cut Davie off from the network that sustains and is sustained by a full-fledged patriotic ideology. He undoubtedly has no objection to the mode of sociomaterial production (since his deliberate stance is to bypass it) that shores him up in Tennessee or in front of a high-toned audience in Chicago. Nearly all the candidates on his list had intervened in rather than bypassed social relations of production in their time. At any rate, it was within that entire network that the "patriotism" of earlier generations could find its function and place. Davie as expatriate, consumer, taxpayer, voter, and investor has (been) moved into so different a network that merely to hang on to the one item on the list that seems sentimentally satisfying will produce, at best, a self-congratulatory simulacrum of community with the illustrious dead.

By force of the ideology appropriate to his place in the world, Davie unwittingly inhabits a country different from merely England. Let us look for a moment at the way he outlines that country, reminding ourselves that it is at those borders of discourse where metaphor and example seem arbitrarily *chosen* that ideology breaks through.

> For when a poet or a literary scholar, *British or American or Australian,* addresses not his fellow-Britons or his fellow-Americans or fellow-Australians but the international community of literary

scholars, that intention shows up at once in the sort of English that he uses. [P. 35; italics mine]

Must we assume that British English, American English, and New Zealand English are on the way to becoming distinct languages, as Romanian and Portuguese once became distinct languages by diverging differently from the parent stock of Roman Latin? [P. 41]

The point is not that the case would be altered (as indeed it would, in interesting ways) if the Caribbean, the Indian subcontinent, and Kenya-Uganda-Tanganyika (the colonial name for Tanzania)—also English speaking—were introduced into the company. The point is that a discourse such as Davie's, ignoring the difference between the linguistic self-concept of national liberation and patriotism, "naturally" or "only by chance" excludes them from the English-speaking Union. Indeed, to alter one of Davie's sentences a little: "[my] suggestion will seem bizarre except to those . . . who [are involved with admission into and granting degrees from U.S. English departments]" (p. 41). Davie's entire argument would have to be recast if the candidate were not "Georges [from] Bucharest" or "Lucille in Vincennes" but Echeruo from Nigeria or Towheed in Pakistan. Of course "all the languages are precious, every one is unique, and so no one is replaceable by any other" (p. 35). But if one examines the figures of foreign-language enrollment in the *Chronicle of Higher Education* or comparable journals, one knows instantly that they are not in fact equally precious, and the demand depends on the politico-economic text. One need only think of the case of Japanese, Arabic, and Persian in recent years. From a somewhat different point of view, one might think of the status of a Shakespeare scholar who has read all of his Shakespeare in Bengali and a scholar of Bengali culture who has had a semester's Bengali in a U.S. graduate school. (This is not an imaginary example, although it "will seem bizarre except to those of us who [are involved in judging fellowship applications on the national level].")

There is disciplinary ideology in Davie's certainty of the secure role of the poet in contemporary society; in Said's conviction that the literary critic rather than the other human scientists are the custodians of sociopolitical interpretation; and, *malgré tout,* in White's admonition that "to appeal to sociology, anthropology, or psychology for some basis for determining an appropriate perspective on history is rather like basing one's notion of the soundness of a building's foundations on the structural properties of its second or third story" (p. 136).

But the most interesting sign of disciplinary privileging is found in Julia Kristeva's "Psychoanalysis and the Polis." At the end or center of delirium, according to Kristeva, is that which is desired, a hollow where meaning empties out in not only the presymbolic but the preobjective, "the ab-ject." (A deconstructive critique of thus "naming" an undifferentiated telos of desire before the beginning of difference can be launched but is not to my purpose here.) The desire for knowledge involved in mainstream interpretation (which Kristeva calls "Stoic" by one of those undocumented sweeping generalizations common to a certain kind of "French" criticism) shares such a hollow center and is thus linked with delirium. Certain kinds of fiction writers and, one presumes, analysands and social engineers try to dominate, transform, and exterminate improper "objects" awakened in the place of the abject. The psychoanalyst, however, wins out over both mad writer and man of politics. "*Knowing* that he is constantly in abjection [none of the problems of this position is discussed in Kristeva's text][12] and in neutrality, in desire and in indifference, the analyst builds a strong ethics, not normative but directed, which no transcendence guarantees" (p. 98; italics mine). This is the privileged position of synthesis within a restrained dialectic: the psychoanalyst persistently and symmetrically sublates the contradiction between interpretation and delirium. To privilege delirium (interpretation *as* delirium) in the *description* of this symmetrical synthesis is to misrepresent the dialectic presented by the essay, precisely in the interest of a politics that can represent its excluded other as an analysis that privileges interpretation. It should also be mentioned, of course, that the indivisibility and inevitability of the archaic (Christian) mother comes close to a transcendental guarantee. To know her *for what she is,* rather than to seek to transform her, is the psychoanalyst's professional enterprise.

I cannot pretend that the born-again recovery of Christianity and particularly Mariolatry in the latest *Tel Quel*s is not disturbing to me. Not only does Kristeva fail to question the sociohistorical symptomaticity of psychoanalysis as a disciplinary practice but she has this to say about the abject mother of psychoanalysis and the messianic role of psychoanalysis as sublation of Christianity:

> *Our* cultural orb is *centered* around the axiom that "the Word became flesh." Two thousand years after a tireless exploration of the comings and goings between discourse and the object [traditional interpretation] to be named or interpreted, an object which is the solicitor of interrogation, we have finally achieved a discourse on discourse, an interpretation of interpretation. For the psychoanalyst, this vertigo in abstraction is, nevertheless, a means of protecting us from a masochistic and jubilatory fall into nature, into the full and *pagan* mother. [P. 93; italics mine]

Who is the excluded other that privileges interpretation? Not the writer, in this case Louis Ferdinand Céline, whose abject-transcending

12. A similar problem is encountered with White's offer of a running narrative as a critique of the narrativization of the discipline of history.

paranoia, otherwise known as anti-Semitism, the analyst-critic interprets for us through a somewhat positivistic analysis of sentence structure. The ideological scapegoat, hanging out on the borders, is that old favorite, Karl Marx. Kristeva makes an unproblematic analogy between the single-person situation of analysis and the vastly multitudinous, multiracial, and multinational (including "pagan" cultures) political arena and gives us a species of Reichian diagnosis of the revolutionary leader's promise of a utopia in the place of abjection. The psychoanalyst by contrast is *poly*topian (not merely the Second Coming of the Hebraic Christ but perhaps also the fulfillment of the Hellenic Homer, who asked the full pagan mother-Muse to sing *in* him the poly-*tropic*—much tricking, in many tropes—Odysseus, at the beginning of his epic). It would be interesting to follow this homogenizing analogy and ask: Who in politics takes the place of the analyst who, knowingly, sometimes participates in the patient's delirium and draws back just enough to offer the healing interpretation which, "removing obvious, immediate, realistic meaning from discourse . . . [reveals] every phantasm . . . as an attempt to return to the unnameable" (pp. 91–92)? White argues that the interpretation of history as sublimely meaningless is "conventionally associated with the ideologies of fascist regimes" (p. 136). "Such a mobilizing interpretation can be called revolution or demagogy," Kristeva writes (p. 92). How can one take such an alternative seriously?

At any rate, to prove that political interpretations cannot be true, Kristeva argues as follows: "Unlike the analytic dynamic, however, the dynamic of political interpretation does not lead its subjects to an elucidation of their own (and its own) truth. . . . Of course, no political discourse can pass into nonmeaning. Its goal, Marx stated explicitly, is to reach the goal of interpretation: interpreting the world in order to transform it according to our needs and desires" (pp. 92–93). One might of course wonder if leading a subject to truth is not a species of transformation of the subject or, yet, if what Marx says about politics is necessarily the truth of all political discourse.

Let us rather investigate Marx's "explicit statement." Is it the eleventh of Marx's *Theses on Feuerbach* that Kristeva quotes in the epigraph? "Up until now philosophers have only *interpreted* the world. The point now is to change it [Die Philosophen haben die Welt nur verschieden *interpretiert,* es kömmt drauf an, sie zu *verändern*]" (italics mine). As close a reader as Kristeva should note that the relationship between interpretation and change in that statement is exceedingly problematic. *Ankommen auf* in this context probably means "what matters" (within philosophic effort). Even in the most farfetched reading, such as "advent" (*ankommen,* or arrival), a contrastive juxtaposition can hardly be avoided. "To interpret . . . *in order to* transform" (italics mine) seems wishful thinking. The point can also be made that these theses, aphoristic statements parodying and imitating Luther, were written in 1845.

Marx had not yet seen a "revolution," not even 1848. It would be like taking an epigraph from *Studies in Hysteria,* basing an entirely unfavorable comparison upon it, and clinching the case with "Freud has explicitly stated. . . ."

I have suggested that in Kristeva's essay psychoanalysis is shown to sublate the contradiction between interpretation and delirium. When Kristeva claims that political discourse cannot pass into nonmeaning, it remains to be asked how it can be posited that the Hegelian dialectic—Marx's morphology—does not accommodate a negative moment, a passing into nonmeaning, in order to accede to truth. I have suggested elsewhere that Marx's theory of practice goes beyond this restrained dialectic.[13] But I have tried to show here that even if Marx is not given the benefit of that doubt and even on Kristeva's own terms, it would be inadvisable to attempt to critique Marx with so little textual evidence. If one wishes to support a major component of one's argument on Marx, he demands at least as much attention as Céline.

I am not altogether comfortable with Louis Althusser's theory of the epistemological cut in Marx's work, although I am moved by his explanations in *Essays in Self-Criticism.* It is, however, well known that the generation influenced by Althusser's teaching, dissatisfied with the failure of 1968 and the subsequent move on the French Left toward a nonrevolutionary Eurocommunism, turned away from the *Capital* and Marx's later writings as endorsed by Althusser and toward, especially, the 1844 manuscripts, as had Jean-Paul Sartre an intellectual half-generation before Althusser; unlike Sartre, this younger generation sought to find in these manuscripts negative proof of an irreducible will to power. When Kristeva writes "this abject awakens in the one who speaks archaic conflicts with his own improper objects, his ab-jects, at the edge of meaning, at the limits of the interpretable [and] it arouses the paranoid rage to dominate those objects, to transform them," she is writing not only of Céline's anti-Semitism but also of the revolutionary impulse (p. 97). What is at stake here is a politics of interpretation.

The ideological exclusion of a "Marx" as other operates also in White's essay. Although no textual analysis is forthcoming, the assertion that Marx was interested in making sense out of history seems to be indisputable. But I am troubled when White submits that this urge to explain history arose in the nineteenth century, that Marx was caught up in that specific moment of historiography's practice, and that the Jews regarded history as a meaningless sublime spectacle until the establishment of Israel. Surely the grand plans of Judeo-Christian psychobiography and historiography should not be thus dismissed! I am not suggesting, as Kristeva does for psychoanalysis, that the discipline of

13. See my "Il faut s'y prendre en se prenant à elle," in *Les Fins de l'homme,* ed. Philippe Lacoue-Labarthe and Jean-Luc Nancy (Paris, 1981).

history in Europe is a fulfillment of these earlier plans. I am merely indicating that the discipline of history did not suddenly fall upon previously virgin ground.

Whatever the truth of the assertion that the pursuit of meaning links Marx with the bourgeois historian (as it links him with the anti-Semitic writer in "Psychoanalysis and the Polis"), it seems bizarre to place him within the change from the sublime to the beautiful without *some* textual consideration. On the other hand, if one sees White's and Kristeva's moves as part of a contemporary academic-ideological network of explaining Marx away by the most general possible means as a foreclosure of exclusion, it becomes less odd. Some questions remain. Does the sublime historian's promise of a perception of meaning*less*ness not assume a preliminary understanding of what meaning in/of history might be? According to White, "the theorists of the sublime had correctly divined that whatever dignity and freedom human beings could lay claim to could come only by way of what Freud called a 'reaction-formation' to an apperception of history's meaninglessness" (p. 134). I will not bring up once again the vexed question of the passage from individual to group psychology here. I will sum up this part of my reading with the following suggestion: If, for political reasons touched upon by Clark and Said in their different ways, it is expedient to valorize the savant who can apperceive meaninglessness, then both Kristeva and White, in *their* different ways, claim "meaninglessness" too easily. I have tried to indicate this in my discussion of Kristeva. In White, "confusion," "uncertainty," and "moral anarchy" are equated with meaninglessness. Such a loose colloquial use deprives the word of any theoretical value.

By way of conclusion I will consider woman as the ideologically excluded other. Although I have some problems with Booth's essay, let me at the outset express my solidarity with his effort to correct this situation.

Almost all the personal pronouns in all the essays are "he." I am not asking for the quick fix of a mandatory "he or she." Just as, if the West Indian were introduced into Davie's script or the Arab academic style into Cavell's hilarious list of (English, French, and U.S.) academic styles, the argument itself would have to accommodate an otherwise unwitting race privileging—I think in twenty years the Japanese will come to inhabit these lists "naturally"—so also, if the "she" is seriously introduced into these essays, the general argument might need to change its shape. I believe it is with this sense of things that I find myself violated by the impregnable agent of an apparently benign statement such as the following by White: "But imagination is dangerous for the historian because *he* cannot know that what *he* has imagined was actually the case, that it is not a product of *his* 'imagination' in the sense in which that term is used to characterize the activity of the poet or writer of fiction" (p. 129; italics mine). The masculist critic might well say, What am I going to do if an objection is brought against the very grain of my prose? Indeed, the feminist critic would urge, if he became aware that the indefinite personal pronoun is "produced-producing" rather than "natural," then he would also realize that, in this specific case, for example, since woman's place within the discipline and as subject of history is *different* from man's all along the race-class spectrum, and since a woman's right to "imagine" history is fraught with perils of a different *kind,* the validity of the critic's entire argument is put into question by that objection. As long as feminism is considered a special-interest glamorization of mainstream discourse (and I am grateful again to Booth for revealing the way feminist approaches are discussed in "academic locker rooms"), this problem will go unrecognized. And *within the tacitly acknowledged and bonded* enclosure of masculist knowledge-production, a partial (masculist) account of intellectual history will, even as it critiques the narrative mode of "doing history," persistently imply that it is larger than the "whole"—the latter being an account that will confront the fundamental problem of sexual difference in material and ideological production. No history of consciousness can any longer be broached without this confrontation.

The problem cannot be solved by noticing celebrated female practitioners of the discipline, such as Hannah Arendt. The collective situation of the ideologically constituted-constituting sexed subject in the production of and as the situational object of historical discourse is a structural problem that obviously goes beyond the recognition of worthy exceptions. This critique should not be understood as merely an accusation of personal guilt; for the shifting limits of ideology, as I have suggested earlier, are larger than the "individual consciousness." Understood as such, my desperation at the smooth universality of Dworkin's discussion of law as interpretation will not seem merely tendentious. For it is not a questioning of the power of Dworkin's thesis; it is an acknowledgment that, if woman as the subject in law, or the subject of legal interpretation, is allowed into the argument in terms of the differential ethico-political dimension of these relationships, then the clarity might have to be seen as narrow and gender-specific rather than universal. (I am of course not mentioning the possibility that the eruption of Judeo-Christian sanctions within the recent debate on abortion shows how questions of sexual difference challenge the secular foundation of Western law.[14]

Let us consider Davie's two quick stabs at feminists before turning to woman in the essays by Kristeva, Said, and Booth. By way of introduc-

14. See, e.g., Joel Feinberg, ed., *The Problem of Abortion* (Belmont, Calif., 1973), and Marshall Cohen et al., eds., *Rights and Wrongs of Abortion* (Princeton, N.J., 1974).

tion, let us insist that the word "patria" is not merely masculine in gender but names the father as the source of legitimate identity. (The appropriation of mother figures into this naming is similarly related to the place of Arendt in White's essay.) One way of explaining this would be to look again at Vico's fable of the origin of civil society—the *patricians*—in *The New Science*.[15] Here I shall point at the accompanying "hieroglyph or fable of Juno hanging in the air with a rope around her neck and her hands tied by another rope and with two heavy stones tied to her feet. . . . (Juno was in the air to signify the auspices essential to solemn nuptials. . . . She had a rope about her neck to recall the violence used by the giants on the first wives. Her hands were bound in token of the subjection of wives to their husbands. . . . The heavy stones tied to her feet denoted the stability of marriage.)"[16]

Davie's first stab comes when he reproaches feminists for not differentiating among women of different countries:

> Where is it acknowledged, for instance, in the vocabulary of feminism that "woman," as conceived by an American writing about Italians, cannot help but be significantly different from "woman" as conceived by an Italian looking at Americans? Or again, an Italian woman may well, we must suppose, be an Italian patriot; but where, in the current vocabulary of feminists, is that dimension of her "woman-ness" allowed for? Let it be acknowledged only so as to be deplored; but let it in any event be acknowledged. At the moment, it isn't. [P. 40]

This is of course a ridiculous mistake. The heterogeneity of international feminisms and women's situations across race and class lines is one of the chief concerns of feminist practice and theory today. To document this claim would be to compile a volume of bibliographical data.[17] And no feminist denies that women's as well as men's con-

15. For an analysis, see my "Explanation and Culture: Marginalia," *Humanities in Society* 2 (Summer 1979): 217 ff.

16. Giovanni Battista Vico, *The New Science*, trans. Thomas Goddard Bergin and Max Harold Fisch (Ithaca, N.Y., 1968), p. 175. Said refers to the Viconian passage on the origin of the patricians without any reference to its sex-fix ("Opponents, Audiences, Constituencies, and Community," pp. 16–17).

17. I will give Davie a start. See Elaine Marks and Isabelle de Courtivron, eds., *New French Feminisms: An Anthology* (Amherst, Mass., 1980); *Signs* 3 (Autumn 1977), special issue on *Women and National Development;* Julia Kristeva, *About Chinese Women*, trans. Anita Barrows (New York, 1977); Nawal El Saadawi, *The Hidden Face of Eve: Women in the Arab World*, trans. and ed. Sherif Hetata (London, 1980); Lesley Caldwell, "Church, State, and Family: The Women's Movement in Italy," in *Feminism and Materialism: Women and Modes of Production*, ed. Annette Kuhn and Annmarie Wolpe (London, 1978); Gail Omvedt, *We Will Smash This Prison! Indian Women in Struggle* (London, 1980); Cherríe Moraga and Gloria Anzaldúa, eds., *This Bridge Called My Back: Writings by Radical Women of Color* (Watertown, Mass., 1981); and Spivak, "Three Feminist Readings: McCullers, Drabble, Habermas," *Union*

sciousnesses can be raised with reference to such notions as patriotism or total womanhood.

The second stab is with respect to Said's mother:

> When his Palestinian parents married, they had to register the marriage with the authorities of what was at that time a British mandate. The British officer, having registered the marriage, then and there tore up Mrs. Said's Palestinian passport, explaining that by doing so he made one more vacancy in the quota of permitted immigrants to Palestine from among the dispossessed of war-devastated Europe. The feminist response to this—"Aha, it was *the wife's* passport that was destroyed, not the husband's"—wholly fails to recognize the outrage that Mrs. Said felt, which her son now feels on her behalf. For if the law had been such that the husband took his bride's name, so that it was the man's passport that was destroyed, the outrage would have been just the same. [P. 40]

If I may descend into unseemly levity for a moment, I will quote my long-deceased father: "If Grandmother had a beard, she would be Grandfather." For the point is precisely that in a patriarchal society there are no such laws.[18]

Said calls for a criticism that would account for "quotidian politics and the struggle for power" (p. 20). At its best, feminist hermeneutics attempts precisely this. Part of the attempt has been to articulate the relationship between phallocracy and capital, as well as that between phallocracy and the organized Left. I refer Said to two representative titles: Zillah R. Eisenstein's *Capitalist Patriarchy and the Case for Socialist Feminism* and the collection *Beyond the Fragments: Feminism and the Making of Socialism.*

I have been commenting on the politics of exclusion. The deliberate politics of inclusion can also turn into an appropriative gesture. We see it happen in Terry Eagleton's *Walter Benjamin; or, Towards a Revolutionary Criticism.* "Let us briefly imagine," Eagleton writes,

> what shape a "revolutionary literary criticism" would assume. It would dismantle the ruling concepts of "literature," reinserting

---

Seminary Quarterly Review 35 (Fall-Winter 1979–80): 15–34, "French Feminism in an International Frame," *Yale French Studies* 62 (1981): 154–84, and "'Draupadi' by Mahasveta Devi," *Critical Inquiry* 8 (Winter 1981): 381–402.

18. And to verify the extension of that turf, Davie might consult an essay by a respected male anthropologist who is not necessarily a feminist, Maurice Godelier, "The Origins of Male Domination," *New Left Review* 127 (May–June 1981): 3–17. A similar objection could be brought to Davie's insistence that there was nothing of the colonizer in the behavior of the British officer. Situationally and personally, perhaps not. But it is not without significance that it was the British rather than the Palestinian who had the power to decide.

"literary" texts into the whole field of cultural practices. It would strive to relate such "cultural" practices to other forms of social activity, and to transform the cultural apparatuses themselves. It would articulate its "cultural" analyses with a consistent political intervention. It would deconstruct the received hierarchies of "literature" and transvaluate received judgments and assumptions; engage with the language and "unconscious" of literary texts, to reveal their role in the ideological construction of the subject; and mobilize such texts, if necessary by hermeneutic "violence," in a struggle to transform those subjects within a wider political context. If one wanted a paradigm for such criticism, already established within the present, there is a name for it: feminist criticism.[19]

Just as Eagleton earlier accommodates deconstruction as a property of the dialectic, so does he accommodate feminism as a movement within the evolution of Marxist criticism.[20] The vexed question of how to operate race-, class-, and gender-analyses together is not even considered, for the safe space of feminist critique within "cultural practice" is assured even as that critique is neutralized by such a situating gesture. In a moment, however, the motives for this accommodation may themselves be situated within an ideological ground. Having praised feminist criticism (carrying his own name on the list by proxy; see n. 20) for its revolutionary-Marxist potential, Eagleton proceeds to trash it in three paragraphs: his main contention, feminism is theoretically thin, or separatist. Girls, shape up!

If I were writing specifically on Eagleton on feminism, I should question this unexamined vanguardism of theory. In the present context, other questions seem pertinent. First, where does this undifferentiated, undocumented, monolithic feminist criticism hang out? The gesture of constituting such an object in order that it may be appropriated and then devalued has something like a relationship with the constitution of a monolithic Marx, Marxism, Marxist critics that we have encountered in most of these essays. Davie's reprimand that *we* do not distinguish among women becomes all the more risible in this context. Even to Booth's benevolent impulse one must add the cautionary word, lest it share a niche with Eagleton's strategy here: woman's voice is not one voice to be added to the orchestra; *every* voice is inhabited by the sexual differential.

19. Terry Eagleton, *Walter Benjamin; or, Towards a Revolutionary Criticism* (London, 1981), p. 98.
20. It is a place—the end of the line of the evolution of Marxist criticism—previously named with his own patronymic: "Let us review some of the names of the major Marxist aestheticians of the century to date: Lukács, Goldmann, Sartre, Caudwell, Adorno, Marcuse, Della Volpe, Macherey, Jameson, Eagleton" (Eagleton, ibid., p. 96). It should be mentioned that Eagleton surrounds the implicit evolutionism of his argument with many apologies to the contrary.

Why is it that male critics in search of a cause find in feminist criticism their best hope? Perhaps because, unlike the race and class situations, where academic people are not likely to get much of a hearing, the women's struggle is one they can support "from the inside." Feminism in its academic inceptions is accessible and subject to correction by authoritative men; whereas, as Clark has rightly pointed out, for the bourgeois intellectual to look to join other politico-economic struggles is to toe the line between hubris and bathos.

Perhaps a certain caution can be recommended to Kristeva as well. I have suggested that she lacks a political, historical, or cultural perspective on psychoanalysis as a movement. I would also suggest that the notion that the ultimate object-before-objectity is invariably the Mother is fraught with the monolithic figure of Woman rather than women heterogeneously operating outside of masculist kinship inscriptions. No neologism is merely etymological. No nomenclature is ideologically pure. It is therefore necessary to question, paleonymically, why the archaic mother is called, precisely, ab-ject. (The argument that it can mean "thrown away from"—as "object" means "thrown toward"—by its Latin derivation is not enough.)

I have tried to read some aspects of the interpretive politics that seemed to produce and was produced by the symposium on "The Politics of Interpretation." I have pointed first at the usefulness of a broader notion of ideology and then proceeded to notice some of the marks of ideology at work: conserving the sovereign subject; excluding a monolithic Marx(ism); and excluding or appropriating a homogeneous woman. But perhaps the strongest indicator of another item on the ideological agenda—the implicit race idiom of our politics—is the explicit charge I failed to fulfill.

In a report on our symposium in the *Chicago Grey City Journal,* Ken Wissoker said about my inclusion in the panel: "She was there, I assume, because she translated Derrida's *Of Grammatology.*"[21] Reading those words, Elizabeth Abel's long and gracious letter of invitation to me came to mind. It was my point of view as a Third World feminist that she had hoped would enhance the proceedings. Apart from a pious remark that the maids upstairs in the guest quarters were women of color and a show of sentiment, involving Thomas Macaulay, when Said and I held the stage for a moment, the Third World seemed ex-orbitant to our concerns. As I reflect upon the cumulative politics of our gathering, that seems to strike the harshest note.

21. Ken Wissoker, "The Politics of Interpretation," *Chicago Grey City Journal,* 24 Nov. 1981.

A Reply to Gayatri Spivak

Stanley Cavell

In taking me to task, Gayatri Spivak sketches what she calls "arguments" that she courteously says I "undoubtedly can anticipate" (p. 353). I understand this as an invitation to say why, if I can, even did, anticipate them, I left myself unguarded with respect to them. I cannot now accept this invitation, so I submit this note of regret.

To leave myself in certain moments unguarded I can see as habitual with me, even a point of honor. In the present case I thought I had been guarded enough in, for example, my closing sentences. In pairing the names of Plato and D. W. Winnicott on the concept of disillusion, I was counting on getting a little credit, not exactly for a worthwhile joke (Spivak is certainly right to take the pairing seriously) but for a juxtaposition surprising enough to make us question what the concept of illusion is that it should be fundamental in the thought of figures so removed (it seems) from one another. So that when, in my final sentence, I say "we must be assured that this promise [of deconstruction, to disillusion us] is based on a true knowledge of what our illusions are," I was counting on being taken to put first, in investigating what our illusions are, the investigation of what our concept of an illusion is, what the uses of this word come to—Why not just say so?

Here are some reasons. I am—I suppose we all are—always looking for ways to distrust words, and trust them, further than we normally are prepared to do. Skepticism, and its ordinary language critics, on my view of them, live essentially on nothing else than these distrusts and trusts. I have learned from the prose of Austin and Wittgenstein and Emerson and Thoreau certain uses of devices like "what you may call" or "let us say" or "so to speak"; but even I get to feeling that they can be used only so many times. For all I know, the idea of using a word "under erasure" is applicable here. But for my purposes every word (just about) would have to occur so. For example, as in the teaching of Austin and Wittgenstein, when philosophers have said such things as "we do not know with certainty that there are things like tables and chairs because we do not really or literally see them but only see appearances or parts of them," they have, unknown to themselves, removed the words "parts" and "appearances" and "see" and "literally" and "things" and "like" and "know" and "certainty" and "really" from their ordinary uses; they have modified their uses so to speak. But if modified, do they mean what they appear to say? Shall we say that those words are all occurring under erasure? (It used to be said that they are occurring in a philosophical language game. Naturally unspecified.) It has occurred to some people that a fitting way to do justice to one's impatience with the words at hand is to realize the idea of erasing all one's words by leaving one's pages blank (just about). This appeals to me. But not enough.

Again, I want the joke because I do not believe that any given theory has the key to our disillusionment, and I felt it a shortcoming of Paul de Man's practice that it seemed (to me) to claim to possess such a thing. Moreover, I felt I had implied this reservation in preempting the word "illusion" early in my paper to refer to one of Wittgenstein's perceptions of our philosophical attachments to theory, a perception of us as inhabiting structures of air (see p. 183).

Something similar should be said about Spivak's remark that "it is not surprising that . . . the one sense of 'turn' . . . that Cavell does not (cannot?) mention is 'trope,' the irreducible turn of figuration that is the condition of (im)possibility of any redemption of voice" (p. 354). I had earlier (p. 196) preempted the word "trope" as follows: "It does not help to picture language as being turned from the world (say troped) unless you know how to picture it as owed to the world and given to it." The point of preempting this concept was to register my dissatisfaction with the theories of figuration I am familiar with. In that context I was suggesting that, for example, the difference between describing something as in waking life and as in dreams (or "literature"?) may be a difference that is a function of voice but is not a difference that is a function of figuration. In the context Spivak cites, where I am reading a sentence of Thoreau's, the absence of the concept of trope signifies that my exhibiting of myself, or betraying of myself, leaving myself unguarded, by turns before the silence of the therapeutic text, is not taken by me to be a function necessarily of my expressing myself figuratively. Again, Thoreau's sentence about sitting quietly in some attractive spot in the woods is not, on my view of metaphor, metaphorical, because it has an ordinary literal realization. No account of its figuration could be right which did not account for that feature of it. (Perhaps such a consideration is irrelevant to Spivak's speaking of figuration. Then that would be part of my difficulty in understanding what she is saying about it).

When I say that "it is as the recovery of [the human] voice (as from an illness) that ordinary language philosophy is, as I have understood and written about it, before all to be understood" (p. 197), I am not talking about all recoveries or all nostalgias of all voices. No doubt some claims made on behalf of the voice are themselves part of the illness (of subservience, of ·unctuousness) from which I have sought recovery. What I was describing was the sense of defending and pursuing ordinary language philosophy on the only ground on which there was (while there was) anyone close enough to it, intimately hostile enough, to require defending it against. This was in practice other analytical philosophers, those for whom Frege's and Russell's visions of a perfect language set out their philosophical hopes. And this perfect language was dominating of what was felt as philosophical Reason, and it was essentially intolerant of voice; it was a discovery of writing. As a development within one strand of the present of philosophy it will have consequences for philosophy as a human enterprise, but they remain unassessed. That they are related to recent discussions of writing I do not doubt; what it would look like to specify the relations I do not know.

Spivak's instruction that "to predicate reality as the death of illusion is to ignore the syntax or practice that passes from illusion to reality via dis-illusion" (p. 353) seems to me, to the extent that I understand it, to be traversing mutually important and fairly familiar ground. I take it to be the burden of Austin's excruciatingly painstaking effort to "dismantle," among other things, the so-called Argument from Illusion in his *Sense and Sensibilia* (Oxford, 1962). ("Dismantle" is Austin's word for what he is doing, in the last sentences of the book.) Austin was so much on my mind as I wrote my paper in question that I perhaps took this too much for granted. Spivak says: "Not to acknowledge that deconstruction distinguishes itself from dialectics precisely by this attention to the syntax that is otherwise ignored in the interest of the semantics of reality is not to speak of deconstruction at all" (p. 353). I do not know about this; I am not in a position to speak in these ways; my paper is about what you may call this inability, even a beginning effort to assess it. Something I am certain of is that I had no intention of providing a "reading of deconstruction" and no wish to "convince" anyone of such a thing.

I think it expresses my inabilities and my prospects here that when I read Spivak's phrase "the semantics of reality" I thought of the following passage from *Sense and Sensibilia*: "Many philosophers, failing to detect any ordinary quality common to real ducks, real cream, and real progress, have decided that Reality must be an *a priori* concept apprehended by reason alone" (p. 64). And her speaking of "syntax that is otherwise ignored" reminded me of Austin's passage a little further on: "Next, 'real' is what we may call a *trouser-word*. It is usually thought . . . that what one might call the affirmative use of a term is basic. . . . But with 'real' . . . it is the *negative* use that wears the trousers. That is, a definite sense attaches to the assertion that something is real, a real such-and-such, only in the light of a specific way in which in might be, or might have been, *not* real" (p. 70). (I do not know whether the imagery of trousers in this passage requires an apology. I mean I do not know whether someone will take offense and, if so, whether an apology would be accepted. Such are the hazards of the politics of superficiality.)

Would it make sense to say here that Austin's "syntactic" attention is, or is not, ignored in the interest of his "semantic" interest? If it would not make sense, is he free, or not free, of "this ideological requirement"? It may be an ideological matter, or attitude, that prevents me from understanding our misunderstandings here as ideological—as opposed, at any rate, to attributing them to impatience, to neurosis, to vanity, to Wittgensteinian bewitchment, or to some further set of cultural differences. (Any term of criticism may, none need, be taken personally.) Suppose it is true, and significant about the American "style of thought," that it has lacked the concept of ideology, as Spivak says on p. 347. Is this like lacking thirteenth-century cathedrals (also true, and significant, of American culture), or like lacking churches of any kind, or like lacking the concept of religion altogether? In the last case you may have a theory of human culture that tells you this is impossible, in which case one tack for you to take would be to look for what concepts "[do] duty" for the absent concept. I think a related cultural difference between American and European intellectual life is that the American (with isolated exceptions) has no sacred intellectual texts, none whose authority the intellectual community at large is anxious to preserve at all costs—no Marxian texts, no Freudian, no Hegelian, no Deweyan, and so forth. Every text stands at the level of professional journal articles, open for disposal. (I am not considering the Declaration of Independence as a candidate for such a text.) If the concept of ideology depends for its usefulness on its functioning within such favored texts, then its absence in American intellectual life would be explained by the absence of such texts, I mean texts so conceived. Since my paper rather deplores the absence of Emersonian and Thoreavian texts as something like sacred common possessions, I should add here that this absence is not wholly, or just, deplorable. But it surely makes for drastic barriers to communication, both within American intellectual life and between American and European thinkers.

The last sentences of my paper toy with issues of illusion and reality of the sort cited by Spivak and Austin, but they do not address them, as though the time for addressing them has past or not yet arrived again. The issue on my mind, thinking of de Man's book, was something else, namely, how to accept a therapy of disillusion (or of dismantling) without succumbing to disillusionment, I mean disillusionment as an attitude, something between discouragement and cynicism. (If we see that politics has been one cure for this, and philosophy another, then we should equally see that they have both, or their degradations have, been causes of it too.) It is in part to refuse this attitude, or refuse it as an attitude (as an ideology, may I say?), that I used old-fashioned phrases of encouragement like "noble promise" and "be given welcome."

Ineluctable Options

Terry Eagleton

In his response to *The Politics of Interpretation,* Walter Benn Michaels convincingly demonstrates that the political "decisionism" of Hayden White and E. D. Hirsch will not really do. White's position, which is not really distinguishable from good old fashioned existentialism, is that history is quite meaningless and that we must simply make a moral and political option for a future which will contrast with this. The point is to be inspired by the chaos and anarchy of the past and fashion a future in which individuals will "endow their lives with a meaning for which they alone are fully responsible" (p. 134).

One problem with this argument is that terms like "chaos," "anarchy," and "meaninglessness" seem to hover indecisively between their moral and epistemological senses. White sometimes seems to mean that history is epistemologically undecidable and sometimes that it has all been a mess. But to see history as a mess is surely a determinate interpretation of a kind and perhaps implies that history is the kind of thing that *could* have had a meaning even if it happens not to have had. Perhaps if White had examined in more detail how precisely history is meaningless, what exactly it is that does not make sense, he might have found himself veering into meaning after all. This, however, might take him rather close to the Marxist case, which is, I suppose, that history is a fairly precise and intelligible sort of mess. So the epistemological meaning of "meaningless" is also necessary: if the "manifest confusion" of history is an epistemological affair, it would not make any difference if history did happen to have a meaning after all, for we could never know it—or at least, given history's "overinterpretability," we could never know that we were knowing it. The future will be different, White hopes: not different in *meaning*, for the past has no meaning to be differed from, but different in the purely formalistic sense of actually *having* a meaning, since we are there to create it. Virtue, so to speak, is intelligibility. But why should the epistemological problem not infect this future as well? What guarantees the meanings I may "responsibly" create against the "undecidability" fate of the past? Perhaps just the fact that I responsibly create them: I can know only what I create and thus can be in orderly possession of my own meanings as I cannot be in orderly possession of the meanings of the past. But the past was not supposed to have any meanings in the first place. Is history anarchic from its own viewpoint as well as from ours? Is it that it really does not have any meaning—the epistemological point—or, as the moral contrast with a desirable nonchaotic future would seem rather to enforce, that I in the present can never appropriate, be responsible for, what meaning history might have?

Perhaps the reason why the past is meaningless is that people in history did not in fact "endow their lives with a meaning for which they alone [were] fully responsible," in which case one wonders why it never occurred to them to do so. Is the past meaningless because its agents were not twentieth-century liberal humanists? Were they not responsible enough, and, if so, might not this historical fact be meaningful? Or perhaps they did produce such responsible meanings, and the problem is that we cannot know whether they did or not because the only meanings we can know are those we produce ourselves. But then why should we not produce responsible meanings for the past as well as for the future? After all, it is not so much that there is too little meaning around when we consider the past but too much: it is susceptible of too many meanings, which is why, somewhat oddly, White calls it "meaningless." White's reason for not producing responsible meaning for the past is a moral one: to do so would be to erase that meaninglessness which inspires us to want to do better ourselves. But how *can* we do better, if meaninglessness is an epistemological as well as a moral condition? How are we not merely going to hand on confusion to our children, in the shape of the undecidability of the past we shall represent to them? What is the value of a future which will extend no further than ourselves? Perhaps responsibility and intelligibility stretch no further than to each generation, marooned as it is between an utterly anarchic past and an equally chaotic future, stranded with a strictly limited liability. But in that case this may have been the position of every generation in history:

Terry Eagleton, fellow and tutor in English at Wadham College, Oxford University, is the author of *Walter Benjamin; or, Towards a Revolutionary Criticism* (1981) and *The Rape of Clarissa* (1982). *Literary Theory: An Introduction* is forthcoming in 1983.

maybe everybody has been producing their own responsible meanings all the way from the Stone Age. White's insistence on acting differently from the past might suggest that they have not, but why should he suspect this? Because history is anarchy and manifest confusion? But that may be just our epistemological problem. One would have thought that for White history was the kind of thing that could not possibly have a meaning in any case—that this for him would just be some sort of error in category; and so it is strange to find him feeling that history's lack of meaning is morally repugnant, equivalent to finding someone's freckles morally repugnant. If meaning is just what we cannot legitimately demand of history, as opposed perhaps to this or that particular meaning, then there is no more reason to find its disorder morally repugnant or, indeed, to use the term "disorder" at all than there is to feel morally repulsed by the fact that history happened on the planet earth rather than on the moon. White's nostalgia for meaning can only not be vacuous if he concedes that it is a protest against history's *moral* anarchy; but he cannot really concede this, for that would be to suggest precisely the kind of determinate interpretation of history which his epistemological position forbids. There is in his essay, I think, a kind of classical, liberal bourgeois contradiction, between, on the one hand, a highly limited notion of individual responsibility—a kind of private enterprise of meaning which will ideally endow history with order—and, on the other hand, a glummer conviction that the result of all this is historical chaos. Even though these two attitudes are in fact sides of the same liberal bourgeois coin, White strives to regulate the contradiction by separating them, relegating the chaos to the past and projecting the more hopeful aspect of the ideology into the future.

In direct contrast to White's decisionism, Michaels himself argues that interpretation is not a political matter because it does not involve free choice. We do not choose the interpretations which convince us: "The whole point of being convinced," Michaels claims, "is that we cannot help believing whatever it is we are convinced of, whereas the whole point of freely choosing is that we might freely choose otherwise" (p. 336). Michaels, in other words, would seem to subscribe to White and Hirsch's (ideological) assumption that the political is primarily a matter of personal choosing and opting; it is just that he denies that *interpretation* is a question of free choice and so denies that it is political.

What does it mean to claim that one cannot help believing whatever it is one is convinced of? It means, I suppose, that to be convinced is to be convinced. Michaels' point is at once an extremely interesting insight and trivially analytic. There is one clear sense in which when I am a Marxist I am not free not to be a Marxist, just as when I am in Oxford I am not free to be in London, or when I am asleep I am not free to not be asleep. This trivializes Michaels' point, but not, I think, greatly so. It is true that beliefs are not things we choose, to the extent that belief does not consist in holding a set of opinions plus a mental act of choosing them; it merely consists in holding a set of opinions. But Michaels' case entails a strange sense of "free." When I adopt a political position freely, I do not usually mean that an act of choosing precedes or accompanies my adopting. It means that I am not forced mindlessly into it by my class interests or by some ideological or pathological obsession, that nobody is holding a gun to my head, that I am in a situation to be able to weigh the arguments and recognize what would count as decisive counterarguments, and so on. "Freedom" describes the material conditions in which my believing goes on: it has a social and political reference rather than the narrowly psychologistic one assigned to it by Michaels. I am not free to be in London when I am in Oxford, and yet of course I may be: given certain material conditions, I may have the time, money, and capacity to get myself there. I am not free to doubt my conviction while I am convinced—this is Michaels' profoundly tautological point—but in another sense whether I am free to take up or lay down a belief depends upon my social conditions. In one sense of "free"—though one later to be qualified—it is surely never possible to hold a belief other than freely, for we would not describe as a "belief" an attitude adopted under *certain* forms of constraint. Michaels tends to identify freedom with a particular ideological and psychologistic model of free, conscious choice—a consumer model, as it were. He does not appear to question this model in general, merely to recognize its inapplicability to interpretation. It is true that we do not choose to believe, but there is an important sense in which belief is not ineluctable either. It is certainly in one sense ineluctable as long as I am having it, just as eating is as long as I am doing it; but Michaels overlooks the sense in which I can still hold my beliefs freely even when I find them magnificently convincing. Indeed, the more convincing I find them, the more freely I hold them. I hold them because I have been convinced by the arguments and the evidence rather than because they are convenient or pleasantly annoying to others or fashionably eccentric. Because I find my beliefs reasonable I would abandon them if they came to seem unreasonable, which is not so easily done with a spontaneous ideological prejudice. To be rationally convinced is thus a "freer" matter than being ideologically controlled. Michaels ignores the relation between freedom and reason—or perhaps it would be more accurate, if less charitable, to claim that it is just this relation which his essay is out to suppress.

I think, then, that both White's decisionism and Michaels' "ineluctabilism" represent opposing simplifications of the question of belief, and I would agree with Gayatri Spivak that what is really lacking here is an adequate concept of ideology. There are reasons other than logical ones why people can't help believing what they believe; and if Michaels is right that in one sense people can't help their beliefs, he ought perhaps also to consider the ideological conditions under which individuals are frequently quite capable of believing and disbelieving something at the same time. There are many people in Britain who, like Donald Davie, deeply respect the monarchy; there are also people who have contempt for it, and in some cases these people are identical. I don't think this can simply be labelled "ambiguity," which would then equally fall under the "ineluctability" rubric: if you *are* ambiguous about something then you can't help being so. It is rather that under certain conditions, and within certain ideological coordinates, people can revere the monarchy, and just the same people, in different practical situations and drawing on alternative dimensions of their experience, can despise it. And of course there are people who do not know whether they revere or despise the monarchy, and people who believe they despise it and unconsciously do not, and vice versa, and both at the same time. Are these beliefs free or ineluctable? In what sense is Davie free not to be a Tory patriot? In the same sense that a medieval bishop was free not to believe in God? The bishop's belief is ideologically determined, but it is still free in the sense that a belief one adopts at gunpoint is not. Because it is ideological determinations which constitute us as free subjects in the first place, ideology is just that realm of "undecidability," as to freedom and necessity, which both White and Michaels overlook. I can also be mistaken about my beliefs, in the sense that I might *think* I can meaningfully doubt whether anything exists but can only do so because I have not seen that there is actually no available language game in which this doubt would find a home and make any kind of sense. Some might want to argue that this is precisely the case with White's belief that the whole of history is meaningless. Because Michaels' concern with belief is purely logical, it tends to homogenize different modes of believing rather deceptively. There are beliefs which I just can't help holding because to do otherwise would involve a radical transformation in my practical forms of social life; and there are beliefs I can help holding fairly easily, such as the opinion that Brighton is a pleasant place; and there is a whole range of much less decidable intermediate beliefs.

Is the political primarily a matter of free choice? Free for whom? White may decide to read history any way he likes, but not everybody is so fortunate. There is nothing in the historical "record," he argues, to determine one reading as more plausible than another. The record, then, is presumably just a heap of bald facts: White's idealism here is the inescapable other face of a positivism. But why think of history first of all as a record, and what are the material conditions which enable this essentially speculative, textual metaphor? White wants to break with history because it is confusion; but there are others for whom history is the present continuation of a practice of struggling against this confusion, a practice which "chooses" us, rather as Michaels' interpretations do. The irresistible character of interpretation is for Michaels, as I have said, a logical point; but there is also a sense in which it is a moral and political one too, in so far as we find ourselves "irresistibly" gripped (while being none the less free for all that) by certain interpretations which are inscribed in a tradition of practices received from the past. Michaels will not extend his antidecisionistic point this far, for this would undermine the epistemological scepticism and political liberalism he apparently shares with the decisionists. His antidecisionism does not stretch to the political itself.

But it is surely the case that you cannot choose the political if you live on Belfast's Falls Road: it has already chosen you in the shape of those British soldiers with an irritating habit of breaking down your front door at two o'clock in the morning and carting half your family away to concentration camps. Of course in one sense you have a whole range of political options here: you could make the soldiers a cup of tea while they beat up your children, for example, or give them a few more addresses. One choice you do not have is to do nothing, for it is not easy to imagine what doing nothing in such a situation would consist in.[1] There is another sense, however, in which you really do not have any choice here. If you and your community are going to have any decent life at all, then you really do not have a choice to not put up some form of political resistance. It is in this sense that desire is absolute. I am not, of course, advocating the madness of putting up resistance *there and then* but speaking rather of some form of collective political resistance. (I should add here, with an eye on the rather comprehensive powers of the British Prevention of Terrorism Act and summoning all the sincerity I can muster, that I am not here advocating armed resistance in the North of Ireland). This is one sense in which political action is ineluctable rather than free and one sense in which the voluntarism which runs throughout some of the essays in *The Politics of Interpretation* is mistaken. Of course what I am describing is a moral rather than a logical necessity, but my point is not just the lame one that *some* form of political option is unavoidable. My point is that history has already rather rigorously delimited those options, and freedom will be the product of acknowledging this necessity.

Political voluntarism tends to leave out of account the fact that the most important form of political action for most people is how they are acted *on*. All the important political action is thus reaction, a point sometimes obscure to those whose social conditions do not yield them a sharp sense of being politically acted on. Political action by a ruling class is just the kind of action that needs and presupposes the reaction of the masses, an action to which their reaction is structural rather than contingent. It is partly because of this structured process of action and reaction that White's classical liberalism—I am responsible for my own actions—won't do, for what "my own actions" are is precisely what is at stake.

1. I am grateful to Dominic Eagleton for this point.

For Michaels, interpretations are ineluctable but political action (by implication) is free. What this overlooks is that there is a sense in which we are not free to not act on the basis of certain interpretations, and this is the surest way in which such interpretations constrain. Not to act, given certain interpretations of history, would be self-contradictory, since it would refute the claims of the interpretation just as surely as my claim to love animals would be implicitly refuted by my practice of torturing them to death. There is surely a point at which the *practical* acceptance or rejection of an interpretation comes to count as a theoretical acceptance or rejection of it as well, and this is another complication of conviction which Michaels' account leaves aside. What would we say of a capitalist who claimed to be fervently convinced of the truth of Marxism without altering his behaviour one whit? Or of a Christian who worked dedicatedly for the triumph of Satan? Is such a person really convinced of the truth of Marxism or Christianity or just labouring under the illusion of conviction? For Michaels, it would seem, either you're convinced or you're not; but I cannot really believe that the unemployed British youth who joins the National Front and sports a Union Jack T-shirt believes in patriotism in the same way that Davie does. I don't mean only that Davie is not, of course, a fascist, nor do I mean that the youth is mystified but Davie is not. Davie is, in my view, every bit as mystified as the youth; the difference is that it seems likely that he really does "love his country," whatever that means, whereas I do not believe that the unemployed young fascist, or many Northern Irish Loyalists, actually give a toss for the Crown. They are of course convinced of *something*, but not of what they think they are.

This is perhaps the place to mention that Davie's defence of patriotism is especially distasteful at a time when families in Britain are mourning the deaths of young servicemen meaninglessly slaughtered in the Malvinas. I don't know whether Davie was in England at the time to witness the lying manipulations of the government and the chauvinistic hatred of the media. ("Kill an Argy and win a Metro!" was how the satirical magazine *Private Eye* modestly parodied the popular press.) If Davie was not in England, he missed an instructive scene; perhaps he would have been able to sustain his distinction between patriotism and chauvinism, though I suspect that even Davie, had he followed the *Sun* and *Daily Mirror,* would have been in for a good dose of deconstruction.

"Explanations come to an end somewhere," Wittgenstein writes. I suppose the hallmark of a certain "vulgar" Marxism is that they come to an end when you act. I hope such a criticism won't be misunderstood as endorsing political inactivity, though I had better be careful: Edward Said describes me as "in cloistral seclusion from the inhospitable world of real politics" (p. 22). I wish Said had told this to the British Labour party before they rejected my application for membership on the suspicion— utterly groundless, I swear!—that I was an active member of a banned political organization. Maybe he would send Mr. Foot a copy of his piece just to soothe him down. T. J. Clark and Gayatri Spivak want it the other way, discerning a certain bad faith in the middle-class Marxist's slightly risible agonizings over the relation between the cultural struggle and a broader politics. "For the bourgeois intellectual to look to join other politico-economic struggles," Spivak writes, "is to toe the line between hubris and bathos" (p. 366). I don't know what a bourgeois (as opposed to middle-class) intellectual would be doing looking to join other people's struggles in the first place; but I must politely refuse to be pinned within my own patch and affirm instead an unreconstructed belief that the place of the socialist intellectual is within political struggle as a whole, not just in the academy. Too vulgar for some, not vulgar enough for others: I wonder if that's what they mean by getting it more or less right?

Where explanation and interpretation "come to an end," surely, is not when we rush out and act but when we arrive at a certain interpretative logjam or sticking-place and recognize that we shall not get any further until we transform the practical forms of life in which our interpretations are inscribed. All conflicts of interpretation are political, but some are more political than others, and the ones I have just referred to are the most political of all. One of the dangers with the title *The Politics of Interpretation* is that the word "politics" is stretched at times almost to meaninglessness—could, in fact, sometimes be interchanged with "social" or "ethical" or "cultural." The concept, in other words, is sometimes emptied of its distinguishing reference to *power,* and only Said's essay seems to me to maintain this constant focus. The word constantly drifts away from power relations toward some milder, more abstract ethical or anthropological sense. But interpretation is surely one place where we sift "softer" from "harder" meanings of the political, identifying those particular interpretative clashes and contradictions which could not conceivably be dissolved, or resolved on one side or the other, without a struggle over the transformation of our social relations—without, therefore, a confrontation with the power structure whose effect is to forestall such transformation.

Index